Sailing East: West Indian Pirates in Madagascar

Sailing East: West Indian Pirates in Madagascar

By,
Baylus C. Brooks

Poseidon

Poseidon Historical Publications
Gainesville, Florida

Sailing East: West Indian Pirates in Madagascar
ISBN: 978-0-359-04792-5

First Edition Paperback

© 2018 Baylus C. Brooks

All rights reserved. No part of this publication may be reproduced, distributed, or transmitted in any form or by any means, including photocopying, recording, or other electronic or mechanical methods, without the prior written permission of the publisher, except in the case of brief quotations embodied in critical reviews and certain other noncommercial uses permitted by copyright law. For permission requests, write to the publisher, addressed "Attention: Permissions Coordinator," at the email address below.

Poseidon Historical Publications

Baylus C. Brooks' Lulu Spotlight page is located at
http://www.lulu.com/spotlight/bcbrooks

Visit http://baylusbrooks.com for upcoming books and events associated with his work

Cover photo: *Map of Madagascar*, by Dr Olfert Dapper (1636-1689) who published a large number of books after 1663. He wrote a history of the city of Amsterdam and furnished the first Dutch translation of Herodotus. But he is known particularly for his many descriptions of foreign lands which he compiled from various sources, without ever seeing the countries he wrote about for himself. This plate is taken from a description of Africa. Location: Österreichische Nationalbibliothek, Vienna, inv. nr. Van der Hem 35:58 and Koninklijke Bibliotheek, Den Haag, inv. nr. 1049B13_071. Date:circa 1668

Table of Contents

Acknowledgements i
Introduction ....…......................... 1

1 - "The Buzzard" Leaves Africa for
    The Indian Ocean 25

2 - Taking of James Macrae's *Cassandra*:
    British East India Company 95

3 - Pirating Bombay, Goa, and Cochin
    In the Arabian Sea 165

4 - The Extraordinary Misunderstood Life
    Of One-Armed Edward Congdon ... 187

5 - *Nossa Senhora do Cabo* &
    The Viceroy of Goa at Bourbon 217

6 - Commodore Thomas Mathews,
    The "Anti-pirate" Squadron, and Dutch
    Engineer Jacob de Bucquoy 241

7 - Richard Taylor Takes up with
    The Spanish at Portobello 293

8 - Trial of the "Buzzard"
    Olivier LeVasseur de la Buse.......... 323

Appendices ....….......... 343
Index 409

Acknowledgements

Writing pirate history the way I do is never simply my own accomplishment – neither does it depend upon a single flawed source. So much that has been written in this genre has handicapped itself by an almost religious devotion to the polemicist newspaper publisher Nathaniel Mist's or "Capt. Charles Johnson's" *A General History of the Robberies and Murders of the Most Notorious Pyrates*. For almost 300 years, this book has dominated the field and, unfortunately, the results of everyone's work. My endeavors have been to forget this flagrantly fickle source and focus entirely on only primary documents.

I tap all and every morcel of evidence within my ability. Consequently, the quite efficient staff of various archives and libraries has aided this project significantly. They include the National Archives in London and the British Library for their India Office Collections. French sources have been enormously helpful, including *Archive Nationales d'Outre Mers, Les Archives Départementales de La Réunion,* and *Bibliotech National de France's Gallica* Research Site. I'd also like to thank the staff of the George Smathers Library of the University of Florida in Gainesville and Glenn Gonzales of Johns Hopkins University Library, particularly for his help with the *Humphrey Morice Collection of the Bank of England*.

Websites have been largely untapped and add more digitized records at a phenomenal pace, literally changing how we historians craft our works. Ancestry.com began their efforts in 2008 and in only five years, they reported 220 million digitized historical documents in just New England alone! Their efforts have thoroughly covered America and England and are expanding. This has significantly changed the availability of all sources, for all time to come – allowing pirate history to enter the realm of social history. Genealogy sites in particular contain a wealth of primary documents that many historians routinely bypass. Ancestry.com, FamilySearch.org, GenealogyBank newspaper collections, Google Books, *Voyages* database, ThreeDecks.org ship information database, Project

Gutenberg, Burney British Newspaper Collection, and a whole host of others are simply too numerous to mention. The value of these sources will be apparent throughout the book.

The research of Dr. E. T. Fox has been essential and you will see numerous citations from his primary source documentation of pirates in *Pirates: In Their Own Words*. Laura Nelson has contributed her research of Olivier LeVasseur, Samuel Bellamy's compatriots in *Whydah Pirates Speak,* and other general pirate research published on her blog at http://petercorneliushoof.blogspot.com/. Arne Bialuschewski of Trent University has done fantastic archival research in multiple countries that heavily contributed to this book. Thanks go to self-described "piratologist" Wayne Hampton of South Africa, who found a significantly relevant document in French and transcribed by UNESCO on their research website.

I would also like to thank Prof. Dr. Jacques Gasser, University of Lausanne, for introducing me to *Les Rapports des capitaines à l'Amirauté de Nantes,* which revealed a great deal more on Edward England. Dr. Gasser's book, *Dictionnaire des flibustiers des Caraïbes: corsaires et pirates français au XVIIe siècle,* details French buccaneers, filibusters, or pirates of the Caribbean. He is also working on Olivier LeVasseur, which promises to reveal much more on this pirate!

Last, but certainly not least, I owe a special thanks to my professors and friends at East Carolina University, the original home of the Pirates! The historians and nautical archeaologists of the Maritime Studies Program have encouraged my natural thirst to unearth and resurface the past – unfortunately, no *actual* gold came from that search! Arrgh! Thank you, all!

Introduction:
A Tale of Two Empires

England laid thousands of miles from its colonies in both the East and West Indies. That's a long way for an empire which required governance – as they say, the difficulties of administering an empire upon which the sun never sets! Still governance was only a small part of their incentive – profit figured much more prominently! Moreover, that administration could have been engineered more effectively, but decided quite early to split its empire in two. For quite simple reasons, the early English Empire evolved from a basically schizophrenic body politic.

England initially created a mess and dealt with cleaning it up later. America remained the last undiscovered (by Europeans, anyway) continent. Founded centuries later, it developed millennia after the classic known civilizations of Europe and Asia. It was a "great wilderness" by European standards when first found. There were no recognizable civilizations or authorities that must be dealt with from their perspective. Europeans viewed America as a vast unclaimed land of treasure - mostly plant, animal, mineral, but occasionally precious metal. The native cultures of America were not comparable with European cultures at first contact and were not as respected as European or Asian cultures had been for centuries! Furthermore, they could offer no significant opposition and required little negotiation for which Europeans might obtain their desired commodities. Europeans often opted to steal from them, or, cheat them in a nominally criminal act of what Europeans touted as "barter."

India, though, was an older, more well-known and intricate civilization – though also viewed as lower on the rungs of racist "civilized" or "European" humanity because of their darker skin and "blasphemous" religion. It had been always "next door" throughout most of England's history. The Indian Ocean was populated all around with cultures rich in gold, diamonds, rubies, sapphires and other jewels, saltpeter, and other commodities – cultures which required more finesse to gain access to those treasures. A latecomer to East Indies profiteering, England had earlier subcontracted administration of its Eastern Empire through a chartered company, but left the West Indies open for individual speculation by their merchant-pirates, drooling at the wealth of the Spanish gold and silver from their mines. Killing and raping was essentially a part of pirating in both Indies, but some companies tended to apologize more often and occasionally cleaned their messes.

The few pirates in service of the English East India Company or EIC, a corporate company very much like modern corporations, were useful to their financial organizations. They were more attuned to the same wishes or fiscal desires for gleaming wealth – still ruthless in their methods. But, of course, any ill feelings could be negotiated between their respective boards of directors. Pirates in the West were usually feared as brutal whereas pirates in the East were more respected, especially by the Dutch, long more experienced than others in the East Indies trade.

The expense-profit balance sheet of the company would supposedly take care of "governing" the East. By contrast, little governing was required in early English America – outright theft needed little guidance – indeed, they avoided regulation! Still the eastern supposedly-more-sophisticated capitalistic method would eventually also prove problematic. This method carried financial benefits, but also enormous social problems that would later plague the Empire. It seems that governing people requires more than simple business acumen, a lesson still lost on modern capitalistic America. For the time being, however, it served its purpose of profit. Massive slave revolts came later – listen up and take heed, America! This is old news!

What exactly happened in America? The West Indies did not begin as a controlled, moderate business affair, with thoughtful governance from 3,000 miles away. Since even before the Stuarts, England set out rudely and roughly for the West Indies to steal Spanish gold and silver. Early American piratical adventurers were not necessarily members of a larger organization, or company – they did not even necessarily owe allegiance to merchants at home. They were mostly individuals who quickly learned to jealously guard, cherish, and defend their individual freedom to rape and pillage the Spanish Empire in the land "beyond the lines of amity." Something that also fervently annoyed Protestant Englishmen, the Spanish held Catholic beliefs like their sometime French allies. Actually, it justified the theft in their view – more pleasant or at least less "immoral."

Only the most unscrupulous of these less-than-devout Protestants crossed the wide Atlantic for such base reasons. Early American heroes: Drake, Hawkins, and Morgan and their ilk became ruthless men, torturing and killing for sport when silver or gold could not "slake their lust," as Barbossa is quoted in film. England, however, enjoyed the glittering proceeds and ignored the crimes of their distant buccaneers.

Still, once England obtained enough Spanish property in the West Indies, it tried to subdue their Frankenstein creations. They found that their own wild thugs began damaging trade for all European nations, not just Spain, France, or Holland. America, all the way across the Atlantic Ocean in the land "beyond the lines of amity," filled with brutal daredevils, *hostis humani generis* or "enemies of mankind," not welcome at home. They proved extraordinarily difficult to control. Again, this stood in stark contrast to the more business-like easternmost branch of the empire on the periphery of the Indian Ocean, although it was still essentially "piratical." Principally, piracy was the most nominal and characteristic feature of the English blueprint when they founded America under the Stuarts and throughout the eighteenth century!

For the best part of a century, many substantial merchants in England and America had become heavily involved in American piracy, gambling on small-scale short-term deadly risks. England waited nearly a century to allow their colonial empire any real measure of control. This effort affected both Indies. In 1696, the old pirate-loving world of Drake and Hawkins faced manigerial, quiet opposition. Resistance to piracy began subtly, beginning almost as if the English government tried to ignore it themselves. In this year, the old aristocratic and unfruitful Lords of Trade were replaced by a formalized body: the Committee on Trade and Plantations, commonly known as the "Board of Trade."

Some scholars follow this trend. Douglas R. Burgess Jr. believes that opposition to piracy in America was a direct result not so much of the Crown, but of their Navigation Acts. These late-17th century regulations mostly concerned England taking control of the Triangular Trade in the Atlantic, especially following the Glorious Revolution of 1688. Specifically annoying to pirate-loving America was the Act of 1696, or the "act for preventing Frauds and regulating Abuses in the Plantation Trade." "Plantation" referred to colonies – mostly in the "woods" of America. There was the provision that certain enumerated goods of the colonies could *only* be transported back to England. These goods were also taxed in England – not for the benefit of the colonies, but for the Crown. We also must not forget the provision in 1696 for establishing Vice-Admiralty Courts in America to try crimes at sea. This provision extremely annoyed American pirates who previously enjoyed the autonomy of their wilderness environment. They could previously comit whatever indiscretions they so chose against the French and Spanish Catholics – and also whosoever chose to be a direct competitor, regardless of flag – without fear of restraint by new laws and enforcers. Speaking of flags – there was to be no more using foreign flags to lie as to allegiances – to fool one's prey, also something that American privateers and pirates heavily used in their ruthless trade. Thus began, as Burgess says, the "Pirate Wars," as in Pirate v. Pirate! "Administrators who in a previous generation," says Burgess, "would have been content to quietly condone piracy... were now actively attempting to root it out."[1] Of course, in America, the die had been set a century ago – criminality was as American as baseball, apple pie, Al Capone, or Donald Trump!

A cultural divide had almost always existed between mother country and colonies, but after the Pirate Wars began, it propagated with increasing relish. Still, the Pirate Wars got off to a slow start because America resisted – jealously guarding its piracy. Even more to the point, many wealthy English

---

[1] Douglas R. Burgess Jr., *The Politics of Piracy: Crime and Civil Disobedience to Colonial America* (Lebanon: ForeEdge, 2014), 51.

merchants, investors, and their fair-weather old-world allies still relied upon the open and illicit opportunities of the western American frontier. Still, a "Revolution" was on its way. Pirates of America would one day be free to decide their own destiny! One such "founding father" might have been… no, I'm not thinking of the smuggler John Hancock, but Henry Every, the loyal English merchant turned pirate!

Henry Every's mutinous actions aboard *Charles II* and his subsequent piracies became a textbook case for the new liberalized Board of Trade. Every initiated his pirate career 6 May 1694 by mutinying against his captain at La Coruna, Spain. He renamed his newly-captured *Charles II* to *Fancy* and cruised along the African coast along a path quite similar to that taken by pirates in 1719: Isle of May to Guinea, then on to Principe Island and Anabon. That December, he crossed the Cape of Good Hope and landed in Madagascar the next month. His entry into the East Indies put him under the auspices of the English East India Company, usually neutral about piracy.

There, Henry Every would have made the acquaintance of "King" Adam Baldridge, pirate factor of New York councilman Frederick Philipse, who, since 1691, made his fortified factory base at Île Saint-Marie or Nosy Boraha, just off the northeast coast. Leaving Madagascar, Every sailed north to Johanna, today known as Anjouan, and captured an EIC ship. Afterward, Every banded together with five other pirates, including Thomas Tew. They took the rich flagship of Great Mughal, King Aurengzeb, called *Gang-i-Sawai* or "*Gunsway.*" They netted 500,000 gold and silver pieces, jewels, and many members of the King's court, including his own daughter.

The pirates, unbizarrely, had not been gentlemen. Several women killed themselves in disgrace at being defiled. *Gunsway* was on its way to the holy city of Mecca and carried religious significance as well. This incident sewed international discord which unfortunately threatened the Mughal's business relationship with the EIC's commercial base in Bombay – Every was costing profits! Agents of the company at Surat were captured and imprisoned even before London knew what had happened. Although Every was never captured, six of his crew had faced trial, a "cause celebre of its time." As Burgess saw it "Henry Every and the Board of Trade would cause a tidal shift in criminality" that would extend across the English Empire of the day – though this shift stalled for decades or longer in Stuart-founded America.[2] The Board of Trade largely formed as a result of a more organized liberal need to condemn Every's piracy – particularly, his crude methods.[3]

Two-thirds of the crew parted with Every and remained at Île de Bourbon, east of Madagascar, while Every and 113 men sailed *Fancy* to New Providence in the Bahamas. The new Board issued proclamations and attempted unsuccessfully to get the pirate-loving governors of America to turn over Every. He fell in with the unscrupulous Bahamian governor, Cadwallader Jones in March 1696. Jones was replaced with a governor just as unscrupulous, Nicholas Trott (not his nephew of the same name, the anti-pirate judge who tried Stede Bonnet), who also later traded with Every and suffered trial himself in London over the affair. Every's remaining crew dissolved into the background. The six who faced trial were eventually captured in Ireland. However, the EIC had promised the Mughal that they would capture Every and all of his crew. Everyone would be sorely disappointed – pirate-loving America hid these pirates well. A folk legend had been created. Not long after, "A Copy of Verses, Composed by Captain Henry Avery, Lately Gone to Sea to Seek His Fortune" appeared in which the pirate called sailors to join him in plundering ships from all nations. Plamen Ivanov Arnaudov writes in his dissertation for the Louisiana State University Department of English that:

> Around 1707, a rogue biography of Avery appeared. Titled "The Life and Adventures of Capt. John Avery, rais'd from a Cabbin Boy, to a King," the narrative had Avery marry a Mogul princess and become King of Madagascar.[4]

---

[2] Burgess, *Politics of Piracy*, 52.
[3] Burgess, *Politics of Piracy*, 41, 52-59.
[4] Plamen Ivanov Arnaudov, *Elements of Mythmaking in Witness Accounts of Colonial Piracy*, PhD Dissertation (May 2008), Department of English, Louisiana State University, 2; Burgess, *Politics of Piracy*, 60-63.

America would have continued growning even further apart from England over their love of piracy, if not for Queen Anne's War, which began in 1702. England warmed once more to pirates, who became desirable once again as privateers in her majesty's service. Still, it was a short-lived love affair. During this war, also, Scotland joined to make "Great Britain" in 1707, basically over the growing influence of capitalism – further inviting ridicule of the unstable policy of piracy. The Pirate Wars could never advance, however, as long as England still needed her crude warrior pirates. Finally, Queen Anne's War ended in 1713 and Britain was free again to visciously prosecute these men. Still, that same year, a British play titled *The Successful Pyrate*, by unknown playwright Charles Johnson, made Every famous again. It was like a siren's call to diminishing pirates of old England or new America. Copies of the play were sold and one of them evidently fell into the hands of future West-Indian pirate Edward England, who would capture a ship, rename it *Fancy*, after Henry Every's famous ship, and sail to Madagascar, even capturing an EIC ship at the island of Johanna, much like Henry Every had done! This play also brought into sharp relief the failures of the now British Empire (since 1707 Act of Union) to subdue piracy and crime in America and around the world. This assumes that they made more than a half-hearted attempt to do that and give up the profit.

Still, in the next couple of years, events grew more extreme between America and England. First, the Jacobite Rebellion of 1715 wedged them further apart and secondly, a catastrophic event of immense proportions! The England-America tenuous cultural gulf widened considerably when 14,000,000 pesos worth of Spanish treasure suddenly found their way within easy reach of these warlike West Indians in July 1715, causing piracy to surge. The Spanish at Porto Bello and Havana waited years to sail because they were desperate to avoid increasingly ubiquitous and notorious British pirates. When they happened to encounter a hurricane just off the Bahamas, eleven heavily-laden vessels smashed into the Florida shores, in shallow water, and kick-started the Golden Age of Piracy in the

Caribbean. Anglo-American pirates, out of work until the next war, greedily fed on the wrecks like vultures on freshly-dead carcasses. Massive greed and discontent nearly severed the ties that bound America to a more radical than ever Mother England, liberally intent upon destroying their uniquely piratical economy – their own century-old Frankenstein creation! This event accelerated the Pirate Wars and an American Revolution almost arrived sixty years early!

The greed of Anglo-American mariners proved an unimaginable phenomenon, in sheer defiance of the Board of Trade's Pirate War! Even the first American newspaper noticed the difference soon after the hurricane of 1715. The Massachusetts newspaper *Boston News-Letter* was the first in colonial America, having initially appeared in 1704. The first mention of the word "pirate" in reference to Englishmen in America, however, hit the pages of this newspaper a bit late in their local reporting arena. In over ten years, despite British anti-pirate influence, this first American "rag" never mentioned an "English" pirate. They covered plenty of French and Spanish privateers and pirates – just not *English*. By contrast, England's journalists – as opposed to *colonial* journalists - covered plenty of news of English pirates. Few readers probably noted the minor dissonance across the 3,000-mile-wide ocean. After the hurricane of July 30, 1715, a warning about Edward "Blackbeard" Thache (best known as Teach) became the first "English pirate" of whom America was willing to acknowledge – probably at Lord Sunderland's insistence, though. The Golden Age of American Greed had finally become too large to ignore! America finally had to admit that Englishmen preyed upon Englishmen and that they were just fine with that:

> One Thomas Barrow formerly mate of a Jamaica brigantine which run away some time ago with a Spanish marquiss's money and effects, is the chief of them and gives out that he only waits for a vessel to go out a pirating, that he is Governor of Providence and will make it **a second Madagascar**, and expects 5 or 600 men more from Jamaica sloops to join in the settling of Providence, and to make war on the French and Spaniards, but for the English, they don't

intend to meddle with them, unless they are first attack'd by them; nevertheless Barrow and his crew robb'd a New England brigantine, one Butler master, in the harbour of Providence and took a Bermuda sloop, beat the master and confined him for severall days, but not finding the said sloop fitt for their purpose, discharged her.[5]

Note that Thomas Barrow saw Madagascar as a shining beacon of piracy – something to be admired. Still, for several reasons, not the least of which was the desire to waste their spoils in peace, this brief American Rebellion of 1715-1718 ended. George I, new German king of England, issued a general pardon or Act of Grace on September 5, 1717. Gentlemanly pirates could retire and keep their spoils – an enticing offer to these wayward businessmen, long accustomed to the smuggling trade while hating the foreign king from afar.

Following this Act of Grace, Gov. Woodes Rogers planned to take charge of the "pirate nest" of the Bahamas, a major British advance in the Pirate Wars. Capt. Vincent Pearse, in HMS *Phoenix* arrived a few months earlier than Rogers. He found 209 pirates willing to surrender by early March 1718. One of those presumably-penitent pirates was a man named "Richard Taylor." A successful American Rebellion would have to wait, but Americans did not so easily give up their criminality.

The rest of this tale is truly a criminal one. Some pirates of the Bahamas "Flying Gang" were not already rich and wanted to continue, even though the 1715 wrecks had been fished out. Charles Vane represents the iconic example of their brood. And, a not-so-penitent Richard Taylor would soon after be followed by Olivier LeVasseur de la Buse, Jeremiah Cocklyn, Edward England, and others, raiding slave traders off the coast of Africa. Most were probably brutish sorts of a lower class of pirate. Afterward, they proceeded to the East Indies to recapture the treasure-filled gilded moments recounted in *The*

---

[5] "America and West Indies: July 1716," in *Calendar of State Papers Colonial, America and West Indies*: Volume 29, 1716-1717, ed. Cecil Headlam (London: His Majesty's Stationery Office, 1930), 139-159.

Successful Pyrate of their own revered American folk hero, Henry Every! They may even have picked up another member of Every's old crew from Madagascar: Jasper Seager.

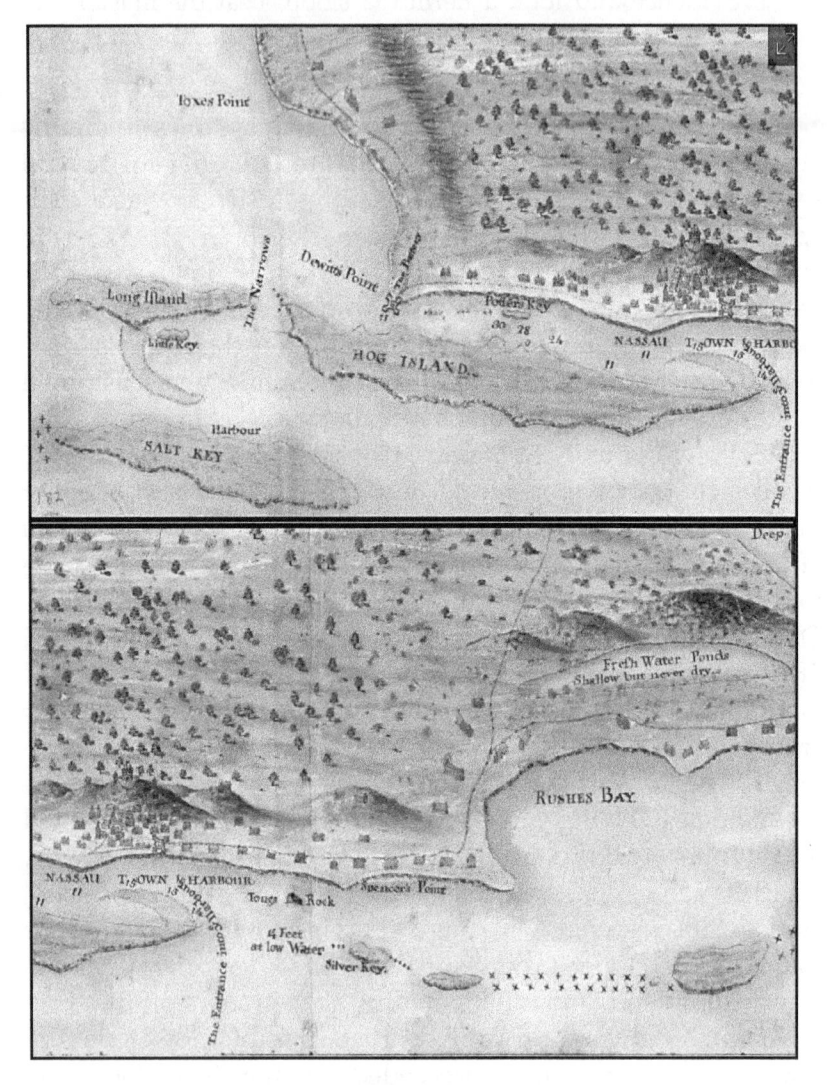

"An exact draught of the island of New Providence one of the Bahama Islands in the West Indies (c1700) – Library of Congress # 74692182. Open Copyright.

The "Madagascar" referred to by Thomas Barrow in 1716 had been, in their fertile imaginations, a shining example of a Pirate Nation! They knew that Madagascar was a place where pirates commanded respect – and these self-important, narcissistic, brigands demanded respect! Many more besides Barrow had wished to turn Providence into a West-Indian version of their ideal. But, it was not to be. Still, the shining beacon of "King" Baldridge's Madagascar remained.

Growing Importance of Madagascar

What was the special lure of Madagascar? What made it so enthralling to these American pirate dreamers of 1719? Respect certainly figured into its reputation, but so did money, women, and jewels! Bored pirates of the West Indies desired treasures more exotic. They wanted more than just lugging high-priced hungry slaves around the African coast with captured cargos of rice and linen! This Charles Johnson playwright fellow told them just where they might find it and how!

Through the early Pirate Wars immediately following formation of the Board of Trade in 1696, Gov. Benjamin Fletcher's New York had become the quintessential American pirate-loving colony. New York councilman Frederick Philipse contracted smugglers, pirates like Adam Baldridge, and other entrepreneurial pirate-merchants from those shores. Wealthy American merchants also traded slaves from Africa and Madagascar and operated short-term factories on the East Indian island outpost. So many slaves had been brought from Madagascar to the West Indies by 1680, that Malagasy slaves composed half of Barbados' slave population – in April 1681 alone, RAC agents reported 900-1,000. By 1698, Edmund Randolph commented from New York that "There were never so many vessels cleared from this port in one year for Madagascar and Curaçoa as now."[6] There were fifteen for Curaçoa and only four for Madagascar that year, with the West Indies still the primary focus for illicit trade. Madagascar, however, was running a close second. Americans weighed the

---

[6] "America and West Indies: August 1698 , 22-25," in *Calendar of State Papers Colonial, America and West Indies*: Volume 16, 1697-1698, ed. J W Fortescue (London: His Majesty's Stationery Office, 1905), 399-406.

new English anti-pirate legislation against long-proven piratical methods and chose the latter.[7]

The great attraction of Madagascar, though, centered upon more than slave profits – remarkably lucrative for Madgascar slaves (as much as 480%). Even more attractive, the Red Sea trade provided instant profits in actual treasure: diamonds, rubies, and other precious jewels! Another New Englander named Samuel Perkins described the average American sailor's experience in the East Indies of the day:

> About five years ago [ca. 1693] I went on board the Resolution, 18 guns and 60 men, Robert Glover, commander, on which I was detained by my uncle, who was boatswain. We sailed from New England at night by way of the Guinea Coast to Madagascar, where we victualled and cleaned, and then sailed to the Red Sea, where we waited for some India ships, but missing them, went to an island called Succatore at the mouth of the Red Sea for provisions, and thence to Rajapore, where we took a small Muscat ship. Glover sailed away in her, having quarrelled with the crew of the Resolution, and Richard Shivers, a Dutchman, was chosen commander. We sailed to Mangalore [Canara Coast of India], where we took, plundered and released a small Moor's[8] ship;

---

[7] Elizabeth Donnan, ed., *Documents Illustrative of the History of the Slave Trade to America, Vol. II: The Eighteenth Century* (Washington: Carnegie Instution, 1931), 549; John Franklin Jameson, *Privateering and Piracy in the Colonial Period: Illustrative Documents* (New York: MacMillan Company, 1923), 187n6; "Frederick Philipse [Filipse] (1626-1702), the richest trader in New York, but perhaps not the most scrupulous; see Henry C. Murphy, in his edition of the *Journal of a Voyage to New York* in 1679-80 of Jasper Danckaerts, pp. 362-365. The ship in which the two Labadist missionaries, Danckaerts and Sluyter, came to America was also named *Charles* and owned by [Dutch-born Margaret and Frederick] Philipse. It was in this year 1693 that Governor Fletcher instituted for him the Philipse Manor. Mary Philipse, who won the affections of young Major George Washington, was his great-granddaughter. It was said that Baldridge's establishment in Madagascar was sustained by Philipse's capital, to obtain for the latter a share in the profits of piracy. Cal. St. P. Col., 1697-1698, p. 108."

[8] Thomas Bayly Howell, ed., *A Complete Collection of State Trials and Proceedings for High Treason and other Crimes and Misdemeanors ... : with notes and other illustrations*, vol. 14 (1700-1708) (London : printed by T.C. Hansard for Longman, Hurst, Rees, Orme, and Brown [etc.], 1816), 155; Often, the reference "Moor" to rich ships of the East Indies was used loosely to refer between both ships of African moors (or Muslims) and ships of the Grand Mughal Empire in India, with whom the East India Company enjoyed trade associations. Indeed, Robert Bradinham, the surgeon aboard William Kidd's *Adventure*, was asked what he meant by the

thence to Calicut, where we took four ships, but finding the people hostile set fire to them and sailed to Cape Comorin. Here we missed the Malacca ships but took a Danish ship, which was rifled, then proceeded to Mauritius and so to St. Mary's, near Madagascar, where we met the John and Rebecca, Captain Hore, with a rich prize taken in the Persian Gulf, and found also a brigantine which had come from New York for negroes. At St. Mary's, which is pretty large and well populated by black people, Captain [Adam] Baldridge, an old pirate, had built a platform of twenty-two guns, but this was destroyed by the blacks when I was in Madagascar nine months ago [ca. 1692/3], and Captain Glover and the rest of the pirates killed. Eleven men in my house were killed at the same time in Madagascar and only myself spared. There was another party of English in Madagascar who defended themselves until Captain Baldridge, who was then absent in his brigantine came and took them off to St. Augustines [San Augustin in SW Madagascar]. I had run away from the Resolution before this happened, and was one of the party that was carried to St. Augustines. From thence she sailed to St. Helena [a volcanic tropical island in the South Atlantic Ocean], where we arrived six months ago, pretending to be a trading ship of New York, and so got water and provisions

---

"Moorish fleet" which they searched from the mouth of the Red Sea, to which he responded "The Natives of India, the Mahometans," a reference to ships of the Mughal Empire *and* African and Persian Muslims. The Indian Mughal Empire extended over nearly all of the Indian subcontinent and parts of Afghanistan at its peak. In the 17th century, Mughal India became industrialized, attaining the status of the world's largest economic power. It then accounted for 24.4% of world GDP, and was the world leader in manufacturing, producing 25% of global industrial output up until the 18th century. The Mughal Empire is considered "India's last golden age" and was heavily preyed upon by pirates. Together with the Ottoman Empire and Safavid Persia, the Mughal Empire was one of the Islamic Gunpowder Empires, owing to their abundance of Potassium Nitrate or "saltpetre." A "moor," however, is generally used today to refer to Muslims from the Mediterranean region, touching upon Africa, the Middle East, and Southern Europe historically – but, not generally to Asians. The early seventeenth-century pirates' favoring of the Red Sea Muslim empires and the riches routinely taken to Mecca probably generated the reference that spread to include Asia, becoming a generally racist term for the dark-skinned inhabitants of most East Indian principalities. "Mocha" or Mocca" refers to a specific coffee port on the modern Yemen Coast within the Strait of Bab-el-mandeb or the mouth of the Red Sea.

[despite Royal African Company or RAC restrictions against the Madagascar trade]. I ran away from her there, and waited on the island for three months until I got a passage home in an East Indiaman. I heard at Madagascar that a little before my arrival fourteen of the pirates had by consent divided themselves into two parties of seven to fight for what they had, thinking that there was not enough for all, and that the whole of one seven were killed and five of the other, so that two men enjoyed the whole booty. I heard and I believe that not only the Resolution but also the Mocha and several other ships were playing the pirate in different parts of the East Indies when I left Madagascar.[9]

Most East-Indian pirate narratives from this time until well into the eighteenth century appear remarkably similar in description. They undoubtedly drew no small amount of salivating hero-worship from easily-invigorated 18th-century pirates of the West Indies, with nothing to lose back there!

America made a habit of investing in East Indian piracy – for both slaves and jewels. American governors routinely issued privateering commissions to mariners who used these "legal" commissions to conduct illegal piracy. Captain Hoare of *John and Rebecca,* mentioned above, for instance had such a commission from the governor of New York to sail against French pirates. Once in the East Indies, he used his semi-legal authority to capture "a Prize (a pritty large ship), belonging to the Mogulls subjects at Suratt, which he had taken at the Gulph of Persia."[10] That the authorities in the colonies could not prevent the illegal pirate trade operated from America is best illustrated by Robert Quarry, writing to the Board of Trade from his post in Philadelphia:

---

[9] "America and West Indies: August 1698, 22-25," in *Calendar*; See primary documents related to "The Case of Henry Every," in John Franklin Jameson, *Privateering and Piracy in the Colonial Period: Illustrative Documents* (New York: MacMillan Company, 1923), 153-189; the full trial of Every's men can be found in volume 13 of Thomas Bayly Howell, ed., *A Complete Collection of State Trials and Proceedings for High Treason and other Crimes and Misdemeanors ... : with notes and other illustrations*, 34 volumes (London : printed by T.C. Hansard for Longman, Hurst, Rees, Orme, and Brown [etc.], 1816-1828); other pirate trials, including William Kidd's can also be found in these volumes.

[10] "Deposition of Samuel Perkins. August 25, 1698 " in Jameson, *Privateering and Piracy,* 176.

Since my last, two seizures have been made, one of East India goods brought from New York without cocket [bill of lading], and supposed to have been run in by a foreign ship from Madagascar; and though a private account was sent from New York of these goods and their value, which was £1,000, yet all that they seized is not worth above £150. Whether this was due to the folly or to the knavery of the officer I do not know; some say that most of the goods were landed before he went aboard [typical illegal tactic used later by smuggler John Hancock of U.S. Constitution fame]. I must repeat that if there were forty officers-more in this bay, they would not be able to secure the trade of the place; nothing can do it but a vessel of force constantly cruising between the Capes.[11]

The Glorious Revolution of 1688 might have chastised the Stuart dynasty, filled with aristocratic arrogance and illegal extravagances, but changes were slow to take place and they did not affect all parts of the Empire equally. The next two decades of the eighteenth century would experience much more liberal Parliamentary reforms in England, but they were slow to take effect in colonies on the fringes – colonies like in America originally formed during Stuart rule and still steeped in conservative Stuart values – later championed by Jacobites or politically-pro-Stuart rebels. Moreover, even under William III's rule, in the latter years of the seventeenth century, piracy and crime enjoyed the latter days of a more official status in the English Empire, still suffering from lingering Stuart extravagance.

William Kidd, reputedly the most famous pirate in American history, was born in Dundee, Scotland in 1654. Kidd settled in the new pirate haven of New York City, following its purchase from the Dutch. There he befriended many prominent colonial citizens, including three governors. These governors, as well as corrupt officials in England, encouraged Kidd's "privateering," and may also have encouraged illicit

---

[11] "America and West Indies: August 1698, 22-25," in *Calendar*; for John Hancock's smuggling, see http://alphahistory.com/americanrevolution/seizure-of-liberty/ .

operations as well. Kidd, though, probably betrayed his partners – thus, no honor among thieves.

In 1695, seven years after the Glorious Revolution and removal of the Stuart monarchy, Robert Livingston of New York, with Lord Bellomont and other men of wealth in England, arranged in London for a potentially-lucrative privateering voyage under Kidd's command. The king himself (William III) was to receive one-tenth of the profits.[12] Kidd sailed from England in April 1696 in *Adventure Galley*, 287 tons, 34 guns, and 70 men. At New York he increased his crew to 155 men (list appears in *Calendar of State Papers*, 1700, 199), and then sailed in September for Madagascar and the East Indies to take pirates. In the summer of 1698, India and the EIC began to complain about Kidd, who had sailed back to America. In November 1698, orders were sent to colonial governors in America to apprehend Kidd as a pirate at the first opportunity. Massachusetts law at the time prevented the penalty of death for piracy, so the Crown had him shipped to England in the spring of 1700 to face trial there. He was charged for the murder of one of his men and for piracy and tried at the Old Bailey. After a reputedly unfair show trial with scant evidence, he was found guilty and hanged on 23 May 1701.[13]

Kidd was not as fortunate as others had been in the East Indies. Clearly, English authorities in London, intending Kidd to be an example to America, felt that he deserved a pirate's death at the end of a rope, perhaps the price he paid for disappointing such prominent business partners, including the king. Pirates were by no means uncommon at the Old Bailey, but England suspiciously tried William Kidd with particularly corrupt relish! Maybe he should have remained at Madagascar!

There were two reasons Madagascar was so useful for these early American pirates before 1700. First, it was a good stopping point for rest and recreation, extra recruits, food, and water or war materiel resupply which aided raids upon the wealthy "heathen" Muslim kingdoms surrounding the Red

---

[12] Other shareholders were Sir Edward Russell, first lord of the admiralty, Sir John Somers, lord keeper of the great seal, the Duke of Shrewsbury, secretary of state, and the Earl of Romney, master-general of the ordnance

[13] John Franklin Jameson, *Privateering and Piracy in the Colonial Period: Illustrative Documents* (New York: MacMillan Company, 1923), 195n1.

Sea. Secondly, and growing ever more important, was a trade intimately related to the new economic system of capitalism – slavery. The slave trade increasingly gained reliance upon Madagascar during the decades straddling the turn of the eighteenth century – Chapter Eight explores the French side of this issue in depth. Of course, it was the peripheral value of the jewels and treasures that later attracted excommunicated pirates of the old "Flying Gang."

Professor Elizabeth Donnan explored documents relevant to the slave trade from 1441 to 1800. Her introduction to the volume on the eighteenth century precisely pinpointed the financial drive at the height of the general slave trade, just at the turn of the century:

> At the opening of the eighteenth century the African slave trade was the foundation on which colonial industry and the colonial commerce of European countries rested. It dominated the relations between the countries of Western Europe and their colonies; it was one of the most important factors in the wars of the century; it played a considerable role in the domestic affairs of the nations involved in it. The century saw the decline of trade by means of joint-stock companies with monopoly grants and an increase in the influence of the independent trader. It saw the growth of industries dependent upon African markets, the opening up of the Spanish American trade, and at the end of the century it saw the development of a humanitarian revolt, which from feeble beginnings grew to power sufficient to convince the world that this traffic was not business but crime, and crime of so intolerable a nature that it must be outlawed by civilization.[14]

For an already felonious America, eager independent merchants found slaves a perfect capital investment. Still, many of these independent merchants could not break into a trade already dominated by the Royal African Company (RAC). Africa provided the bulk of slaves for primary slave traders in this traditionally reprehensible business. They

---

[14] Donnan, *Documents Illustrative of the History of the Slave Trade*, II: xiii.

contracted at Guinea, Anomabo, Sierra Leone, Cape Coast Castle, or Whydah, aka Ouidah, Judah, or Juddah. Merchants even carried slaves to the East Indies from these ports. The RAC usually received the best treatment from African slave traders. Thus, African slaves were expensive.

Important for most of these less scrutinizing independent traders, like those in the American colonies, Madagascar was still an important and attractive source of cheaper slaves. Unlike most West African ports who despised pirates for their disruptions to the trade, slave-trading pirates at Madagascar actually became useful to less scrupulous American independents:

> Madagascar was politically divided among dozens of competing kingdoms, and captives in the internecine warfare became slaves to the victorious parties. For many coastal inhabitants, the pirates represented a welcome presence as potential allies in the increasing internal warfare. The pirates were excellent warriors and had access to firearms, important factors in the slaving wars that were spreading rapidly throughout the island.[15]

Engaging in the lucrative slave trade encouraged many merchants to overlook and even encourage the pirates' eccentricities. American colonial merchants, especially from New York, stationed known pirates as factors on Madagascar to broker slaves and other goods. Colonial goods shipped to Madagascar came a long way and were expensive, but Madagascar-based pirates obtained slaves easily and cheaply. The cheap cost of labor would have made a modern capitalist jealous! This lucrative pirate business respect is what Thomas Barrow had later been hoping to regain in the West Indies when he vowed to make the Bahamas "another Madagascar." It was all about respect in the pirate economy of America. This is why pirates seldom if ever used aliases, for they did not wish to hide their identities at all, but rather, advertise them!

The general rendezvous location, or primary trading outpost, that was chosen, was the island of Île Saint-Marie, on

---

[15] Kevin P. McDonald, *Pirates, Merchants, Settlers, and Slaves: Colonial America and the Indo-Atlantic World* (Oakland: University of California Press, 2015), 82.

the northeast side of Madagascar. Two agents of New York councilman Frederick Philipse operated there: Adam Baldridge and Lawrence Johnson. Baldridge, a known murderer and pirate since 1685, and Johnson "married local women on St. Mary's or Île Saint-Marie, and exercised considerable power over the locals, while guarding themselves by building a fort with twenty-two guns."[16] The number of guns actually varied widely in different reports. Still, pirates had developed a highly-organized "pirate-smuggling state" on the tiny East-Indian locale and began creating their own unique culture.

Kevin P. McDonald argues in *Pirates, Merchants, Settlers, and Slaves* that these West-Indian pirates developed their own identity on Madagascar as "Red Sea Men." The Jamaican-New York nexus pirates there blended their West-Indian ways with local Malagasy culture. This will be evident in Olivier LeVasseur's relationship with the locals as witnessed by Jacob de Bucquoy's anthropological observations, detailed in chapter six. The Board of Trade feared a pirate state was in the making, reporting "1,500 men, forty to fifty guns, and seventeen ships at the settlement of St. Mary's alone."[17] Many of these pirates...

> ... were universally male, and their national background was mainly English and Dutch, with a mix of French and, increasingly, African and African-American. Many were veterans of the Caribbean and Pacific campaigns against the Spanish, including members of the *Cygnet* and *Batchelor's Delight*, the first of over thirty Atlantic pirate ships that would sail to Madagascar.[18]

One contemporary English author (probably Daniel DeFoe) enthusiastically regarded Madagascar pirates as having formed a "regular government" and encouraging England's tacit approval.[19] Col. John Biddulph in *Pirates of Malabar* described the merchant's or pirate's criminal immunity in the

---

[16] Tim Travers, *Pirates: A History*, 164.
[17] McDonald, *Pirates, Merchants, Settlers, and Slaves*, 83.
[18] McDonald, *Pirates, Merchants, Settlers, and Slaves*, 83.
[19] Daniel DeFoe?, *A True Account of the Design, and Advantages of the South Sea Trade* (London, 1705).

East Indies admirably well in one paragraph – an explanation that applied equally to studies of the West Indies as well as the East:

> But the chief cause of [pirates'] immunity lay in the fact that it was the business of nobody in particular to act against them, while they were more or less made welcome in every undefended port. They passed themselves off as merchantmen or slavers, though their real character [note: more reputable than non-slavers] was well known, but they paid royally for what they wanted; and, as gold, silver, and jewels were the principal booty from which they made their dividend, many a rich bale of spices and merchandise went to purchase the good will of their friends on shore, who, in return, supplied their wants, and gave them timely information of rich prizes to be looked for, or armed ships to be avoided. They prided themselves on being men of honour in the way of trade; enemies to deceit, and only robbing in their own way. The Malabar coast [southwest Indian coast] was scandalized when [William] Kidd broke the rule, and tricked or bullied people out of supplies [this was probably the impression that got him hanged]. Officials high in authority winked at their doings from which they drew a profit, and when armed squadrons were sent to look for them, the commanders were not always averse to doing business with the freebooters [as referenced in chapter six].[20]

During Queen Anne's War (1702-1713), the East India Company made repeated requests for permission to seize pirates from 1707-1708. Forced into moving against their own financial interests, the Crown compiled several pages of information directly related to pirates then living on Madagascar in 1709. They finally discussed reasons for reducing the pirates of Madagascar, but little discussion about chastising them occurred. Their candid discussion of 15 December 1709 bluntly indicated the financial desires of a Pirate Mother Nation that felt remorse for her lost militant children – and the profit that they created. Pirates were resourceful and could help them fight the Catholic nations of

---

[20] John Biddulph, *The Pirates of Malabar and an Englishwomen in India Two Hundred Years Ago* (London: Smith, Elder, & Co., 1907), ix-x; Note that Biddulph, like almost every pirate history author since 1724 has been infected by Johnson or Mist's *A General History;* most usually repeat the many errors of that author.

France and Spain during the current war. That the Crown also coveted their treasures:

> Certain Pyrates having found the Island of Madagascar to be the most proper if not the only place in the world for their abode, and carrying on their destructive trade with security etc., and being since increased to a formidable body are become a manifest obstruction to trade, and scandal to our nation and religion, being most of them, English, at least 4/5ths... [and] form themselves into a settlement of robbers, as prejudicial to trade as any on the coast of Africa. It seems morally impossible to reduce them by force, for the pyrates have, by their liberality in bestowing part of their booties on the inhabitants [natives of Madagascar], so gain'd their love and esteem that, should any superior force be sent to reduce them, they might readily march up far into the country and be safe. Fair means is the only way to reclaim them; and in order to it endeavours of that nature have been used, but so ill managed that several of the pyrates who relied upon promises (and even Proclamations) and thereupon surrender'd themselves, having lost some their lives, all their effects, and been treated in a most inhumane manner, it is not to be expected the rest should come in without more ample security for the safety both of their lives and treasure, but have declared they are still willing to come in, on condition they were rendered secure to their satisfaction. [And, for the treasure part:] And though their treasure has been all got by robbery, yet since it can never be restored to the owners, having been taken (mostly, if not wholly) from the subjects of the Great Mogull, etc., and now lies buried or useless in or near Madagascar, it's much better they should be **permitted to bring it to England with safety, where it may do good, etc., and the pyrates be reclaimed and become bold and skilful mariners and subjects of H.M. etc**. Proposes that a person of considerable quality, well known to them, be sent with a pardon and conditions of surrender; and escort them to England with a squadron of 4 or 5 H.M ships, etc.[21]

---

[21] "America and West Indies: December 1709, 1-15," in *Calendar of State Papers Colonial, America and West Indies: Volume 24, 1708-1709*, ed. Cecil Headlam

Another memorial from the same month on "Suppressing the Pirates att Madagascar" regarded their "Rich," faithful, and always reliable English pirate friends. It states in its second paragraph:

> And understanding further that since the said Pirates have obtained great Riches their Affection (which is natural even to the Worst of Men) for the Account of their native Countrey is so reviv'd in them (and that more especially on Account they have receiv'd of Yr Majts. Most mercifull Disposition & glorious Reign) as makes them most earnestly desirous to return to their Duty & Allegiance, & to lay out their Money, & settle themselves in Great Brittain..."[22]

Even though England had liberalized a bit, they still had a long way to go – and the war stalled that effort. The money and the new war was clearly the draw – not any desire for justice for their neighbor states. That the world *beyond* England was a wild "uncivilized" place was never in question – neither was corruptive influence of the treasure on even the home government, willing as they were to forgive... for the right price. A deposition of the same day in 1709 told of *Carlisle*, Capt. John Brehoit of Carolina, who had, in 1700 left for Madagascar to pirate. Brehoit was captured and imprisoned, but the crew "cut cables and escaping the guns of the Fort sailed away to Africa and amassed good treasure by piracy at Madagascar."[23] The captain spent months in a Lisbon prison, was released, went to England and there met shipwright Peter Dearlove, whom he had known from prison in Lisbon. Dearlove was then currently incarcerated at Marshalsea for piracy. The two men connived with Lord Fairfax, with a shipbuilder named Fraeme, and Col. Elias Haskett (another one-time corrupt governor of the Bahamas). The three of them worked to:

(London: His Majesty's Stationery Office, 1922), 540-556.; British Library, Add MS 61590 and Add MS 61611.
[22] British Library, India Office, "A Memorial for Suppressing the Pirates att Madagascar & Preventing their further Piracies & Depredations...," Dec 1709, Add MS 61590, ff. 114.
[23] "America and West Indies: December 1709, 1-15," in *Calendar*.

... draw in the Lord Rivers and several other gentlemen to the expence of many thousand pounds in providing and equipping ships for going upon such pretended wreck, matters being so concerted that Haskett was to go Commander in Chief of the said ships, and Dearlove the pilot. But Breholt only acted behind the curtain, that his ill charectar might not defeat their reall design, which was to get out to sea and then to carry the said ships to Madagascar, upon a Scotch pardon for the pyrats there, that Breholt pretended to have gott.[24]

Ah, the monetary benefits of capitalistic freedom or free-from-prying-eyes enterprise! Governance be damned! Little had changed since Kidd and Every's day through to the first two decades of the eighteenth century – again, in both East and West Indies. The primary difference lay in the fact that the English East Indies was administered almost exclusively by a company and not the Crown – since 1600! "Crime" was merely a minor consideration on the corporate balance sheet and, thanks to smuggling, much of it was tax free! Furthermore, they were in direct competition with their French, Dutch, and Portuguese company counterparts. All was fair in love, war, and capitalism! Not surprisingly, one or more sides in such ruthless and often devious business negotiations inevitably felt cheated and the Malagasy people occasionally made their discord known. At the turn of the eighteenth century, the local natives again rebelled, destroyed the fort, and killed seven English and four Frenchmen.[25]

Despite the dangers, Île Saint-Marie had gained almost mythical status with elaborate riches flowing through the local economy of that port. The EIC offices in Bombay made it worse by exaggerating the numbers, but they suggested that a general pardon might convince the remaining pirates, living comfortably as virtual kings, to retire from their business. Why this pardon would presume to work better than others wasn't really the question to ask – how much profit it would turn was.

---

[24] "America and West Indies: December 1709, 1-15," in *Calendar*.
[25] Travers, *Pirates: A History*, 165-166.

The Royal Navy arrived a decade earlier and delivered the pardon to the remaining English pirates, who well knew how to use it for cover of their operations. Pirates remained at Madagascar and kept the legend alive, made even more noticeable in numerous British petitions to obtain the vast wealth still in the sands of Île Saint-Marie. Some took the pardon and retired wealthy men, repeated later by Edward Congdon, as revealed in Chapter Four. Some were probably killed by the natives, also a part of Chapter Four and Congdon's horrific tale, but it did not keep younger pirates from later dreaming the same dream. Gilded visions of jewels and endless parties, not entirely realistic, called like a siren to bored West-Indian pirates, ejected from their "second Madagascar" by Woodes Rogers in 1718. Cocoa, sugar, and bothering to steal trifles – even slaves, who required food and maintenance - from the Royal African Company grew stale and bothersome. A contemporary ballad provided the lyrics:

> Where is the trader of London town?
> His gold's on the capstan
> His blood's on his gown
> And it's up and away for St. Mary's Bay
> Where the liquor is good and the lasses are gay.[26]

Beginning with Olivier LeVasseur de la Buse or the "Buzzard," we'll now explore the tale of the last West Indian pirates who, cornered by social progress, drawn by legend, and such gilded bejeweled "get rich quick" fantasies of the last generation of buccaneers, sailed east for Madagascar to seek their fortunes!

A note about dates: the Gregorian Calendar Reform effected an 11-day change after September 1752 in Great Britain and her colonies (see Naish letter in Appendix). For most of the events in this book, from an English perspective, those changes are not important to the actors themselves. But, Catholic nations made nearly the same change in 1582 and comparing French and Spanish dates, (Denmark, since 1700) with English, for instance, *can* be a significant issue for those historical actors. I have indicated the difference between these Catholic dates (and Danish), such as 3 March 1720, with [J: 20 Feb] for instance to adjust for this 11-day difference to 18th-century British standard, or old Julian calendar. You can easily adjust for the 11-day difference in the modern British Gregorian calendar yourself, assuming it matters to you!

---

[26] Travers, *Pirates: A History*, 165-166.

Chapter 1: LeVasseur

"The Buzzard"
Leaves Africa for the Indian Ocean

As with the "Buzzard's" haphazard entry into the *East Indies*, no one knows exactly when Olivier LeVasseur de la Buse, "la Bouse," or the "Buzzard" (old meaning of French "La Buse")[1] began his pirate career in the *West Indies*. As pirates go, that's not much of a surprise – they tended to emerge from the backdrops of nascent colonial civilizations in the "Wild Frontier" waters of both Indies. Still, two records, both French, for LeVasseur in both Indies told that he was born in Calais, France of a good family and that he was educated. There is little reason to dispute this, aside from his apparent "bad boy" attitude.[2]

Depositions from the survivors of Samuel Bellamy's *Whydah*, wrecked at Nantucket, Massachusetts 26 April 1717,

---

[1] The modern meaning is "the nozzle." Old French term could mean variously: brute, fawn, critter, flock, fauna, cattle, or beast. The variant term "la Bouse" found in some texts means "Cow, beef, or bull dung" in modern French. There appears to be no historic connotation. Also "de la Buse" denotes a place, as in "from the Buse," but no place has yet been identified as "la Buse." The most likely answer is that the term is a derogatory epithet, denoting his behavior, as "brute" or "beast." His family name is LeVasseur or Le Vasseur and that name will be used throughout this book.

[2] These trial records were researched and retrieved by researcher Laura Nelson. They will be detailed later in Chapter 8.

tell of LeVasseur's early consortship with Benjamin Hornigold, the "common pirate" and leader of the Bahamas' "Flying Gang." The New Englander Samuel Bellamy and his close associate, Palgraves Williams, both hailed from devoutly religious Massachusetts when they took up piracy. Hornigold himself, had family in Massachusetts and a possibly Puritan background, which may have led them to sharing habitation on the destitute Bahamas as the "Flying Gang," founded primarily by Puritan New Englanders in the late seventeenth century.[3]

One of the *Whydah* survivors, John Brown was a Jamaican taken from Capt. Kingston's ship sometime in April 1716. Benjamin Hornigold in *Benjamin* and Oliver LeVasseur in 8-gun *Postilion* pirated his vessel west of Cuba. This is the first heard of the "Brute" or "Buzzard," but he was not the first "brutish" LeVasseur to enter the West Indies.[4]

As an interesting side note, an older LeVasseur was sent by French authorities from St. Christophers in 1640 to Saint Domingue and actually lent Tortuga its infamous "buccaneer" reputation. A French text from 1857 told that this LeVasseur governed quite undemocratically:

> Le Vasseur governed as a despot, and inspired terror in the inhabitants; the slightest faults were punished by suspending the culprits to a large iron crane which he had named "Hell," as he had called the fort where he held them in prison, "Purgatory."[5]

John Brown remained aboard "Lebous' [La Buse or LeVasseur's]" ship for about four months while near Hispaniola - roughly May-August 1716. After the cruise at Hispaniola, a dispute broke out between Hornigold and Bellamy – Bellamy taking some men onto *Mary Anne,* a sloop originally given to him by Hornigold after taking the French vessel (7 April) at Port Mariel, Cuba.[6] They then parted. Brown

---

[3] Laura Nelson, *The Whydah Pirates Speak* (CO: Laura Nelson, 2015-2016), 49-50.
[4] Nelson, *The Whydah Pirates Speak*, 49-50.
[5] *L'Art de Vérifier Les Dates* (Paris: M. Marquis De Fortia, 1857), 72.
[6] This is possibly the source of the idea given to Johnson for the erroneous Thache-Hornigold pupil-master relationship told by him in *A General History*. This tale involved Hornigold "gifting" *Queen Anne's Revenge* to Thache, similar to Hornigold "gifting" *Mary Anne* to Bellamy. The Timberlake deposition shows that Thache and Hornigold each possessed vessels of equal size and power. There is, therefore, no reason to assume any master-pupil relationship between them.

is one of two witnesses to this event of Hornigold being forced out by his subordinates in late summer 1716. Shortly thereafter, Hornigold found a brief consort in Edward "Blackbeard" Thache.[7]

Like Bellamy, LeVasseur also decided to part ways with Hornigold. He then joined Hornigold's old partners, Bellamy and Williams for the better part of eight months until March 1717. He parted from Bellamy before the fateful event that destroyed *Whydah*. Sailing north for the summer to pre-Maine-Nova Scotia waters, he there made a name for himself as a brutal man – not unlike the earlier LeVasseur in Tortuga and was perhaps nicknamed "la Buse" for these qualities.

An excerpt from the *Boston News-Letter* issue of 22 July 1717 demonstrated LeVasseur's alleged ruthlessness with Capt. John Frost of Piscataway, New Jersey on the 4th of July:

> [Capt. Frost] sent his Mate, who was received by the Pirate[,] sword in hand, Designing to have cut him down, if it had been the Master, for offering to run from him... Morning, Frost went on board the Pirate, where he was treated roughly... Then the captain of the Pirate sent Frost on board his own Ship, where he was accosted by the aforesaid Quarter Master with several others, he (being stript to his shirt) was unmercifully cutt, beaten and threaten'd to be skin'd and barbequ'd.[8]

Newspapers, however, have a way of amplifying a person's worst characteristics. LeVasseur was more concerned with profit than causing pain for pain's sake – nowhere near the ruffian pirate Edward Low. Moreover, people from whom one steals do not speak well of their thief when they are able to tell their story. Oddly enough, the victims *are* usually quite alive – with all of their fingers, ears, and toes – and able to tell their tale, contrary to the popular "dead men tell no tales" traditional pirate mantra. The only way to accurately describe LeVasseur's crew, as represented in this article, was "motley." As we shall see, mixed crews were a consistent characteristic of LeVasseur and his associates, well into their travels in the East

---

[7] Brooks, *Quest for Blackbeard*, 255-261.
[8] *Boston News-Letter*, 22 Jul 1717, 2.

Indies. This haphazard impression came not simply from their alleged brutal ways, but more so because Frost described them as a mixed crew, sailing a vessel of "20 guns, 250 tons, 170 men, of all Nations."[9] While this is, by no means, unusual in the maritime Atlantic world, it appears to occur more often with pirates. Still, LeVasseur's tendency to incur the brutish reputation that gave him is nickname remains somewhat consistent throughout his pirate career.

Colin Woodard, author of *Republic of Pirates* and staff writer for *Press Herald*, a local paper in his native Maine, wrote about the "Machias" or "Mechisses River" pirate. He believes this may have been Olivier LeVasseur de la Buse on the coast of Maine in 1717, contrary to *A General History*'s assertion that it was Samuel Bellamy. Capt. Charles Johnson, found by Arne Bialuschewski to be the probable pseudonym of Nathaniel Mist, was the author of this somewhat embellished work, fully titled *A General History of the Robberies and Murders of the Most Notorious Pirates*.[10] It was first published in London in 1724, but did not initially include a passage on Samuel Bellamy until 1728. *A General History* applied great verbage to *Whydah* being in this region, which was probably *not* the case. Woodard quoted *Whydah* expert Kenneth Kinkor as saying that Bellamy was far too busy and too far south in April 1717 (then on his way north from the Caribbean) to have visited this Machias Bay region. Woodard, however, claims that the detail in the text suggests that another pirate had visited there, though not Bellamy. LeVasseur, he believes, was that pirate – an intriguing suggestion.[11]

As Woodard observed, in the *Boston News-Letter* article of 22 July 1717, LeVasseur's men, then northeast of Cape Codd, "told the sloop's captain, John Frost, that they were headed for the New England coast [Massachusetts then included northern

---

[9] *Boston News-Letter*, 22 Jul 1717, 2.
[10] Arne Biaaluschewski, "Daniel DeFoe, Nathaniel Mist, and *A General History of the Pyrates*," Papers of the Biographical Society of America, 98 (March 2004), 21-38; Also discussed in: Baylus C. Brooks, *Quest for Blackbeard: The True Story of Edward Thache and His World* (Lake City: Baylus C. Brooks, 2016) 171-180.
[11] Colin Woodard, "Ayuh, ye mateys! Did the pirates of the Caribbean build a lair in Down East Maine?," *Press Herald*, 22 Jul 2012, https://www.pressherald.com/2012/07/22/ayuh-ye-mateys__2012-07-22/ (accessed 30 Jun 2018).

Maine, where Machias Bay is located] where they 'had a consort ship of 20 guns' — possibly a reference to the *Whydah*."[12] Woodard accurately argues that LeVasseur parted with Bellamy before *Whydah*'s destruction. After all, LeVasseur's crew mentioned to Capt. Frost in July their intended rendezvous with the likely *Whydah* after its wrecking at Cape Codd the previous April. LeVasseur was unaware of Bellamy's death – thus, he believed that *Whydah* still sailed. Then, Woodard claims, LeVasseur sailed north and may have visited the Machias River area before he had heard about the Whydah's destruction in April 1717 – he then built his encampment there, described in detail by *A General History*:

> They entered ["River Mechisses" or Machias River] as agreed, and run up about two Miles and a half, when they came to an Anchor, with their Prizes. The next Morning the Prisoners were set ashore with Drivers, and Orders to assist in the building Huts; the Guns were also set ashore, and a Breast Work raised, with Embrazures, for the Canon on each Side the River, this took up four Days: A Magazine was dug deep in the Earth, and a Roof rais'd over it by the poor Slaves the Prisoners, whom they treated after the same Manner as the Negroes are used by the West-India Planters. The Powder being secured, and every Thing out, they hove down the Sloop, cleaned her, and when she had all in again, they careened the Whidaw, by the largest Prize.[13]

Note that the treatment of Europeans "after the same Manner as the Negroes are used by the West-India Planters" was a hot-button issue with European sailors of the time. To be treated like a West-Indian slave was the most demeaning treatment that they could imagine. This made LeVasseur appear more evil to readers of this narrative and this may have been the intent of the author.

Woodard's theory has merit… assuming that a pirate had indeed visited this area in 1717. Still, there is, of known sources, no primary reference to pirates at Machias Bay in 1717.

---

[12] Woodard, "Ayuh, ye mateys!"
[13] Charles Johnson, *A General History*, 4th ed. (1728), 223-224.

Moreover, the tale of Samuel Bellamy at "Mechisses" in *Whydah* was certainly false, which does not represent the author of *A General History* favorably. Nathaniel Mist, as the controversial author of *A General History*, may have elaborated as he had done often. He may simply have drawn detail from the pirates Peter Rodrigo and John Rhodes' story from 1675 for his narrative.[14] Furthermore, the Nine Year's War provided even more geographic detail with Sir William Phips' recent expedition against French Acadia in the English-claimed "Province of Main" and to the "River Mechisses" in April 1690. In other words, plenty of detailed data on the Machias region was available to early polemical and controversial writers like Nathaniel Mist. He may have been mistaken or he may simply have lied – he did it before – about Samuel Bellamy, too![15] The present lack of primary evidence for the "Mechisses" or "Machias" pirate story as it relates to LeVasseur continues to frustrate Woodard and other supporters of this flamboyant and controversial secondary book as reliable history. Primary documents, however, appear more than adequate to supply the necessary information.

After the incident with Capt. Frost in July, LeVasseur abandoned his alleged "base" at Machias Bay and sailed to Madeira in September 1717. There, he experienced a near deadly encounter the next summer after perhaps leaving New Providence in a 6-gun sloop. This encounter involved HMS *Scarborough* at Isla Morro Blanco, appropriately on Friday, the 13th of July of 1718 (date in *Scarborough's* log), a favorite tiny careening island in the Grenadines just off Venezuela. That incident left "Capt. L. beur [buttery?] ye Pyrate"'s and his eighty men without their Brazilian prize. LeVasseur's master and eighteen of his crew were captured as the pirate sloop escaped with sixty men, leaving a quarter of their mates in the prize to face the Man-of-War. Capt. Francis Hume had towed the Brazilian ship to Nevis in the northern Windwards. The ship was condemned there at 6 p. m. of 6 July under Judge

---

[14] Declarations of Thomas Mitchell. May 24, 1675, and Edward Youreing. May 24, 1675, Case of Rodriguez and Rhodes, in John Franklin Jameson, *Privateering and Piracy in the Colonial Period, Illustrative Documents*, 1970 reprint (New York: Augustus M. Kelly, Publishers, 2008), 41-42.

[15] Brooks, *Quest for Blackbeard*, 329-339.

William Wooddrop, but Barbados argued with them over jurisdiction. LeVasseur's captured men were transferred to and jailed in Barbados by Gov. Lowther, but later escaped. Interestingly, Barbados fought with Nevis over jurisdiction and dispensation of the Brazilian prize ship, named ironically *Blanco*. Barbados Gov. Lowther believed "all pirates goods belong to the King" since *Blanco* was captured in their territorial waters. He accused Wooddrop of acting "illegally."[16]

LeVasseur did not appear in known records again this year. He then probably joined with William Moody (re: Snelgrave, 1734; *see also London Journal* in Appendix) until he arrived on the African coast in March of 1719. Here, he joined Howell Davis, fresh from burning the RAC's Fort James and capturing *Guinea Hen*, at Gambia River and later, Jeremiah Cocklyn in Sierra Leone River.

As earlier alluded to, the somewhat embellished *A General History* has been a difficult companion for pirate historians. As Johnson-Mist related his glitzy tales, he often gave great detail that presumably only an eyewitness would have been aware – the problem is that he also added inaccurate flamboyant detail to please his readers and sell copies, which caused the impression of his "eyewitness" accounts to seem, at best, suspicious. Still, aside from flashy newspaper accounts, he frequently used Admiralty documents to prepare his narrative, which alluded to its presumed accuracy. On the chance that it may be true, this lengthy passage might offer details on LeVasseur's presumed first meeting with Davis:

> After [Davis and probably Richard Taylor] had done as much Mischief as they could, and were weighing Anchor to be gone, they spy'd a Ship bearing down upon them in full Sail; they soon got their Anchor's up, and were in a Readiness to receive her. This Ship prov'd to be a *French* Pyrate [*Murrane*] of fourteen Guns and sixty four Hands, half *French*, half *Negroes*; the Captain's Name was *La Bouse* [LeVasseur];

---

[16] National Archives, London, Master's Log of HMS *Scarborough*, ADM 51/865 & Captain's Log of HMS *Scarborough*, ADM 52/227; "America and West Indies: November 1718," in *Calendar of State Papers Colonial, America and West Indies: Volume 30, 1717-1718*, ed. Cecil Headlam (London: His Majesty's Stationery Office, 1930), 381-397.

[LeVasseur] expected no less than a rich Prize, which made him so eager in the Chace; but when he came near enough to see their [Davis'] Guns, and the Number of their Hands upon Deck, he began to think he should catch a *Tartar*[17], and supposed her to be a small *English* Man of War; however, since there was no escaping, he resolved to do a bold and desperate Action, which was to board *Davis*. As he was making towards her, for this Purpose, he fired a Gun, and hoisted his black Colours; *Davis* returned the Salute, and hoisted his black Colours also. The *French* Man was not a little pleased at this happy Mistake; they both hoisted out their Boats, and the Captains went to meet and congratulate one another with a Flag of Truce in their Sterns; a great many Civilities passed between them, and *La Bouse* desired [of] *Davis*, that they might sail down the Coast together, that he *(La Bouse)* might get a better Ship: *Davis* agreed to it, and very courteously promised him the first Ship he took, fit for his Use, he would give [the ship to] him, as being willing to encourage a willing Brother.[18]

---

[17] Tartary, "the land of the Tartars" (modern "Tatar") - a name used primarily by Turko-Mongol peoples after the Mongol invasion and the resulting Turkic migrations. Tartars were a Turkic people, native to a region east of the Caspian Sea. Ghengis Khan's horde was a mix of Tatars, Mongols, Turks, etc. Here, used figuratively for "savage, rough, irascible person" (1660s). To catch a Tartar "get hold of what cannot be controlled" is recorded from 1660s. The implication here is that Davis' excessive armament indicated to LeVasseur that Howell Davis' vessel armament was extensive by comparison to his or "uncontrollable."

[18] Charles Johnson, *A General History of the Robberies and Murders of the Most Notorious Pirates,* 2nd edition (London: T. Warner, 1724), 184-185; Note that the 1726, two-volume edition may not have been written by Mist, as he left for France in exile about this time. This author is not of the opinion that Nathaniel Mist ever left London while writing his original pirate essays. Most of the details that he discovered probably came through the Admiralty offices at Whitehall, some details he may have picked up from the docks on the Thames, and perhaps visitors to his print shop on Great Carter Lane. Otherwise, the outspoken Jacobite Mist was quite busy answering court summons and raising cash to pay his fines. He used "filler" and elaborated on facts where none existed, especially on the pirates whose trial documents were not readily available to him. His detail on Blackbeard, Stede Bonnet's early history from which he stole data from Samuel Bellamy, and the Frenchman Jean Martel are glaring examples of this onerous practice. On the pirate documents closer to London, he was able to easily obtain them from his usual government sources – the trial records for Bartholomew Roberts at Cape Coast Castle, for instance, which he quotes extensively – CNN and other journalists have their government sources!

Owing to its rarity and relevance, this passage is convenient; however, it is one of the few excerpts that will be borrowed from the questionable "Johnson" for this book. Other primary sources, including the deposition of *Guinea Hen's* captain, William Slade of Barbados, more than adequately cover most of the detail. Indeed, Slade's deposition may have served as his source for this passage. Johnson, though, tended toward sensationalism and distortion of those facts. Pirate historians should mostly be wary of Johnson.[19]

Any narrative provided by the irresolute Johnson should be verified, if possible. Doing so affords an opportunity to explain the strengths and weaknesses of various primary sources available to the pirate historian. Many sources can directly answer this particular verification task on the Davis-LeVasseur meeting – three of them remarkably confirm Johnson and one appears to not – others simply can't be trusted. One must determine the strengths of these sources before using them.

Primary sources usually evolve directly "from the source," or an eyewitness, and are more reliable than secondary ones, like Mist's or Johnson's book. Still, care must be taken with newspaper data in particular, for many are unfortunately misreported and are essentially secondary in content. Some erroneous newspaper accounts wholly distort facts. Furthermore, newspapers often shared their news with other papers, causing multiple reports of the same information. This applies a false sense of confirmation of any erroneous reports through sheer repetition. In this case, one particular account tends to conflate Davis and Edward England, further confusing the timing of Davis' whereabouts. This particular article from the *Weekly Packet* (24 Oct 1719) of London will be analyzed in Chapter Two, in which we explore England's early career.

The reason this excerpt of Johnson's was used here was that Howell Davis in *King James* (prob former *Loyal Merchant*, Mathew Golding, commander) most likely *did* meet Olivier LeVasseur at

---

[19] Compare Johnson's passage with *Weekly Packet* of 5 December 1719, transcribed in E. T. Fox, *Pirates in Their Own Words*, 378-381.

Gambia River about early-mid March before heading south (following trade winds) to Sierra Leone River, as Johnson said. LeVasseur indeed had found a better vessel there with the help of Jeremiah Cocklyn. This happened at least a couple of weeks before Cocklyn also found an even better ship in *Bird* galley of London, Capt. William Snelgrave. An apparently accurate newspaper report, also from the *Weekly Packet*, supports this as well as a deposition from a prisoner of Howell Davis. Still, only after careful analysis, both of these sources were determined as essentially reliable.

Depositions *can* be more reliable than newspaper accounts, depending wholly on the witness, of course. As with troubled newspaper reports, the reliability of any deponent must also be determined from the surrounding detail. They can also be cross-verified with other sources, such as personal letters and accounts. All sources have their own characteristic bias, which must be identified and accounted for at all times. This is an important step and adequate time should be spent on source analysis before using them. After careful consideration of these primary sources, the details can then come through.

There were two versions of William Snelgrave's account that need to be considered. Both of them are from the perspective of an eyewitness, but one written in 1719, at the time of the event. The other is a version of that story written fifteen years later in a book published in 1734 – and any source published *after* 1724 could have been infected by Johnson's *A General History*. Snelgrave's later narrative also suffers from the possibility of memory loss – the narrative of 1719 should be judged more reliable on that point. A confusing statement in Snelgrave's later published narrative created a problem, owing possibly to the fifteen years of faulty memory of Snelgrave; plus there are technical problems in his narrative. Snelgrave related in his book of 1734 that after his capture in early April:

> On the same day also arrived one Captain Davis, who had been pirating in a sloop, and taken a large Ship at the Cape Verde Islands. He coming into Sieraleon with her, it put

the other two Pyrates into some fear, believing at first it [Davis' prize] was a Man of War.[20]

This is Snelgrave's introduction for Davis; he noted that Davis appeared to arrive coincident with his own capture on 4th of April. His letter of 1719 did *not*, however, say this. LeVasseur was already with Cocklyn then, which created great confusion for the historian, reading Johnson's assertion that Davis and LeVasseur met and traveled to Sierra Leone together. This had possibly occurred earlier; Snelgrave's narrative is unintentionally misleading because of his misperception. Davis had probably gone back out of Sierra Leone River after his earlier arrival, captured the "large Ship [*Eagle*?]," and returned after Snelgrave was captured. By Snelgrave's statement, it seemed that Davis had arrived at Sierra Leone separately, although one should not blame Snelgrave for this easily-made error. Other sources still verify Johnson's account.

Weekly Packet of 5 and 12 December 1719 may have issued a rather accurate report from the African Coast. A competitor's newspaper would have been readily available to Nathaniel Mist, publisher of the *Saturday Evening Post & Weekly Journal*. The report of 12 December told that Howell Davis, after capturing Fort James on James Island (now called Kunta Kinteh Island) in Gambia River earlier that winter, met a "Brigantine [that] also first began in the West Indies, and most of the Men also came from Providence, but were pardon'd."[21] The article then tells that Davis and the "brigantine" sailed into Sierra Leone and took several ships that we know from Snelgrave's letter of 30 April 1719 were primarily the acts of Davis, Cocklyn, and LeVasseur. The "briganteen" was undoubtedly *Murrane* and its captain was Olivier LeVasseur.[22]

---

[20] William Snelgrave, *A New Account of Some Parts of Guinea and the Slave Trade* (London, 1734), 199.
[21] *Weekly Packet,* 12 Dec 1719; National Archives, London, Pearse to Admiralty, 3 Jun 1718, ADM 1/2282; while LeVasseur does not appear on Pearse's list in ADM 1/2282, his quartermaster in April 1719, Palsgrave Williams does and was indeed pardoned there Feb/Mar 1718.
[22] William Snelgrave, "William Snelgrave to Humphrey Morice," 30 April 1719, *Humphrey Morice Papers,* microfilm: 4 rolls (Marlborough, Wiltshire: Adam

A corroborating report on the early March Davis-LeVasseur consort theme appeared in Richard Luntly's later deposition. The details sound suspiciously like Johnson's paragraph on Davis' meeting with LeVasseur. On the 23rd of December 1718, as Luntly told, he "could not be contented with staying in the Island of Barbados, and Use the Home Trade; but [he] must Ship [him]self for Guiney."[23] He found a sloop of that island, aptly named *Guinea Hen,* Capt. William Slade who was heading for the Gambia River. He signed on and sailed with Slade, arriving 8 February 1719 in that river. They soon met with two pirates there, 26-gun *King James,* Capt. Howell Davis, and *Buck,* possibly then under Richard Taylor, both recently come from New Providence Island in the Bahamas.

Soon afterward, perhaps near the 1st of March, while still at Gambia River, Luntly told that another pirate joined with Davis by the name of "Captain L'Bouse." This agreed with Johnson and *Weekly Packet's* report of 12 December 1719. "L'Bouse" or Olivier LeVasseur then consorted with Davis until they sailed to Sierra Leone, "where happened to be another pirate lying there."[24] This pirate was Jeremiah Cocklyn in *Rising Sun,* verified by both of Snelgrave's narratives, 1719 and 1734.

Incidentally, Johnson made it sound as though Davis and LeVasseur had never before met, but it's quite possible that they had. LeVasseur's then-quartermaster, Palsgrave Williams had surrendered to Capt. Vincent Pearse of HMS *Phoenix* while in the Bahamas during the pirate-pardoning phase of early 1718. Davis presumably sailed on Woodes Rogers' sloop *Buck* from that location only a little later, before he wound up pirating ships in the Cape Verde Islands off Africa. They probably crossed paths in the Bahamas.

Snelgrave annotated his tale of 1734 with the story of Jeremiah Cocklyn's departure from pirate captain William Moody, who used to sail this *Rising Sun* (36 guns in November 1718 at St. Thomas). Olivier LeVasseur and Jeremiah Cocklyn actually had

---

Matthew Publications, 1998); perhaps the 4-gun brig (tender to *Rising Sun*) formerly commanded by Richard Frowd.

[23] "The Last Speech and Dying Words of Richard Luntly (Edinburgh, 1721)," in E. T. Fox, ed., *Pirates in Their Own Words* (Fox Historical, 2014), 119.

[24] "The Last Speech and Dying Words of Richard Luntly," 119; The primary strength of Luntly's deposition is his account of Davis and Roberts from Africa to Brazil and back to the Windward Islands 1719-1720.

both left William Moody's command circa February 1719 and sailed to Africa. Cocklyn took Moody's 36-gun ship, *Rising Sun*, from him and sailed to Sierra Leone. LeVasseur, who left after Cocklyn, mutinied and took Moody's remaining brigantine, *Murrane*. He may have taken *Amity* and *Glasgow* off Carolina (*see London Journal* in Appendix), and then apparently sailed to Gambia, where he first encountered Davis 8th of March. Cocklyn had several smaller merchant vessels that he had taken in 36-gun *Rising Sun* off Sierra Leone when his old shipmate LeVasseur showed up about 22nd of March in an augmented 30-gun *Murrane* with Davis in *King James*.[25]

Snelgrave probably learned about this from the pirates themselves in 1719, but may have heard this from elsewhere in the fifteen intervening years before publication of his book – just not Johnson, apparently. Snelgrave's impression was that Cocklyn left his former commander because Moody was too much of a gentleman:

> There were, at the time of our unfortunate arrival in the above mentioned river, three pirate ships, who had then taken ten English ships in that place. As it is necessary for illustrating this story, to give an account how these three ships came to meet there, I must observe that the first of them which arrived in the river was called the *Rising Sun*, one Cocklyn commander, who had not with him above twenty-five men. These having been with one Captain [William] Moody, a famous pirate, some months before in a brigantine which sailed very well and took the *Rising Sun*, they were marooned by him, (as they call it) that is forced on board that ship and deprived of their share of the plunder taken formerly by the brigantine. These people being obliged to go away in her with little provision and ammunition, chose Cocklyn for their commander and made for the River Sierra Leone.[26]

As Johnson asserted, LeVasseur did not like *Murrane* and was searching for another when he and Davis met up with

---

[25] National Archives (UK), Deposition of William Slade, 3 Jun 1719, CO 31/15, ff. 13-19.
[26] William Snelgrave, "William Snelgrave to Humphrey Morice," 30 April 1719, *Humphrey Morice Papers,* microfilm: 4 rolls (Marlborough, Wiltshire: Adam Matthew Publications, 1998).

Cocklyn in *Rising Sun*. The French pirate captured Lambert's *Sarah* or *Duke of Ormond* soon after arriving in Sierra Leone River in March, and discarded *Murrane*. Cocklyn also found one that he liked better, as Luntly said, "a Galley belonging to London," 120-ton *Bird* galley, Capt. William Snelgrave. So, Luntly was also a witness to the events at Sierra Leone, some of which had preceeded Snelgrave's observations.[27]

Therefore, the LeVasseur-Davis premise appears valid. Davis and LeVasseur may indeed have met at Gambia River, and then sailed to Sierra Leone, together, in March, *before* 4th of April, when Cocklyn captured William Snelgrave in *Bird*. This exercise demonstrates that history is no less a science than physics!

Davis and LeVasseur arrived from Gambia at Sierra Leone River, with *Guinea Hen* sloop in tow, by 22nd of March – fifteen days after Cocklyn (7th March), who, according to Snelgrave, rejoiced at seeing LeVasseur again. Together, Cocklyn and LeVasseur then took "Segnor Joseph, a black gentleman [Catholic priest]... several Bristol and other ships arriving soon after were likewise taken."[28] These differences in narratives are quite subtle, so misreporting in newspapers easily confused facts.

The tale of William Snelgrave is quite valuable for not only the particulars of these pirates and their interactions, but it also establishes a baseline for understanding their personalities, and the well-deserved epithet of "brute" or "la Buse" for Olivier

---

[27] "The Last Speech and Dying Words of Richard Luntly," 119.
[28] Snelgrave, "Snelgrave to Morice," 30 Apr 1719; Snelgrave, *New Account*, 197; William Moody, born about 1694, took *John and Thomas* on 5 Nov 1718, using 36-gun *Rising Sun;* after Cocklyn and LeVasseur left him about March 1719, may have taken *Scarborough* frigate near St. Christiophers only a month later. He was later hanged at Cape Corso Castle, Africa, in February, 1722; From E. T. Fox on Pyracy Pub (http://pyracy.com): On August 23 1720, William Bournal was tried in Bermuda. Bournal was charged that he had "in the Month of June in the year 1718 at the Bay of Honduras and within the Jurisdiction of the Adm.lty of Great Britain, and at divers other times and places after, join wth or enter yourself on board a ship called the *Rising Sun*, whereof one William Moody a noted Pirate was Commander". Bournal cruised with Moody "in and about the West Indies for the space of two Months", before leaving his crew to join "one Joseph Thompson another Noted Pirate" on a sloop called the *Eagle* (CO 37/10, f. 170); fot more on "Segnor Joseph," see Arne Bialuschewski, "Black People under the Black Flag: Piracy and the Slave Trade on the West Coast of Africa, 1718–1723," *Slavery and Abolition* Vol. 29, No. 4, December 2008, 463-464, 470n16.

LeVasseur. Although, Jeremiah Cocklyn may have been the greater brute; they were certainly suited for one another!

Captain William Snelgrave's
A New Account of Some Parts of Guinea, And the Slave Trade

William Snelgrave was probably born in Ringwood, Hampshire, England – just one place of origin for many English Snelgraves or Snelgroves. His family was somewhat prolific in England at the time and there is some difficulty in determining his exact birth or baptism among the many listed on *Ancestry.com*. Still, a wealthy mariner by this name subscribed to Joseph Harris' *A Treatise of Navigation* in 1730 and Thomas Riley Blanckley's *A Naval Expositor* in 1750 (we find later that this 1750 record is for his son, William, who was also a mariner). Assuming that the 1730 reference is for the same William Snelgrave probably born around 1680, *FamilySearch.org* shows his likely baptism on 21 January 1681, son of William, in Ringwood, Hampshire, England. *Voyages* database also shows a "William Snelgrave" in command (apparently, Capt. Negus was replaced) of *Eagle* in 1704, the adventure upon which William's father also died in Virginia. This man's son William, who sailed *Eagle* home from Virginia, then, would have been 23 years old, if born in 1681, and was probably the mariner of whom we search. The history thus follows from 1704.[29]

Mariner William Snelgrave early became involved in the slave trade, joining Capt. Jonathan Negus and his father, 1st mate William Snelgrave, as purser in *Eagle* galley, obtaining £3,000 of insurance in London on 25 January 1704, stopping at Old Calabar in Guinea in spring 1704, suffered numerous sick,

---

[29] Ancestry.com, U.K. and U.S. Directories, 1680-1830 [database on-line] (Provo, UT, USA: Ancestry.com Operations Inc, 2003); "England Births and Christenings, 1538-1975," database, *FamilySearch* (https://familysearch.org/ark:/61903/1:1:NK6D-RY5 : 11 February 2018, William Snelgrove, 21 Jan 1681); citing RINGWOOD,HAMPSHIRE,ENGLAND, index based upon data collected by the Genealogical Society of Utah, Salt Lake City; FHL microfilm 0994051 IT 3-5.

young William's first "slave mutiny," and finally delivering 302 slaves to Virginia by October. Capt. Negus, who probably fell ill, passed command to the elder William Snelgrave before leaving Africa for Virginia, where the elder William then died. The younger William then returned *Eagle* to London by spring of 1705. After some years, he returned again to Calabar in 1713, this time as captain of *Anne,* owned by "Messrs. Bradley" of Virginia, and then delivered 395 slaves to Antigua. Trading slaves at Whydah in 1717 as master of South Sea Company's vessel *Prince,* he delivered 186 slaves to Jamaica and 167 to Portobello. Two years later, as captain of London merchant Humphrey Morice's vessel 120-ton, 16-gun, and 45-man *Bird* galley, he was captured by pirates in 1719 and lost *Bird* to them. In 1734, three years after Humphrey Morice possibly committed suicide, Snelgrave told of this encounter in section III of his *A New Account of Some Parts of Guinea and the Slave Trade* (London, 1734).[30]

Not to be deterred, the spirited slave-trader Snelgrave took out the then-usual commission as privateer in 1719 and returned to Cape Coast Castle in Morice's 200-ton, 16-gun, and 45-man *Henry,* taking 367 slaves to the Americas by the next year. He returned almost annually to the African Coast for his employer. Again, he saw Bight of Benin, Jacquin, Cape Lopez and Annobon in another vessel of Morice's, the much larger 300-ton *Katherine* with 606 slaves for Pernambuco and Antigua in March 1727. Snelgrave is best known for his experiences at the Bight of Benin in 1727, told in "History of the Late Conquest of the Kingdom of Whidaw by the King of Dahomè," or Book I of his *New Account,* pages 1-156. He returned there again in *Katherine* in 1730, delivering even more slaves to the Americas. As one of the more successful perpetrators of the horrid slave trade, it is perhaps more gratifying to discuss the

---

[30] William Snelgrave, *A New Account of Some Parts of Guinea and the Slave Trade* (London, 1734), 193-288; *Voyages* database; Elizabeth Donnan, ed., *Documents Illustrative of the History of the Slave Trade to America, Vol. II: The Eighteenth Century* (Washington: Carnegie Instution, 1931), 7, 342n1; Robin Law and William Snelgrave, "The Original Manuscript Version of William Snelgrave's 'New Account of Some Parts of Guinea,'" History in Africa (Cambridge University Press), Vol. 17 (1990), 367-372; Ancestry.com databases; National Archives, London, Ship: Henry (Master William Snelgrave), 1719, HCA 32/62/44; Humphrey Morice was also governor of the Bank of England..

alleged "good captain" Snelgrave's capture by pirate Jeremiah Cocklyn in 1719, detailed in "Book III."[31]

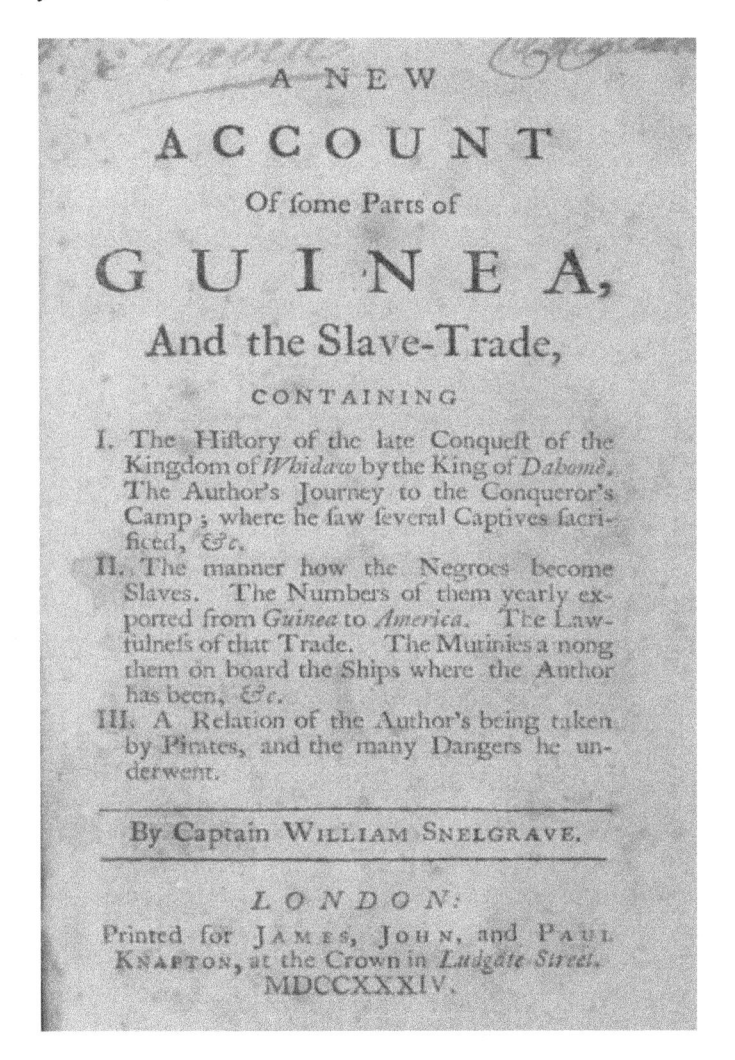

A NEW ACCOUNT Of some Parts of GUINEA, And the Slave-Trade,

CONTAINING

I. The History of the late Conquest of the Kingdom of *Whidaw* by the King of *Dahomè*. The Author's Journey to the Conqueror's Camp; where he saw several Captives sacrificed, &c.

II. The manner how the Negroes become Slaves. The Numbers of them yearly exported from *Guinea* to *America*. The Lawfulness of that Trade. The Mutinies among them on board the Ships where the Author has been, &c.

III. A Relation of the Author's being taken by Pirates, and the many Dangers he underwent.

By Captain WILLIAM SNELGRAVE.

LONDON:

Printed for JAMES, JOHN, and PAUL KNAPTON, at the Crown in *Ludgate Street.*
MDCCXXXIV.

Snelgrave told in his book of 1734 that he was given command of *Bird* by Morice in November 1718. This was his first run for Morice, apparently also the Calabar veteran's first visit to Sierra Leone, and he was eager to please this new

---

[31] Robin Law and William Snelgrave, "The Original Manuscript Version," 367; *Voyages*.

employer. Still, fate dealt him more than one serious blow. Humphrey Morice is regarded as the 1720's foremost slave merchant, subject of an entire chapter in James A. Rawley's *London, Metropolis of the Slave Trade*. He also had repeated issues with pirates. In 1715, Morice commissioned *Whydah* galley, and appointed Dutch Captain Lawrence Prince to command her. This ship was taken in 1717 by pirate Samuel Bellamy. Following that event, Morice, with Micajah Perry, Woodes Rogers, Samuel Buck, other merchants of Bristol, and Secretary Joseph Addison, called for extended anti-piracy legislation in America. Still, many merchant captains who encountered pirates sailed for Humphrey Morice; he lost at least four cargoes and/or ships to pirates in 1719 alone!

Richard Blincko, for example, sailed for the prominent slave-trader Morice in *Heroine* galley since 1715, a ship that Morice owned in partnership with Director of the South Sea Company John Fellows (apparently an in-law of Blinckos'). He also owned *Elizabeth*, captained by John Thompson, the year after pirates burned his *Jacob and Jaell*. Both of these ships were also taken by these same pirates and appeared on Snelgrave's list of April 1719, displayed later in this chapter. Morice also part-owned *Princess*, Capt. Abraham Plumb[32], taken by pirate Howell Davis and on which Bartholomew Roberts served before turning pirate. James and Jeremiah Pearce also sailed in the slave business for Morice, who encountered the pirate ship *Cassandra*, captained then by Richard Taylor, and delivered to the Spanish. Morice and his associates had frequent undesirable contact with these pirates.

Whig member of Parliament from 1713-1731 and a political liberal for his day, Morice was also an investor in the East India Company and a governor of the Bank of England. The influential Humphrey Morice played a vital if indirect part in opposing piracy in general. By 1730, the year before his death, Morice instructed Capt, Jeremiah Pearce, then in command of *Judith* snow, to "Let your Great Guns and small Arms be loaded and in readiness for use and Service upon any

---

[32] Former captain of *Little London* (Dec 1709, Mar 1711, & 1712) and 120-ton, 6-gun *Kent* galley c. 1712, and *Mermaid* (1716), all of the Guinea slave trade to Jamaica (CO 142/14).

Occasion" during his voyage.[33] He may have been disturbed by past pirate activity or the French who encroached on England's African trade. Concerned then merely with logistics of earlier voyages, he made no similar instruction to Snelgrave in 1721 or 1722. Morice ended his own life in 1731, possibly wrought by £150,000 of massive debt and facing charges of corruption and fraud concerning the Bank of England.[34]

In preparation for his 1719 cruise to Sierra Leone, Snelgrave sailed for the Netherlands (just across the channel from Kent, England) with fellow Morice employee, Capt. Richard Blincko in *Heroine*. During a sudden storm on the night of 11 December 1718, they both ran aground about three miles from Hellevoetsluis (small port a few miles south of Rotterdam) in mud, "a lamentable accident" which slightly damaged their ships and cargo.[35] They lightened their ships and found *Bird* had been stuck in seven feet of the mud. Snelgrave and Morice wrote each other every few days while the crews dug a 300-foot trench to free *Bird* and *Heroine*. Bad winter weather fought the efforts of both captains. Snelgrave had just signed aboard *Bird's* crew, yet, because he ran aground, lost a cooper, carpenter, and five sailors who believed that they would lose their wages. "The officers and people left are very hearty," Snelgrave wrote on the 17th, "but ye cold weather pinches every one that wee are not half men, however

---

[33] Humphrey Morice, "Morice to Jeremiah Pearce," 31 Mar 1730 and Snelgrave voyages of 1721 and 1722, *Humphrey Morice Papers*, microfilm: 4 rolls (Marlborough, Wiltshire: Adam Matthew Publications, 1998).

[34] Humphrey Morice, "Morice to Jeremiah Pearce," 31 Mar 1730 and Snelgrave voyages of 1721 and 1722, *Humphrey Morice Papers*, microfilm: 4 rolls (Marlborough, Wiltshire: Adam Matthew Publications, 1998); James A. Rawley, *London, Metropolis of the Slave Trade* (Columbia: University of Missouri Press, 2003), 40-80; Statistics given by Rawley: in 1720, Morice had 8 vessels in the slave trade, when most had only a few or one; by 1726, he had 7 of London's total of 87 slave ships, designed to carry 2,500 of an intended 26,440 slaves, or 9.4 percent to America; Morice, Richard Harris, and Francis Chamberlayne and 46 others owned 24.4 percent of the total London slave trade, with Morice owing the most.

[35] William Snelgrave, "William Snelgrave to Humphrey Morice," 13 Dec 1718, *Humphrey Morice Papers*, microfilm: 4 rolls (Marlborough, Wiltshire: Adam Matthew Publications, 1998); The nearby port of Rotterdam ("muddy water") grew into a port of importance, becoming the seat of one of the six "chambers" of the Vereenigde Oostindische Compagnie (VOC), the Dutch East India Company.

ye hopes of getting ye ship afloat again & into ye Haven bouys uss up."[36]

Sierra Leone River portion of William Snelgrave's Map of West Africa, 1734

Snelgrave and Blincko finally caught a sufficient tide high enough to get them off the mud. They then completed their transactions with Bastiean Molewater, Morice's business associate in Rotterdam.[37] They obtained their cargo for intended trade at Africa and both returned to Great Britain, encountering repeated weather difficulties along the southern coast of England. Finally, *Bird* and *Heroine* put in for repairs at Kinsale, Ireland. There, they completed fitting and provisioning of their ships and *Bird* left 10 March 1719 on this fateful voyage to Sierra Leone. He arrived there in less than three weeks time on the 4th of April.[38]

---

[36] William Snelgrave, "William Snelgrave to Humphrey Morice," 13, 17, 20, 22, and 27 Dec 1718, *Humphrey Morice Papers,* microfilm: 4 rolls (Marlborough, Wiltshire: Adam Matthew Publications, 1998).

[37] Wife of Bastiean Molewater: Megtelina Blockhuijs, son Bastiean baptised 12 May1709 in Rotterdam.

[38] William Snelgrave, "William Snelgrave to Humphrey Morice," 30 April 1719, *Humphrey Morice Papers,* microfilm: 4 rolls (Marlborough, Wiltshire: Adam Matthew Publications, 1998); Snelgrave wrote this letter to Morice while still on the Sierra Leone River and still with the pirates. He states in this letter that he arrived at

"The day that I made the land," wrote Snelgrave, "which I was with in three leagues of the river's mouth, it became ca'm in the afternoon."[39] Seeing a smoke on shore, often a signal of welcome to passing ships, Snelgrave sent his first mate Simon Jones in the pinnace to investigate. Jones, experienced with the region, was to follow the smoke and see where it led – if there were a town. As Snelgrave was unfamiliar with Sierra Leone, he relied partly on Jone's knowledge of the region plus "Capt. Gordon's Journall," apparently notes of a previous visitor.[40] As he said, he "went by that tell twas dark, and anchord of[f] ye Cape 1 1/2 mile from the shore."[41]

Snelgrave instructed Jones to ask the natives how affairs stood up river. As the map shows, two towns, Boure and Boulon K., indeed, sat on that river, but these men were more likely to encounter Europeans first. The Sierra Leone River is twelve miles wide at the entrance. The depth throughout most of it is shallow, requiring ships to hug the starboard shore, leading them directly to a privateer village at that location.[42] Perhaps unknown to Snelgrave, this village lay southward on the starboard shore, just behind the cape, near future Freetown, on Frenchman's, St. George's, or Kru Bay – known also as

---

the river on 4th of April, whereas his book states the 1st of April. The presumption is that the letter is more accurate.

[39] William Snelgrave, *A New Account of Some Parts of Guinea and the Slave Trade* (London, 1734), 200.

[40] David Richardson, ed., *Bristol, Africa and the Eighteenth Century Slave Trade to America*, Vol. 38: The years of expansion, 1698-1729 (Bristol: Bristol Record Society, 1986), 9; Capt. John Gordon of Bristol, captain of *Prince of Mindleheim*, owned by John Goodwin & Co., sailed to Africa 24 Feb 1708 and returned to London, 26 Jun 1708. He traded in Africa from 1702-1715 and was acquainted with Humphrey Morice and William Snelgrave. See: "Journal, May 1726: Journal Book C.," in *Journals of the Board of Trade and Plantations: Volume 5, January 1723 - December 1728*, ed. K H Ledward (London, 1928), 251-270.

[41] Snelgrave, "William Snelgrave to Humphrey Morice," 30 April 1719.

[42] John Hamilton Moore, *A new and complete collection of Voyages and Travels: containing all that have been remarkable from the earliest period to the present time ... With an account of the rise and progress of navigation among the various nations of the earth ... comprehending an extensive system of geography, describing in the most accurate manner, every place worthy of notice in Europe, Asia, Africa, and America ...* (London, Printed for the proprietors and sold by A. Hogg, 1778), 475.

"Pirate's Bay" from 1721 when Bartholomew Roberts later revisited.

Jones returned and informed Capt. Snelgrave, not surprisingly, that "no people lived there," or no natives, anyway.[43] Also, the smoke, he alledged was made by some travelers who were roasting oysters on the shore. Jones indicated that they would be gone before he could get a mile from the ship. Also, Jones inferred that as night closed on him in the pinnace, it would soon be too late for him to return to *Bird* if he had gone too far. Snelgrave reluctantly accepted his report, but suspected there was more to the story. Suspiciously, sunset was not for two more hours after Jones' return to *Bird*.[44] Jones simply made excuses for not going into the mouth of the river, but why? Well, he was lying.

"Evening," as Jones defined it, was five p.m. With some daylight yet and despite Jones' reticence, Snelgrave took *Bird* into the mouth of the river.[45] Just as dusk came on, they spied a ship at anchor a little further up, perhaps at Frenchman's or Pirate's Bay. Just after dark, they themselves anchored there at about 7 p.m. As the men ate their dinner, others on watch informed him of some unknown men approaching in a boat. Snelgrave hoped that some white merchants may have spotted them and had come to trade. As a precaution, however, he sent his first mate Jones to get the crew ready with weapons to defend the ship. This had been a grave error.[46]

As the sounds of the boat came closer, *Bird's* second mate hailed into the darkness over the water. The answer came back, "*Two Friends*, Capt. Elliot of Barbados." Jones told Capt. Snelgrave that he knew Elliot and this vessel. Snelgrave urged caution, however, and was proved right when, after another hail, the answer came back with a volley of pistol shot. Snelgrave marveled at the audacity, if not insanity of these revealed pirates![47]

---

[43] Snelgrave, *A New Account*, 200.
[44] Snelgrave, *A New Account*, 201.
[45] Note that Snelgrave does not mention doing this in his letter of 30 Apr 1719 to Morice. He said that he anchored 1.5 miles from the cape and *there* the pirates came to *Bird* in a boat – not within the river; Sunset on 1 April at 8:46 N lat. = 18.15.
[46] Snelgrave, *A New Account*, 201-202.
[47] Snelgrave, *A New Account*, 202.

Snelgrave ordered the guns to fire, but then found that Jones had been feeding him misinformation with plans to betray him to the pirates. *Bird's* men later told Snelgrave that they would have taken up arms, but the chest had been moved – as it turned out, by Jones. The pirates then began to board,

> ... firing their pieces several times down into the steerage and shot a sailor [Hugh Ross] in the reins [kidneys], of which wound he died afterwards. They likewise threw several granado-shells, which burst amongst us so that it is a great wonder several of us were not killed by them or by their shot.[48]

Snelgrave and his loyal men resisted, but to no avail. After the pirate boarding party had taken the ship, they found Capt. Snelgrave and asked him why he tried to fight:

> The Quarter master of ye pirates came down into ye Steridge, asking were was ye Comdr. [I] told him I was[.] he asked me what was ye reason I order'd a great gun to be fired at ye boat and ye people to defend ye ship, I replied it was my duty, upon wch he clapt a pistoll to my breast, but putting it one side with my hand it fir'd under my arm[.] he then beat me with his Cuttlash unmercifully, and order'd me with ye people on deck[.] as soon as came up, ye boatswain of ye pirates told me they never gave quarter to any Comdr. who offer'd to defend his ship, and strikes at me with his broad sword but God was pleased to cause ye blow to [strike] on ye quarter deck, otherwise [I might] had been cleft down[.] then they beat me again, but all my people beg'd [the pirates] not abuse me, saying they never were with a better Comdr. upon wch they left of[f] and fell to beating them[.] Mr. Richardson was cut on ye head wth several others that suffer'd. They had turn'd their boat adrift haveing drank damnation to one ye other if they did not take ye ship, so order'd me to send one of my boats with 4 hands to take up theirs but if they did not return declar'd would pistoll me[.] Mr. Jones offers readily to go & tho' very dark [he] luckily found her, but as he came along side would have had ye people given 3 chears, they had more prudence then to comply for not one would have been left alive if they had done it. By this time ye Pirates ship was come down and fir'd at uss, then they sent me onboard, Mr.

---

[48] Snelgrave, *A New Account*, 205.

Jones going with me, I was treated civil enough, and they told me should have no further hurt to my person, provided ye people gave me a good character.[49]

The quartermaster then straightened Snelgrave and told him that his life would be spared, so long as none of his crew complained of him. Meanwhile, the pirate vessel had unmoored and drifted down river towards *Bird*. When their boarding party began shooting in the air out of celebration, the pirates on the ship mistook this for them being slaughtered by *Bird's* crew and gave them a broadside. The pirates on *Bird's* deck looked surprised. Snelgrave mentioned to the pirate quartermaster that they could call to their ship with the bullhorn, to which the quartermaster again thought to kill him, but took his advice instead.[50]

When the misunderstanding was corrected, Snelgrave asked permission to tend to his men. The quartermaster agreed. Soon, his captain called from the pirate ship to send Snelgrave over. When the wounded Snelgrave made it over the gunwale, he found himself before Capt. Jeremiah Cocklyn of *Rising Sun*, a rather short, stout man.[51] The pirate addressed him:

> I am sorry you have met with bad usage after quarter given, but it is the fortune of war sometimes. I expect you will answer truly to all such questions as I shall ask you, otherwise you shall be cut to pieces. But if you tell the truth and your men make no complaints against you, you shall be kindly used.[52]

Another man whom Snelgrave recognized with four pistols in his girdle and a broadsword in his hand then walked up to Snelgrave. He told him that his name was James Griffin and that they had been school-fellows. Although Snelgrave remembered him well enough, but having heard that it was sometimes unwise to be familiar with pirates, he acted as though he did not. As it turned out, Griffin was a forced man,

---

[49] Snelgrave, "William Snelgrave to Humphrey Morice," 30 April 1719.
[50] Snelgrave, *A New Account*, 207, 210.
[51] Nationa Archives, London, Information of William Snelgrave, 20 Jan 1721, HCA 1/54, f. 128; Snelgrave in this deposition tells that the ship that took him was "Maroon," obviously *Murrane*; See Appendix for whole document.
[52] Snelgrave, *A New Account*, 212.

lately mate to David, brother of Capt. James Creichton of Bristol, both of whose vessels, *Queen Elizabeth* of London and *Nightengale* of Bristol, were then captured and in the river. There, also, was *Two Friends,* Capt. William Elliot of Barbados, the name used as a ruse by the pirates earlier. This pleased Snelgrave, who immediately owned that he knew the man. Then, Griffin asked for a bowl of punch and led Snelgrave to the cabin with Capt. Cocklyn where they drank and toasted one another – then, of course, as with most of these pirates, the health of the Pretender, James III.[53]

Snelgrave was given the use of a hammock to rest his wounded body and Griffin stood watch over him. Soon, the inebriated pirate boatswain who had earlier attempted to beat out his brains with a pistol butt found him there. Griffin asked him what he wanted and the man answered "to slice his liver, for he was a Foul Dog!"[54] Griffin fought the man off and later, asked Cocklyn to talk sense into the boatswain. Snelgrave, realizing that it may be beneficial to him, even defended the pirate and asked the others not to have him whipped. And, yet again, according to Snelgrave, the hostile man assaulted him![55]

At 8 a.m. on the 5th of April, Snelgrave's former 1st mate, Simon Jomes, who had joined the pirates with nine others of Snelgrave's crew, went over to *Bird* and began tossing their cargo overboard – money and necessaries being most desired by the pirates. Not surprisingly, these pirates and their new recruits often tricked others into signing their articles, as Snelgrave wrote in his letter to Morice:

> The next day [Jones] persuades yᵉ people to enter saying I design'd it my self, so he got 9 to do it. God only knows whether this man had any hopes of meeting with pirates here when he advis'd to touch at this place, for Thos. Christopher one yᵗ has enter'd & afterwards repented told me wth tears in his eyes, yᵗ he said to him yᵉ day before came in here[, Simon Jones] was in hopes to meet with pirates.[56]

---

[53] Snelgrave, *A New Account*, 214-216; *Voyages* database.
[54] Snelgrave, *A New Account*, 217.
[55] Snelgrave, *A New Account*, 218.
[56] Snelgrave, "Snelgrave to Morice," 30 Apr 1719.

Then, one of several private merchants at Sierra Leone, Capt. Henry Glynn, heard that Snelgrave had been taken. The popular Glynn was, by 1721, the governor for the Royal African Company's Fort James in Gambia River. Glynn came aboard *Bird* with Capts. Howell Davis and Olivier LeVasseur, with whom he had then been trading, to see him on board *Rising Sun*. These were captains of two other pirate vessels that had lay hidden from view in the river by an arm of land that jutted out into it. From his letter of 1719, Snelgrave believed at first, probably from the reactions of the other pirates, that Davis had arrived to Sierra Leone River after he had been taken, but Davis had been there all along with LeVasseur. Indeed, as Snelgrave soon discovered, there were a total of three pirate ships in that river when he first arrived. He would not have escaped alive if he had not eventually surrendered![57]

Snelgrave found Davis a generous man, who kept his crew in order. He noted that he rather liked him, as well. His opinion of the cruder Cocklyn, however, was different. He also regarded Davis as unwilling to either consort with or join the other two, which he found to Davis' credit:

> Neither had he consorted or agreed to join with the others when I was taken by Cocklyn, which proved a great misfortune to me (as will appear afterwards), for I found Cocklyn and his crew to be a set of the basest and most cruel villains that ever were; and indeed they told me after I was taken that they chose him

---

[57] Snelgrave, "Snelgrave to Morice," 30 Apr 1719; Snelgrave, *A New Account*, 224; Before 1704, Glynn had worked for the RAC at the Bunce or Bence Island fort. Afterward, he conducted private trading on that river, with his partners, Mead, Pearce and Jones and with the occasional pirate. For some years the firm had great success, its warehouses and barracoons being casually scattered amongst those belonging to the great companies along fifty miles of the river. His neighbor was John Leadstone, "Old Crackers," a retired early pirate. In 1722, Glynn became the RAC factor at Fort James in Gambia River, a master of *Clarendon,* but died in spring 1723; a substantial study of Henry Glynn and Robert Plunkett can be found in J. M. Gray, *A History of the Gambia* (Cambridge: University Press, 1940); Dr. John Atkins in Donnan, *Documents of the Slave Trade,* II: 264; John Atkins wrote "The private Traders are about 30 in number, settled on the Starboard [right or south] side of the [Sierra Leone] River; loose privateering Blades, that if they cannot trade fairly with the Natives, will rob"; Interestingly, a "Henry Glynn" appears as captain of *Mermaid* in the Guinea-Jamaica slave trade in 1710/11 and 1713 and "Henry Glinn" appears on Capt. Vincent Pearse's list of 209 pirates [ADM 1/2282] who surrendered at New Providence, the Bahamas in Feb/Mar 1718.

[Cocklyn] for their commander on account of his brutality and ignorance.[58]

Davis allegedly argued for Snelgrave, saying that if *he* had been taken by Snelgrave and that "I had defended my ship against him, he should have doubly valued me for it."[59] Snelgrave noted that Davis and Cocklyn nearly came to blows over differences in temperament and for slights received, readying their ships to fight one another – and would have if Glynn had not interceded with an offer of the liquors aboard *Bird* to Davis. Davis and his crew came aboard that night to take advantage of the offer, and almost all was consumed by these boozing brigands![60]

Shipping record from Jamaica in 1713 showing Henry Glynn, captain of 70-ton, 10-gun *Mermaid* of London, coincident with Peter Skinner (see Chapter Two) of 90-ton, 12-gun *Tunbridge Galley* of Bristol, both from Guinea, Africa. Source: CO 142/14.

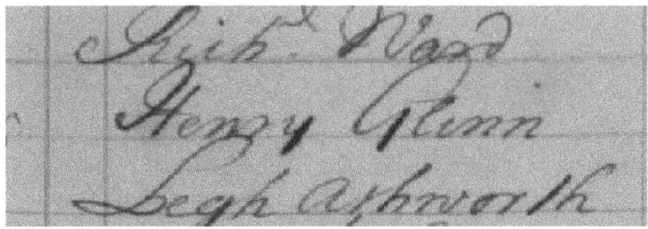

"Henry Glinn" appeared on the last page of Capt. Vincent Pearse's List of pirates who surrendered at New Providence, Bahamas Feb/Mar 1718. The "Legh" or Leigh Ashworth whose name appeared after Glinn was a consort of Henry Jennings in 1716. Source: "Vincent Pearse to Admiralty," 3 Jun 1718, ADM 1/2282.

On the morning of the 6th of April, LeVasseur and his men were allowed aboard the *Bird* prize to join the others in their

---

[58] Snelgrave, *A New Account*, 199.
[59] Snelgrave, *A New Account*, 226.
[60] Snelgrave, *A New Account*, 226.

plunder. They consumed the few liquors and food that had been left from the previous soiree. Afterward, all of the pirate captains had gone ashore to the home of Capt. Glynn. Glynn was a possible former pirate himself who surrendered to Capt. Pearse in the Bahamas early in 1718. He had lived at Sierra Leone in past decades as a trader and pirate/privateer facilitator, sometimes as RAC official. Snelgrave then described the pirate town: é

> Around [Glynn] gathered, and flourished for more than thirty years, a settlement of interlopers, loose privateering blades," of various nationalities, who supplied the wants of the visiting pirates, storing provisions and liquor, employing ship-repairers and armourers, building a jetty (now hidden beneath the western arm of the stone pier), and converting some of the mud-flats into safe careening yards. They kept a trained troop of grumettas [native soldiers] for their protection, employed many slaves, and had good friends amongst the natives along the river and the coast.[61]

Capt. F. T. Butt-Thompson, author of the quote above, taken from *Sierra Leone in History and Tradition,* helps to demonstrate that pirates, privateers, RAC officials, and other trusted servants of the Crown, were rather interchangeable in the eighteenth century. Pirates of this period were not criminals, *per se,* but rather, briefly-errant mariners of varying experience and wealth living in a harsh environment and remote wilderness. Survival and profiting in such places required unconventional means and activities. Piracy, for them, was merely an active means of gaining capital – a derivation of frontier free enterprise.

Another Sierra Leone merchant of the privateer town, Edward Hogbin (b. 1687) of Dover, Kent, made his fortune from his association with pirates. Hogbin lived at the privateer community from 1718-1721, and he witnessed Cocklyn taking Snelgrave's *Bird* galley in April 1719 and *Henry and Temperance,* Capt. Henry Owen of Barbados in 1720. Snelgrave deposed 20 January 1721, in which he claimed that Hogbin had come aboard *Bird* to discuss arrangements with Cocklyn, Davis, and

---

[61] Capt. F. T. Butt-Thompson, *Sierra Leone in History and Tradition* (London: H. F. & G. Witherby, 1926), 52; Snelgrave, *A New Account*, 238-239.

LeVasseur for some of *Bird's* goods, as did many of other residents there. After the pirates left at the end of April, Snelgrave demanded to examine the goods that Hogbin had received. These included "several peices of harlem Strippes, Nittacrees, blew Bafts, Cotton Romalls" and other goods to the value of £50.[62] Snelgrave had to pay Hogbin a third of their value, or £16-16-8, for the return of these goods. Hogbin actually extorted a 33.3 percent commission on storage of stolen merchandise from Snelgrave. This was simply the profit-motivated commerce of most privateer-pirate merchants at Sierra Leone – for a third of the proceeds, but with little expense and risk.[63]

Snelgrave found Henry Glynn an agreeable sort and asked the pirate quartermaster to be allowed to go to Glynn's and speak with him, to which he assented. When Snelgrave arrived, he complained for a second time that his necessaries and clothing had been destroyed. The captains all agreed to allow Snelgrave one of the vessels that they had no use for, with some of the cargo useless to them still aboard, also probably for a one-third value for salvage. The pirates also proposed to take him with them down the Guinea Coast where he might trade these items for gold, or have other merchandise from the other French and Portuguese ships that they would take along the way.[64]

For some strange reason, the pirates could not understand Snelgrave's refusal, assuming ignorantly that these gifts were generous, illegal or not. Capt. Davis again appeared the lone voice of reason amongst them and defended Snelgrave's choice. Afterward, they grudgingly agreed to give him only what belonged to him and his ship's cargo that remained. They then told Snelgrave that he might have LeVasseur's old brigantine *Murrane*. Meanwhile, they allowed Snelgrave to stay aboard *Two Friends*, which they had fitted out as a storeship,

---

[62] National Archives, London, Deposition of William Snelgrave, 21 January 1721, HCA 1/54, ff. 127-129.
[63] National Archives, London, Deposition of Edward Hogbin, 16 May 1721, HCA 1/54, f. 125.
[64] Snelgrave, *A New Account*, 239-240.

still under William Elliot. Snelgrave found their changed behavior quite remarkable:

> And now, the tide being turned, they were as kind to me as they had been at first severe. So we got the brigantine along the side of the prize and as bale goods and eases came to hand, we got them into her. Only now and then we lost some by the ill-nature of two or three leading pirates, for if we could not receive the goods so fast as they expected with the few people I had of my own then with me, they would let them drop overboard.[65]

Thinking on LeVasseur's disposal of *Murrane*, Snelgrave here diverts to a past event the pirates related to him concerning *Murrane,* which LeVasseur had first taken from Capt. Moody and did not like very much. He had desired another ship. This event happened "some weeks" before *Bird* came into the river on 4th of April. It involved two captains of ships taken and burned by Davis and LeVasseur (Cocklyn was busy with *Two Friends*) who had luckily escaped into the woods. These two captains had first escaped and hidden from the pirates, but later attacked and killed someone at the home of "Mr. Jones" over provisions, perhaps a partner of Glynn's. The story came up because these same two captains caused them trouble again by trying to steal their slaves and incite others against them. The stories of how these two captains, John Bennet and John Thompson, came to so annoy these pirates, Snelgrave found interesting. Embedded within this tale is also revealed LeVasseur's late March search for *Duke of Ormond*.[66]

Robert and Jane, Capt. John Bennet, bound from Antigua to the coast of Guinea, was taken February 1719 at Cape Verde Islands by Howell Davis. Davis restored Bennet's ship which unfortunately for Bennet then came into the Sierra Leone River about early March, where Capt. John Thompson of *Jacob and Jael* of London had arrived before him.[67] They carried their ships up river to "Brent's Island" (Bunce Island; the fortified settlement of the Royal African Company) perhaps to see Gov. Robert Plunkett

---

[65] Snelgrave, *A New Account*, 243-244.
[66] Snelgrave, *A New Account*, 245-247; *Weekly Packet*, 12 Dec 1719.
[67] Southampton Archives (UK), SC9/4/81, Examination of Richard Vavastour, 25 Jul 1719; Vavastour was a crewman of John Thompson's on *Jacob & Jaell*, who was held for "six weeks," meaning that pirates had been at Sierra Leone since about 15 March. He took passage on a French ship to the island of Guernsey, then to Southampton, arriving 24 Jul 1719.

about slaves for their cargo. When Cocklyn approached them about 7th of March, flying the "Jolly Roger," they brought their ships very near the shore, entrenched under the fort's guns, and having landed ammunition, resolved to defend them against the pirate who they saw coming after them.[68]

LeVasseur in brigantine *Murrane* and Howell Davis in *King James* then approached the RAC fort on 22nd of March. LeVasseur desperately wanted to be rid of William Moody's old ship since before he met Davis at Gambia. He had hoped Bennet or Thompson's vessel might suit him better. Robert Plunkett's forces at the fort began firing at the pirates to protect the two ships under their walls. The pirates together took the day. Seeing the futility of the fight, Bennet and Thompson fled into the woods (presumably on the mainland) with the aid of Gov. Plunkett. These two captains hid from the pirates there, with only rice and oysters to sustain them.[69]

Out of anger, Levasseur and Davis burned both captain's vessels. They also kidnapped Gov. Plunkett, who would endure the same treatment under Bartholomew Roberts two years later. LeVasseur did not get a new ship that day, but soon found another to his liking, *Sarah* of London, Capt. Jonathan Lambert, a vessel captured by them shortly afterward. This vessel LeVasseur took and named *Duke of Ormond*, thereby happily scrapping his distasteful old *Murrane*. Snelgrave occasionally makes such diversions rich in detail.[70]

---

[68] Snelgrave, *A New Account*, 247; Information of Edward Green, 271; Bunce Island (also spelled "Bence," "Bense," or "Bance" at different periods) is an island in the Sierra Leone River. It is situated in Freetown Harbour, the estuary of the Rokel River and Port Loko Creek, about 20 miles upriver from Sierra Leone's capital city Freetown ("Journal, May 1726: Journal Book C.C," in Journals of the Board of Trade and Plantations: Volume 5, January 1723 - December 1728, ed. K H Ledward (London: His Majesty's Stationery Office, 1928), 251-270; "[Capt. Bonham states] the Company have no forts there, though they formerly had one, which was of no use, because ships could not come within 15 or 16 miles of it"). It had only a skeleton crew operating the 22-gun fort for the first two decades of the 18th century. In 1728, Portuguese raiders took the island and fort away from the British. It came back to private British hands in 1750 when a London corporation, Grant, Sargent, & Oswald, purchased it for the South Carolina and Georgia slave trade.

[69] Snelgrave, *A New Account*, 247; National Archives (UK), Robert Plunkett to RAC, 30 April 1719, T 70/19, f. 165.

[70] Snelgrave, *A New Account*, 247-248; National Archives (UK), Deposition of William Slade, 3 Jun 1719, CO 31/15, ff. 13-19, and Robert Plunkett to RAC, 16 Apr 1719, T 70/6, 97–98; *Weekly Packet*, 12 Dec 1719; *Boston News-Letter*, 4 Apr 1720; Snelgrave, "Snelgrave to Morice," 30 Apr 1719; Henry Hunt, 190-19; Donnan,

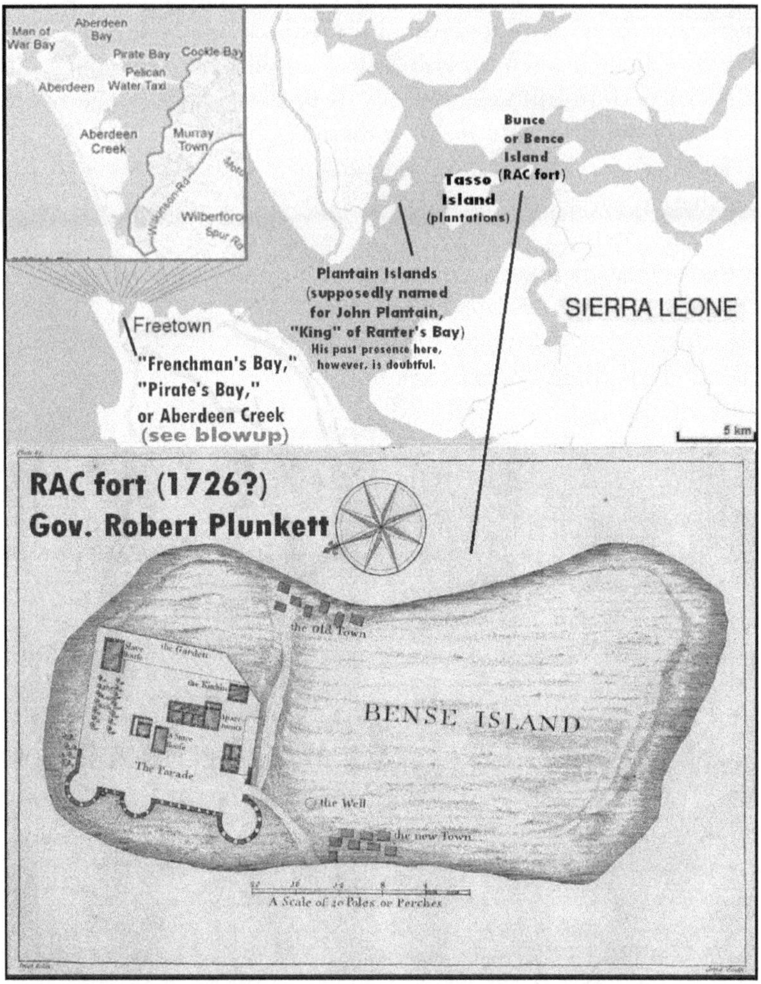
Man of War Bay
Aberdeen Bay
Pirate Bay
Cockle Bay
Pelican Water Taxi
Aberdeen
Aberdeen Creek
Murray Town
Wilkinson Rd
Spur Rd
Bunce or Bence Island (RAC fort)
Tasso Island (plantations)
Plantain Islands (supposedly named for John Plantain, "King" of Ranter's Bay) His past presence here, however, is doubtful.
SIERRA LEONE
Freetown
"Frenchman's Bay," "Pirate's Bay," or Aberdeen Creek (see blowup)
5 km
RAC fort (1726?)
Gov. Robert Plunkett
the old Town
the Garden
The Parade
BENSE ISLAND
the Well
the new Town

Almost two weeks since arriving in *Bird* and being captured, on about 16th of April, a ship came into the mouth of the river and caused some concern. The lost French vessel *Saint Antoine,* Capt. Clinet de Vitry, had entered the Sierra Leone River to take readings and gauge their position. As they saw

---

Documents of the Slave Trade, IV, 24; 22-gun *Sarah* galley of London, Capt. Lambert, became *Duke of Ormond*. The article and Snelgrave's letter to Morice both state that Snelgrave's *Bird* and Capt. "Lamb" or Lambert's *Sarah* were made pirate ships. RAC records (Donnan) insinuate that Lambert was stranded on the coast for up to a year. It states on 6 Apr 1720 that "Capt. Lambert joined with Mr. Wm. Younge on a Trading Voyage to Windward… Will consign the Negroes to Mr. James Bowles at Puttuxent River in Maryland.".

several ships within the river, they hoped to enlist their aid and approached unawares. The pirates feared she was the 40-gun man-of-war *Launceston*, who was due to be in these parts, because the approaching vessel never seemed to fear them. When they realized she was a French merchant, the pirates fired a warning to surrender. *Saint Antoine* did as *Bird* and did not immediately strike their colors. Still, the pirates took them:

> And because the [French] captain did not strike [his flag] on their first firing, they put a rope about his neck and hoisted him up and down several times to the main-yard-arm till he was almost dead. Captain Le Bouse [LeVasseur] coming at that instant, luckily saved his life; and highly resenting this their cruel usage to his countryman, he protested he would remain no longer in partnership with such barbarous villains. So to pacify him, they left the Frenchmen with the ship in his care; and[,] after the cargo was destroyed.[71]

LeVasseur found the ship worthless, however, and ran her ashore. Her crew then joined the other refugees at the privateer town.

By the 20th of April, the *Bird* had been completely refitted by the pirates. Snelgrave was invited to the naming ceremony the next day, not out of disrespect, they assured him. They merely wanted to share their good cheer. They all gathered aboard the former *Bird* and when the time came, "Captain Cocklyn [yelled] aloud, 'God bless the Windham Galley,' we drank our liquor, broke the glasses, and the guns fired." Firing the guns, however, elicited some commotion:

> The ship being galley-built with only two flush decks, the cover of the scuttle [hatch] of the powder-room was in the great cabin and happened at that time to be open. One of the aftermost guns blowing at the touch hole, set fire to some cartouch boxes that had cartridges in them for small arms, the shot and fire of which flew about us and made a great smother. When it was over, Captain Davis observed there had been great danger to us from the scuttle's being open; there being [in a room underneath more than] twenty thousand weight of gunpowder. Cocklyn replied he wished it had

---

[71] Snelgrave, *A New Account*, 259-260.

taken fire, for it would have been a noble blast to have gone to Hell with.[72]

The pirates, still intoxicated with the spectacle, set fire to Cocklyn's old *Rising Sun* and watched the great blaze. They wanted to burn three others, but Capt. Davis prevented them. As a result, Capts. Elliot and Davis had resolved to be done with these hothead pirates, Cocklyn and LeVasseur. Capt. Glynn readily agreed.

Capt. Elliot asked Snelgrave to briefly come aboard his ship. Snelgrave diverted a stop at Capt. Glynn's house to do so. There, Elliot asked him to write a certificate that the great many illegal items stowed aboard his ship were not taken by him, for he planned to make a break for it when possible – he planned to sever his unwilling "partnership" from these pirates. Snelgrave readily assented to this.[73]

While they spoke, a boat carrying the three pirate captains came alongside *Two Friends*. Davis, in seeing Snelgrave about Elliot's vessel, asked him to come aboard his ship for a drink or two. Snelgrave tried to refuse, because he wanted to talk to Glynn about saving what he could of his cargo. Still, he felt that he best not refuse any of these men. That was almost the worst decision he could have made!

At night, while drinking aboard Davis' vessel, *King James*, someone sent a slave to fetch more rum from below. The slave had to use a candle because of the darkness. Unable to see clearly in the dark, he brought the flames too close to the bunghole and set the rum on fire. The first barrel set another barrel on fire because it had been carelessly left open as well and both exploded like cannon! The fire threatened to engulf the tar and pitch as well, which would have been even more disastrous. Confusion was everywhere, with most men leaping overboard into boats, a few fighting the fire, and some slower sailors too afraid to jump overboard because the boats had already left and they could not swim.[74]

---

[72] Snelgrave, *A New Account*, 263-264.
[73] Snelgrave, *A New Account*, 265-266.
[74] Snelgrave, *A New Account*, 267-272.

From: "William Snelgrave to Humphrey Morice," 30 April 1719, *Humphrey Morice Papers*

Pirates Names			
Windham	Capt. Cocklin	34 Guns . 90 Men	late ye Bird Gally
King James	C. Davis	32 Guns . 130 Men	
Duke Ormond	C. Le Booze	22 Guns . 95 Men	late Sarah gally

	Ships taken by these.		
1. Mons. Channel	Society	London	Plunder'd, but little
2. Jno. Bennet	Robt. & James	Do.	Burnt
3. James Chrichton	Nightingall	Bristol	Plunder'd
4. John Thompson	Jacob & Jaell	London	Burnt
5. Henry Morris	Parnall	Bristol	Plunder'd
6. [William] Elliot	Two Friends	Barbados	Carried wth. ym. for a tender
7. Davd. Chrichton	Queen Elizabeth	London	Plunder'd but little
8. James Nisbett [Nesbett]	Edwd. & Steed [Edwin Stede]	Barbados	Plunder'd
9. Jonathn. Lamb[ert]	Sarah Gally	London	taken for a privateer
10. Wm. Snelgrave	Bird Gally	Do.	Do.
	Saint Antonio		Plunder'd & run ashore
11. Do. [Clinet de] Vitry	[Saint Antoine]	St. Malos	
12. ___ Willson	Dispatch	African company	Plunder'd

Added from *Voyages* database

	Owner	tons	guns	Destination
	Becher, John	50	///	Kingston, Jamaica
				Jamaica
	Ruddick, Noblet			Barbados - Va
		60		Barbados
				Barbados
	Humphrey Morice	120	16	
	Beauvais, Le Fer	120		

Baylus C. Brooks   59

Richard Taylor, master for Davis's sloop *Buck*, with fifteen men, eventually conquered the flames and extinguished the fire at about ten o'clock that night. Taylor and his fellows were badly burned when they came to the deck. The surgeons came to dress their wounds. Still, Snelgrave was obliged to remain aboard until morning, with no boats left available.[75]

Two days later, the 22nd, RAC ship *Dispatch*, Capt. Wilson[76] was caught by the pirates as she sailed into the river. They argued over whether to burn his ship, but decided to spare her. They gave it back to Wilson, after picking out choice items.[77]

The sale of Snelgrave's items was held the afternoon of the 26th of April aboard his former ship, *Bird* – now Jeremiah Cocklyn's new *Windham* galley. Snelgrave had refused their ealier invitation and remained at Glynn's house, drying his goods and negotiating with other men for the return of others, The pirate crews, however, had grown fond of Snelgrave during the past month and had been generous with him, loading a canoe with many of his things during the sale.

Events of the 26th during the sale, as usual with these pirates, turned ugly, as Snelgrave later learned from others. Drink flowed and tempers flared. When Snelgrave's gold watch was put up for sale, it caused a stir. Many bid upon it, some of them out of spite to Capt. Davis, who made it known that he wanted it. One ran the price to a hundred pounds and bought it. Afterward, another pirate said he believed the cases of the watch were of inferior gold. The buyer demanded use of a "touch-stone" to test the gold's purity. He baulked at the copperish color of the "touch" and denied its purity.[78]

Snelgrave explained afterward that the "touch looking of a copperish color (as indeed all gold cases of watches do on the touch by reason of the quantity of alloy put in to harden them)."[79] "This pretense," he said "served the turn of this villain, who thereupon exclaimed against me, saying I was a greater rogue than any of them who openly professed piracy, since I was so sly

---

[75] Snelgrave, *A New Account*, 272.
[76] Donnan, *Documents of the Slave Trade*, II, 240-241; *Voyages* database; "Capt. Wilson" was probably the "James Willis," with Samuel Petts of *Dispatch*, who was mentioned by James Phipps of Cape Coast Castle in a letter dated 17 April 1719, in which he told of "a Few English Interlopers on the Coast to Vie with."
[77] Snelgrave, *A New Account*, 275-276.
[78] Snelgrave, *A New Account*, 277-278.
[79] Snelgrave, *A New Account*, 278.

as to bring a base metal watch and endeavor to put it off for a gold one."[80]

The pirates believed the liar and began to make grave threats at Snelgrave. James Griffin, his old school-mate, however, defended him. Capt. Davis merely laughed it off, but others swore to flog Snelgrave when they went ashore. Fortunately, they never made good on that threat.

Three days after the pirates sailed away on the 27th, he penned a letter to his employer Humphrey Morice and sent it by *Queen Elizabeth*, Capt. David Chrichton or Creighton, to report the damage done to their trade. This report contained remarkable detail on the pirates, their ships, and twelve vessels captured by them. See the chart on page 59.[81]

Where was Edward England during all of this? There is some speculation that England was living in a house perhaps at the "privateer settlement" on Frenchman's Bay, "Pirate's Bay," or Aberdeen Creek (1792 Scots settlement). Assuming England was at Sierra Leone during Snelgrave's captivity in April 1719, it is interesting that Snelgrave did not mention him. Furthermore, French depositions inform us that England still cruised the French Windwards of the Caribbean until at least 5th of April [J: 25 Mar] when he captured Jean Collin of 8-gun *Le Bon Secour*, just as his vessel approached Martinique from France.[82]

---

[80] Snelgrave, *A New Account*, 278-279.
[81] Snelgrave, *A New Account*, 276; .
[82] Deposition of Jean Collin of *Le Bon Secour*, 19 Oct 1719, [J: 8 Oct], Rapports de navigation des capitaines au long cours et au cabotage enregistrées par l'Amirauté (1692 - 1779), *Les Archives départementales de Loire-Atlantique*, B 4579, 30-31 ; Thanks to Dr. Jacques Gasser, author of newly-published *Dictionnaire des flibustiers des Caraïbes,* for contributing the French depositions on Edward England; T. N. Goddard, *Hand Book Of Sierra Leone* (Edinburgh: Riverside Press, n.d.), 17-18; "[Pirate's Bay] gained that name not only from the settlement of freebooters that for some time lay alongside it, but also from the deeds enacted there in the May of 1683, when Jean Hamlin, the famous French filibuster who had turned pirate, took seventeen Dutch and English ships in the river"; The following amusing account of the pillaging of Bunce Island is given by Mr William Smith, surveyor to the Royal African Company, who visited Sierra Leone in 1726 : "Roberts having three ships under his command, put into Sierra Leone for fresh water, and finding a trading vessel in the Bay of France [Frenchman's Bay], took her thence and carried her into another near the Cape, which is very deep and has a long narrow entry. This the author in his survey has called Pirate's Bay, because when Roberts had rifled that ship he set fire to her; and part of her bottom was to be seen at low water when Mr.

For the most part, England did not have good opportunities to associate at length with Cocklyn, LeVasseur, or Davis before sailing east. This does not help with the question of what caused the disrespect or disassociation with England after taking *Cassandra* the next August 1720 at the Island of Johanna (Chapter Two). Perhaps they found him too "gentlemanly" and "fair" in his dealings, as he demonstrated with Capt. Macrae – much like the reputation of their former commander William Moody. They may have thought of him as less of a pirate. The general behavioral charcteristics of these variably-natured pirates shape up rather well with these extended observations.

Finally, Snelgrave's account explained his later intelligence on how Richard Taylor left Davis and why:

> As to Davis, having discovered a few days after they left the River Sierra Leone [27th April] a conspiracy to deprive him of his command, which was carried on by one [Richard] Taylor — that was master of the ship [*Buck*] under him — he timely prevented it, but he and some others left their ship and went on board the *Windham Galley*, Captain Cocklyn.[83]

Davis, according to Richard Luntly (still a captive of Davis'), then parted from Cocklyn in *Windham/Bird* and LeVasseur in *Duke of Ormond*, much annoyed by those rogues. Just as they were about to leave, Cocklyn coerced Richard Taylor into overthrowing Davis' command, but Davis found out, and booted Taylor from their company, forcing Taylor to remain with Cocklyn.

Howell Davis may have remained in Sierra Leone a few days longer. His crewman, Walter Kennedy took Taylor's old

---

Smith was there. The next day Roberts sent up a boat well armed to Governor Plunkett desiring to know if he could spare him any gold dust or powder and ball. Plunkett sent word he had no gold to spare, but that as to powder and ball he had some at his service if he would take the trouble to come for it. Roberts, considering this reply, anchored with his ships the next flood before Bunce Island, and a smart engagement followed between him and the Governor for several hours together, till Plunkett, having fired away all his ammunition, fled in his boat to a small island called Tombo. But, being overtaken by the pirates, was brought back again to Bunce Island, where Roberts swore heartily at him for his Irish impudence in daring to resist him. Plunkett, finding the bad company he had gotten into, fell acursing and swearing faster than Roberts, which raised much laughter amongst the pirates, who bid Roberts hold his tongue, for that he had no share at all in the palaver [court of judicature] with Plunkett. However, it is said that by mere dint of swearing Old Plunkett saved his life. When Roberts had rifled the warehouses, he went aboard and sailed out of the river next ebb, leaving Plunkett again in possession of the fort, which the pirates had much damaged."

[83] Snelgrave, *A New Account*, 280-281.

command of *Buck* there and they made yet another attempt on Plunkett's RAC fort. Three vessels (one of 46 guns, *Royal Rover?*, another of 28, *King James*, and one of unstated power, *Buck*) of a black flag on which "represented a man asleep and a skeleton with one hand a clock, a sword of the other" tells the tale, as the flag usually associated with Kennedy and possibly also Davis. After leaving the river, a vessel of the Marquis de Prié of Belgium (a founding investor of the Ostend Company), 32-gun *Marquis del Campo*, Capt. Matheus Gerrebrants, "had been taken under the imperial flag on June 12 [J: 1 Jun] on the coast of Guinea, by an English pirate named Jean Davids [Davis], a native of Bristol, and that my captain had been killed with several officers and sailors in the action which lasted forty hours."[84]

In *Royal James*, Edward England appeared to first operate off West Africa in the Gambia River region as late as May, while Davis and Kennedy followed Cocklyn, Taylor, and LeVasseur from Sierra Leone. Another French deposition mentions an English pirate namd "Jan l'Inglan" which is phonetically equivalent to "England." His presumed deeds on the "Coste Gigni [Guinea]" at "Cap de Trois Pointes" in September and afterward will be presented for debate in Chapter Two.

After trailing just behind the reprobate pirates LeVasseur and Cocklyn, Davis captured *Royal Rover*, "a New England sloop," which he made his new flagship of 32 guns. While still in *King James*, he also took Abraham Plumb's vessel *Princess* on 6th of June. Contained therein on *Princess* was reputed a crewman named Bartholomew Roberts, known also as Thomas and John, and become the most renowned pirate of the West Indies. Luntly's deposition mostly told about his adventures with this Bartholomew Roberts.[85] Snelgrave also reported an eyewitness

---

[84] Deposition of François Negré, commander of *Le Lesabes de Nantes*, 9 Sep 1720 [J: 30 Aug], Rapports de navigation des capitaines au long cours et au cabotage enregistrées par l'Amirauté (1692 - 1779), *Les Archives départementales de Loire-Atlantique*, B 4579, 92-95 ; Adolphe Levae, *Recherches historiques sur le commerce des Belges aux Indes* (Brussells : Wouter, Raspoet et cie,1842), 75.

[85] "The Examination of Thomas Lawrence Jones, 13 February 1724, HCA 1/55, ff. 50-52," "The Examination of Richard Moor, 31 October 1724 (addenda 5 November 1724), HCA 1/55, ff. 94-97," in E. T. Fox, *Pirates in Their Own Words* (Fox Historical, 2014), 155-160, 207-213; *England, Births and Christenings, 1538-1975*. Salt Lake City, Utah: FamilySearch, 2013; Note: A single hit in Familysearch.org for "Jerimiah Cockline" is found in St. Peter, Kent, England, bap. 28 Jan 1691, son of

account, though not his own, of the final days of his pirate friend, Capt. Howell Davis at Principe Island:

> Davis's crew, after plundering the ship, restored her to Captain Plumb again. After this, Captain Davis went for the island Princess [Principe], belonging to the Portuguese, which lies in the Bay of Guinea. Here the pirates gave out [that] they were a King's ship, but the people soon discovered what they were by their lavishness in purchasing fresh provisions with goods, but the governor winked at it on account of the great gains he and others of the chief of his people made by them. But at last, some putting him in mind that if this affair should come to the King of Portugal's ear it might prove his ruin, he plotted how to destroy Davis and his crew in order to color over what he had so basely permitted in allowing them a free trade after discovering they were pirates.[86]

Note that Howell Davis and Henry Glynn were both considered by Snelgrave reasonable men. Some only pirated until they could find a way out – but others were less polite. Cocklyn and LeVasseur, likewise, left their former commander, William Moody, because, in their eyes, he was "too gentlemanly."

A new breed of pirate had evolved on the Bahamas and elsewhere since the pardon was issued 5 September 1717. Pirates who came from more cultivated, higher class colonies of Jamaica, Antigua, Bermuda, and others – pirates like Edward Thache, Henry Jennings, Stede Bonnet, Leigh Ashworth, James Carnegie, and Edward James tended to engage in piracy because of the massive amount of treasure spilled on the Florida shores from the hurricane of 1715. They sought profit. This event wrecked eleven Spanish ships, carrying 14,000,000 pesos in silver alone, in shallow water – easy pickings. Still, their activities, the resistance from the home government, and their fantasy of the Madagascar pirates of old, over time generated a desire for a more base and criminal-type pirate – delinquent, if you will. Samuel Bellamy, Palsgrave Williams, Jeremiah Cocklyn, Olivier LeVasseur, and others, some hailing from mainland proprietary colonies, from similar Puritan stock and class as the early "Flying Gang" on the Bahamas, continued to reign over and terrorize the oceans of the world.

At Africa, they terrorized the Royal African Company, particularly the freshly piratical Howell Davis in February 1719 with the taking of Fort James on Gambia River. The RAC received

---

Jerimiah and Mary. There were no hits for "Thomas Cocklyn" of any spelling as he is often reputed to have been called.
[86] Snelgrave, *A New Account*, 281-282.

few letters from their factors on that coast for nearly three years! But, it would be the pirates' final hurrah, ending with the capture and death of Roberts at Africa in 1721.[87]

Snelgrave's account is a veritable treasure trove of piratalia! Another topic of interest detailed by Snelgrave's experiences lay with LeVasseur's quartermaster, Palsgrave Williams, who, with LeVasseur and Samuel Bellamy had taken *Whydah*, Capt. Lawrence Prince a couple of years before. Williams still sailed with him, although he had captained his own vessel for so long, he now resented being *just* a quartermaster.[88]

After the pirates had all gone and left the Sierra Leone River the most serene it had been in nearly two months, Capt. William Snelgrave gathered with other captains still licking their wounds. Henry Glynn, Capt's Bennet and Thompson, who came out of the woods, and Capt. David Creichton of *Elizabeth*, worked to refit *Parnall* snow, Capt. John Morris, which the pirates allowed its captain to keep. They also went to several merchants residing there to demand the "gifts" the pirates had given them. Capt. Glynn's brother Robert and partners, Mead and Pearce, obliged, but many had not. Thus, Snelgrave returned to England four months after being captured. As he wrote to Morice, "Capt. Glyn & my selfe with about 12 of my people shal come about 10 days hence in ye Parnall snow Capt. Morris bound for Bristol."[89] True to his word, Snelgrave and sixty others left the Sierra Leone River 10th of May 1719 on *Parnall*. After eleven weeks of grueling passage around the Atlantic and two deaths of his fourteen

---

[87] Baylus C. Brooks, "Proprietaries, Privateers, and Pirates: America's Forgotten Golden Age," Master's thesis from the Department of History, Maritime Studies, East Carolina University, 2016; John Milner Gray, *A History of the Gambia* (Cambridge: University Press, 1940), 158, National Archives, London, Robert Plunkett to RAC, 16 Apr 1719, T 70/6; *Weekly Packet,* 12 Dec 1719; *Boston News-Letter,* 4 Apr 1720; Henry Hunt, 190-19; Donnan, *Documents of the Slave Trade,* IV, 24; 22-gun *Sarah* galley of London, Capt. Lambert, became LeVasseur's *Duke of Ormond* . The *Weekly Packet* article contains a mass of misattribution and cannot easily be trusted. In fact, the article completely ignores the presence of Cocklyn and LeVasseur. Still, it is possible since the article states that both Snelgrave's *Bird* and Capt. Lambert's *Sarah* were made pirate ships. RAC records (Donnan) state on 6 Apr 1720 that "Capt. Lambert joined with Mr. Wm. Younge on a Trading Voyage to Windward… Will consign the Negroes to Mr. James Bowles at Puttuxent River in Maryland."
[88] Snelgrave, *A New Account*, 258.
[89] Snelgrave, "Snelgrave to Morice," 30 April 1719.

remaining crew, they arrived safely in the ship's home port of Bristol on 1 August 1719. He lived a fairly long life for his day and died a "gentleman" approximately 62 years old on 21 February 1743 in Mile End, Stepney, Middlesex, England, leaving wife Elizabeth, son William who followed his lead as mariner, and daughters Mary Ann and Elizabeth.[90]

It should be noted that London merchant Humphrey Morice had many connections in the merchant business – slave and otherwise. He had business interests in the East India Company, too. He was mightily interested through two of his associates, Capt James Pearce of the vessel *John* and Jeremy Pearce of the snow *Ruby*, both of whom were present in Jamaica when Richard Taylor and his crew sought a pardon from the governor there (see Chapter Seven). Morice also owned ships captained on occasion by Capt. Richard Blincko - vessels also captured at this time by Howell Davis, Jeremiah Cocklyn, Richard Taylor, and Olivier LeVasseur!

Most interesting is an article that appeared in the *Weekly Packet* of 5 December 1719. The uncanny detail of events that had occurred only a few months before *and* had been so well-described in William Snelgrave's letter of 30 April 1719 to Humphrey Morice *and* the added detail of Morice's other employee, Richard Blincko and his vessel, *Heroine, and* the fact that Morice lost both *Heroine* and *Bird* that summer probably mean that Snelgrave or Morice was the informant. It is probably also the original source for the Davis-LeVasseur meeting scenario used by Johnson. This article appears transcribed in E. T. Fox's *Pirates in Their Own Words*, 378-381.

On Jacobitism, Stuart Anti-Government Conservatism and Pirate America

One wonders... why *King James, Duke of Ormond* and *Windham* as names for pirate vessels? Why toast the health of the "Pretender," James III? James Butler, 2nd duke of Ormond and Sir

---

[90] William Snelgrave, "Snelgrave to Humphrey Morice," 1 Aug 1719, *Humphrey Morice Papers in the Bank of England;* National Archives, London, England & Wales, Prerogative Court of Canterbury Wills, William Snelgrove, 21 Feb 1743, PROB 11/732/98; See also *Morice v Snelgrave*, C 11/794/2; Snelgrave got the ship name wrong in his book and called it *Bristol* rather than *Parnall* of Bristol, which he stated in his letter to Morice in 1719.

William Windham were both popular Jacobites of the day, adherents of James III, the "Pretender." So does this have anything to do with the tendency of pirates to be politically independent and anti-government? According to Snelgrave's narrative of his capture, it did.

Snelgrave noted that all three of the pirate captains: Howell Davis in *King James,* Olivier LeVasseur, then taking command of *Duke of Ormond,* and Jeremiah Cocklyn, preparing to outfit *Bird* or *Windham,* were Jacobites. They supported the claim of the ousted Stuart dynasty over that of the Hanoverian King George I. Davis named his ship, *King James,* after the would-be King James III. They even claimed to be serving under his authority, supposedly possessing his personal commissions. Pirates regularly drank to the "Pretender's health." As Snelgrave noted, they were "doubly on the side of the gallows, both as traitors and pirates." They even referred to King George as a "son of a whore" and a "cuckoldy dog."[91]

LeVasseur was French; he was born in Calais, France. Catholicism defined his nation. It dominated his upbringing, as it had influenced the Stuarts of England, until the interruption of William of Orange, the Protestant Dutch king and husband of Mary Stuart, daughter of James II. Parliament in 1688 had used this marriage as a bandage for the wound they caused by delegitimizing monarchial succession in England. The "Glorious Revolution" was bad for Stuarts, but the recent political insurrection surrounding the accession of the German George I was absolute treason to Stuart conservatives and their allies! James Butler, 2nd duke of Ormonde was one such conservative patriot – as viewed by Jacobites, followers of James III or the "Pretender."[92]

---

[91] William Snelgrave, A New Account of Some Parts of Guinea and the Slave Trade (London, 1734), 193-288; Richard Sanders, *If a Pirate I Must Be...: The True Story of Black Bart, King of the Caribbean Pirates* (Skyhorse Publishing Inc., 2007), 31.

[92] A good explanation of the divisive politics reminiscent of the Trump administration in today's America is found in Frank O'Gorman, *The Long Eighteenth Century: British Political and Social History, 1688-1832* (London: Arnold, 1997), 43-51; Extreme conservatives or Tory Jacobites of 1715, at the time of the hurricane that set off massive piracy in America, were quite similar to the extreme "Neo-Confederate" Republicans of today's America, with similar rebellious anti-government ideology. Racism, however, was the new element then and still highly significant today, owing to America's unique economic reliance in the 17th-19th

68   Sailing East

Born the son of Thomas Butler, 6th Earl of Ossory and his wife Emilia, James Butler was grandson of James Butler, 1st duke of Ormonde. Raised in Ireland as a Whig, he yet schooled in France and afterwards at Christ Church, Oxford. He served with distinction in the military and attained political office. But, when Parliament attempted in January and February 1689 to declare that James II had abdicated his throne, thereby putting William of Orange and his Stuart wife Mary on the throne, he voted against both motions. Even though the conservatively-horrid deed had been successful, he yet served William III with similar distinction. Butler appeared to be loyal to his nation, whatever its politics. Ormonde was appointed Commander-in-Chief of the Forces and colonel of the 1st Regiment of Foot Guards. In the Irish Parliament, Ormonde and the majority of peers supported the conservative or Tory (monarchial) interest. His position as Captain-General imbued him with great influence during the crisis brought about by the death of Queen Anne in 1712. Shortly preceding her death, Ormonde began exhibiting definite Jacobite leanings. When the Jacobite Rebellion of 1715 (coincident with an uptick of British piracy in America) broke out, Ormonde was accused of supporting it. Rebels invoked his name with the cheer "High church and Ormonde." The rebellion resulted in Butler's impeachment for high treason by Lord Stanhope on June 21, 1715. He then fled to France and joined the "Pretender," or the would-be James III.[93]

Many wonder at Jacobite names of pirate ships: *King James*, *Royal James*, *Windham* (for Sir William Windham, a Jacobite whose arrest is attributed with causing the failure of the Jacobite Rebellion of 1715), and *Queen Anne's Revenge*. All of them carry a stubborn Jacobite political message – similar to that of other conservative manifestos – for the early eighteenth century, that phrase might have been "Stuart rule will rise again!" Obviously,

---

centuries upon chattel slavery. Still reeling from Parliament's assertion of power over the monarchy in 1688, it was no coincidence that Jacobite conservatives again rebelled in 1715, as the Confederacy in America did in 1861 over slavery, or Trump voters did in 2016 essentially in reaction to an African-American president. Racism remains America's most persistent illness.
[93]; "James Butler, 2nd Duke of Ormonde". *Oxford Dictionary of National Biography*. Retrieved 11 May 2012; The hurricane on 30 July 1715 spilled a tremendous amount of Spanish silver on the east coast of Florida and essentially started the uptick in piracy. Those mariners in America who felt betrayed by Whigs in Parliament, essentially favored conservative or Jacobite politics. They greedily opposed liberal reforms against piracy, seen as a valid path to riches in Stuart-founded America.

the insinuation is to illustrate the descent of conservative West Indian slaving descendants of Carolina from these same Jacobites. Many privateers and pirates in America and the West Indies, founded on Stuart traditions and Jacobite in ideology, harbored this same resentment of the new king, George I of Hanover, a foreign German Protestant who did not even speak English! This ideology translated directly to the Confederate States of America's ailing mourners with the euphemism "The South Will Rise Again!" Jacobitism was clearly a matter of conservative pride and America still excells in it![94]

Illustrating this, wealthy South Carolina gentleman and pirate Richard Tookerman ordered his crew to fire a salute to James III (exiled in France with many of his supporters like Ormonde after 1715) on his, the "Pretender's," birthday. Tookerman was not afraid to dine with Jamaican elite in Port Royal, including the governor's own son and local widow, Mrs. Pendergrass. He signaled to his first mate to fire *Adventure's* guns by waving a handkerchief from Mrs. Pendergrass' window as they sat enjoying a meal at her dining table. He did this twice without hesitation and with direct instructions to the contrary from the Royal Navy in Kingston Harbour. Capt. Edward Vernon of HMS *Mary* learned of his misdeeds in South Carolina, Virginia, and the Leeward Islands. He arrested him and returned him to England, but Tookerman successfully sued Vernon for false arrest and won![95]

Not all Tories, conservatives, Catholics, or loyal Stuarts were prone to give up their lives and country for the cause. Historian E. T. Fox describes three levels of Jacobitism:

> The first consisted of "hard-core, ideologically committed Jacobites... [who] brought up their children to follow the true [Stuart] path after them." The second layer were those who were driven to Jacobitism by disillusionment with the Hanoverian regime and whose allegiance might therefore be temporary,

---

[94] Windham information from: Lloyd Charles Sanders, *The Possibility of a Stewart Restoration on the Death of Anne: The Stanhope Prize Essay for 1880* (London: T. Shrimpton, 1880), 19.
[95] Baylus C. Brooks, *Quest for Blackbeard: The True Story of Edward Thache and His World* (Lake City, Florida: Baylus C. Brooks, 2016), 453-468.

while the third was comprised of "adventurers," "desperate men" who turned to Jacobitism to repair their own misfortunes and who had "little or nothing to lose and everything to gain if the Jacobites won, which guaranteed their enthusiasm for the cause when it was in the ascendant."[96]

Tookerman's story revealed one basic truth. Radical conservative Jacobites had not lost every adherent to the cause after 1715, even in the courts of Great Britain. Author Colin Woodard even raised the possibility that pirate Charles Vane had negotiated directly with powerful Jacobite politicians and military officials. Still, pirates, especially more gentlemanly types, were perhaps more capitalistic "adventurers" than ideological radicals. Though they certainly harbored conservative political resentments, profit stood out as most important, as it would for generations to come in America. This factor probably best tells the tale of pirates' Jacobite tendencies – and, indeed, the later rebellion for "freedom" in America.[97]

As a Frenchman from "a bourgeous family [who] received an excellent education," LeVasseur symbolically honored the sacrifices of James Butler, then in exile in France with his so-called "Pretender" king, James III.[98] *Duke of Ormond* was a name befitting this particular pirate as well as any other Jacobite name. It had special meaning to the French compatriot of these conservative English rebels in the Americas.

Cocklyn, Taylor, and LeVasseur After Sierra Leone

Previously in 1719, Thomas Samson, master of *Comrade Galley*, prepared his vessel to depart London for a voyage to Barbados and a return to London by way of Guinea on the African coast. On *Comrade's* return voyage from Barbados and while on the coast of Africa, he and his ship met their fates at the hands of our subject pirates. On 7 June 1719, *Comrade* took on fresh water

---

[96] E.T. Fox, "Jacobitism and the 'Golden Age' of Piracy, 1715-1725," International Journal of Maritime History, XXII, No. 2 (December 2010), 278.
[97] Colin Woodard, *The Republic of Pirates: Being the True and Surprising Story of the Caribbean Pirates and the Man Who Brought Them Down* (Orlando, 2007), 102-103, 196 and 230-231.
[98] Laura Nelson, *The Whydah Pirates Speak* (Colorado: Laura Nelson, 2015), 50.

for their return to London five leagues or 15 miles east of Anomabu (Dutch) on Africa's Ghana Coast. Two pirate vessels approached and captured them there: 26-gun *Speedwell* (same ship as *Bird/Windham*, though he'd reportedly lost some guns), commanded by Jeremiah Cocklyn, and 22-gun *Duke of Ormond*, Olivier LeVasseur de la Buse. This event gave Richard Taylor another vessel of his own to command – *Comrade*.[99]

Three men detail events that led Olivier LeVasseur to the East Indies from the African coast. These came from actual eyewitness accounts given in official depositions – from captives of the pirates themselves and forced into labor aboard their vessels. One account even comes from an insurance investigation deposition in plague-ridden Marseilles, France of the 1720s![100] A wealth of data has been uncovered from myriad other sources that detail the events that occurred once these West Indian pirates stretched their canvas for the Cape of Good Hope and rounded it for Madagascar and the Mascarenes. More than just LeVasseur was discussed, but the focus of this chapter has been on him.

One of these captives, Richard Moor, originally served as surgeon's mate on board *Comrade*. Moor would be forced first into service of Jeremiah Cocklyn on his vessel, *Speedwell* (former *Windham/Bird*). Moor's deposition, made 31 October 1724, quite a few years later, gives great detail during the many years that he was kept by these pirates. Caution must be observed, however, in gathering information from the aging faulty memory of Moor, a man held captive by these pirates for nearly four years

Historians cannot choose their eyewitnesses, the conditions under which they tell the tale, or the timing of their testimony. There are other eyewitness testimonies that disagree with Moor on some facts concerning the events that led pirates to the East Indian island of Madagascar. Still, Moor happens to testify to the longest period of time involving the "Buzzard's" and his pirate consorts' leaving the African coast for the glistening treasure of the East Indies.

Moor also represents one of the more valuable crew members sought by pirate ships - surgeons. A surgeon repaired battle

---

[99] Nelson, *Whydah Pirates*, 50.
[100] 40,000 died in Marseilles itself and a further 90,000 in the rest of Provence out of a total population of 400,000.

wounds, a common event in piracy. Pirates who often engaged in battle eagerly desired their services. For example, Edward Congdon, another pirate who plied the East Indies, kept three surgeons from various ships he had captured and later traded them for a French pardon (see Chapter Four). Incidentally, Congdon had lost an arm and once had need of a good surgeon himself, perhaps as a result of his chosen profession as pirate.

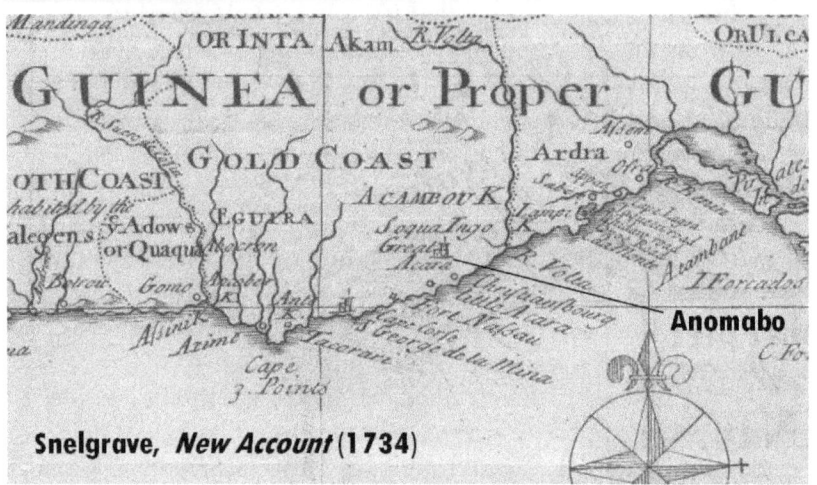

West African Guinea Coast, showing location of Fort Anomabu, annotated by the author. Source: William Snelgrave's *New Account*, 1734.

Taylor, Cocklyn, and LeVasseur heavily armed *Comrade*. The three then sailed to Whydah, just down the Gold Coast from Sierra Leone. Pirates routinely augmented their armament from their many prizes. They also lost armament through battles, misfires, or negligence; thus, the number of reported guns might vary. Also, they traded vessels regularly, as will be evident; and also thus, we find that Taylor and Cocklyn briefly traded vessels. *Speedwell/Windham/Bird*, then under Richard Taylor, *Duke of Ormond*, under LeVasseur, and *Comrade*, under Cocklyn, sailed east to a point about fifteen miles from Fort Anomabu and took Humphrey Morice's *Heroine* of London, Capt. Richard Blincko.[101]

The second of these captives who left valuable depositions was a foremast-man on board *Heroine*. John Matthews of Chilham, Kent, was a former fisherman at Faversham when, in 1719, he joined Richard Blincko's crew "then in the River of Thams and

---

[101] "The Examination of John Matthews, 12 October 1722, HCA 1/55, ff. 201-21" in E. T. Fox, *Own Words*, 193-194.

bound on a voyage to Guinea."[102] Matthews, like Moor, made mistakes and omissions in his testimony. He was a bit more illuminating for researchers concerning the brief period he spent with pirates, though he failed to mention seemingly important details like French and Portuguese vessels encountered by them. For instance, he described the "Island of Coreno" or Corisco as "a desolate Island upon the said Coast where the pirate ships usually harbor and refit."[103] Richard Moor, by contrast, lightly touched upon foreign vessels and testified that:

> [On 22 June 1719, at Whydah, the pirates] took five sail of French and Portuguese Vessels and plundered them and then proceeded to an uninhabited Island called Corista [Corisco] upon the sd Coast of Guinea and thereall the sd three [*Speedwell/Windham/Bird*, *Duke of Ormond*, and *Comrade*] Ships were hove down and cleaned.[104]

Heroine was refitted at Corisco as a pirate. Richard Taylor desired this ship and a shuffle again occurred, with LeVasseur dropping *Duke of Ormond*, or Lambert's former *Sarah*, for *Comrade*. Jeremiah Cocklyn retained his *Speedwell/Windham/Bird*.

Lastly, another vessel, recently arrived from France, had just barely avoided being captured that 22 June at Judah. It was the French vessel named *Le Victorieux* or *Victory*, Capt. Guillaume Hais of Nantes, that the pirates later used to capture *Cassandra*. The detailed record left by Hais and his crew for insurance purposes with Messrs. Pont-Leroy & Company of Marseilles not only supplemented the depositions of Matthews and Moor, but also answered a lot of age-old questions about these pirates. It told a great deal about many vessels of foreign nations assaulted by these men.

---

[102] Matthews, 193.
[103] Matthews, 193.
[104] "The Examination of Richard Moor, 31 October 1724 (addenda 5 November 1724), HCA 1/55, ff. 94-97," in E. T. Fox, *Pirates in Their Own Words* (Fox Historical, 2014), 208; ACCIM [Archives de la Chambre de Commerce et d'Industrie de Marseilles] f° 169-177(f° 169) Juillet 1720, Prise et abandonnement du vaisseau le Victorieux, capitaine Hais de Nantes, N°22,170; This document, discovered by Wayne Hampton of Edenvale, Gauteng, South Africa, shows that the pirates entered Whydah or Judah harbor on 22 Jun 1719; translation from French for this book made by Baylus C. Brooks.

Taking of *Le Victorieux*, Capt. William Hais of Nantes

A uniquely detailed document found on a UNESCO website by a researcher in South Africa tells about *Le Victorieux*, yet another of three vessels, based on the name *Victory*, all of which had been pirated on the coast of Africa in the summer of 1719. The original is located in a Marseilles commerce archive in France. This report of Capt. Guillaume Hais of Nantes also fills in details involving the length of time that these pirates remained on the African Coast and Olivier LeVasseur's capture of *Indian Queen*, Capt. Thomas Hill, in which vessel LeVasseur would sail to Madagascar. The story evolved in two parts, the first being *Le Victorieux's* arrival from Nantes on the African Coast to their first encounter with these pirates at the slave port they called "Judah," or Whydah, on the Gold Coast.[105] The second part, about LeVasseur's capture of *Indian Queen*, shall be elaborated at the end of the chapter. For now, the following paragraphs detail the initial voyage of *Le Victorieux* and the harsh experiences they encountered as a result of pirates on the African Coast, as indicated by Moor's last quote.[106]

Before the Golden Age of Piracy, Nantes, on the Brittany Coast of France, enjoyed an economy based on local products: salt, wine, and fabrics. Recent failures in these markets and the surge of activity from West-Indian sugar and the slaves needed to produce that commodity encouraged France to enter the slave trade. From 1707 to 1793, Nantes sailed from its port 42 percent of total French slaving vessels, accounting for 450,000 African slaves shipped to the West Indies. It is this context in which we find Capt. Guillaume Hais (William Hays) and his vessel *Le Victorieux*

---

[105] Portuguese Fort of São João Baptista de Ajudá (1680) at Judah or Ouidah (Fida, Whydah, Juda, Hueda, Whidah).

[106] ACCIM f°169-177(f° 169) Juillet 1720, Prise et abandonnement du vaisseau le Victorieux, capitaine Hais de Nantes, N°22. *See also* "Edouard Haize second Capne on the ship the Victorious of Nantes," 16 May 1720 [J: 5 May], Rapports de navigation des capitaines au long cours et au cabotage enregistrées par l'Amirauté (1692 - 1779), *Les Archives départementales de Loire-Atlantique*, B 4579, 64-69 ; *Note :* the depositions spelled the name in varous phonetic equivalents of Hays, Hais, and Haize.

(or *Victory*) of Nantes, preparing for a slaving voyage to the Coast of Africa, just after Christmas 1718.[107]

View of the port of Nantes before the Revolution (attributed to Ozanne Nicolas)

Le Victorieux fitted out at Paimboeuf, some twenty-five miles down the Loire River from Nantes. They departed 30 December 1718 for the African Coast. Two days into their journey, the ship "suffered an impetuous and contrary wind," ruining the small mast and parrel (hoops, rings, or chain encircling the mast and securing the yards). This was not a good omen for them and significantly slowed the vessel's progress. Not until 24 February 1719 [J: 13 Feb] did they weigh anchor at Cape Mesurado, 300 miles southeast of Sierra Leone in modern Monrovia. There, they intended to take in wood, water, and rice.[108] After remaining six days, they had found only wood and set sail, following the southerly trade winds, for Rio de Junco in modern Margibi, Liberia, twenty-five miles further down the coast. This locale also resulted in a failed attempt, so they sailed to Petite Sestre (current Sobo?), anchored, and sent their boat ashore under a junior officer to make proposals for trade with the local King. Here, they not only failed to get rice, but received a bit of trouble:

> The negroes of this place came aboard the boat to ask what they wanted. The officer on board replied that they came there to treat for rice, that on this answer the said negroes asked a man to

---

[107] Olivier Pétré-Grenouilleau, *Histoire et Géographie Contemporaine* (Plomelin: Éditions Palantines, 2008), 92.

[108] *Ozyra Glabberima*, or a red-husked rice grown by the Baga in interior regions of Africa was popular with slavers as it lasted longer on sea voyages than *Ozyra Sativa*.

go with them to make the request to the King. As is the custom, the officer ordered Pierre Meunier of La Rochelle to go with them. Hardly was this sailor on the ground, when the negro seized him and fired on the boat, wounding in the thigh a sailor named Jean Moisson of Quiberon. The officer of the boat withdrew from shore to advise his captain, who sent his canoe and his armed boat, to attack the negroes enough to establish order and for the purpose of imposing respect, but the negroes fired on the boat as soon as they saw them within range of their arms, which obliged the people of the said boats and canoes to retire on board. It was deemed better to abandon this Pierre Meunier, a man who exposes the rest of the crew, who are not enough to make a landing under such conditions, the negroes being too numerous, and the landing too difficult.[109]

When *Le Victorieux* departed Petite Sestre and landed at Grand Sestre (Grand Cess today), seven leagues further south, they learned the reason for this attack. The natives at Grand Sestre were friendly and arranged to sell them rice and water for a small gift. They also "told them that what they had experienced [at Petite Sestre] was the result of the English [pirates] that went there every day under the French flag, to make incursions on their coast and take them off under the pretext of trading."[110] The local men told them that they would get Pierre Meunier back for them, that they were sure he would not be harmed. They would give him to the next French ship that came there, to which a thankful Capt. Hais left them gifts and a note for other French ships to remind them to retrieve his sailor, Meunier. They then weighed anchor and sailed with the easterly "Guinea current" for Whydah or Judah to obtain their main cargo of slaves.[111]

Judah, Ouidah, or Whydah came on their horizon 22 March 1719 [J: 11 Mar] and they anchored in the harbor there before their principle town, Sabee. Six days later, Capt. Hais went ashore to

---

[109] M. Balthazard-Marie Emerigon, *Trâite des Assurances et des Contrats a la Grosse* (Marseilles: Jean Mossy, 1783), 89; ACCIM f°169-177(f° 169) Juillet 1720, 169-170.
[110] ACCIM f°169-177(f° 169) Juillet 1720, 170.
[111] ACCIM f°169-177(f° 169) Juillet 1720, 170 ; Robert Harms, *The Diligent: A Voyage Through the Worlds Of The Slave Trade* (NY: Basic Books, 2002). 99-100; "In the seventeenth century French merchants from Normandy had established two trading posts here, which they called Little Dieppe and Little Paris, where they purchased ivory and malaguetta peppers… [the ship followed] the Guinea current, which would carry them all the way to Whydah and beyond."

negotiate, leaving his first officer and brother Edouard Hais, in command of *Le Victorieux*. Two months passed without incident.

On the 22 June 1719 [J: 11 Jun], however, "at four or five o'clock in the afternoon... Three rogue ships entered the harbor under the English flag, and distinguished themselves only when they were near the said vessel *Le Victorieux*."[112] They began immediately to capture more prizes. The deposition of Capt. Helle Lavigne, commander of of 90-ton, 10-gun *Le Preni de Nantes* read:

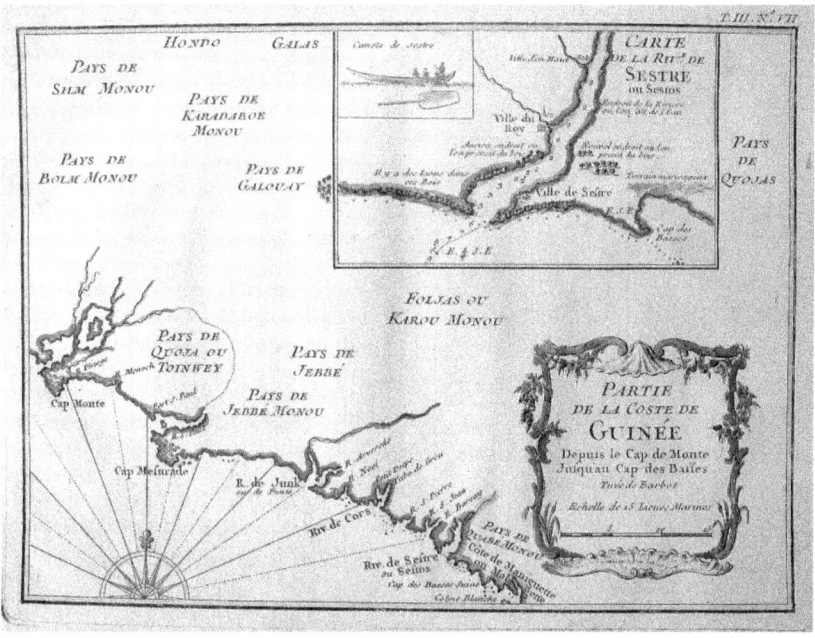

Antique Copperplate Engraving. *Partie de la Coste de Guinee Depuis le Cap de Monte Juiqu'au Cap Des Basses* (about 30-40 miles NW of Cap de Palmes, or Cape Palmas), by, Jacques Nicolas Bellin. Date: 1764 - Public Domain

> ... he arrived at night on the 21st of the [August 1720] [J: 10 Aug], where he found more ships of the river of Nantes... began to make his trade there till the 30th of September [J: 19 Sep], following that on the evening he heard from the officers of the fort [Anomabu] that four ships [two pirates and two of their prizes] appeared, among which were a brigantine and a corvette, which anchored at two places.[113]

---

[112] ACCIM f°169-177(f° 169) Juillet 1720, 170-171.
[113] "Judah," ~5 Sep 1720 [J: 25 Aug], Rapports de navigation des capitaines au long cours et au cabotage enregistrées par l'Amirauté (1692 - 1779), *Les Archives départementales de Loire-Atlantique*, B 4579, 95.

Capt. Lavigne also told that another merchant he met at Grand Sestre told him earlier in late July that the pirates, then just arrived at Judah, had given him a pass to trade on this coast. That French captain intimated to Lavigne that he must also obtain such a pass. Interesting to note here, is that these pirates appeared to control the trade of large areas of the African coast at a single time. Lavigne had missed the earlier action, but he would later meet one of these pirates face-to-face!

The pirates anchored at Judah consisted of a 40-gun vessel (*Comrade*, Cocklyn), a 32-gun vessel (*Speedwell/Windham/Bird*, Taylor), and "an 8-gun sloop," probably *Duke of Ormond*, LeVasseur. They raised black flags and began firing at Capt. Hais' ship. First mate Edouard Hais "cut two cables on the bitts and set sail."[114] There were only thirty crew aboard, half of whom were sick and in no shape to fight.[115]

The pirates had been busy since arriving at Judah that afternoon. As Hais fled, they passed five ships, apparently prize vessels of the pirates, "three of which were Portuguese, one English, and one French from La Rochelle." The English one belonged to Humphrey Morice. She was *Heroine*, master Richard Blincko. Two of the pirates followed *Le Victorieux* for a half an hour. First mate Hais sailed westward from Judah for five days, then on the 27th [J: 16 Jun], anchored and wrote to the captain, his brother, about where he had gone and why. Capt. Hais responded to his brother's letter on 10 July [J: 29 Jun] and *Le Victorieux* sailed back to Judah to finish their business and retrieve their captain. Still, the water was low and they had difficulty getting over the bar, so Hais sent a boat on longer trips ashore for provisions. Meanwhile, the crew was sick and getting sicker by the day.

Obviously, these groups of pirates maintained contact even at a distance. Capt. François Negré of *Le Lesable* was chased from Sierra Leone River all across the Gold Coast by his pirate nemesis, Howell Davis. Their eastward course showed them battling the pirate near Cape Appolonia on 19th June [J: 8 Jun] (meanwhile, "Pevas" or Davis' consort "Pierre Roberd [Bartholomew Roberts?] of Jamaica" took Capt. Montigne, then *l'Anne de Sables*, Capt. Francois Moreau, on the 20th [J: 9 Jun]), to the forts at Cape Coast, just a day after LeVasseur, Taylor, and Cocklyn had departed, and

---

[114] ACCIM f°169-177(f° 169) Juillet 1720, 171..

[115] John Matthews, 193; John Matthew's deposition pairs the pirate commanders with their ships at this time.

Anomabo by the 6th of July [J: 25 Jun], and by *Trois Pointes*, to Judah by 21st of July [J: 10 Jul]. Negre reported that Davis' men were in search of *Le Victorieux* "who had evaded the pirates [Cocklyn, *et al*], to give them this second" chance to supply Davis with free human cargo, "without paying the country's fees"![116]

Now set upon by pirate Howell Davis, *Le Victorieux* cut another cable and moved off as on 22 June, leaving his boat and men in the bay. The pirates "took their boat with seventy iron bars and several casks full of water - which said boat was delivered to the pirates by a sailor [on the boat] named Jacques Carré [French phonetic of Carey?], Irishman who took sides with them."[117] The pirates later ransomed these men, by whom Capt. Hais learned some detail of their nemeses. Then, Davis also moved away from Judah to meet his final fate at Principe Island.

Meanwhile, Capt. Richard Blincko spent a month or so with Cocklyn, Taylor, and LeVasseur, witnessed the near capture of *Le Victorieux* on 22 June, and learned valuable information. Two days after this incident began, on the 24th of June, they would part from him with his ship, *Heroine*, then under Richard Taylor's command.[118] He believed he needed to share this information with the director of the East India Company, because they informed him that "Maurxicios [Mauritius]" was their eventual destination, an island east of Madagascar in the EIC's legislative domain:

On the 24th of June sailed from Widdaw three Pirates:

	Men	Guns
Oliver LaBous In the Conrade	130	40
Jeremiah Cocklin In the Bird	110	36
Richard Taylor in the Heroine	80	40

---

[116] Deposition of François Negré, 9 Sep 1720, 94 ; Deposition of François Moreau, 18 July 1720 [J: 7 Jul], Rapports de navigation des capitaines au long cours et au cabotage enregistrées par l'Amirauté (1692 - 1779), *Les Archives départementales de Loire-Atlantique*, B 4579, 82. *See A General History*, 2nd ed., 186-187 for similar data on Howell Davis' voyage to Cape Appolonia, Trois Pointes, and Judah – but, not specific to any French vessels – just Dutch and English.
[117] ACCIM f° 169-177(f° 169) Juillet 1720, 171.
[118] Taylor then gave *Speedwell/Windham/Bird* back to Cocklyn, who didn't like *Comrade* for some reason. LeVasseur then gave up the weaker *Duke of Ormond* for *Comrade*.

80   Sailing East

> The Three Captns. did affirm to me that they were going to the Island of Princess [Principe] in order to refitt their Ships & there to Proceed to the Coast of Brazile & from thence to the Island of Maurxicios [Mauritius] & that there were several other Pirates to Join them at that Place in order as they Said To Settle there and yt. There had been three other Sets of Pirates [England's three (*Royal James, Queen Anne's Revenge,* and *Flying King*) and Davis fresh from Sierra Leone with four (*King James, Buck, Royal Rover,* and, from Moreau deposition, another sloop of 10 guns and 80 men under "Pierre" Roberts "of Jamaica")] on the Coast of Guinea making altogether abt. 10 Sail.
>
> Richard Blincko[119]

Why Mauritius? Mauritius, about 550 miles east of Madagascar, had been claimed directly by the Dutch, at Madgascar, but barely settled by them. More to the point, perhaps, it also figured prominently in the tales of Henry Every and his men as a slightly populated Dutch colony that welcomed pirates, or likely anyone willing to trade for their timber. Like La Bourbon, Mauritius possessed a creole community of mostly Malagasy slaves from Madagascar, but had been abandoned, for a second time, by the Dutch in 1710, leaving that community in peace. In 1715, it was claimed by the French, but not yet settled in force by them. LeVasseur, a probable member of an elite French family from Calais, may have envisioned Mauritius as a place of French rebirth, an untouched place where they could make their own pirate community.[120]

Blincko was released by them 24 June, without his ship. *Voyages* database, however, shows that Richard Blincko completed his voyage in a different vessel. He did not get *Heroine* back in order to accomplish this task. Blinkco also had seventeen of his crew taken, including Matthews. Regardless, Blincko was able to contract a ship, collect his cargo of slaves and departed Africa on 15 July 1719. He sailed to Maryland to obtain a shipment of tobacco and returned to London.[121]

It seems that Jeremiah Cocklyn did not yet go to Principe Island, as told to Blincko, for Cocklyn still desired the elusive *Le*

---

[119] British Library, India Office Records, Letter 274, Captain Richard Blincks to the Court reporting on the movement of pirates on the coast of Guinea who have gone to Mauritius. IOR/E/1/10 ff. 455-456v: Date unspecified (ca. June 1719).

[120] Megan Vaughan, "Slavery and Colonial Identity in Eighteenth-Century Mauritius," *Transactions of the Royal Historical Society* Vol. 8 (1998), 195.

[121] Henry Hunt, 192; *Voyages* database.

Victorieux. He returned again to Whydah to take her. On 28 July 1719, two of the pirate ships once again bore down on Hais' sick crew while at anchor at Whydah, forcing First Mate Hais to cut yet another 4th cable to escape. For another five days, Hais and crew waited to return, with the men growing sicker and sicker by the hour. Just under a week later, on 2 August, Hais came back to conclude his business, contracting 450 slaves, of whom 90 died from sickness before they left on 15 September, in company of a Portuguese vessel. They had no further encounter with pirates, some of whom left again for Principe Island and may have been distracted by Davis' lethal encounters there.[122]

Meanwhile, Richard Taylor (with deponent Richard Moor aboard) and Olivier LeVasseur (with John Matthews) sought to clean at Corisco Island where the three vessels "were hove down and cleaned." After cleaning and resting at Corisco Island throughout August-September, Olivier LeVasseur then sailed in *Heroine*, intending to rendezvous at Anabon. LeVasseur then proceeded southward for the Angola coast, but would again rejoin Cocklyn after this pirate's capture of Capt. Hais' *Le Victorieux*. Jeremiah Cocklyn quite stubbornly seems to have continued on the hunt in *Speedwell/Windham/Bird*, still chasing the large queasy-crewed slaver *Le Victorieux*. He and LeVasseur, however, were briefly distracted by another French ship, *Le Solide*. Richard Tayor, still, had returned to Judah or Whydah 30 September. Taylor apparently agreed with Cocklyn and LeVasseur to rendezvous at Anabon Island, a French island located off the coast of Gabon.[123]

Capt. Guillaume Hais had serious thoughts on his mind as he sailed away from Whydah with his cargo of slaves. His thirty-odd crew and cargo was dwindling and sick – only growing sicker. Capt. Hais' thoughts concerned "the pitiful condition of his ship and crew, which was fatigued by work, of the little food and

---

[122] ACCIM f°169-177(f° 169) Juillet 1720, 172.
[123] Matthews, 194; Matthews states that LeVasseur traded his ship for Jeremiah Cocklyn's and Blincko's 24 June letter indicates that he sailed in *Comrade*. Cocklyn also appears to have been absent for most of their time at Corisco. Moor states that, before leaving, they left *Comrade* at Corista, while Matthews contradicted this testimony and told that LeVasseur sailed away from Corista in *Comrade*. Still, Hais asserted that *Comrade* was never part of the negotions over ships between Cocklyn, LeVasseur, Thomas Hill and himself at Cape Lopez, so Moor's version is accepted here, especially since *Comrade* was the vessel on which he originally sailed.

heavy weather which they had suffered."[124] His ship possessed no more cables and only one useless anchor. Their Portuguese consort encouraged Hais to make for São Tomé and allow his crew to heal and refresh themselves. Still, they had already loaded slaves – a perishable cargo and must get them to the French West Indies Islands. "They did their best to reach São Tomé," noted the deposition, "but the winds having always been contrary, as well as the tides, they were obliged to anchor at Principe Island" on 11 September 1719, fortunately already vacated by all the pirates.[125]

Here, the Portuguese governor of Principe, being a good capitalist pirate (as opposed to humanitarian), promised to give the sick crew food and assistance as long as Hais could pay for their provisions. He then offered a deal: Hais would sell one of the governor's friends his ship and cargo. Portuguese crew would man the nearly crewless vessel and would ship the slaves to Brazil rather than the French Windward Islands. Under normal circumstances, this would have been unacceptable – but, these were not normal circumstances. The sick would stay at Principe and the capable French seamen arranged to continue working *Le Victorieux* under Portuguese ownership. Sixteen of Hais' crew joined them in that voyage with Guillaume Hais staying on as captain; he would run "the risks of the ship and the Portuguese, [and] of the mortality of the blacks."[126] Staying three weeks, they almost missed the pirates, particularly Cocklyn, still determined to capture them. Indeed, when *Le Victorieux* again set sail on 4th of October, they had reason to believe the danger was gone.

While Hais negotiated at Principe Island, an again-rejoined pirate pair of Cocklyn and LeVasseur, on 25 September 1719, captured Capt. Alexander Patterson, commanding 60-ton *Le Solide* of Dunkirk, on her way to Martinique, trading slaves for factor Nicholas Morel. This is a fascinating deposition in that it told great detail of pirates of the time, of whom about 20 had recently left New Providence after the "pirate island nation" had been retaken by Woodes Rogers in 1718. Even more explicit, the deposition gave their names as "Jerémie Coquelin" and "La Bas, nom de guerre, and family name, Olivier LeVasseur de Calais." While hunting *Le Victorieux*, Cocklyn had apparently renamed *Speedwell/Windham/Bird* again to *Defiance*, then then said to have 40

---

[124] ACCIM f°169-177(f° 169) Juillet 1720, 172.
[125] ACCIM f°169-177(f° 169) Juillet 1720, 172.
[126] ACCIM f°169-177(f° 169) Juillet 1720, 172.

guns. LeVasseur was also with him, in *Royal Ranger* [apparently, the pirates' new name for *Heroine*, although no eyewitness had called it that at Cape Lopez], also of 40 guns. "Coquelin's," or Cocklyn's, 250 *motley* crew were said to be of English, French, and Dutch extraction. They took from Patterson...

> ... 600 subjects of trade [slaves], 30 fine fuses, hundred pieces of Indian [?], about 3000 lbs. powder, 125 ancres of brandy and various other goods suitable for the slave trade of which he had already taken about 150 young and old that he currently had on board, being besides that [he was] very mistreated and several petty officers of his crew having been threatened several times; further declares the captain that the two ruffians who took him told him that they left Providence 20 sails, vessels or brigantines, that they intended to make the race for some time again at the coast of Guinea and to go then to their new general rendevous at St. Helena then to refit to go to the Indies [were they implying the East Indies?] and the South Sea, proposing they do not make [act of] grace [surrender] to no one.[127]

Cocklyn and LeVasseur kept Patterson for about two weeks and informed him that he was their 39th capture; and there were four more after him: two Dutch and two Portuguese. Chillingly, he recounted in his deposition to the officials at Martinique that they cut masts, took sails, and let them go "after having cut the arms and legs of the crew!"[128] Hopefully, this was an exaggeration or this author's mistranslation from the French! *La Solide* was able to deliver 169 slaves to Martinique and Saint Domingue. The most fascinating detail from this deposition surrounds the pirate's stated "new general rendezvous" of St. Helena, a lonely isle in the middle of the Atlantic – a second choice after losing New Providence to Gov. Woodes Rogers and the new Bahamas Company?

After this brief diversion and disposing of *Le Solide*, the pirates split again. LeVasseur headed south toward Angola in

---

[127] "Statement by Sieur Alexandre Patterson, Captain of the Solid, Dunkirk, about the looting of his ship by the pirates near Cape Lopez (17 December 1719)," FR ANOM COL C8A 27 F° 5, ff. 5-6; *Heroine* had probably been renamed *Royal Ranger* by LeVasseur, since there was little time to refit a new pirate vessel in the few days in which they left *Le Victorieux* and took *Le Solide*.
[128] "Statement by Sieur Alexandre Patterson."

84   Sailing East

Heroine/Royal Ranger and Cocklyn in *Defiance/Speedwell/etc* back to Principe Island again in search of *Le Victorieux*. Again, they intended to rendezvous later at Anabon.

What was Richard Taylor doing? Capt. Helle Lavigne, commander of *Le Preni de Nantes,* may be able to tell us. While Cocklyn and LeVasseur were occupied with *Le Solide,* a pirate ship again raided Judah on 30 September, taking *l'Union de Nantes,* Capt. Jacques Nadreau. Lavigne heard the rumors and arrived that night to speak with the directors ashore. After departing, on 2nd of October, two days en route for Anabon, he and a Portuguese ship were also taken – most probably by Taylor. Lavigne told little about this pirate, except that he pillaged his cargo. The pirate kept him near Judah until 11 November 1719, and then ordered him to follow, as the pirate had to leave – probably to rendezvous with LeVasseur and Cocklyn. Moreover, Lavigne would meet fellow French pirate captive Guillaume Hais of *Le Victorieux* quite soon!

Five days out of Principe Island, thirty leagues windward of the island, while manned by the Portuguese, in the company of the same Portuguese ship that had followed *Le Victorieux* from Whydah, *Le Victorieux* lost sight of their Portuguese consort. Still, they continued their journey till the following day, at four o'clock in the afternoon. Then, Hais' look-out warned that a distant ship was taking a parallel course. They thought at first that it was their lost Portuguese consort looking for them, but soon feared she was *Defiance/Speedwell/etc* under Cocklyn. Indeed, at seven o'clock that evening he approached within range, fired cannon and hoisted his black flag. Jeremiah Cocklyn in *Defiance* or *Speedwell/Windham/Bird,* fresh from capturing Patterson and the last four ships, once again found its elusive prey. The fact that *Le Victorieux* got away from him so often may have deeply annoyed Cocklyn – he was nothing if not tenacious. This time, he had taken them by surprise, with no way out. Jeremiah Cocklyn's *motley* (mixed) pirate crew cheered![129]

Cocklyn finally had his prize and ordered *Le Victorieux* to bring to and prepare to be boarded. Twenty-five pirates landed on Hais' deck to take *Le Victorieux,* Capt. Hais, and five other men. Edouard Hais observed that *Defiance/Speedwell/etc* was a pirate of then thirty-four guns, having two hundred men. Two days later, Cocklyn told them that they were heading to Anabon to give *Le*

---

[129] ACCIM f°169-177(f° 169) Juillet 1720, 173.

Victorieux to another pirate – Olivier LeVasseur.[130] Richard Moor confirmed at least part of this, yet still referred to Cocklyn's vessel as "*Speedwell*":

> And the sd Ship *Speedwell* about 5 Days after she was come from Corista [Principe?] took a French Vessell called the *Victory* (whereof one Captain Hays was Commander) and plundered her and brought her to Cape Lopez and there fitted her out for their service and manned her with the Company of the *Speedwell* and gave *Speedwell* to the sd Captain Hays, and from Cape Lopes they proceeded in the sd Ship the *Victory* under the Comand of the sd Cocklyn to Madagascar.[131]

Before arriving at Cape Lopez, however, Cocklyn took an English ship of Bristol, loaded with 200 slaves, the timing and approximate slave count of which matches with *Peterborough*, Capt. John Owen. Cocklyn took this opportunity to lighten his burden. He rid himself of all the newer Portuguese crew of *Le Victorieux*, most of the English crew, sixteen in number, including two French sailors of *Le Victorieux* named Jean Detern and Etienne Bond with a servant named Provost (another crewman of Hais, Joseph Pascal turned pirate and joined Cocklyn). He and Pascal forced all these men onto the Bristol ship. Cocklyn again prepared to deliver his prize *Le Victorieux* to Olivier LeVasseur at Anabon to trade with his vessel.[132]

Le Victorieux had broken her bowsprit in the recent battle, delaying Cocklyn again. He searched for a suitable place to put in and replace her bowsprit with the one from *Defiance* or *Speedwell/Windham/Bird*. He realized that they had already passed Anabon in the action, so instead, sought the road to Angola.

A rather confused newspaper report may include one earlier English capture, Capt. Binglove, about 15 leagues from Cape Lopez, en route to LeVasseur's position. The article gets details quite distorted and, thus mentions *Heroine*, "Capt. Jerry [Jeremiah Cocklyn?] Commander," [LeVasseur commanded *Heroine* at Cape Lopez] 36 guns and 200 men, and a "large French built Ship [*Le*

---

[130] ACCIM f°169-177(f° 169) Juillet 1720, 173.
[131] Moor, 208-209.
[132] ACCIM f°169-177(f° 169) Juillet 1720, 174.

Victorieux] which they had taken some Days before."[133] It also mentions an apparently absent *Merchant*, "Le Buck Commander," 40 guns and 180 men; and also *King James*, "Davis Commander," 56 guns, 200 men. These pirates had apparently recently left the the first two pirates, who may have been Cocklyn and Taylor. "Le Buck" may have been "La Buse" and "Davis" was, of course, Howell Davis.[134]

Following the capture of *Le Victorieux*, Cocklyn then came upon LeVasseur in *Heroine* at Cape Lopez, on the coast of Gabon, as Moor reported. LeVasseur was not at the agreed upon rendezvous. He had chased a South Sea vessel away from Anabon, passing along Gabon and the Angolan Coast when he caught and captured her. She was the 250-ton, 28-gun South Sea's *Indian Queen*, owned by Walter and Richard Lougher, master, Capt. Thomas Hill, then coming from Guinea with slaves for Jamaica. LeVasseur was in the process of switching vessels with Capt. Hill when Cocklyn found him. Richard Taylor must have joined them there after the 11th of November, accompanied by his prize, *Le Pren*.

Two weeks later at Cape Lopez, Cocklyn in newly refitted 38-gun *Le Victorieux*, now styled *Victory*, took 20-gun *l'Afriquain de Nantes*, commanded by the recently deceased (28 Sept.) Pierre Dosset, who had previously been taken in *La Concorde de Nantes* by Edward Thache, three years before, on 28 November 1717.[135]

A contradiction between depositions should be settled. Having gone with LeVasseur on *Heroine/Royal Ranger*, John Matthews had earlier sailed away from Richard Moor, who was probably then still aboard Richard Taylor's *Comrade*. Matthews told in his deposition that LeVasseur did not keep *Comrade* for long, for "in her passage thither," apparently while passing along the Angola Coast, he "met with an English Merchant ship called the Indian Queen."[136] He said LeVasseur made a pirate of this larger vessel and gave *Comrade* by way of consolation to Capt. Hill. Moor asserted that they disposed of *Comrade*, but did not say how. Matthews told that LeVasseur "put all the men of the said

---

[133] *Weekly Journal and Saturday Evening Post*, 26 Mar 1720; Cocklyn sailed in *Defiance*, not in *Heroine*.
[134] *Weekly Journal and Saturday Evening Post*, 26 Mar 1720.
[135] "Judah," ~5 Sep 1720, Rapports de navigation, *Les Archives départementales de Loire-Atlantique*, 96.
[136] "The Examination of John Matthews, 12 October 1722, HCA 1/55, ff. 201-21" in E. T. Fox, *Pirates in Their Own Words* (Fox Historical, 2014), 192-195.

ship Indian Queen onboard the [*Comrade*] with him except seaven whom he detained onboard his new ship."[137] Still, Moor and Hais probably offer more accurate information on this small detail – Matthews probably did not. *Comrade* had long been discarded.

Another problem must be arrested. Charles Johnson, not in his first, second, or third edition, but in the 1726 enlarged, two-volume fourth edition of his *A General History,* had attributed the capture of this *Indian Queen* to the pirate "Captain Condent" of the "*Flying Dragon,*" a man whom we now know to be Edward Congdon of the *Dragon* (see details in Chapter Four). This further confuses the detail. John Matthews' and Edouard Hais' depositions, however, assured us that Olivier LeVasseur was responsible for taking *Indian Queen*. This passage in *A General History* was woven together by disparate events of separate pirates, but may partly be based upon some actual evidence refering to Edward England:

> [Condent] from this went to the Guiney Coast, and took Captain Hill in the Indian Queen [actually taken by Olivier LeVasseur – the following may belong to Edward Congdon:] [After supposedly taking *Indian Queen*,] In Luengo Bay [Luanda in Angola?] [Condent or England] saw two Ships at Anchor, one a Dutchman of 44 Guns, the other an English Ship, called the Fame, Captain Bowen [420 tons EIC ship, Capt. William Brown (Jan 1700); Capt. John Pinnel, d. 1721 at Cape of Good Hope of "yellow janders"], Commander; they both cut and ran ashore, the Fame was lost, but the Dutch Ship, the Pyrate, got off [captured] and took with him. [Back to LeVasseur:] When he was at Sea again he discharged Captain Hill, and stood away for the East-Indies. [Congdon again:] Near the Cape he took an Ostend East-India Man, of which Mr. Nash, a noted Merchant in London, was Supercargo. Soon after he took a Dutch East-India Man, discharged the Ostender, and made for Madagascar.[138]

---

[137] Matthews; National Archives, London, Wills of George Lifseord, Taylor, and John Redman, prob. 24 Jun 1720 and 6 Sep 1718, PROB 11/574/446 and PROB 11/565/176; Deposition of Jan Viau - Lt. aboard L'Afriquain de Nantes - 250 tons, 20-guns, commanded by Pierre Dosset, Rapports de navigation, *Les Archives départementales de Loire-Atlantique*, B 4580, 74-76.

[138] Charles Johnson, *A General History of the Pyrates: From Their Rise and Settlement in the Island of Providence, to the Present Time,* Vol. II (London: T. Woodard, 1726), 142; Authorship of the added pirate stories in this edition's Volume II is disputed – it may be that the original author (Nathaniel Mist, using the pseudonym of Charles Johnson) was unavailable at the time (exiled in France). Note also that this passage tells of older pirate crews on Madagascar joining more recent

John Matthews, Richard Moor, and Edouard Hais offer absolutely no detail to confirm Johnson's story about "Captain Condent." Indeed, none ever mentioned "Condent,"any variant spelling, or even Edward England! They expressed, by contrast, great detail about Capt. Thomas Hill and *Indian Queen*. Johnson should have been aware of this. Where Johnson got some of his information on Edward Congdon is not much of a mystery – for the supergargo James Naish wrote a letter to his owners telling of his capture – Johnson knew him! This letter has, however, sadly been misplaced by the British Library (see Chapter Two).

Being more generous, Johnson may have simply gotten confused – at least on this point. Captain Thomas Hill was certainly in command of *Indian Queen* when captured by Olivier LeVasseur, in *Heroine, and* it happened off the Angolan Coast. There is a port there called "Luanda," probably Johnson's "Luengo." These are facts that Johnson may have conflated. Still, Nathaniel Mist, or the controversial author identified as "Johnson" probably followed his nominal practice of supplying scant historical evidence and then heavily elaborating upon the detail, supplying "alternative facts" to enhance his narrative. Much of *A General History's* data probably evolved from hearsay told by inebriated mariners at the Thames River docks or in Wapping coffee houses, often frequented by them. But, not this time, as Naish's letter was readily available to him. Still, Johnson, or rather Mist, might simply have been confused between separate events, as well as between three separate pirates. The only commonalities are that they all sailed to Madagascar in 1720 and were previously off Angola. He then applied this detail to fill in embarrassing gaps in his history of "Captain Condent," as he did with "gentleman-pirate" Stede Bonnet.[139]

While at Cape Lopez, Cocklyn and LeVasseur, having collected numerous slaves from the vessels they captured, especially *Le Solide*, decided to let most of them go. They generously gave Capt. Hill 140 slaves, and then put the remaining 4-500 ashore at Gabon. Most quickly disappeared, blending back

---

arrivals (in this case, the pirate "Condent" according to Grey, but also possibly LeVasseur, by what we learn from Matthews' deposition. It is also possible that LeVasseur and Edward Congdon met after LeVasseur parted with the others on the African Coast, although one might expect Matthews to mention this.

[139] Brooks, *Quest,* 329-339; the section "Mist's Piracy" describes some of *A General History's* many problems.

into the indigenous population, although displaced as they were from their own nations.

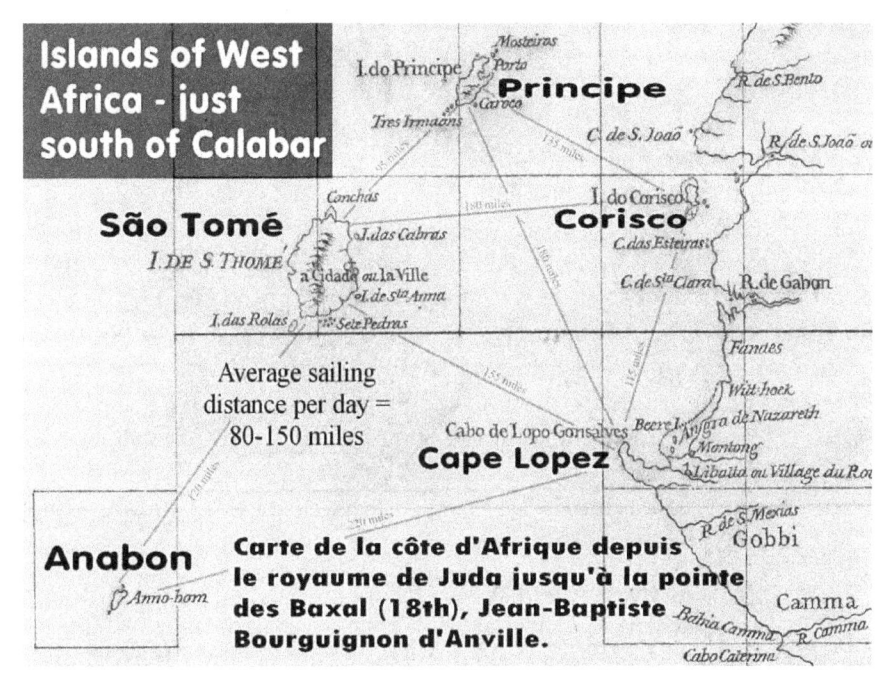

Islands of West Africa - just south of Calabar

São Tomé
Corisco
Principe
Anabon
Cape Lopez

Average sailing distance per day = 80-150 miles

Carte de la côte d'Afrique depuis le royaume de Juda jusqu'à la pointe des Baxal (18th), Jean-Baptiste Bourguignon d'Anville.

The pirates also disputed with each other whether or not to give Capt. Hais one of their prizes, or to – as the deposition states rather ominously – "degrade said Hais and his crew." Edouard Hais' deposition intimated the ship or crew were to be drowned – perhaps another translation discrepancy? It was decided that Hais should take Blincko's former *Heroine* "because all the masts were worthless,"as Moor indicated. John Matthews asserted that Hill received *Comrade* from LeVasseur, but this is not true. LeVasseur may already have been in the process of trading his *Heroine* for *Indian Queen* when Cocklyn, then Taylor and thus, Matthews, found him at Cape Lopez.[140] Depositions from these 18th-century

---

[140] ACCIM f°169-177(f° 169) Juillet 1720, 175; "Edouard Haize second Capne on the ship the Victorious of Nantes," 16 May 1720, Rapports; Matthews is off on dates and intricate detail in most of his deposition; moreover, he was later arrested by Capt. Richard Kirby as an active pirate and may have lied to avoid serious self-incrimination, therefore Moor's, as well as Hais' extremely detailed deposition is given precedence. Edouard Hais said that his brother received *Heroine,* not *Comrade;*

mariners, not always the most reliable witnesses, explain the confusion. The pirates then sailed away, LeVasseur in *Indian Queen* and Cocklyn in *Le Victorieux*, newly styled *Victory*, apparently with its *beauprés*, or bowsprit unmolested, as Hais asserted.[141]

Capt. Hill and Capt. Hais decided to go ashore and water their respective gunless "hulks," as the pirates had left them. Hais still had ninety slaves and Hill had his gift of 141 from LeVasseur – allegedly taken from *Le Victorieux*. First Mate Edouard Hais collected another 30-40, which he offered to trade for the 141 that pirates had taken from *Le Victorieux* before giving them to Hill. He recognized some of them on the deck of Hill's *Heroine* – about 35 in number. Capt. Hill returned these slaves only, but refused to return the rest of them, pretending they did not belong to Hais.[142]

The Hais brothers examined one of the English ships stripped by the pirates. They discarded it and Richard Taylor brought them another, Helle Lavigne's *Le Preni* captured earlier at Judah with another 120 slaves still aboard:

> Capt. Hais treated with the said Captain [Lavigne of *Le Preni de Nantes*] some Beef, flour and some rolls of tobacco, and that after a little work and refit they left on 7 December 1719 for the Isle of Sao Tome [chased away, of course, by one of the pirates] to take on water, arriving there the ninth of the same month and left on the 22nd with a hundred and fifty blacks, healthy and sick that remained to them and made the route for Martinique with Captain Lavigne and a Dutchman.[143]

These pirates were possibly getting bored, for, after leaving the pirates at Cape Lopez, with Guillaume Hais' old crew and cargo aboard, and while on route to São Tomé to water, Capt. Lavigne's previously-captured *Le Preni de Nantes*, was again

---

furthermore, we know that Richard Blinkco/Humphrey Morice had lost their ship, *Heroine* to the pirates, who never returned it.

[141] ACCIM f°169-177(f° 169) Juillet 1720, 173; Moor, 208; note that *Victory*, the French ship that took *Cassandra* at Johanna Island was the former *Le Victorieux* of Nantes and not *Petersborough* of Bristol.

[142] ACCIM f°169-177(f° 169) Juillet 1720, 175.

[143] ACCIM f°169-177(f° 169) Juillet 1720, 175-176; Lavigne completed his cruise in *St. René of Nantes*. Curiously, this document mentioned a Dutchman, as Johnson had in his book.

Baylus C. Brooks 91

chased on 7th of December – most likely by Richard Taylor – was he just messing with them?[144]

Capt. Guillaume Hais and his French-Portuguese crew changed their plans once again for the French West Indian Islands – the trip to Brazil was deemed unwise. First Mate Edouard "Haise, [ship master] Andre Thomas, and [bosun] Jacques la Mountain" took passage from Martinique with *La Sainte Agnes* for the return to Paimbouef and make their report, arriving there on 13th of May. Lavigne returned 1st of September 1720, four days before making his report. His voyage was rather successful, despite his misdealings with these pirates – 335 slaves total! Still, 161 sacks of cocoa, 14 bales and two Gallolin of assorted cotton and indigo, were thrown in the sea! Furthermore, he only lost one sailor, Samuel Fox, to the pirates. Several more died of disease, however.

Seldom do pirate researchers discover such detail of the victims of these voyages. Pirates may not have directly killed their victims, but indirectly, they were responsible for most – through delayed medical attention, starvation, dehydration, and the like – assessed not as pirate problems, but merely as "perils of the sea!" Capt. Hais' crew obituary report becomes a deadly reminder. Out of 99 men aboard *Le Victorieux*, 57, or more than half, had died, including:

> Scrivener Jerome Trequin, Jean Gautier, Rene Henry, Jean Riou, Michel Robin, Mathieu Derien, Louis Chamaillé cooper, Guillaume Bonet caulker, Jean Roulet, Jean Valegon, Belgian Louis Joyaux pilot, Henry Lebars, Ferens (Laurent ?) Aucourne chaplain, Juon (Yen) Adré, Jean Dalene, Jacques Kuarcé, Pierre Galisseau, Yves Moissan, William Hwil, Jaques Federic, François Anapie, Pierre Marechal, Jean Leguen, Jacques Gaches gunner, Roger Maindin, Jean Fournier forestaller (buyer), Jean Desse, Jean-Baptiste Lacroix, Thomas Bourg, Jacques Masse, Jean Verne, René Mirapel, Herve Sansleur, Pierre Mérier «pistonelle» surgeon, Pipet, Jean Raimbaud, Jean Billardois, Lequin, Pierre Aubard, Lajolly, Nicolas Laminot, Barthelemy Raphily, Pierre Michelot lieutenant, Pierre Trial (of Malta), Mathieu Roger, Pierre Mirapel, Daniel Delaurent, Pierre

---

[144] "Judah," ~5 Sep 1720, Rapports de navigation, *Les Archives départementales de Loire-Atlantique*, 96.

Benito, Jean Baure, Mathieu Renou, François Quinsel, François Bonnegrace.[145]

Messieur Marquis de Feuquieres, governor of the French Windward Islands, learned almost immediately of offenses by these pirates. Probably with reason, he took it as an example of cultural prejudice. The first day of 1720, he reflected a general dismay at English pirates' bias against particularly French vessels:

> The Council will see by this report, which has been confirmed to us by the Captain of a small vessel of Nantes [not *Le Preni de Nantes*, who arrived there 22 February], just arrived eight days from Guinea, belonging to M. de Montadouin... who has not been able to report all night. His cargo has been pillaged of 57 negres; the appalling disorder which the pirates have caused at the coast of Guinea, and of which consequence it is to remedy it, we take the liberty of representing that we do not believe that there is a more secure means than weapons at Bress, and Rochefort two or three frigates, good vessels to give them the Hunting without which they may destroy absolutely all the commerce of France. Our seas are covered with these vagabonds[;] they have plundered us of the ships that went from this isle to Quebec and others that sailed from here to Saint Domingue and it comes back to us every day of the stories of their disorders and of the different cruelties that they excrete.[146]

These three pirates may have kept their promise to attempt "Brazil," or at least the South American coast before making for the East Indies. Three pirate vessels matching Cocklyn, Taylor, and Levasseur appear off the Guyana coast, 10 December 1719, anchored two leagues off Cayenne, sending three men ashore. Still, they could not fool the inhabitents into thinking they were legally commissioned and did not stay long.[147]

While the others moved south toward Angola, England may have raided a French vessel at "Cap de Trois Pointes" just west of Judah 11 September 1719. He later moved in that direction as well, capturing *Callabar Merchant* on 11 December. He held that vessel for nine weeks at "Old Calabar, Cape Lopez, and Anabona

---

[145] ACCIM f°169-177(f° 169) Juillet 1720, 176.
[146] Secretary of State for the Navy - Correspondence on arrival from Martinique 1717-1727: Feuquières (François de Pas de Mazencourt, Marquis de), Governor General of the Windward Islands, EN ANOM COL C8A 27 F ° 1, 1 Jan 1720, ff. 1-2.
[147] Decision on a letter from d'Orvilliers dated December 10, 1719. (June 30, 1720), FR ANOM COL / C14 / 12 F ° 48, *Archive Nationales d'Outre Mers*.

Island."[148] He was running slightly behind Cocklyn, LeVasseur, and Taylor, following the trade winds south from first entering the Gambia region in May. No known evidence pairs the four pirates before rounding Cape of Good Hope for Madagascar in 1720. Since these other three had spent a significant amount of time together, and in apparently constant contact, yet still apart from England, in the same locations off West Africa, this may suggest that the three subjects of this chapter did not always get along with the late-comer Edward England. He may have been more of a loner, like Congdon. It may have been his Irish heritage – after taking Howell Davis' command, Bartholomew Robert's crew rejected taking a man from a captured Samuel Carry's vessel simply because he was Irish! All of this could explain England's behavior and treatment by the others after taking *Cassandra*.[149]

LeVasseur, Taylor, and Cocklyn probably intended to make sail for the East Indies alone, then to Madagascar and, perhaps to Mauritius afterward, as they told Richard Blincko. Once there, LeVasseur wandered briefly from Madagascar, missing out on one of the greatest – or most renowned – captures of pirate history: the East India Company's *Cassandra*. Furthermore, the new member of the group, Jasper Seager, a probable elder resident of Madagascar, did not know Edward England until his arrival there roughly coincident with the others, by late spring. Unlike Richard Taylor, Olivier LeVasseur, and Jeremiah Cocklyn, Seager held no prejudice against partnering with Edward England to take *Cassandra*. LeVasseur, having stranded himself on an island just northwest of Madagascar, missed out on that adventure!

The next chapter will involve even more great literary confusion, but still some new information, offered by HMS *Salisbury's* midshipman-turned author Clenment Downing. All of this confusion must be eliminated before we can find the true history of these pirates. Downing experienced many events with pirates directly, but was still much devoted to Capt. Charles Johnson's recent (1724 - only 13 years for Downing, published in 1737) extravagant tales, the bane of the modern pirate researcher!

---

[148] David Richardson, ed., *Bristol, Africa and the Eighteenth Century Slave Trade to America*, Vol. 1: The years of expansion, 1698-1729 (Bristol: Bristol Record Society, 1986), 81.
[149] *Boston News-Letter*, August 22, 1720, 2.

A Compendious
HISTORY
OF THE
INDIAN WARS;
WITH
An Account of the RISE, PROGRESS, STRENGTH, and FORCES of
Angria the Pyrate.
ALSO

The TRANSACTIONS of a Squadron of Men of War under Commodore *Matthews*, sent to the *East-Indies* to suppress the PYRATES.

To which is annex'd,

An ADDITIONAL HISTORY of the Wars between the *Great Mogul*, *Angria*, and his *Allies*.

With an Account of the LIFE and ACTIONS of JOHN PLANTAIN, a notorious Pyrate at *Madagascar*; his Wars with the Natives on that Island, where having continued eight Years, he join'd *Angria*, and was made his chief Admiral.

By CLEMENT DOWNING,

Midshipman on board the *Salisbury*; afterwards Lieutenant of the *Victory Frigate*, *Fame Gally*, and *Revenge Grab*, part of the Squadron employ'd by the *East-India* Company to attack *Angria*; and sometime ENGINEER in the Service of the Great Mogul.

London: Printed for T. COOPER, at the *Globe* in Pater-noster Row.   M.DCC.XXXVII.
(Price bound 2 s. 6 d.)

Chapter 2: *Cassandra*

Taking of James Macrae's *Cassandra*: British East India Company

Edward England appears to have begun his pirating career in the eastern Caribbean, making quite the propitious start. Still, there has been a great deal of confusion regarding this "Irish" pirate. Charles Johnson claims him to have come from Jamaica serving under a pirate named Capt. Winters.[1] Another literary singularity of Johnson's has him capturing the *Cadogan* snow, Capt. Skinner, off Sierra Leone, Africa in early summer 1718, taking 37 slaves. Howell Davis, who supposedly began his journey to piracy that day, was also *supposedly* Skinner's first mate. Johnson tells a long tale of how Skinner was abused by Capt. England, tortured, and eventually killed. He elaborates novelistic dialogue in England's conversation with an old unwelcome acquaintance: "*Ah, Captain* Skinner! *Is it you? The only Man I wished to see; I am much in your Debt, and now I shall pay you all in your own Coin.*"[2] Afterward, in his origin for Howell Davis, Johnson says Skinner's first mate Howell Davis took *Cadogan's* cargo to Barbados and was arrested. After his release, he found no work and headed for

---

[1] Woodard, *The Republic of Pirates,* 250; Colin Woodard gives his name as "Christopher Winter." Other likely candidates would be Robert Winter of *Johnston* frigate (1713-1715) or Peter Winter, captain of *King Solomon* (1711-1715), both in the Jamaica trade at the right time.

[2] Charles Johnson, *A General History of the Robberies and Murders of the Most Notorious Pyrates,* 2nd ed. (London: 1724), 114-115.

New Providence, recently retaken by the Crown. Captain Woodes Rogers "having fitted out two Sloops for Trade, one called the *Buck*, the other the *Mumvil Trader; Davis* found an Employment on Board of one of them."[3] Davis mutinied and took 14-gun *Buck* and then became a pirate himself, heading for the Cape Verde Islands and the African Coast... so told Johnson... actually the newspaper publisher Nathaniel Mist!

This entire passage was inspired by possible newspaper error, literary manipulation of data, and, undoubtedly, Mist's furtive imagination! However, the timing and certain details can be fairly confirmed on Capt. Skinner's appearance at Africa, which indicates that Mist, aka Johnson, based his elaborate musings upon actual data – in this case, unreliable newspaper reports. Also, those reports offered absolutely no connection to Edward England. Furthermore, Howell Davis appeared in none of these particular records! Moreover, *Moville Trader*, the vessel Johnson listed as *"Mumvil Trader,"* actually belonged to Thomas Porter and "Othneil" Davis, who had surrendered at New Providence Island to Capt. Vincent Pearse in Feb-Mar 1718 and again in South Carolina. This certainly identifiable pirate Davis then served the Crown as a privateer, taking numerous Spanish prizes in the next Spanish war.[4]

There is no reason, however, to suspect that there was not another Davis, perhaps named Howell, who signed aboard of Rogers' other vessel, *Buck*. Furthermore, the primary pirate involved in the *"Cadogan"* – actually, *Coulston* - incident, was Edward Congdon of *Dragon*, not Edward England – ironically, according to the same newspaper sources! Indeed, there is *no* primary evidence, except perhaps the confused *Weekly Packet* article mentioned earlier, showing that Davis and England had ever met under such circumstances before Davis became a pirate – which was in February 1719, *before* England had even reached the African Coast! We know that Johnson, or controversial Jacobite newspaper publisher Nathaniel Mist, read his competitors' newspapers, after all. This part of the chapter seems like it goes on interminably, but if the reader will please be patient, it may clear up a lot of oft-asked and oft-

---

[3] Johnson, *A General History*, 175-176.
[4] Brooks, *Quest for Blackbeard*, 558-559.

debated, long-held questions about Edward England *and* why we should *not* use *A General History* as a primary historical source.

Voyages database, collated from primary sources, tells much richer detail. These diassassemble, degrade, and desintegrate Johnson's narrative for the notorious origins of the Edward England-Howell Davis pairing. For starters, this database does not show a *Cadogan* in the time period explored. The only *Cadogan* in the database was captained by Richard Baugh and sailed in 1731. It, as well as newspapers, *does* show the voyage of *Coulston*, however, from the time it departed Bristol on 3 December 1717 until it returned 28 September 1718 – nearly ten months. *Coulston's* captain was indeed named Skinner – Peter Skinner. As expected, this date range straddles the August edition of the *Weekly Packet* and the July edition of the *Post Man Historical,* two English newspapers, and covers nearly a year of a round-trip voyage for this ship. In other words, only one voyage was possible for 1718.

The earliest report from *Weekly Packet* told of "two Pirates of 30 Guns each" while the *Boston News-Letter* issue of 17 November lists the pirates as "Dragon, Capt. Conwel [Congdon], the Rover, Capt. Butscher [La Buse?] and a Sloop of twelve Guns and 170 Men." England's name is not specifically mentioned – though he *could* have been the unnamed captain of the 12-gun sloop – still, he had been otherwise occupied in the Caribbean. Was Mist reading his competitors' newspapers closely enough? Newspapers mention "Sera [Sierra] Leone," an African river. There is some vague supposition in pirate history circles that Capt. England may have later briefly settled in the "privateer village" there circa March-early May 1719, but this is suspect – again, he was on the other side of the Atlantic. The timing is way off as England was still in the Caribbean until mid-April! He was not otherwise noted as being in this location the year before – when and where Johnson claims.[5]

---

[5] *Voyages* database; *Weekly Packet*, 2 Aug 1718; *Boston News-Letter*, 17 Nov 1718, 1; Note that neither newspaper article mentioned a *Cadogan,* only *Coulston,* although the BNL article conflated captain with ship. It may be that Johnson or Mist used *Cadogan* to hide his invented tale. William Snelgrave also deposed (20 Jan 1721)

98   Sailing East

The ship in question was certainly *Coulston* of Bristol, 70-tons, 4 guns, built in 1717 and named for Francis Coulston, a former partner with Robert Tunbridge, owners also of *Berkeley* galley. Capt. Peter Skinner was definitely *Coulston's* captain in 1718; however, the detail which Johnson included appears to have been inspired by these newspaper reports that do not mention Edward England by name. Moreover, Johnson erroneously pairs him with Howell Davis before it was even possible! Of course, the artistic journalist appears to have added flamboyant narrative, as he did with others of his subjects.

> *Bristol, July 28.* Yesterday Morning arriv'd the Lydia and Sarah, Capt. Briant, in six Weeks from Barbadoes, and brings News of the following Ships arriv'd there; viz. Boyle-Frigate, Capt. Webb, Sarah and Elizabeth, Capt. Wilcox, Boston-Merchant, Capt. Briscoe, and Pearl, Capt. Barnsdale, all of and from this Port; Parnel, Capt. Morris, and Coulston, Capt. Skinner, from the Coast. The Coulston and Society, both of this Port, were plunder'd by two Pirates of 30 Guns each, at Sera-Leons. They took thirty seven Slaves out of the Coulston, and a considerable Quantity of Gold. They did but little Damage to the Society. It is thought they design to range the Coast, and then go to Brasil with their Negroes.

"Bristol, July 28," *Weekly Packet*, 2 Aug 1718, "two pirates of 30 Guns each." This repeated identical data from the *Post Man Historical Account*, 29 Jul 1718.

> *London, August 1.* Letters from Barbadoes bring the unwelcome News, that Three Pirate Ships, viz. the Dragon, Capt. Conwel the Rover, Capt. Butcher, and a Sloop of twelve Guns and 170 Men, have taken the following Merchant Ships; namely, the Margaret of London, Capt. Castle, the Society, Capt. Webber, and the Skinner, Capt. Coulston, both from Bristol, a Bristol Sloop, Capt. Wardner, a Dutch Ship, and another, whose Names are not known.

"London, August 1," *Boston News-Letter*, 17 Nov 1718, "Three Pirate Ships," with the ship and captain erroneously conflated.

about a man named "Edward Hogbin (who then lived on Shoar there [Sierra Leone])" who was probably conflated with Edward England.

Documents held by Bristol Record Society show that Peter Skinner sailed 130-ton, 4-gun *Berkeley* galley in 1708 for "Robert Tunbridge & Co.," delivering 310 slaves to Jamaica by April 1709. He made a similar run the next year with possible supercargo Edward Saunders for *Berkeley's* owners: Robert Tunbridge and "Co." or Robert Berkeley, John Webley, Francis Coulston, and Issac Crumpe. Again, in 1710, he repeated this same route. His next voyage for "Robert Tunbridge & Co." occurred in 1713 in 100-ton, 12-gun *Tunbridge* galley, making the same run he made from 1708-1710, this time for Barbados, again in 1714 for Jamaica, and in 1716 for Barbados. Owners then were listed as: Robert Tunbridge, John Duckinfield, and John Hitchins. *Berkeley* galley had then been transferred to Capt. John Owen, later captain of *Peterborough,* also captured by pirates. These records show that Skinner's first run in "*Coulstone*" occurred in 1717, with mate Hugh Vaughan. Owners were: Robert Tunbridge & Co., Edward Saunders, Nathaniel Bushell, James Smith, and Samuel Wyat. This voyage was completed in October 1718 after transacting the final slave sale with Robert Harper of Barbados. None of the data from the Bristol Records or from the British Naval Office mention Skinner's death on this voyage or from any pirate torture. These records show a great deal of detail, but they don't even mention pirates – like other vessels listed in this same source! This is odd, indeed, for such an infamous incident.[6]

Primary source records available from Ancestry.com tell that a Peter Skinner of Bristol married Mary Carpenter in 1712 and that he was a mariner, well-acquainted with the Tunbridges of Bristol. He made his will in 1713 in which he left everything to his new bride and made his "loving friend Robert Tunbridge of the City of Bristol" executor. This Skinner is

---

[6] David Richardson, ed., *Bristol, Africa and the Eighteenth Century Slave Trade to America,* Vol. 1: The years of expansion, 1698-1729 (Bristol: Bristol Record Society, 1986), 11, 14, 19, 24, 34, 41, 52, 61, 75; Note that Joseph "Stetton," or Stratton, who appears as captain of *Prince Eugene* who dealt in pirated goods with Edward Congdon in 1720, sailed as master of Skinner's former command, *Tunbridge,* for the African/Jamaica trade in both 1717 and 1718.

definitely the renowned captain of *Coulston*, the reports of whose death were possibly exaggerated, but not far off the mark. Lastly, the will was probated 23 June 1719, a full year *after Coulston* delivered her cargo to Barbados. Wills were not always probated in a timely fashion, however, and it would be desirable to verify his date of death, if possible. This is important, though – he probably died in 1719, *after* his alleged pirate encounter and *not* in 1718 – after a decade as mariner for Robert Tunbridge. Foremost in this debate, however, his first mate Hugh Vaughan took over his Barbados run on *Coulston* for 1719! Also, while there is no specific indication of piracy in these detailed records, there is also no indication that *Coulston* was *not* captured by pirates, just probably not evilly-minded ones who tended to speak like a comic book villain! Lack of a specific record leaves the question quite open.[7]

Most likely, Skinner did not die the way Johnson said he did – but could have died from maybe disease, quite common in eighteenth-century voyages, especially for mariners in the African Slave Trade. He may have contracted such a contagion during his 1718 voyage mentioned by the *Weekly Packet*. Pirates were known to torture captains and crew to extract information and Skinner may, indeed, have endured this; but, no evidence even hints at this and it's also just as likely that he contracted malaria or dysentery on the coast of Africa or from the Africans chained in the cargo hold of his vessel. Johnson, however, deftly utilized Skinner's story for his own purposes: clearly, enhanced drama – we know that he used it often to enhance his flamboyant tales. One practical goal might include a dramatic device for the vivid entrance of the newspapers' known pirate Howell Davis in his burlesque pirate drama.[8]

Mist, as Johnson, wrote that Edward England gave *Cadogan* to newly-createed pirate Howell Davis and allowed him to proceed to Barbados. Once Davis arrived at Barbados he

---

[7] National Archives, London, Will of Peter Skinner - probated 23 Jun 1719 - PROB 11/569/170; *Voyages;* NA (KEW); *Coulston* was previously (1712) a privateer under William Trestain; other ships owned by Robert Tunbridge and captained by Peter Skinner were *Berkeley Gally* (1708-1711), previously registered as a privateer under Capt. Edmund Saunders (HCA 26/14/35), and *Tunbridge Gally* (1712-1715), registered 17 Jul 1712 as a privateer (HCA 26/16/137).
[8] *The Weekly Packet* (London), 24 Oct 1719; death rates varied between 15-25%; Bialuschewski, "Black People," 464.

"related to these Merchants the unfortunate Death of *Skinner*," and that England supposedly gave him the vessel, "upon which *Davis* was seized and committed to Prison, where he was kept three Months," definitely dramatic![9] Again, Mist certainly invented this fiction.

Skinner's chief mate was plainly listed as Hugh Vaughan, *not* the impossible Howell Davis. Skinner and Vaughan sailed together from Bristol, arrived at Sierra Leone in late winter to early spring 1718, purchased 41 slaves there, 123 at Calabar, and delivered them to Barbados 9 June 1718. They lost 8 slaves of the 41 promised to Barbados (a loss of 19.5% - average was about 15-25% for 17th-early 18th centuries), nominal for these types of Middle Passage trips. *Coulston*, then under master Hugh Vaughan, sailed for York River, Virginia to deliver 123 slaves there. Again – *not* Howell Davis.[10]

Neither newspaper article ever mentioned Edward England's name, still, Mist, alias "Johnson," included this elaborate narrative to complete his ornate tale on Capt. England, including the infamous torture and death of Peter Skinner:

> [England's crew] laid hold of the Captain [Skinner], and made him fast to the Windless, and there pelted him with Glass Bottles, which cut him in a sad Manner; after which they whipp'd him about the Deck, till they were weary, being deaf to all his Prayers and Intreaties, and at last, because he had been a good Master to his Men, they said, he should have an easy Death, and so shot him thro' the Head.[11]

Again, this excerpt cannot be confirmed or denied without further evidence, but judging from his many "mistakes," Johnson or Nathaniel Mist should *not* be trusted. Johnson also claimed England to be a moderate man, though this passage is

---

[9] Johnson, *A General History*, 2nd ed., 175.
[10] *Voyages* database; Elizabeth Donnan, *Documents Illustrative of the History of the Slave Trade to America*, Vol. 4 (Washington: Carnegie Institute, 1935), 183.
[11] Johnson, *A General History*, 115.

not moderate, but quite cruel, reminiscent more of Edward Low. That West-Indian pirates would even have allowed their crew to react this way is not completely unheard of, but still unlikely.

Mist apparently read the confusing reports of *Daily Post* of 17 October 1719 and *Weekly Packet* of 24 October 1719 and assumed that England and Davis knew one another – then he added flourish. His flamboyant false narratives, sold to us as actual history, have truly distorted pirate history for nearly 300 years! The only thing worse than repeating an error is enhancing that error to make it even more saleable to avid readers, who cared not so much for truth as a good story! "Elaborations" or "alternative facts" are still simply lies! More to the point, Charles Johnson, or Nathaniel Mist, had relied on the same newspapers and Admiralty reports for his basic information – which he would then manipulate. Mist never needed to leave his printing offices on Great Carter Lane, except for the occasional stroll to Whitehall to look at Admiralty reports and modify their content for his quite popular book. The same reports, for the most part, we can still read today – including the numerous ones that he missed! Reliance upon *A General History* has done a grave disservice to actual, professional pirate history.

The Known Edward England

As to what the records *did* actually tell about Edward England, he began his career a bit later, in early December 1718, just over a week after Edward "Blackbeard" Thache's death in Ocracoke Inlet, North Carolina. Contrary to hypotheses which placed him in the Bahamas even earlier, no primary sources yet indicate this.[12] No place of recent

---

[12] Colin Woodard, *Republic*, 248n; Note: specific assertion of Edward England as Charles Vane's new quartermaster in early 1718 (from: *A General History*, Vol. 2, 4th ed., 1728, 362) and both allegedly surrendered to HMS *Phoenix*; National Archives, London, Captain's log of HMS *Phoenix* (1715 Oct 8-1721 Oct 6), ADM 51/690; Entries for 22 Feb - 11 Apr 1718 at New Providence, but before departure for Virginia show detailed activity of pirates and their vessels, but no specific names, specifically no indication of Edward England's presence; moreover, Pearse's list of 209 surrendered pirates shows Charles Vane, but not Edward England. Where did this assertion come from? See Appendix for *Phoenix* log (ADM 51/690) entries.

departure is ever mentioned for him in primary sources, although Jamaica would be appropriate point of origin for an early pirate or wayward merchant in the Americas.

Edward England set out in a 12-gun brigantine with about 90 men and took a vessel belonging to Lt. Col. William Leslie of Barbados. England had a smaller sloop with him functioning as tender as they made their way through the Windward Islands – same locale frequented later by Bartholomew Roberts and near where Edward "Blackbeard" Thache captured *La Concorde* of Nantes, or *Queen Anne's Revenge*. He then set out eastward for the Guinea coast of Africa. Along the way, near Barbados, he took the ship *Christiana* of Boston, Capt. Jonathan Bull and their sloop tender on 5 December 1718.[13]

Bull made his deposition the following 17th of January to Gov. William Hamilton of Antigua. Bound from Surinam (NE South America) to Boston, as Bull declared, he was captured only an hour after the pirates had sunk Lt. Col. Leslie's ship. The following evening:

> ... [England] took a vessel [1st capture of *Victory* of London?][14] bound to Barbados from Guinea with 250

---

[13] "The Examination of Henry Hunt, 27 September, 1720, HCA 1/54, ff. 115-116," "The Examination of Richard Moor, 31 October 1724 (addenda 5 November 1724), HCA 1/55, ff. 94-97," "The Examination of John Matthews, 12 October 1722, HCA 1/55, ff. 201-21" "Captain Mackra's ship taken by Edward England, *The Post Boy*, 25-27 Apr 1721" in E. T. Fox, *Pirates in Their Own Words* (Fox Historical, 2014), 190-192, 207-213, 192-195, 271-276; "America and West Indies: November 1718," in *Calendar of State Papers Colonial, America and West Indies: Volume 30, 1717-1718*, ed. Cecil Headlam (London: His Majesty's Stationery Office, 1930), 381-397; *Boston News-Letter*, 22 Jul 1717; *BNL*, 29 Jul 1717, 2; *BNL*, 5 Aug 1717, 2.

[14] *Boston News-Letter*, 4 Jul 1720; Probably 90-ton, 10-gun *Victory*, Capt. William Rideout. *Voyages* database shows that *Victory* loaded with 256 slaves at Africa, and then delivered 219 to Barbados on 2 Aug 1718. She left for her homeport on 8 Sep 1718, but no date of her return is given, although she is not shown as captured. However, *BNL* of 4 Jul 1720 reports: "London, April 11. We hear that the African Company have received an account from the Coast, that since their Letters from thence, the *Peterborough* Gally of Bristol, Capt. Owen, and the *Victory* of London, Capt. William Rideout, were fallen into the Hands of the Pyrates, who had plunder'd the latter and let her go, but had taken the former and fitted her up for a Pyrate." It is reasonable to assume that Rideout's *Victory* may have made other ports of call to collect a return cargo and lingered until being captured 6 Dec 1718 by Edward England. Even stranger, *Voyages* shows a second voyage in summer of 1720 for this *Victory* of London with both captains Rideout and "John Bull" aboard. Edward

negroes, and some small time after another ship from Madera [Madeira] bound for Barbados with provisions *etc*. On 28th they took a small sloop belonging to Martinico [Martinique] *etc*. Believes they intend to fit out the Guinea man for their man of war somewhere near St. Vincents [to southward of Martinique]. When they sent him and his men off in their own vessel, they had on board 5 commanders with their men, including the Commander of a briganteen belonging to Piscataqua taken about 18th Dec. They were about 125 in number when he left them.[15]

French records have largely been ignored in investigating these pirates, but they can be quite helpful, especially in regards to English pirate disdain for the French – prejudice clearly defines the period! One such deposition of Pierre Jouane of the diocese of St. Malo, en route to Saint Domingue from Martinique in *Le Mercure*, or *Mercury*, probably related details of the taking of this "small French sloop" referred to by Capt. Bull.

By the end of November 1718, Jouane and his consort, one Daguerre, in 30-ton *Marie* of Martinique, having debarked from Martinique to go to St. Domingue, encountered an English pirate of 40 tons ten leagues from Samana Bay, just south of Scot's Bay on eastern Hispaniola. The pirate carried 8 guns, and had 70 men. He had a prize with him, another English Bermudian vessel (*Christiana* of Boston, Capt. Jonathan Bull?), whom he had previously taken. The pirate took this ship, "having the 10th of December, at eight o'clock in the morning, chased the ship, seized it the same day at four o'clock in the evening, and having cut off the great mast, took all that was in that ship, even the old and new sails, with an old jib and a sail of fortune." Supposedly, this unnamed pirate cruelly

---

England must have let this ship go. Again, it was captured by pirates (probably not Edward England this time – Roberts?). The captains Rideout and Bull both had been captured by pirates the year before and were captured again - together!

[15] "America and West Indies: December 1718, 11-19," in Calendar of State Papers Colonial, America and West Indies: Volume 30, 1717-1718, ed. Cecil Headlam (London: His Majesty's Stationery Office, 1930), 404-424; occurence of vessels named *Victory* and conflation with Hais' *Le Victorieux* in regards to Edward England's history have confused his alleged early interaction with Taylor, LeVasseur, and Cocklyn.

mistreated Jouane and Daguerre, and then relieved them of *Mercury*.[16]

Another pirate afterward harassed Daguerre's *Marie* yet again, but let them go. The unlucky pair of Jouane and Daguerre continued on their journey south around Hispaniola, approaching Cape Tiberon, when they were taken yet again ten leagues from the cape at La Grange by the 8-gun brigantine...

> ... of which the captain was an Irishman, and the crew numbering one hundred men of different nations, the said brigantine's men having boarded Jouane took his anchors and oars, and his canoe. Hence it was not without difficulty that Jouane and Daguerre attained the Cape de Saint Domingue [Tiburon], or they made their declaration.[17]

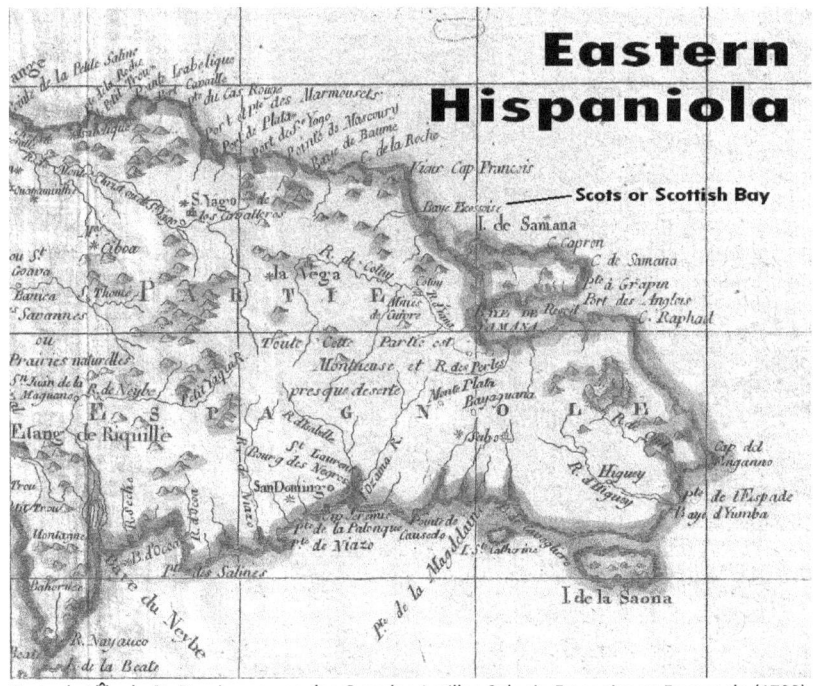

Carte de L'Île de St. Domingue une des Grandes Antilles Colonie Francoise et Espagnole (1780), from Raynal, G., *Atlas de Toutes les Parties Connues du Globe Terrestre, Dressé pour l'Histoire Philosophique et Politique des Établissemens et du Commerce des Européens dans les Deux Indes*, 1780.

---

[16] FR ANOM COL C8A 26 F° 133, 14 février 1719, ff. 252-256.
[17] FR ANOM COL C8A 26 F° 133, 14 février 1719, ff. 252-256.

The following month of January, after crossing to the northward of Hispaniola, England took the snow *Eagle* of New York, Commander Robert Leonard, perhaps while crossing the Atlantic to the African coast. They sailed in latitude of 23 degrees. Robert Leonard of *Eagle* made his deposition when he arrived in Antigua before Gov. Hamilton on the 24th of February 1719, just ten days after Pierre Jouane made his at Saint Domingue. Leonard testified that, similar to Henry Hunt's later treatment, England "beat him with his cutlass for not bringing to at first shot."[18] He also said that the pirates "threatned to sink his vessell and throw him overboard with a double headed shot about his neck, if he concealed where his money was."[19] Note that pirates, including Edward "Blackbeard" Thache, often made such threats, but rarely carried them out. The pirates had informed Leonard that they had taken a French pirate in Scots Bay [*Bahía Escocesa*] at the north end of Hispaniola. Leonard also recognized the sailing master of the pirate vessel, Alexander Ure, who sailed with him about six months ago as boatswain.

Another deposition of John Bois, Carpenter of the *Wade* frigate, — Edwards Commander, spoke of engaging Edward England near Samaná Bay, where *Mercury* was earlier taken. England's ship then had 26 guns instead of the 12 mentioned earlier near Barbados, and Bois told that he was Irish. He may have upgraded his vessel along the way from Barbados, perhaps Capt. Rideout's *Victory* of London, with added armament, as they indicated that they would:

> These plundered another vessel, and sent deponent and one Isaac Wackee on board because they refused to go with the pirates. The pirates had on board about 130 white men, and about 50 Spaniards, negroes and Indians, 26 guns and 4 swivel guns, commanded by Edward England an Irishman. They designed to go to the latitude of Barbados to get bread or flower and a better ship, and from thence to the coast of Guinea and Brazil. Sumana Bay and Scots Bay and the Island

---

[18] "America and West Indies: December 1718, 11-19," in *Calendar of State Papers Colonial, America and West Indies: Volume 30, 1717-1718*, ed. Cecil Headlam (London: His Majesty's Stationery Office, 1930), 404-424.
[19] "America and West Indies: December 1718, 11-19."

of Mona [*Isla de la Mona*, west of Puerto Rico] are places of rendezvous for the pirates.[20]

Edward England tacked back to the French Windward Isles that spring to take Capt. Jean Collin of 8-gun *Le Bon Secour* near the island of Martinique. On 5th of April, 1719,

> ... the English [pirate "l'Ingland"], of 24 guns and six pivots [swivels], and two hundred crewmen, who took all his cannon, thirty-two casks of flour, 7tt. of Bordeaux wine, 150 flats of butter, 20 arras[?] of bacon, 6 barrels of beef, and all their bread loaves and wines of provisions.[21]

This French deposition absolutely destroys *A General History's* fiction on yet another erroneous mentor-pupil literary devices of Nathaniel Mist's, similar to the false pairing of Edward Thache with Benjamin Hornigold to take *La Concorde of Nantes*. Edward England was nowhere near the African Coast when Howell Davis became a pirate at least two months earlier!

Presumably, England then set sail for the coast of Africa, probably right after taking *Le Bon Secour*, in order to arrive on the African Coast in time to take Henry Hunt by May 1719. By that time, Jeremiah Cocklyn, and Olivier LeVasseur, with recently-liberated Richard Taylor left Sierra Leone River, leaving Howell Davis to again attack the RAC fort there. Still, Edward England's confusion with Howell Davis has become an extremely complicated and *awfully* annoying 300-year-old conundrum, owing to erroneous newspaper articles, an unscrupulous journalist, and his greatly distorted *A General History*!

---

[20] "America and West Indies: December 1718, 11-19;" Mona Passage, or simply The Mona, is an 80 mile strait that separates the islands of Hispaniola and Puerto Rico.
[21] Deposition of Jean Collin of *Le Bon Secour*, 19 Oct 1719, 9 Sep 1720, Rapports de navigation, *Les Archives départementales de Loire-Atlantique*, B 4579, 30.

Identifying English ships
In the African Trade

Until 1698, the Royal African Company or RAC enjoyed a monopoly on the West African slave trade and kept fairly complete records, but in that year parliament ended RAC's monopoly. This opened the trade to many individual merchants and other ports besides London, Liverpool, and Bristol. Individual merchants from small provincial ports without detailed knowledge of Africa participated – for a ten percent surcharge to the RAC until 1712; however, they did not keep the most accurate records. With tighter focus, they worried more about their individual short-term profit – their "bottom line." For this reason, vessels caught by pirates in 1719 are rarely mentioned in English records, except in the rarer personal correspondence, like those from Snelgrave to Morice. Many of these events undoubtedly slipped through official notice. Shipping lists and newspapers can help, but as we've seen, many of those are missing or haphazardly reported. More valuable are computer databases that collate many known primary records, including those of government – such as *Voyages* database. It turns out that there is a great amount of information in the "spaces between" or incidental records created by the brief interactions between merchant, ship captain, port authorities, and the letters, depositions, and newspaper blurbs generated by that contact. For instance, Snelgrave's letter of 30 April 1719 was quite rich in detail and crossed some tees and dotted eyes on many captures, especially belonging to Humphrey Morice, that year. Collation of Bristol records with those of London and personal references fill gaps and help to complete pirate history faster than any single contemporary author, no matter how conscientious, would be able.

Again, newspapers can be annoyingly inaccurate compared with other more reliable sources! The *Daily Post* and *Weekly Packet*, both of London reported piracies at Gambia River that involved Edward England. *Daily Post* had word from Gambia that a ship called *Royal James*, Capt. Edward England, "a Pirate of 30 Guns and 160 Men, had burnt four Ships in that River, and plunder'd three more; had also taken two others, and fitted them up for Pirates, one of which they call the Flying King."[22]

This news item was dated 17 October 1719 – quite late for similar items of Howell Davis who raided Fort James and generally wreaked havoc in the same river earlier. Edward England's vessel *Royal James* can be identified through *Voyages* database as a ship of the South Sea Company named *Pearl*, 24-year-old Capt. Edward Tizard, having boarded slaves at Fort Anomabu for Kingston, Jamaica in December 1718 and was taken by pirates while on route to that destination. So, this probably accurate detail on *Pearl's* capture placed it in the Caribbean, around the time that England made his way there from Hispaniola that spring – *before* arriving on the African Coast. Before the discovery of French depositions concerning Edward England or "l'Ingland" by Dr. Jacques Gasser, the missing time gaps for this pirate have truly annoyed researchers – and exposed the fancified creations of less-diligent ones. This is probably the reason that many researchers offer his theorized residence at the "privateer town" around the time of Snelgrave's capture at Sierra Leone as a "bandage" for this historial absence "wound."

A second report of 22 October told of England's capture of an Ostend vessel, a Dutch vessel, and *Loyalty* of Glascow, Scotland, Capt. Mungo Graham, and owned by Richard Graham. This Dutch vessel may have been *Jacoba Galeij*, commanded by Jan Cornelissen and owned by Phillipus Bonket of Amsterdam, which intended to purchase slaves in West-Central Africa and St. Helena, and which could be England's *Fancy*, used to take *Cassandra* in the East Indies. *Loyalty* had purchased her slaves in Gambia and Sierra Leone, places of familiarity to these pirates.[23]

The Weekly Packet report contained greater detail of a single event on 25 March 1719 to which many events of May and June were appended. This particular article served as Charles Johnson's source for his detailed listing given for Edward England. Still, this *Eagle* [not Robert Leonard's vessel], taken 25 March 1719 in that listing, was likely one of Davis' captures, definitely *not* England's

---

[22] *Daily Post*, October 17, 1719.
[23] *Daily Post*, October 22, 1719; *Voyages*, http://www.slavevoyages.org/; the other vessel fitted for a pirate was *Sarah* galley of London, Capt. Lambert, which England carried to Sierra Leone.

110   Sailing East

(still in the Caribbean) and *not* at Gambia, since Davis was nearer then to Sierra Leone with Cocklyn and LeVasseur. This is probably the "large Ship" that Snelgrave mentioned and that Cocklyn, LeVasseur, and their crews briefly mistook for a Man of War. Also important is that *Sarah's* captain Henry Hunt deposed that he saw *no* pirates at Gambia from 1 March until he was taken at Gambia by England in late May, fresh from the Caribbean!

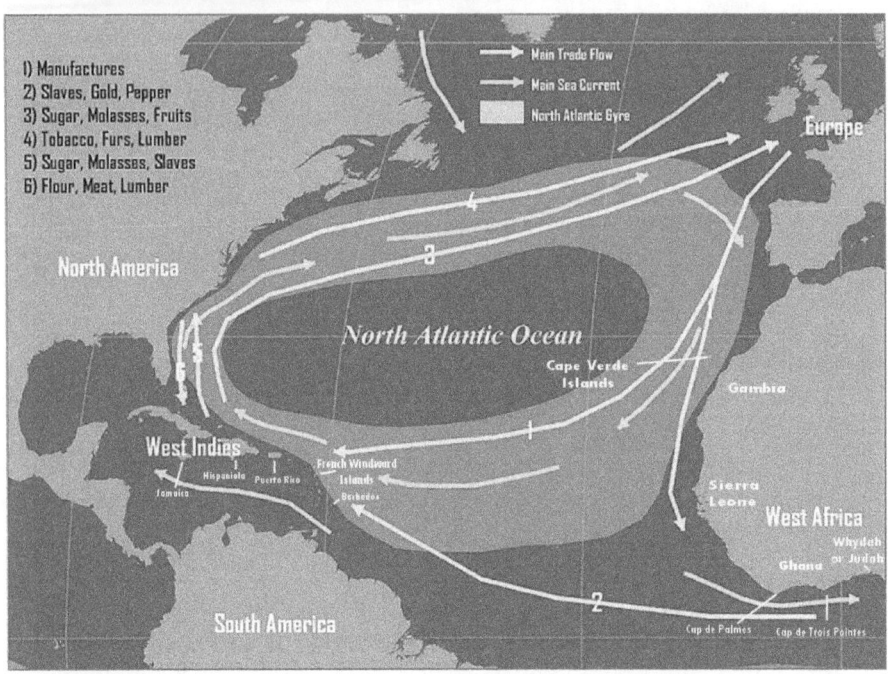

Atlantic Ocean – Trade Winds Map, in Jean-Paul Rodrigue, *The Geography of Transport Systems*, 4th ed. (New York: Routledge, 2017). Annotated with locations concerning Edward England by Baylus C. Brooks.

Although blaming Charles Johnson, er… Nathaniel Mist, is convenient, he cannot be wholly blamed for the mistakes of other journalists. These newspaper reports have caused confusion as to where Edward England began on the African Coast. They also confused England *with* Howell Davis – which probably influenced Mist to erroneously and flamboyantly pair them in his book, with ultra-notorious and fictional delight! England's arrival on the African Coast occurred late, about late May 1719, when Hunt was taken. Howell Davis, who arrived there about three months earlier, was not involved with these late May captures at Gambia River. England left a plethora of documentary evidence cruising in the Windwards in spring, then followed the traditional Atlantic trade route up the coast of North America, jumping over to Africa with the easterly trade winds to the Cape Verde Islands and the Gambia region. Most mariners would then follow those winds southward.

Again, this newspaper article rightly identified *Royal James* as Edward Tyzard's *Pearl*. Of specific importance, it does not give the date of capture for *Pearl*. Indeed, *Voyages* database tells that she delivered her cargo of 201 slaves on 11 February 1719 at Kingston, Jamaica. She most likely was captured afterward, perhaps while returning to her home port in Great Britain and before April when he took *Le Bon Secours*. So, *Pearl* could, indeed have been captured by England, *Eagle* pink of William Rickets was not, and the rest of the article describes England's activities afterward on the African Coast in late May 1719:

> We have reciev'd the following List of Ships taken by the Pirates this Year, In the River of Gamboa [Gambia], which tho' very particular, we are well assur'd our Readers may depend upon as authentick. The *Eagle* Pink, Capt. [William] Rickets Commander, belonging to Cork, was taken [by Davis nearer to Sierra Leone?] March the 25th, having 6 Guns and 17 Men on board, seven of which turn'd Pirates[;] The *Charlote*, Capt. Oldson [Branson Oulson], of London, was taken May 26th [def. by England], having 8 Guns and 18 Men, thirteen whereof turn'd Pirates. The *Sarah*, Captain Stunt [Hunt], of ditto, was taken [def. by England] May the 27th, having 4 Guns and 18 Men, whereof three turn'd Pirates. The *Bentworth*, Capt. Garner, of Bristol, taken [prob. by England] May the 27th, having 12 Guns and 30 Men, 12 whereof turn'd Pirates, The *Bank* [or *Buck,* but not Davis' old 14-gun *Buck*] Sloop, Captain Sylvester, of Gamboa, was taken [prob. by England] May the 27th, having 2 Guns and 2 Men, who both turn'd Pirates. The *Carteret*, Capt. Snow of London was taken [prob. by England] May the 28th, having 4 Guns and 18 Men, whereof 5 turn'd Pirates. The *Coward* Galley, Captain Creed, of ditto, was taken [def. by England] June the 17th, having 2 Guns and 13 Men, whereof 4 turn'd Pirates [info from Creed deposition]. The *Mercury*, Captain Maggot, of ditto, taken [prob. by England] May the 29th having 4 Guns and 18 Men,

5 whereof turn'd Pirates. The *Elizabeth and Katherine*, Captain Bridges, of Barbados, was taken [prob. by England] June the 27th, having 6 Guns and14 Men, whereof 4 turn'd Pirates.

The 3 first were sent to Jamaica, Virginia, and Maryland, the two last made Pirates, and the rest burnt. They were taken [Again, not *Eagle*...] by the *Royal James*, Captain Edward England, formerly the *Pearl*, Captain Tyzard; she now mounts 30 Guns, and 160 Men. The *Mercury* is now call'd the *Queen Ann's Revenge*, and carries 14 Guns, and 30 Men. The *Elizabeth and Katherine* is nam'd the flying King, has, 8 Guns and 14 Men, Robert Sample Commander.[24]

Sarah, Capt. Hunt is of particular interest in this investigation because of his eyewitness account that May-June. Still, contrary to this, *Sarah* had *not* become 22-gun *Duke of Ormond*, later used by Olivier LeVasseur. Chapter One clearly details Snelgrave's letter showing *that Sarah* of London had to have been Capt. Jonathan Lambert's vessel, captured at Sierra Leone by Cocklyn and LeVasseur.

The deposition of Capt. Henry Hunt, then master of another *Sarah* galley of London, 4 Guns and 18 Men, showed that he had arrived at Gambia 1 March 1719.[25] Again, he encountered no pirates for the next two months as he loaded his cargo – certainly, he should have noticed if pirates had been there – they'd have been the ones shooting their loud guns at other ships in the same river and causing some commotion. The timing was coincident with the incidents involving Jeremiah Cocklyn, Richard Taylor, Howell Davis, and Olivier LeVasseur well over 400 miles away at Sierra Leone River between late March and early May.

---

[24] *The Weekly Packet* (London), 24 Oct 1719; Captain of 100-ton *Pearl* was Edward Tyzard or Tyzack, born in Dorset, England in 1694. His father, Edward, son of Perigrin, was a Quaker merchant who was killed falling from a mast in 1700. Edward Jr. became a merchant as well, he captained *Pearl* before in February 1714, but became captain of *Success* of New England by January 1715. After his capture in *Pearl* in 1719 by Edward England, he moved to St.Olave, Southwark where he married in All Hallows, Staining, London to Mary Smith on 30 August 1720. He died 28 Aug 1743 in All Hallows Barking or Tower Hill of "Convulsions" and was buried in Ratcliffe, Devonshirehouse.

[25] Donnan, *Documents of the Slave Trade*, II: 421; probably the brother of merchant William Hunt of Little Tower Street, London.

Edward England steared the former *Pearl* along the Atlantic trade winds to North Africa, and then to Gambia River, so Henry Hunt would not miss the displeasure of his company that late spring day. Hunt deposed that he had taken on 133 slaves when "on or about the 27th of May following[,] a pirate Vessel called the *Royal James* [Capt. Edward England, 30 guns, 160 men]... came into the River with two other English Ships[26] which had been taken by the sd Edward England" and manned with pirates.[27] England had been busy on this voyage. One of these sloops was very likely *Bank* or *Buck* (not Davis' old sloop) of Gambia, Capt. Sylvester, captured with only two crew and two guns that same day. It likely had been a messenger packet for the fort there. *Daily Post* of London added that he burnt four ships (*Charlotte, Bentworth, Bank/Buck,* and *Coward* galley, Capt. Thomas Creed[28]) in Gambia River, plundered three: *Carteret* snow, Capt. Thomas

---

[26] These ships might be any of the following, listed in *The Weekly Packet* issue of 24 Oct 1719: "The *Charlote*, Capt. Oldson, of London, was taken May 26th, having 8 Guns and 18 Men, thirteen whereof turn'd Pirates... The *Bentworth*, Capt. Garner, of Bristol, taken May the 27th, having 12 Guns and 30 Men, 12 whereof turn'd Pirates, The *Bank* Sloop, Captain Sylvester, of Gamboa, was taken May the 27th, having 2 Guns and 2 Men, who both turn'd Pirates." Note that this "*Buck*" mentioned by Henry Hunt cannot possibly be Howell Davis' vessel, because he came in that vessel from New Providence. Furthermore, these ships all were later burnt by the pirates, presumably after finding larger ships. Hunt states in his deposition that the other vessel was *Charlotte*.

[27] *Daily Post* (London, England), Saturday, October 17, 1719; Issue 13; "The Examination of Henry Hunt, 27 September, 1720, HCA 1/54, ff. 115-116," in E. T. Fox, *Own Words,* 191; "Deposition of Henry Hunt and [surgeon] Thomas Blackston," in "America and West Indies: January 1724, 1-15," in *Calendar of State Papers Colonial, America and West Indies: Volume 34, 1724-1725*, ed. Cecil Headlam and Arthur Percival Newton (London: His Majesty's Stationery Office, 1936), 1-18; Still, this would not be Hunt's first encounter with pirates, as commander of *Delight*, he endured capture again in 1723. *Charlot* is found in the appendix.

[28] Capt. Thomas Creed, son of Margaret, married Sarah and lived in Ratcliffe, Stepney, Middlesex, with son Thomas born in 1717. Former captain of *Sarah* and *Foreward* galleys, this mariner was born about 1684 and died 1721. He left a will in Ratcliffe. He should not be confused with the longer-lived mariner, Thomas Creed of probably Kent, wife Elizabeth Horsey (later married Elias Cornish), master of HMS *Scarborough* and later served aboard HMS *Lyme*. Note: there is some confusion over the vessel or captain names between different newspaper articles, in reference to "Capt. Creed's" vessel, *Weekly Packet,* 24 Oct 1719 and *London Journal,* 24 Sep 1720; see note 31.

Lynch[29], and took two, one being former *Elizabeth and Katherine*, Capt. (Thomas?) Bridges of Barbados, now *Flying King,* under pirate Robert Sample, the other the former 50-ton *Mercury,* Capt. Henry Mackett of London, "Maggot," or "Market," according to Hunt (who first purchased slaves in Madagascar for Barbados), now *Queen Ann's Revenge.*[30] Hunt tried to escape by cutting loose his anchor, but to no avail. England's men...

> ... beat him with their Cutlaces and threatened to kill him for endeavouring to escape from them and also threatened to burn his sd Ship, and soon afterwards they forced [Hunt] to go on board of the Buck sloop [Captain Sylvester] and ordered him to take Charge of her as Pilote of her and threatened to blow out his Brains if he suffered her to touch the Ground.[31]

Hunt alleged he was threatened and beaten. This negative influence upon him must be taken into account when analyzing this source. By contrast, Hunt also deposed that "on or about the 5th of July 1719 the generous pirates delivered to the Examinate his aforesd Gally and Negroes and permitted him to sail away with them."[32] Thomas Creed added that Hunt also sailed away with "several brass Panns & bottles" that belonged to him, as well as some goods from Thomas Lynch's *Carteret.* [33] The Ostender, Dutchman, and *Loyalty* reported by *Daily Post* of 22 October 1719 may have been captured after Hunt was released, again, likely that same month.[34]

Hunt was not only beaten, but later, was arrested, as well, thanks to England's capture of him – and fellow merchant

---

[29] A Capt. Thomas Lynch commanded *Mary & Constance* in Jamaica trade in July 1713.

[30] *Daily Post* (London, England), Saturday, October 17, 1719; Issue 13; *The Weekly Packet,* 24 Oct 1719; *American Weekly Mercury,* 17 Mar 1720, 3; *AWM* reports Buck/Bank as "Buck of Gamboa".

[31] Henry Hunt, 191-192.

[32] Henry Hunt, 192.

[33] National Archives, London, Information of Thomas Creed of Stepney, Middlesex, 27 Sep 1720, HCA 1/54, f. 115.

[34] *London Journal,* 24 Sep 1720; This "Capt. Creed" supposedly commanded *Anne,* taken at the same time as Hunt's *Sarah.* According to *London Journal,* "Capt. Hunt, being taken by the same Pyrates some few Hours before...," implying that *Sarah* and *Anne* were taken the same day. This was in error, as the Information of Thomas Creed of Stepney, Middlesex, 27 Sep 1720, HCA 1/54, f. 115 states "Thomas Creed's" *Coward* was taken the next month on 17th June. This is confirmed by *Weekly Packet,* 24 Oct 1719. *Anne* was Creed's current vessel, after his encounter with pirates.

Thomas Creed. Creed's deposition accused him of having joined the pirates and stolen his goods. Creed deposed he was captured by pirates about twenty days after Hunt in only "two fathoms of water," who was then being forced to pilot for the pirates. He claimed that if Hunt had not directed their sloop, Creed's *Coward* would never have been captured. Hunt and Oulson suffered trial the next year primarily because of Thomas Creed's accusation against them found in his deposition of 27 September 1720. *Coward's* former captain Creed convinced authorities that Hunt and Oulson may have turned pirate.

The following year, Henry Hunt visited the Admiralty Office to obtain a Mediterranean pass and was arrested for piracy. He was then incarcerated in Marshalsea Prison, awaiting arraignment. Boyer's *The Political state of Great Britain* showed:

> On *Monday*, the last Day of this Month [in 1720], at a Sessions of the High Court of *Admiralty*, holden at the *Old Baily*, for the Trial of Crimes committed on the High Seas, Captain *Hunt* of the *Delight* [a different vessel; Hunt commanded *Sarah* galley when taken], and Captain *Oldson* [Oulson], of the *Charlotte* [captured before *Sarah*], Merchant Ships, were tried for Piracy: But' it appeared that they themselves were taken by the Pyrates, and were of Necessity obliged to assist them in the Direction or managing their Ships, to save themselves from being Shot: The Owners appeared on the Part of these Gentlemen, gave them very good Characters, and told the Court, that they were well satisfied with their Conduct; and the chief Witness varying much in his Evidence [in other words, Capt. Creed allegedly lied], they were honourably acquited.[35]

The Hunt-Creed incident was the first report of any kind known on Edward England on the African coast. There are still few details until he took *l'Heureaux Avanturies* in September at *Cap de Trois Pointes*. From here, he finally ventured out to take

---

[35] "Information of Thomas Creed"; A. Boyer, *The Political State of Great Britain*, Vol. 20 (1720), 385.

Callabar Merchant in December, maybe joining with Cocklyn and LeVasseur near Cape Lopez, cruised off Cape Town that winter, and then sailed for Madagascar by spring of 1720. Before we continue with this part of the tale, though, we must divert our attention to correcting even more confusion affecting Edward England's story – the dreaded Plantain "fake news!"

Yet Another Ripple in Reality!

Pirate Edward England's activities from July-December 1719, with one possible, are essentially unknown. Johnson has certainly been of no help, but his narrative was not the worst. That dubious honor falls on the flamboyant narrative of an ex-pirate told to an ex-navy midshipman who recorded every fascinating word. He later related the tale in a book of 1737. Convoluting the narrative even further, this author had read Charles Johnson's *A General History*, believed every word of that one, too. He then tried to reconcile his work with these stories and detail, as many have since. Johnson knew no more than we today of England's activities from Gambia in May, to *Cap de Trois Pointes* in September, until he met *Callabar Merchant* in December – and he did not account for the two months that England held the ship before sailing for Madagascar. So much of the secondary material written since 1724 has been so universally infected by Johnson that it is all practically worthless! Every reference leads back to that one infectious source. Thus, this author's strenuous attempt to sort out the convoluted maze initially created by Nathaniel Mist masquerading as Charles Johnson and return pirate history to the realm of professional historical care!

England's history contains serious gaps, but they need to be filled with primary sources, not hearsay or fantasy! We know that he did not make the trip to the East Indies in *Royal James* and few primary sources hint at the possible acquisition of the Dutch ship *Fancy* in which he seemed to have made that voyage. This ship, maybe *Jacoba Galeij*, would be rather important in the tale involving the renowned James Macrae's *Cassandra*. Therefore, *Fancy* is primary in the investigation of

Edward England. It is also the single thread onto which this gigantic web of distortion is tied.

Clement Downing's *History of the Indian Wars,* told the stories related by this verbose veteran pirate who alleged that he served under pirate captain Edward England – but he probably did not. It may still offer some vague clues – though clues which must be treated wih great caution. This pirate's tale may have simply been another invention about the early history of Edward England, famous in the East Indies for his renowned ship *Fancy* and for being at the taking of *Cassandra.* Still, this informer also may have been earlier "informed" by his pirate acquaintances on Île Saint-Marie, Madagascar and could have been at least privy to certain singular details. At least part of his narrative may be valuable, even if he was never with England at the time. Still, it's not much to go on.

Clement Downing, a midshipman on HMS *Salisbury,* was part of Comm. Thomas Mathews' squadron that visited the island of Madagascar, an island bigger than the whole of Great Britain, almost two years later and detailed in Chapter Six. They encountered this pirate called John, James, or William Plantain (we'll use John). Downing says Plantain claimed to have left Rhode Island in a pirate sloop called *Terrible*, under John Williams, and they sailed for the African coast. Contrary to England's earlier position of captain as illuminated from primary records, Plantain's alleged narrative indicated that after capture of a larger vessel *Prosperous,* en route to the Guinea Coast, he met Edward England as a mate of another prize ship, *Onslow*. Plantain, like Johnson, was quite fond of "tall-tale" invented introductions!

Capt. Williams supposedly kept the ship and let go their two smaller craft. Plantain related through Downing that the experienced England allegedly desired to join the pirates and was made captain of *Onslow*:

> The *Prosperous* had on board a considerable number of *Eaft-India* Bales, which they hoisted up on Deck, and cut open; the Quarter-master distributing the same amongst the Pyrates. They arrived in a short time on the Coast of *Guinea*, and kept

all the trading Ships from carrying on any manner of Commerce at *Gambo* [Gambia], and the other Ports on that Coast. Here they met with the *Onslow*, whom they fought a considerable time; but the Pyrates being well mann'd, boarding her, made sad Havock of her Crew, and brought them to cry out for Quarter, which is but very indifferent at best; so when they had taken her, they made one of their number whose Name was *England*, a Man who had been Mate of several good Ships, Captain of her.[36]

This narrative, if from Plantain (1722), may indicate possible knowledge of England's activities at Gambia River in May 1719. If from Downing's (1737) recollections, it may be colored by Johnson (1724). Existence of this *Prosperous,* also, cannot be directly verified.

This narrative told that England was not a pirate until captured by pirates at the African Coast. The problem is that primary sources already tell of England in command of his own pirate flotilla when he left the Caribbean in April. Plantain's narrative ignores a long list of primary sources that tell of England pirating in the Windward Islands and sailing to Africa *after* having taken numerous vessels, including *Pearl/Royal James,* and amassing a large crew already.

Plantain's tale is unnecessarily fraught with complications – but not all due to Plantain. One should be careful with the history given indirectly for Plantain through Downing. Was Downing partly at fault? Was he relating Plantain's conflated accounts of himself or tales Plantain told of others – men who Plantain got to know well at Madagascar – and Downing simply misunderstood? Plantain may also have been intentionally lying to Downing to inflate his own ego! Downing also was not the first pirate historian to conflate all he heard with Johnson's widely-published tales.

A 360-ton, 26-gun *Onslow,* Capt. Michael Gee, had been reported taken by pirates 8 August 1721. It was retaken by HMS *Swallow* in January 1722, but lost in a storm on the Guinea Coast. This appears, at first, to perhaps agree with at least part

---

[36] Clement Downing, *A Compendious History of the Indian Wars... with Account of the Notorious Pirate John Plantain at Madagascar...* (London: Printed for T. Cooper, 1737), 105-114.

of Plantain's story. Still, this occurred two years too late and the narrative was probably the experience of another person who visited Madagascar, say in late summer of 1721. This visitor may perhaps have served aboard *Onslow* or under Bartholomew Roberts, as "Charles Johnson" reasonably gave him credit for the 1721 capture of *Onslow,* which Robert's renamed as his fourth *Royal Fortune*. This visitor might simply have heard about the capture and then told Plantain about *Onslow* not long before he relayed the story to Downing. Downing then may have attached the tale to England's story to further impress upon the officers of *Salisbury* the great deeds of his alleged former captain. Plantain met Downing in late April 1722, so there was plenty of time for anyone with knowledge of Robert's capture of *Onslow* to get word to Madagascar. There's always the possibility of two ships by that name or that *Onslow* was taken twice and there remains no record of the first capture – again, another unlikely complication in the flow of logic. Ship-owning capitalists kept up with their ships![37]

Downing related that Plantain was supposedly present when the surgeon Moor, another person who Plantain should have gotten to know well, was taken from *Comrade,* Thomas Samson, after June 1719. This would imply that Plantain was with Jeremiah Cocklyn, Olivier LeVasseur, or Richard Taylor then. He said that one Roberts was then quartermaster, but John, or Thomas (later, Bartholomew), Roberts was quartermaster probably under Howell Davis, so this part may not have come from Johnson and may be someone else's experience. These men had also split from Davis by May at Sierra Leone. He also mentioned a vessel that the pirates kept and renamed *Defiance,* of 300 tons, capable of mounting 30 guns. Most intriguing, this vessel could have been *Speedwell/Windham/Bird* of Jeremiah Cocklyn, which would agree with the Patterson deposition of September 1719 in Martinique. Plantain might have heard about the piracy of *Le Solide.*

---

[37] *Voyages* database; *New England Courant,* December 17, 1722, 2; Johnson, *A General History,* 2nd ed., 254.

Plantain knew many details of different pirates' forays off Gambia River and later, along the more southern Gold Coast. Still, Plantain spent months talking and carousing with these same men at Île Saint-Marie, or Nosy Boraha, from 1720 to 1722 (assuming he was in England's and/or Congden's crew) before Downing arrived with the fleet that April. Indeed, he seemed to be with Edward England and his crew at the time the fleet arrived! The details may have been fresh in his mind, albeit swirling with alcohol as they must have been. Contradicting Downing-Plantain's narrative of sailing with Jeremiah Cocklyn, Richard Taylor, or Olivier LeVasseur before they arrived at Madagascar, was pirate captive Richard Moor, himself. Moor was with Taylor at the time, said he arrived at Île Saint-Marie with the pirates when "there [he] saw one Plantin who appeared to be and was... intimately acquainted with many of the Pirates."[38] Moor apparently did not know Plantain before arriving at Madagascar. Moor said that Plantain had served under Edward Congdon in *Dragon* and he had been left behind there when Congdon was poisoned by the natives to prevent their fleeing to Île de Bourbon (see Chapter Four). If Moor was correct, then Congdon's part is the only excerpt told by Plantain that actually *might* be his own experience.[39]

Plantain may have certainly embellished his story to Downing to include more on his pirate resume with details from the various pirates he would have met on Madagascar. Also possible, Downing may have conflated the various tales told to him. Thoughts of an author who despised pirates is not the best filter for discerning the truth from a pirate's probably-already-enhanced tale and Downing's second-hand interpretations of Plantain's behavior are clearly biased as well as contrary to Downing's sense of military honor.

The history that Downing relates on Plantain is replete with derogatory language that could express this bias. After all,

---

[38] Moor, 212.
[39] Moor, 212; Clement Downing, *A Compendious History of the Indian Wars... with Account of the Notorious Pirate John Plantain at Madagascar...* (London: Printed for T. Cooper, 1737), 105-114; note that Richard Moor, in his deposition, also claimed that Plantain served as well on the *Dragon* under pirate captain Edward Congdon, who was then (after Jan 1721) a resident of Réunion Island; Downing also mentioned that Plantain claimed to be "a part" of *Cassandra's* crew, but that is by no means confirmed.

Downing later testified against Comm. Mathews himself and may have been a loyal navy man. Some people of the British East India Company (EIC) and Royal Navy might express distaste with any "un-gentlemanly" pirate – some. Bias in this Downing-related testimony has tempted many, like Patrick Pringle (*Jolly Roger,* 1953), to completely disregard Plantain's oral history in Downing's book. This is not entirely reasonable. Some details, especially about Congdon and *Dragon,* allegedly mentioned by Plantain should probably not be completely dismissed. Details about England's early history in any reasonable context, however, can simply not be accurately determined with this source.

Plantain had left his residence to meet the fleet when they arrived at Charnock Point, today known as *Pointe de Larrée,* just across the water from Île Saint-Marie. Some pirates, including Edward England, had escaped inland (mainland Madagascar?) to avoid them before "King" Plantain left for Charnock Point. Plantain had known England, but England was not present to verify or deny Plantain's story when related it to Downing. "King" Plantain must have been quite self-assured, with his accompanying retinue of native warriors. He probably tried to impress and entertain these officers and men with extraordinary elaborations to impress them and to befit a "monarch" like himself. Still, Plantain told an interesting tale and delighted the officers of HMS *Salisbury.* This early history of Edward England associated with *Onslow* should, however, as Patrick Pringle rightly suggests, be dismissed.[40]

As to how Edward England located his *Fancy,* however, Plantain offered another tall tale that may have had some

---

[40] South Sea Company ship 360-ton, 26-gun *Onslow,* Capt. Michael Gee, taken by pirates summer 1721 - CO390/7: The National Archives (London), Colonial Office CO 388/25, 376 and 379; this does not preclude an earlier capture; Capt. John Dolling, then Thomas Creed, masters of 45-ton, 2-gun *Coward,* w/16 crew, captured by pirates in summer 1719 – CO 390/7: The National Archives (Kew, UK) Colonial Office; page 115: "HANS BURGEN, the Dane, was born at Copenhagen, and had been brought up a Cooper; but coming to London, he entered himself with Capt. Creed for Guinea - the Ship being taken by the Pyrates, he agreed to go with them, and became a Comerade to King Plantain;" pirates burned Creed's *Coward,* 27 May 1719.

elements from perhaps someone's actual memories. Not long after their battle and alleged capture of *Onslow*, as Plantain related to Downing, England came upon the famed "Dutch Interloper" which he says became the renowned *Fancy*:

> ... not long after they took the Onslow they mastered a Dutch Interloper, with whom they bad a smart Battle, and had not the Sloop come to their Assistance, they would have been obliged to let her go. But the Sloop coming up, and pouring a great number of Men on board, they soon over-powered them. This Ship they liked exceeding well, and were resolved to keep her, calling her the *Fancy*; and Capt. England having a mind to her, they allowed him to command her.[41]

Again, having no doubt spoken a great deal with Edward England, Plantain may have related what was told to him, rather than what he had experienced himself – or just invented his own facts. This may seem like belaboring the point, but it must be kept firmly in mind when telling the tales of this self-important flamboyant "King." He told that England's crew daily increased in number, and avoided keeping their prizes. They might have done this for two reasons: first, they already possessed vessels of sufficient strength to take almost any ship, and secondly, they may have imagined attracting too much attention from the Admiralty and EIC. There might soon be a Royal Navy squadron after them if they did. Plantain said that England offered his crew another plan and dealt significantly

---

[41] Downing, *A Compendious History; Voyages* database at http://www.slavevoyages.org; Plantain called *Fancy* a "Dutch Interloper" and Capt. James Macrae described her as "Dutch built... about three hundred Tons." The consensus seems to be a Dutch slaver. *Voyages* slave trade database lists only one such Dutch vessel lost in 1719 to pirates, Jan Cornelissen's *Jacoba Galeij*. Dutch admiralty records show that "Jan Cornelissen managed to bring his ship safely to the bay [Ponta Praiàe] of São Tomé. Cornelissen could not prevent his ship from falling into the hands of pirates. After more than three weeks with them, he got the *Mediterrian*, an English frigate that was exchanged by the pirates for the Dutch or Zeelandic *Jacoba Galeij*. Moreover, the two hundred bought-in slaves were returned to him, with which he continued his smuggling journey to St. Eustatius," from 67n138 NA, AA 2542, Resoluties admiraliteit Zeeland, December 14, 1720; ZA, DIB 44, January 27 and March 10, 1721; AC, July 25 and August 24, 1720 in Rudolf Paesie, "Lorrendrayen on Africa: The illegal goods and slave trade on West Africa during the eighteenth-century trade monopoly of the West India Company, 1700-1734," Doct. dissertation presented to Leiden University (De Bataafsche Leeuw, Amsterdam: 2008), 66-67, 357-79.

with Howell Davis (Johnson influence on Downing here or perhaps England met with Davis at Sierra Leone circa June-July?) and Bartholomew Roberts from July 1719 and that they captured *Fancy* together (again, with critical cap on...):

> Now Capt. England propos'd a new Voyage to them, which might be the making of them all very rich... First they proposed to burn the *Terrible* Sloop, being old and leaky, and not fit to beat about the Cape... These Pyrates had now got the *Fancy* [named perhaps for Henry Every's ship] under the Command of Capt. *England*, and a small Brigantine called the *Unity*, which they named the *Expedition*, and gave the Command to one *Johnson* that was with them; tho' one Quarter-master serv'd for them all.[42]

According to this narrative, if any of it *was* true, Howell Davis must already have made his bold and failed attempt to fool the inhabitants of Principe Island. Davis pretended that he was a Royal Navy man to fool the Portuguese. They knew better, killed him, and Thomas, or Bartholomew Roberts had taken his place. This definitely occurred no earlier than August of 1719. Without knowing anything about England's activities from July-December 1719, there's little reason to object, other than the corrupt character of the witness. There's no *other* reason to believe that England would *not* have consorted with Davis after leaving Gambia that July.

Plantain's tale states that England desired to round the Cape of Good Hope and go to Madagascar, but Davis' replacement, Thomas or Bartholomew Roberts, disagreed. This part of Plantain's tale seems more reasonable – if true:

---

[42] *Ibid.*; *Unity* is not on *Voyages* database; however BNL of 13 Dec 1720 mentions a sloop *Unity* from Jamaica, Capt. William Wade, who informed Philadelphia about pirates around Jamaica - 32 in number, he said. He may have had some personal experience with them that gave him this knowledge. It did not mention, however, that he had then lost his vessel. *Unity* appears under three different captains in RAC records from 1698-1708 in Donnan, *Documents*, II: 31-33. *London Journal*, 6 Oct 1722 mentions a slave ship *Unity*, Capt. Plumsted, from Guinea to Jamaica, taken by a Spanish pirate and lost 250 slaves; *note alao* that if England had joined with Davis at Sierra Leone roughly June-July, this passage may carry more weight!

And being in great Dispute how and which way they should dispose of each other, went on shore on the Coast of Guinea, and there held a fresh Consultation, when some were for going with Capt. *England,* and some with Capt. *Roberts*... They had now six or seven Ships with them, on which account it was resolved, that *England* and *Roberts* should separate, for fear of a Civil War amongst themselves. *England* was to take the *Fancy*, the Snow [45-ton snow *Carteret*, Capt. Thomas Lynch?], and the Ship they called the *Victory* [taken by Jeremiah Cocklyn], and go away for the East-Indies; and *Roberts* and the rest were to continue and range about those Seas, as they thought fit.[43]

There are currently, however, no primary sources that place England together with Davis or Roberts. The mention of *Victory* in this excerpt is probably an attempt to tie that vessel with *Fancy* in Plantain's story, since vessels of both those names later captured *Cassandra* at the Island of Johanna. It also appears from more trustworthy primary sources that Edward England usually operated separately from maybe Davis and Roberts, and certainly LeVasseur, Taylor, and Cocklyn – about two months behind them to north. Still, as stated, it cannot yet be fully discounted. Until more evidence is found, at least it can function as a possible theory to explain the timing around Edward England's gaining command of the Dutch ship *Fancy*. This is rather common in amateur pirate history. Many theories were entertained as to Edward Thache's origins, some rather far-fetched, until the Jamaican Anglican Church Records were found detailing his likely wealthy family in the capital of Spanish Town.[44]

As mentioned earlier, one French account tells of an English pirate "Jan l'Inglan" attacking Jacques Hego, commander of *l'Heureaux Avanteuries* with a flotilla of three pirate vessels. These consisted of "one of twenty-six pieces of cannon [*Royal James*?], one of twenty-two, and the other of

---

[43] *Ibid.*; These events must have followed Howell Davis' death on Principe Island – when Bartholomew Roberts took his command. Note that the *Victory* mentioned here cannot be either *Le Victorieux*, Capt. Guillaume Hais, captured later by Jeremiah Cocklyn, or *Victory* of London, Captain William Rideout, which ship they released. Again, this confuses Edward England's early placement with the other three pirates.
[44] Brooks, *Quest for Blackbeard.*

twelve pieces of cannon."[45] This took place on 15 September 1719 [J: 4 Sep], three leagues from *Cap de Trois Pointes*, just west of Judah – the pirate detained him for only nine days. One may conclude that this previously unknown English pirate's name may have been "Inglan," or "England." And, still another report of Yves Chery, pilot of the ship *La Sureté* de Nantes came from Judah on 20 October 1719 [J: 9 Oct] of a similar three English pirates along England's route southward. Like Howell Davis, England led his own flotilla down the West African Coast. Note that Richard Taylor remained near Judah through October, until November, and may have met Edward England at this time.[46]

By the way, captive Richard Moor had referred to a "Dutch sloop" while his group of pirates were at the Island of Corisco. Moor deposed that nine of *Comrade's* crew had been sent ashore for water and were detained by "Natives upon the Account of some Injury which they had reced by one Captain Plummer." He added that "the Master [presumably of *Comrade*] and chief mate and two boys had their Liberty and were put on board of a Dutch sloop and one Stephen King the Boatsns Mate was forced" aboard Cocklyn's *Speedwell/Windham/Bird*. The "Dutch sloop" appears to have been another pirate vessel, which could have been England's *Fancy*, and would fit well with the latter part of Plantain's narrative – assuming that these pirates met up with England at Corisco or later at Anabon Island. Still, these pirates had taken *many* vessels of various nations, including Dutch ones and we don't know for certain if Edward England had even laid eyes on them until meeting up with them at Madagascar. The most probable theory is that he

---

[45] Deposition of Jacques Hego, commander of *l'Heureaux Avanteuries*," 13 Jul 1720 [J: 2 Jul], Rapports de navigation des capitaines au long cours et au cabotage enregistrées par l'Amirauté (1692 - 1779), *Les Archives départementales de Loire-Atlantique*, B 4579, 79-80.

[46] Yves Chery, pilot of the ship *La Sureté* de Nantes, September 1720, Rapports de navigation, *Les Archives départementales de Loire-Atlantique*, B 4580, 2-3.

came upon *Fancy* alone (again, probably *Jacoba Galeij* near São Tomé), before rounding the Cape of Good Hope.[47]

Leaving the African Coast

Edward England's activities since sending Henry Hunt, captain of *Sarah,* away on 5th of July 1719 may have included meeting with Howell Davis at Sierra Leone, then to the Gold Coast in September, and taking *Callabar Merchant* in December. He may have consorted with Davis and Roberts, but we don't know that. Charles Johnson offered little in the way of substance, only to say that he believed England arrived in the East Indies by the beginning of 1720, and then cruised the Malabar Coast that spring before returning to the island of Johanna near Madagascar to take *Cassandra*.[48] Oddly enough, he paired England with Levasseur and not Roberts, who descended from Davis. He wrote that England…

> … sail'd down to Whydah Road, where they found another Pyrate, one Captain la Bouche, who getting thither before England arrived, had forestall'd the Market, and greatly disappointed their Brethren… Captain England, after this Baulk, went into a Harbour, clean'd his own Ship, and fitted up the *Peterborough*, which he call'd the *Victory* [not the one that took *Cassandra,* although Johnson may have hoped it was]; they liv'd there very wantonly for several Weeks, making free with the Negroe Women, and committing such outragious Acts, that they came to an open Rupture with the Natives, several of whom they kill'd, and one of their Towns they set on Fire. When the Pyrates came out to Sea, they put it to a Vote what Voyage to take, and the Majority carrying it for the East-Indies, they shap'd their Course accordingly, and arrived at Madagascar, the Beginning of the Year 1720.[49]

---

[47] Moor, 208; Jeremiah Cochlyn traded *Speedwell* for this ship, renamed *Victory,* before they sailed to Madagascar.

[48] Predictable trade winds east of Africa blow from northeast during November to March. The winds blow exactly the opposite direction roughly in 6-month intervals from May to September. So, arrival in the East Indies from the west was usually timed in spring – departures six months later. From the Indian or China Coast, a return to Madagascar involved following the east-west current at the equator.

[49] Johnson, *A General History*, 2nd ed., 117.

Still, this probably did not happen. England could have captured *Peterborough* – he may even have captured Capt. Rideout's *Victory*, but he probably did not rename *Peterborough* to *Victory*.[50] Johnson simply had to tie Capt. James Macrae's letter (a primary source document) into the narrative and the name *Victory* was a part of that narrative. England actually arrived in the East Indies, first at Madagascar, no earlier than late March-early April 1720, probably already in *Fancy*. Cocklyn sailed *Le Victorieux,* another completely different *Victory,* to Madagascar separately. These two vessels completed the necessary components of the story told by James Macrae.

> We hear that the African Company have receiv'd an account from the Coast, that since their Letters from thence, the Peterborough Gally of Bristol, Capt. Owen, and the Victory of London, Capt. Rideout, were fallen into the Hands of the Pyrates, who had plunder'd the latter and let her go, but had taken the former: and fitted her up for a Pyrate.

"London April 11," *Boston News-Letter,* 4 Jul 1720

Now that that is out of the way... again, England's first reported position on the African Coast was Gambia River from May-July 1719. French records place him probably at the Guinea Coast in September. English primary records show that the next and last act of Edward England, before rounding the Cape of Good Hope and presumably in *Fancy* was reported to have taken place on 11 December 1719. Comparitively, there's a great deal of primary-source data on this last single event. It's

---

[50] *Voyages;* Boston News-Letter, July 4 & July 18, 1720; *Peterborough* was a 120-ton vessel of Bristol, owned by John Duckinfield & Co. Another vessel was captured on the coast of Guinea probably late in 1719, similar time to *Peterborough,* a vessel called *Europe,* Capt. Bound, with slaves intended for the "River Plata in the Spanish West Indies." England, Cocklyn, LeVasseur, and Taylor, however, were probably too far south of Guinea at the time. This must have been the act of another pirate. Another vessel of Humphrey Morice, 80-ton *Swallow,* Capt. John Fitchett, left London in November 1719 and may have been involved about January 1720 by this same band of pirates, after moving south from the Gold Coast.

fascinating that so much detail exists for this man's actions on 11 December and he had been so documentarily silent for so long. Then again, the prolific wordsmith Lt. Gov. Alexander Spotswood of Virginia had been involved with *Callabar Merchant*! Indeed, was there enough wax and twine in all of Great Britain and America to hold this governor's letter bundles together?

Callabar Merchant, 90-tons, Capt. Thomas Kennedy, had been fitted out in Bristol in September 1719 for the slave trade and sailed to Guinea to purchase slaves by 11 November. Its previous voyage in 1718 ended in Jamaica, but this one was due in Rappahannock River, Virginia. A month later, four and a half months since Henry Hunt last saw him sailing away – and a few months after his *theorized* meeting involving Davis and Roberts on Corisco's shores – *and* while still on the coast of Africa, near "Old Callabar" or the border region between modern Nigeria and Cameroon – Edward England took *Callabar Merchant*. He kept them prisoners for nine weeks while slowly moving south down that coast to Cape Lopez and Anabon Island where he finally released them.

A great deal of iron-gall ink was spilled in this incident. Secretary of the Treasury Charles Stanhope wrote to Board of Trade secretary William Popple 22 March 1720 over the concerns of five merchants, composing Francis Stevens & Co., owners of *Callabar Merchant*. After Kennedy finally arrived in Virginia in April, Spotswood wrote James Craggs, Secretary of State, about this incident on the following 20 May. Kennedy made his deposition 14 November before Henry Watts in Bristol. Kennedy's 1st mate later made his deposition 24 March 1721, after returning to London. Lastly, John, Lord Carteret wrote four days later to the Board of Trade.

England gave Kennedy and his 1st mate Alexander Bradford "21 Negroes, 2 iron guns and a small hawser," pirate contraband which Kennedy handed over to Lt. Gov. Alexander Spotswood when he arrived at York River, Virginia, 20 April 1720. Bradford's deposition contained some unique information, part of which read:

> That about the 11th day of Xbr.[December] att the Dawning of the Day in the Same Year the Said Ship in the prosecution of her Voyage

being near to Old Callabar on the Coast of Guinia had the Misfortune to fall near Three Ships and a Brigantine wch proved to be all pirats one of which having Twenty Guns mounted And two hundred Men whose Commanders Name was England came up with them, And Hoysted a black Flagg with Death's head in itt And Fired at the Callabar Merchant and Soon entered on Board her by force of Arms and Beat and Abused Several of the Said Ships Company and threatned to Burn the Ship with her Cargoe. And forced the Master Thomas Kenedy with the Ship and her Company to goe with them into the River of Old Callabar and whilst there the pirats fitted their Ships and Cleaned them. All which time the Master and Company of the Callabar Merchant were prisoners and the Ship in the possession of the said piratts and that the said pirats After they had fitted their Ships and Cleaned them Departed from that river forceing the Callabar Merchant to Saile with them to Cape Lopas [Lopez], and from thence to the Iland of Anabona and near the Said Iland[.] After having been Nine Weeks in the possession of the Said Pirats and their prisoners all that time Did Obtain Liberty to Depart from them and proceed on their Voyage to Virginia and at their Departure they put on Board Twenty one Negro Men wch they gave the Master as a Satisfaction for the Damage they had done him the Said Twenty one Negroes were all new Negroes for they could Speak no Europian Language.[51]

Bradford's deposition was taken by a justice given as "Ra: Harsery" who had taken many such depositions in London of that time. England detained *Callabar Merchant* for nine weeks, or over two months, until approximately 15 February 1720! If England then aimed to go to Madagascar by the beginning of the year, he was quite late by our modern calendar. Kennedy lost:

> One Hundred and Thirteen Copper barrs, Six Iron Barrs, Six Peaces of Photas, Twelve peaces of large Topseals [topsails], Twenty four peaces of romalls [cloth], Thirty peaces of Cuthleas, Ninty ps. of Brawles, four hundred forty five Bunches of Beads, Between three and four hundred wieght of Nailes, Between four and five hundred

---

[51] National Archives, London, Correspondence with the Lieut. Governor of Virginia (Spotswood), 1720-1726, CO 5/1319; David Richardson, *Bristol, Africa, and the Eighteenth-century Slave Trade to America,* Vol. 38 (Bristol: Bristol Record Society, 1986), 71, 87; Elizabeth Donnan, *Documents Illustrative of the History of the Slave Trade to America*, Vol. 4 (Washington: Carnegie Institure, 1935), 95-97; CO 5/1319, f. 53.

weight of pewter, one hundred and four Laced Hatts, Seven plain Hatts, Ten barrells of powder, one hundred and Eleven Tradeing Guns and Several other Goods damaged [plus ship's stores – a total of about £1,200].[52]

Charles Grey, in *Pirates of the Eastern Seas* also copied Johnson, but he had access to sources that many western writers did not. Also, he blessedly and clearly indicated the information he obtained from his differing sources. According to Grey, East India Company records revealed more detail of Edward England and/or his associate's activities as he finished with *Calabar Merchant* and rounded Cape of Good Hope, in Dutch hands at the time. This detail involved Dutch ships, but none that were *said* to be captured by England:

> On the 11th December 1719 the Pirates took and plundered the *Calabar Merchant*, which they let go without any further harm and in February [1719/20; note this was two months later – definitely Edward England's doing] attempted a Dutch ship near Cape Town [South Africa]. This ship which came in on the 29th February [1719/20] reported that 'The Pyratt ship could not hav had less than 250 men aboard.' They came up with the Dutch ship with their Black Flag flying at the Mast head and gave notice that if the Dutchman did not instantly strike, they would give no quarters. They made great use of their small arms, the shot flying so briskly that the Dutch Captain went below leaving his crew on the deck by themselves. "The fight lasted for seven glasses on the first day and for six on the second. The Pirate was not beaten off until his foremast was within one foot of the Dutchman's Ensign staff, when her chase guns raked him and made him withdraw." A few days later another Dutch ship reported that she had been chased by a Pirate shewing the Black Flag.[53]

---

[52] Donnan, *Documents Illustrative of the History of the Slave Trade*, 96; *Voyages* database; Va. Hist. Soc., *Collections*, II, 343; *Callabar Merchant's* owners were listed as: Francis Stevens, Abel Grant, Thomas Melton, Samuel Allen, and Samuel Fry.

[53] Charles Grey, *Pirates of the Eastern Seas* (1618-1723), *a Lurid Page of History* (London: S. Low, Marston & co., ltd, 1933), 307-308; National Archives, London, War Office Campaign Medal and Award Rolls 1793-1949 (WO 100), WO 100/75, accessed through Ancestry.com; The author Charles Grey was possibly the grandson of Sir Charles Edward Grey (1785-1865) who served in the 71st Highlanders from 1833-1842 in India. The author Charles Grey also served from 1889 to 1902 in 1st K R R Corps, regiment 3495. Sir George Fletcher MacMunn, a colonel in the Indian forces and an author himself, edited *Pirates of the Eastern Seas*, published in 1933, for Grey. Another article written by Grey concerning the "Taking of the Cassandra" was published in the ninth volume of the journal *Indian State Railways Magazine*, in

Neither of these Dutch ships was reported captured and so, probably could not be *Fancy*. If *Jacoba Galeij* was the vessel that became *Fancy*, he may well have captured her at São Tomé not long before his capture of *Callabar Merchant*. Several subsequent captures would augment his weaponry. Remarkably, the name of his vessel was never mentioned in the plethora of detailed documents that evolved from this action – an action that lasted nine weeks! "Charles Johnson," or Nathaniel Mist, erred once again, but Charles Grey, even moreso – probably due to reading Johnson! This excerpt refers to Edward Congdon and best belongs in Chapter Four, but the tale of the EIC's disdain for Ostend vessels and their crew is relevant to the taking of *Cassandra*.

Johnson confused Edward England and his "Capt. Condent," or Edward Congdon, who arrived in the East Indies a year later. In his first, second, and third editions, Johnson, or Mist, only mentioned "Conden" once. In his fourth, two-volume edition, Mist or someone added an entire section on "Capt. Condent" in which he included this entire excerpt that was heavily conflated with Cocklyn, LeVasseur, and Taylor and some, with Edward England. This passage is annotated for explanation:

> When he [Congdon] was at Sea again he discharged Captain Hill [captain of *Indian Queen*, actually taken by LeVasseur], and stood away for the East-Indies. Near the Cape he took an Ostend East-India Man, of which Mr. Nash [Naish], a noted Merchant in London, was Supercargo. Soon after he took a Dutch East-India Man, discharged the Ostender, and made for Madagascar; at the Isle of St. Mary, he met with some of Captain [John] Halsey's Crew, whom he took on board with other Stragglers, and shaped his Course for the East-Indies, and in the Way, at the Island of Johanna, took, in Company of two other pyrates he met at St Mary's, the Cassandra East-India Man, commanded by Captain James Macragh [Congdon was not involved – this was Edward England; the rest of the passage is neither Congdon nor England...]; he continued his Course for the East-Indies, where he made a very great Booty, and

---

Bombay in 1936. Grey had composed *Pirates of the Eastern Seas* as a supplement to Charles Johnson's *A General History*, as he said. He carefully indicates in his text the difference between Johnson and other sources, including records from the East India Company, whose India offices were in Bombay. He likely had access to journals, log entries, and other official papers. Still, he handicapped himself by using Johnson's book as the basis for his own.

returning, touch'd at the Isle of Mascarenas, where he met with a Portuguese Ship of 70 Guns, with the Vice-Roy of Goa, on board. This Ship he made Prize of, and hearing she had Money on board [*Nossa Senora do Cabo* taken by Seager, LeVasseur, and Taylor – Congdon was then a resident of that island and casually offered to negotiate afterward], they would allow of no Ransom, but carried her to the Coast of Zanguebar, where was a Dutch Fortification, which they took and plunder'd, razed the Fort, and carried off several Men who enter'd voluntarily [actually, LeVasseur and Taylor in Mozambique].[54]

What a mess Johnson created here! *Evening Post* of 23 Jun 1720 referred to an Ostend, Belgian, or Flemish 250-ton *Prince Eugene,* the name for the refitted *Camberwell Galley* of England (aka *Charles VI*)[55], Capt. Jean de Clerck, supercargo James Tobin, owned by "Messrs." Charles & Jacques Maelcamps[56] of Ghent since 1715. This ship, manned by an English crew, made the first voyage for what would become the Ostend East-Indies Company (GIC) to the Indian Malabar Coast.[57] They then returned from

---

[54] Charles Johnson, *The History of the Pyrates : containing the lives of Captain Mission. Captain Bowen. Captain Kidd ... and their several crews...*, Vol. II. By Capt. Charles Johnson, author of vol. I. ... London : Printed for, and sold by T. Woodward ..., [1728], 143.

[55] "England and the Ostend Company," *English Historical Review,* v.22 (1907), 255-264; *Records of the Madras government, Despatches from England:1715-1718,* 142; "The Ship Camberwell Galley [26 guns; 400 tons (1710)] went some while since from hence to Ostends she is there call'd the Charles [VI] Galley and We hear is design'd for the East Indies one David Naigle appear'd here to be her master but it is said Cap'. [James] Tobin or one Myers is to command her."

[56] Ostend East-India Company (Dutch: Oostendse Compagnie, or Generale Indische Compagnie or GIC, French), 1722-1731: seven directors chosen from leading figures in trade and finance: Jacques De Pret, Louis-François de Coninck and Pietro Proli, from Antwerp; Jacques Maelcamp (1685-1741), Paulo De Kimpe and Jacques Baut, from Ghent; and the Irish Jacobite Thomas Ray, a merchant and banker based in Ostend, a place known for its pirates and slave smugglers. The GIC was abolished by the Treaty of Vienna, signed on 16 March 1731 by Holy Roman Empire ministers, including Prince Eugene of Savoy.

[57] Gijs Dreijer, "Bargaining for Shelter: An Entrepreneurial Analysis of the Ostend Company, 1714-1740." Master's thesis submitted to the Dept. of History, Leiden University, (2017), 23, 26-29; "In 1720, when the first voyage to Canton was made by merchants later associated with the GIC, the merchants tried to pay the Chinese tea merchants with fake silver. This swindle almost led the merchants to be expelled from Canton, and the reputation of GIC merchants declined in the period between 1720 and 1724... Many of these [piratical] merchants, especially the Irish and the Scottish (35% of GIC crews), established themselves in Ostend in the early eighteenth century [Thomas Ray was a major Irish investor in the GIC who settled in Antwerp in 1715, fleeing Britain after the Jacobite Rebellion]. Some Irish merchants

China, loaded with 1,600 boxes of tea, silk, and porcelain, via Surat, passed the Cape of Good Hope when they were taken by an unnamed 38-gun, 280-man pirate (probably Edward Congdon; 40-gun, 320-men, according to Naish) on 20 February.[58]

Another ship of the Ostend Company, 69-man, 400-ton *House of Austria*, Capt. Joannes de Vos, supercargo James Naish, had departed Ostend on 6 February 1719 in company of *St. Joseph* and *Wirtemburg*, Capt. Van Maestricht. *House of Austria* traveled to China, and was then captured on its return in February 1720, just hours before *Prince Eugene*. The pirate "seized the best Silk Stuffs, and the Gold Dust on board," amounting to 14,000 florins. The "Dragon pirate" then put Capt. de Clerck, his chaplain, some of his 43 crew, and James Tobin, as Supercargo of *Prince Eugene*, aboard *House of Austria* and let her sail to Ostend. She reached Dover first where Capt. Naish made his report to the EIC on 15 June. He allegedly reported also that his first mate, a Londoner named Andrew Kennedy of Rotherhithe, was killed fighting this pirate (will prob. 21 June). Naish then proceeded to Ostend, arriving 1 July 1720. The Maelcamps reported 38.03, 7.85, and 8.20 percent loss from 1719 to 1721, partly due to piracy and cheating Asian merchants, but also from overflooding of the Asian tea trade. Even with these problems, the failure of the English South Sea Company in 1720 opened a vacuum in the market. The Maelcamps joined with other investors to form the official Ostend Company in 1722 to fill the English mercantile void, much to English disdain.[59]

---

had already traded in the early eighteenth century from other piracy nests such as St. Malo or Dunkirk."

[58] *Daily Courant*, 28 Jun 1720; Jelten Baguet, "De Oostendse Compagnie, haar directeurs en de Oostenrijkse Bewindvoerders. Een casuïstisch e analyse van hun onderlinge interactie (1722-1731)," Master's Thesis submitted to the Dept. of History at the University of Ghent, Belgium (2015), 21-31.

[59] K. Degryse and Jan Parmentier, "Merchants and captains: a prosopographical study on the merchants, supercargoes and naval officers of the Ostend trade to East-India and Guinea (1716-1732)," *Collectanea Maritima*, 6: pp. 119-241 (1995); British Library, India Office, Letter 139: James Naish on board the House of Austria off of the coast of Dover to the Court reporting that their ship was taken by the pirates after some resistance, 15 Jun 1720, IOR/E/1/11 ff. 226-227v; British Library, India Office, Letter 43: Consul Daniel Foulis at Ostend to Thomas Woolley reporting that the House of Austria , St. Joseph and Wirtemburg have set sail from Ostend, 6 Feb 1718/9, IOR/E/1/10, f. 66; British Library, India Offce, Letters 140-141 George Clifford in Amsterdam to Thomas Woolley forwarding a letter from Consul Daniel

134   Sailing East

Congdon, detailed more fully in Chapter Four, later traded two Ostend surgeons that he said he took from two vessels, so this was probably accurate. Nathaniel Mist could have known the sometime-supercargo Naish, who lived part-time in London. But with three groups of pirates sailing east about the same time, he should have read the records more closely before compiling this story! Most likely, he just needed extra data for his fragmentary tale of "Capt. Condent" – still, Edward England's history is already confusing enough!

Illustrating this, Nathaniel Mist's own newspaper, *Weekly Journal and Saturday Evening's Post,* printed an article about *this* Flemish *Prince Eugene* vessel that somewhat sounds like Edward England was responsible and *not* Edward Congdon. His issue of 25 June 1720 revealed that a pirate with England's recent history and itinerary recently fought a powerful Dutch vessel that bested him:

> The Pirate plundered, and was in possession of her [*House of Austria*] seven Days, and then let her pursue her Voyage; but several of the Men both English and Flemings, went along with the Pirate, who gave out that he was bound for the East-Indies to cruise for Purchase. The said Pirate before he took this Ship, met and attacked a Dutch Ship of 50 Guns, who gave him such a sharp Reception, that after a long Fight, in which several of his Men were killed, he was obliged to sheer off.[60]

Owners of *Prince Eugene* presumed that Edward Congdon "brought Prince Eugene to Madagascar" – a loss keenly felt by the Marquis de Prié.[61] This passage reflects the data discovered by Charles Grey in EIC records wrongly conflating Edward England's futile battle with the Dutch vessel – because, after all, he needed to be associated with a Dutch vessel before meeting *Cassandra*! Again, this pirate was actually Edward Congdon.[62]

Foulis at Ostend and a cargo list of the Prince Eugene ship recently returned to Ostend from China, 11 July 1720, IOR/E/1/10 ff. 234-235v; National Archives; London, Prerogative Court of Canterbury and Related Probate Jurisdictions: Will Registers; 21 Jun 1720, PROB 11/574; James Naish, brother of Hugh Naish, merchant at Fort St. George, was later made Consul in China and Canton President for the EIC. James Naish had long been embroiled in legal problems for smuggling gold from China.
[60] *Weekly Journal and Saturday Evening's Post,* 25 Jun 1720.
[61] Levae, *Recherches historiques,* 79.
[62] H. C. V. Leibbrandt, *Precis of the archives of the Cape of Good Hope,* Vol. 1 (Cape Town, W. A. Richards, 1896), 279; Dutch records recorded this Dutch vessel

England was possibly a daydreamer, fascinated by Every's exploits. He appears to have sought to re-live them. He could have planned to make the jump for the Cape after finishing with *Callabar Merchant*, but then got distracted off Cape Town with rich Dutch diversions. He then might have surprised Cocklyn, LeVasseur, and Taylor when he showed up at Madagascar in *Fancy* with *John Gally*. He may have done many things before he rounded the cape, but we simply know so little. That's the frustrating part of this Irishman's story, made even more complicated by *A General History's* mystifying muddlements!

Once Edward England finally rounded the Cape after the beginning of March, following the 6-month interval of trade winds (see page 126n48), what did he do? Well, there's no relief from fantasy here, either. The events leading up to the taking of *Cassandra* have long been confused. Depositions of both Richard Moor and John Matthews offered few details and there are no depositions from an actual captive of England's to illuminate these events. England probably arrived at Île Saint-Marie unannounced and unexpected *after* LeVasseur, Cocklyn, and Taylor – maybe distracted at the Cape. Richard Moor's deposition clearly stated that he sailed *Fancy* accompanied by *John Gally*[63], and arrived before Cocklyn died, then he burned *John Gally*, in that order. Again, more depositions from some of England's crew are desperately needed to illuminate these details. If he and his crew had not been stranded on Madagascar, such depositions may have come forth.[64]

---

as possibly *Assenburgh,* pursued, but not taken, 22 Feb [J: 11 Feb] 1720. This vessel and the timing also relates to Edward Congdon.

[63] *Voyages* database: *John Gally*, Capt. Thomas Dunckley (and Edward Coward in 1718), a balandra of 120-160 tons (data from three sorties) owned by the South Sea Company trading slaves in Jamaica and Portobello, captured also in 1716 en route to Jamaica and 1717, both times by a Spanish pirate.

[64] Charles Grey, *Pirates of the Eastern Seas* (1618-1723), *a Lurid Page of History* (London: S. Low, Marston & co., ltd, 1933), 307-308; National Archives, London, War Office Campaign Medal and Award Rolls 1793-1949 (WO 100), WO 100/75, accessed through Ancestry.com; The author Charles Grey was possibly the grandson of Sir Charles Edward Grey (1785-1865) who served in the 71st Highlanders from 1833-1842 in India. The author Charles Grey also served from 1889 to 1902 in 1st K R R Corps, regiment 3495. Sir George Fletcher MacMunn, a colonel in the Indian forces and an author himself, edited *Pirates of the Eastern Seas,* published in 1933, for Grey. Another article written by Grey concerning the "Taking of the Cassandra" was published in the ninth volume of the journal *Indian State Railways Magazine*, in

"King" John Plantain, by way of Downing's book, however, is all we have to rely upon – and that is unfortunate. Plantain offered more detail of the Every-fan Edward England allegedly making his first eastern venture in his own *Fancy* to the fabled pirate haven of Madagascar – the reputed "kingdom" of seventeenth-century pirates. England's first landing of his sickly crew was supposedly – and reasonably – at San Augustin[65] on the southwest coast – quite a bad anchorage, according to Plantain. Downing was also an experienced sailor who had visited this location a year before he met the "retired" pirate in HMS *Salisbury*, so he would have tempered any wild notions in this part of Plantain's narrative. Indeed, this early part was assuredly more *his* memory than Plantain's – affected by his literary choices. Still, Madagascar was *not* West Africa, Gambia River, Sierra Leone, or anything to which England's crew might have yet been accustomed:

> CAPT. *England* took to the *Eastern Seas* and came away for *St. Augustine's Bay*, on the Island of *Madagascar*, and his People being very sickly, the Doctor had them sent on shore for the Recovery of their Healths; but several died. Here they cleared their Ship as well as they could, *St. Augustine's Bay* [SW Madagascar] being a Place not extraordinary convenient for Shipping to lie in, on account of the Foulness of the Ground in the Bottom of the Harbour, and the irregular Sounding, on which account a Ship can no ways come to anchor there, to continue any time; nay, not so much as four or five Hours: For 'tis a hundred to one, should the Anchor go in the Ground, or amongst the Rocks, if ever 'tis got up again. But there is a Road to the Southward of the Harbour, where you may anchor in six or seven Fathom Water [traditional anchorage]: Here is smooth Riding, and the Inhabitants will

---

Bombay in 1936. Grey had composed *Pirates of the Eastern Seas* as a supplement to Charles Johnson's *A General History*, as he said. Thankfully, he carefully indicates in his text the difference between Johnson and other sources, including records from the East India Company, whose India offices were in Bombay. He likely had access to journals, log entries, and other official papers while there – but none that mentioned Congdon by name. Still, like many others, he handicapped himself by using Johnson's book as the basis for his own.

[65] Also known as *Ianantsony*; the Malagasy word is *Anantsoño*. It is a town and commune or *kaominina* in Madagascar. It belongs to the district of *Toliara* II, which is a part of *Atsimo-Andrefana* Region. The Portuguese made attempts to settle Madagascar in 1528, but were repulsed by natives. Though they claimed the western coast in 1641, they focused rather on Mozambique, 250 miles west. The first English settlement here was near Toliary under William Courteen and Thomas Kynneston from 1644 to 1646. It failed due to fever, dysentery, and hostility from the Malagasy. This was coincident with the French settlement near Taolagnaro, Fort Dauphin, directly opposite, on the eastern side from 1643-1674. San Augustin became the standard first landing of most ships crossing from the Atlantic into the Indian Ocean.

come off to trade with you; but be careful how you trust them, for they are a more politick and cunning People than the Negroes of the *Guinea* or *Gold Coast*, very crafty in their way of Trade, and private in their Intentions, [they will] speak you fair, but intend to murder you at the same time. They have five or six petty Kings near one another, who are in Alliance together. Here Capt. *England* lay in the Road and repaired all his Rigging, and got a Supply of Provisions.[66]

Downing was nothing if not an accomplished author! His detail paints an excellent, if biased, picture of life at Madagascar. Edward England had thus arrived in the land of his heros, sick and injured. He may have remained at St. Augustin for weeks.

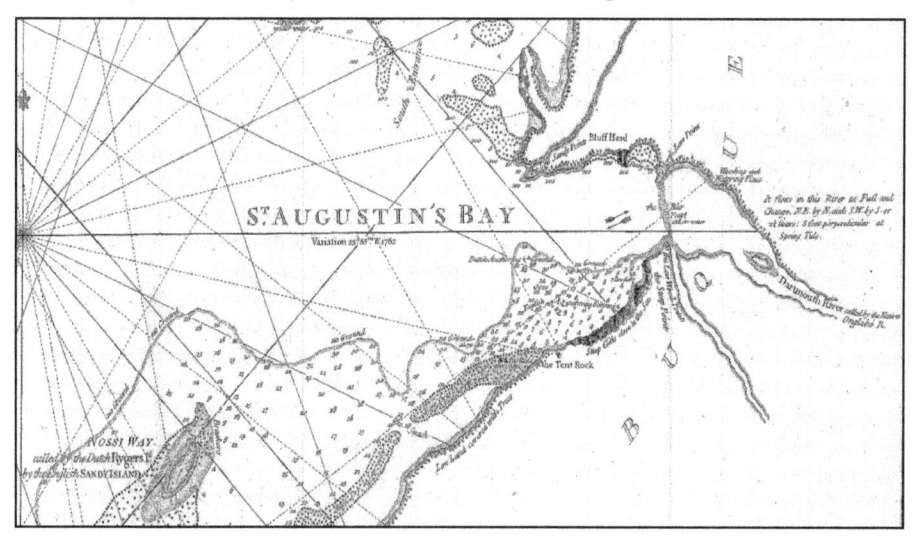

From: A fine and scarce sea chart of St. Augustin's (Anantsoño) and Tullea (Toliara, Toliar, or Tolear is a town and bay just north of St. Augsustin) bays, amongst the finest anchorages on the west coast of Madagascar, published by the leading chartmakers of Laurie & Whittle, Robert Laurie & James Whittle (London, 1794).

Sailing East
"Four Rogue Privateers"

Following the defeat of the Spanish Armada in 1588, an event no more surprising to anyone than to Queen Elizabeth I herself, a merchant trading company to the East Indies formed under her successor and first Stuart king, James I of England and James VI of

---

[66] Downing, *A Compendious History*, 110-111.

Scotland, in 1600. England was free of hostilities with Scotland, broken her Holy Roman and Spanish shackles, and felt free to conquer the globe – with pirates, of course! The Stuarts began England's "Golden Age" in America by stealing Spain's colonial possessions and continued sending "Sea Dogs," ancestors of eighteenth-century pirates to quell the land "beyond the lines of amity." Thus occupied, King James could not be bothered with the administration of such a vast territory as the East Indies, so he subcontracted that administration through a private company.

The "Governor and Company of Merchants of London trading with the East Indies" or just "English East India Company" (EIC) operated almost autonomously from the English Crown. They possessed a monopoly that certainly ensured success, with the singular right to transport silver from England to conduct the trade. Throughout the seventeenth century, the company increased its hold on India, establishing three distinct presidencies: Surat, Madras, and Calcutta. At that time, the primary trade centered, ironically, not on spices as the west had desired for centuries, but on saltpeter. This was a vital ingredient in gunpowder, the abundance of which "fueled most of the European wars from the mid-seventeenth century through the eighteenth."[67]

The recent defeat of the Spanish Armada opened global trade to other nations who once feared Spain's power. In the spice trade, the EIC simply could not compete with the more powerful "United Dutch East India Company," "Oude Westindische Compagnie," or "Vereenigde Oost-Indische Compagnie" (VOC), which had developed coincident with the EIC. Like the EIC, they also formed by assuming the immense powers of their state. The VOC, in the power vacuum left by Spain (who focused more intently upon the gold and silver of the West Indies and South America), as well as the most powerful company on the West African Coast, also became the dominant company vying in the East Indies spice trade. They established authority over the Spice Islands while the EIC focused more on the Indian subcontinent. The eighteenth-century Dutch legal system, as well as their EIC counterparts, somewhat ignored the crimes of *kapers* (privateers), *vrijbuiters* (freebooters), and *rovers* (pirates). As Dr. Virginia Lunsford writes, and which will be quite clear in chapters three

---

[67] Stephen R. Bown, *Merchant Kings: When Companies Ruled the World, 1600-1900* (New York: Thomas Dunne Books, 2010), 105-110.

and six, the Dutch legal term *zeeroverij*, or piracy, "contains a myriad of categories for maritime robbery, ostensibly mitigating and obfuscating the fundamental character of the crime."[68] In fact, many "crimes" of this period scarcely reflected modern criminality.

Several other nations bought into the same game, but the French *Compagnie des Indes Orientales* (CDI), established in 1664, became the most important third player in the East Indies. They established Pondicherry on the Indian Coast and most of the islands of the southern Indian Ocean, including Madagascar and the Mascarenes. Their first attempt to establish a colony on Madagascar at Port Dauphin failed shortly thereafter. Still, the Portuguese losses in the East Indies opened the door for them in the eighteenth century, both, nominally again in Madagascar, and, more fully in the Mascarenes, including both Île de France (modern Mauritius) and Île de Bourbon (modern Île de Réunion).[69]

Edward England v. Henry Every?

The next portion of Edward England's tale offers heretofore unknown details about this group's time in the Indian Ocean during the spring-summer of 1720. Jeremiah Cocklyn, probably with Richard Taylor aboard *Victory*, had sailed for Madagascar. Olivier LeVasseur in *Indian Queen* also sailed for that destination, but probably diverted northward. After watering at St. Augustin, and then landing at Île Saint-Marie, Taylor and Cocklin were later joined by two other pirate ships called the *Fancy* and the *John Gally* under the command of Edward England," about late March-April 1720. There, "the said Cocklyn died" and "they burnt ye *John Gally* and took her men on board the *Victory* and *Fancy.*"[70] These pirates also met local pirate resident of Île Saint-Marie, Jasper Seager.

Yet another Johnson-esque error must be properly tidied up here – this time due probably to Clement Downing. Before taking

---

[68] Bown, *Merchant Kings*, 105-110; Virginia W. Lunsford, *Piracy and Privateering in the Golden Age Netherlands* (New York: Palgrave MacMillan Publishers, Ltd., 2005), 178.
[69] Bown, *Merchant Kings*, 105-110.
[70] Moor, 209.

Cassandra at Johanna, Edward England and his crew were reputed to have explored northward to the Red Sea and the western Arabian Sea. Richard Moor, captive eyewitness to these events, however, never mentioned this. Neither did John Mathews on LeVasseur's *Indian Queen*. Their tales delve right into the taking of *Cassandra*. True that none of the eyewitnesses sailed with England, but was this true or simply mere Every-*Fancy* fantasy?

This Every-esque excerpt is probably another unnecessary effort of Clement Downing's efforts to reconcile the fantastic musings of others. It was perhaps conflated by Downing with gilt stories of pirates like William Kidd, Thomas Tew, and, again, Henry Every – especially Every, with whom Edward England obviously fancied himself. So many similarities to Every's legendary tale and half-hearted attempts to reconcile Johnson's corrupt narrative should make for more than a little trepidation.

Supposedly, England's men happily found that legendary stories of diamonds, rubies, gold, and other precious jewels had been true – as most pirate fantasies go. Truthfully, the East Indies produced more of the commodities traditionally viewed by pirates – and us – as "treasure" than the ubiquitous silver, sugar, cocoa, slaves, and rum of the West Indies. Here follows Clement Downing's contemporary tale of the *alleged* "Moor" or Mughal ship which *allegedly* made England so rich and famous in Downing's mind (before taking *Cassandra* made him infamous in the eyes of British EIC authorities):

> From hence [England] came on the Coast of *Ethiopia* [northeast Africa], with his two Ships [*Fancy* and *Expedition (John Gally*?)], and went to the *Portuguese* [who were then building a fort at Delagoa; see Chapter Six] at *Massembeach* [Mozambique], who supposed them to belong to the English East-India Company. After they had got a fresh Supply of Provisions, they sailed to the Island of *Johanna*, where they lay some time, and then cruised off the *Streights Mouth* of *Babelmondon* [Straits of Bab-el-Mandeb], or the *Red-sea*, where they took a Moors Ship, richly laden, coming down from *India*. They then made the best of their way for *Madagascar*, and went to *St. Marys Island* [Île Saint-Marie just off northeast coast of Madagascar, adjacent Antongil or "Ranter's" Bay], where none of their Fraternity had been for many Years [not actually true; probably where they found Jasper Seager], and were very joyfully received by the King. This Island joins to the Continent of *Madagascar*, and is generally a Place of Residence for Pyrates. Here they made a sad Massacre of the poor Moors Men [Downing presumed, and did not personally witness this ruthless act], [who] they had taken in the Ship above-

mentioned, and abused their Women in a very vile manner [as in Henry Every's story]. Some say, that Capt. *England* kept one or two of the Moors Women for his own Use, there being some of Distinction amongst them [as in Every's story], whose Fathers were in high Posts under the Great Mogul ... THEY brought the Moors Ship's Cargo to a quick Market [for the natives], and made Sale of what they could; and Part of the rest they cast in heaps on the Beach, to be spoil'd by the Winds and Weather. The Sloop, they found, was not answerable for their Purpose; on which account they [hauled] her [toward] shore, and sunk her, with some part of her Cargo on board, which was neglected by the Inhabitants, who knew not the Value nor Use of those rich Commodities. They took up their Winter-Quarters at this Place, and replenished their Store: Before they sunk the Moors Ship, they made a Sort of a Hulk of her, and hove down their other Ships the *Fancy*, and Snow, which they called the *Expedition* [or *John Gally*?], and made a clean Ship; this was in the Year 1719 [ended in March 1720].[71]

Compare this long and detailed passage to that given for Henry Every's earlier voyage in the introduction to this book. The *déjà vu* feeling is hard to ignore – again, England was theoretically enthralled with Every.[72]

Richard Moor, in his deposition, gave no long history of proceeding to the Red Sea and capturing the famed "Moor" ship, again making this portion of England's history, as told by Downing, suspect. Note that Charles Johnson had not included this particular detail, either, but did still have England arriving earlier in the East Indies and sailing along the Malabar or Indian Coast before taking *Cassandra* – which cannot be sufficiently disputed for lack of evidence. Still, Downing perhaps regaled his

---

[71] Downing, *History of Indian Wars*, 110-113; Obviously, Clement Downing is narrating part of John Plantain's history. He offers side-notes without warning and his own bias against "notorious" pirates.

[72] Two calendar changes in Great Britain and its colonies, which complicates dating: the first was to change the start of the year from Lady Day (25 March) to 1 January; the second was to discard the Julian Calendar in favor of the Gregorian Calendar. Dates given by eyewitnesses such as Moor, Matthews, and Downing are often confusing, partly due to faulty memory and partly due to idiosyncrasies of and changes in the calendar being used. The problem that historians have is a temporal one – explaining the interval of "Winter-quarters [Dec-March]" of 1719 until 8 August 1720 when *Cassandra* had been taken. Part of the interval can be explained by 25 March 1720 actually ending the year of 1719 for those in the early eighteenth century.

readers with "fake news," though probably unintentional – for him. This was perhaps the case for his questionable ex-pirate and rather loquacious and self-flattering informant Plantain.

Primary sources better agree on timing and make the additional Every-fantasy portion unnecessary. England, Cocklyn, LeVasseur, and Taylor all left, perhaps not all together, from the west coast of Africa sometime around February-March 1720. In close agreement, James Phipps, captain-general of Cape Coast Castle, and John Stevenson wrote from that location on the African Coast to the Royal African Company that "Pyrates design to range on the Coast to Windward till end of Febry, then for the Coast of Brazil, and thence to Madagascar."[73] As learned from Grey's EIC study, Edward England may gone there as well, but we have no primary sources to show this. Phipps and Stevenson also mentioned "2 large French Ships" taken by the others, certainly a reference to *Le Victorieux* of Guillaum Hais and perhaps Alexander Patterson's *Le Solide*. This would delay Cocklyn, LeVasseur, and Taylor's arrival at Madagascar to *no earlier* than late March-early April, maybe even as late as May. John Matthews, then aboard LeVasseur's *Indian Queen,* confirms this in his deposition. There was really little time for a sortie to the Red Sea – Downing may have been mistaken, or he fancied the 17th century tales – or Plantain *modified* his tales more than earlier believed.

Preparing for Battle

Moor deposed that Cocklyn died and was succeeded by Richard Taylor as commander of 46-gun *Victory* (we will use this name instead of *Le Victorieux* from here on). *John Gally,* as he said, was burnt and her men taken aboard *Victory* and *Fancy*. Edward England, however, is mentioned as the captain of *Victory* when the taking of *Cassandra* occurred, as stated in John Barnes' journal – entry of 8 April 1720. Perhaps Taylor was demoted to quartermaster, owing to personality conflicts or because Seager was more experienced. Possible pirate resident of Madagascar, and presumably more experienced, Jasper Seager, could have

---

[73] "James Phipps and John Stevenson to the Royal African Company, Cabo Corso Castle, Jan. 12th, 1719(20)" in Elizabeth Donnan, ed., *Documents Illustrative of the History of the Slave Trade to America, Vol. II: The Eighteenth Century* (Washington: Carnegie Instution, 1931), 242-243.

assumed command of *Fancy*, and as commodore for them all, at this point.

Jasper Seager is an historical enigma. His name does not appear in documents related to this particular group of pirates before sailing to Madagascar in 1720. He appears not to have come from the African Coast with the others. Still, he assumes command of *Fancy*, and possibly as commodore over both of the two ships that take *Cassandra*. If his name had not appeared in Chief Mate John Barnes' journal from *Greenwich* as captain of *Fancy* on the dated entry for 7 August 1720, before hostilities began on the 8th, he would not have been considered as all that important. His credit from historians is undeservedly and comparatively slight after taking *Cassandra*. He is not as perceptible in most narratives after the pirates take the Viceroy's ship (see Chapter Five) at La Bourbon, despite the Viceroy's own account – Richard Lasinby's account, of course, came from aboard *Victory* and not *Cassandra*, then under Seager's command.

Owing purely to speculation, Seager may be regarded as an older man of great experience, perhaps already a pirate inhabitant of Madagascar when the others arrived. It is known that one Thomas Seager was in Henry Every's crew, had not returned with others, and had possibly settled on Madagascar in the mid-1690s.[74] Perhaps another Seager served in Every's crew or in Kidd's? To his credit, Charles Johnson predicted that Edward England's crew searched for Every's old crew when they arrived at Île Saint-Marie. Evolving from this reasonable speculation, it may also be that later pirate crews consisted of mixes between elder pirate residents of Madagascar and the recent arrivals to the island. Charles Grey also alludes to this in *Pirates of the Eastern Seas*. As an older pirate residing on Madagascar who once possibly served with Henry Every, Jasper Seager could have been viewed by these younger pirates as legendary as Every himself. It should be noted that an early article by Grey, published in Bombay, India on the "Taking of Cassandra" gave Jasper Seager the primary credit for

---

[74] "William III: November 1696," in *Calendar of State Papers Domestic: William III, 1696*, ed. William John Hardy (London: His Majesty's Stationery Office, 1913), 428-449; Calendar of State Papers show that one Thomas Seager was part of Henry Every's crew, one of the few men captured in Ireland and executed in 1696/7. Over 200 of Every's crew remained on Île de Bourbon before *Fancy* returned to the West Indies – some may have made their way back to Madagascar.

her capture, not Edward England. Indeed, from Barnes' journal, it was Seager in *Fancy* who engaged Macrae for so long and so diligently while England in *Victory* chased Kirby's *Greenwich*.[75]

Olivier LeVasseur had, however, disappeared from the group before this happened. John Matthews, aboard *Indian Queen* when she arrived in the East Indies, indicates that LeVasseur and his crew were shipwrecked and stranded on the Island of Mayotte for much of the time after their arrival (they may even have arrived alone), building a canoe from the remains of Capt. Thomas Hill's former vessel. Matthews didn't mention a rendezvous on Île Saint-Marie, perhaps confirming that they arrived in the East Indies separately. He said they headed straight for Mayotte, intending to careen their vessel there. Plantain-Downing ignored LeVasseur as well, perhaps because LeVasseur was not engaged during the capture of Macrae's *Cassandra*. If even aware of LeVasseur's presence at Mayotte, it is reasonable to assume that Seager, Taylor and England simply left him to his own devices with the wounded *Indian Queen*. We have Matthews' words to tell the tale; also the five pirates of *Indian Queen* who went aboard *Greenwich* 30 July 1720. These men had stranded themselves on the island of Johanna for some time before *Greenwich* arrived and took them onboard – how long is uncertain. So, it can be said that *Indian Queen* was at least indirectly involved in the *Cassandra* incident.[76]

Johanna or Anjouan lies just 50 miles northwest of Mayotte, so Edward England and Jasper Seager would have to have sailed passed Olivier LeVasseur and *Indian Queen* to take *Cassandra*. LeVasseur probably limped back to Île Saint-Marie[77] on his ragged makeshift canoe from Mayotte Island, having missed out on *Cassandra* – a late d'Artagnon riding his "Buttercup," a fourth "rogue privateer" if you will.

For long-time captive Richard Moor, there was little confusion about the pirate management at the "Battle of Johanna," or the "Taking of *Cassandra*." Leadership among these pirates was fleeting, at best. Taylor was unseated by Edward England before they reached Johanna and probably made quartermaster – why is uncertain. After the battle, England is then deposed by Taylor, who then takes command back from *him*. Then, Lasinby's tale

---

[75] Johnson, *A General History*, 118; Charles Grey, "Taking of the Cassandra," *Indian State Railways Magazine*, 9: 3 (Bombay, Apr-Sep 1936), 211-215.
[76] Matthews, 194.
[77] Nosy Boraha, today – capital: Ambodifotatra; Îsle Saint-Marie is 60 kilometres (37 miles) long and less than 10 kilometres (6.2 miles) wide.

began, with Taylor then in charge. Later, following their adventures on the Malabar or Southern Indian Coast, Taylor again loses command to LeVasseur. No one, however, appears to have challenged the likely elder Seager's authority. Indeed, the various narratives and clues as to the events of the Battle of Johanna reveal much political intrigue and deception – mostly because of the infighting *between* the pirates! Most bouts involved Richard Taylor, but those of more political import involved, of course, bureaucrats, paper, and an overuse of quill and ink![78]

Battle of Johanna or Taking of the *Cassandra*

The British Library Archives, Indian Office Records describes *Cassandra* as 380 tons, 26 guns, and carrying 76 crewmen. She had left Portsmouth, England on 21 Mar 1720, headed for Bombay. She was commanded by Capt. James MacRae, who was unfortunately interrupted by pirates after three months journey to Johanna on 8 August 1720. The archives contain a few references to *Cassandra* and her captain's career, which included sailing with Capt. George Pitt to Benkulen on 250-ton, 20-gun *Swallowfield*. Pitt briefly served as East India Company president at Fort St. George on Sumatra (1723-1725), and finally became the governor of Madras, on the southeastern shore of the Indian sub-continent.

Future governor James Macrae was born into poverty in Ayrshire, Scotland. Ayrshire, one of the most agriculturally fertile regions of Scotland, was part of the the southwest coast and south of the Antonine Wall – briefly occupied by the Romans during the reign of Emperor Antoninus Pius. It is a maritime community partly composed of mainland, and three smaller islands. Of definite historical note, Ayrshire's Turnberry Castle dates from the 13th century or earlier and may have been the birthplace of Robert the Bruce.

---

[78] Moor, 209.

Macrae's father died when he was young, forcing James to seek employment to support his mother and himself. He began herding cattle while his mother found work as a washerwoman in a suburb of Ayr. Local musician, Hugh Maguire, fared well financially and it is thought that he may have helped James Macrae with his educational expenses. By 1692, Macrae went to sea and did not see his home for another 40 years.

Macrae found his calling as a mariner in London. There, he married his wife Elizabeth and worked his way up. He became captain of *Brice Galley* in 1709, owned by William Browne, Captain Randal Brice of London, and Abraham Elton Jr. of Bristol, merchants. His association with Browne may have introduced him to the East India Company, who hired him ten years later as captain of *Cassandra* in 1719. He then began preparing *Cassandra* for the voyage ahead, requesting permission to carry £500 worth of elephant's teeth. He also sought a license to carry £100 worth of white lead on the *Cassandra* as part of his private trade allowance.[79]

Macrae then said "goodbye" to his wife in London, who would maintain regular correspondence with her husband. *Cassandra* joined with three other captains and their ships to make the voyage: William Upton (b. 1682) of *London*, Thomas Gilbert of *Chandos*, and Richard Kirby of *Greenwich*. They received their final instructions 9 March 1720 and set sail on the 21st. *London* and *Chandos* would separate from *Cassandra* and *Greenwich* while rounding the Cape. Macrae and Kirby together arrived at the Island of Johanna the 25th of July, accompanied by an Ostend vessel, 220-ton *Stahremberg*, Capt. Richard Gargan, they met along the way.[80] Almost immediately, they contacted some runaways on the beach of Johanna from LeVasseur's *Indian Queen*, then stranded on Mayotte:

> WE arrived the 25th of July last, in Company of the *Greenwich*, at Joanna, (an Island not far from Madagascar) putting in there to

---

[79] British Library, Indian Office Records, IOR/E/1/10 ff. 564-565v : 23 Dec 1719; IOR/E/1/11 f. 92 : [5 Feb 1720]; James Macrae's biography from *Dictionary of National Biography* (England), "James Macrae (1677?-1744)," 720-721.
[80] British Library, IOR/E/3/100 ff. 138-41: 9 Mar 1720; *Stahremberg*, likely named for Count von Stahremberg , researched by Degryse & Parmentier, "Merchants and captains," 176, 226; Gazetteer of the Bombay Presidency. v. 26, pt. 1, 259n1; "Haremberg [Stahremberg]" arrived on 23 Oct 1720 at Surat.

refresh our Men, we found fourteen [exaggerated] Pyrates that came in their Canoes from the Mayotta, where the Pyrate Ship to which they belong'd, viz. the *Indian Queen*, two hundred and fifty Tons, twenty eight Guns, and ninety Men, commanded by Capt. Oliver [LeVasseur] de la Bouche, bound from the Guinea Coast to the East-Indies, had been bulged and lost. They said they left the Captain and 40 of their Men building a new Vessel to proceed on their wicked Design.[81]

The wayward men, actually about five in number and *not* fourteen (Macrae most likely inflated this number), including John Matthews, came aboard Kirby's ship on 30 July "from the shore" and told him their story, related in his deposition of October 1722:

> That upon their arrival [on Mayotte] [Matthews] and four others found an opportunity in the night to get away from thence in a small Canoe belonging to the Blacks... to the island of Johanna... they stay'd about two months [roughly 30 May-30 July 1720] before ... a Mercht ship called the *Greenwich* bound to the East Indies arrived... they desir'd to be entred as foremast Men onboard [Kirby's] ship which the said Capt. agreed to and hired them at five and twenty shillings a Month for the rest of his Voyage.[82]

Capt. Richard Kirby consulted with his consort Macrae on this stranded pirate, *Indian Queen*, which was new to the region, and possibly a danger to their EIC shipping. Macrae related in his letter of 16 November 1720 to the EIC that he determined "I concluding that it might be of great Service to the East-India Company to destroy such a Nest of Rogues."[83] Presumably, Matthews informed Macrae and Kirby of the other pirates besides LeVasseur, shipwrecked on Mayotte. Still, *Indian Queen* was lost two months earlier (circa May-June 1720) and this was the only known pirate ship in the area at that

---

[81] "Substance of a letter from Captain Mackra, dated at Bombay, Nov. 16, 1720" in *The Post Boy*, 25 & 27 April, 1721.
[82] "The Examination of John Matthews, 12 October 1722, HCA 1/55, ff. 201-21" in E. T. Fox, *Pirates in Their Own Words*, 193.
[83] "Captain Mackra's ship taken by Edward England, *The Post Boy,* 25 Apr and 27 Apr 1721" in E. T. Fox, *Pirates in Their Own Words*, 272.

time. Regardless, Macrae and Kirby expected little trouble from forty stranded and probably desperate pirates and allegedly readied their ships to sail in pursuit.[84]

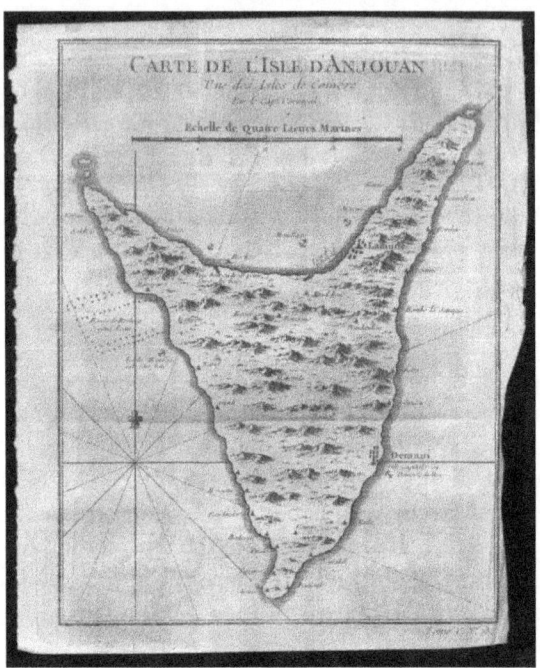

Bellin, *Carte de L'Île D'Anjouan* (Johanna) (1764)

According to *Greenwich's* first mate's log, the five men escaped from the pirate ship *Indian Queen* had not been quite as innocent as they appeared to Capt. Kirby. On the 31st, one of them died and was buried in "Brown's Garden" ashore of Johanna. The morning of 2 August, an Italian man enlisted aboard *Greenwich* who had known these men. This Italian man, who incidentally would later desert *Greenwich* in September 1721, accused them of having been pirates themselves, not just captives. First mate Barnes wrote "our Capt. Order'd their hammocks to be Searched, in w[hi]ch were found gold dust, silver Spoons, D[itt]o. Buckles, a silver barr and other things of value."[85] Capt. Kirby then ordered the valuables confiscated and the pirates put into irons.

---

[84] Matthews, 193.
[85] British Library, "Greenwich: Journal, John Barnes, Chief Mate," India Office Records, IOR L/MAR/B/488A, 6 Oct 1719-13 Jul 1722.

About eight in the morning of 7th of August, just as Macrae and Kirby were to begin their alleged search for LeVasseur, two ships appeared in the road.[86] By 12 noon, Barnes recorded that *Cassandra* weighed anchor to investigate, followed by *Stahremberg*. At that point, he said, they received quite a surprise, confirming their worst fear. The newcomers were two more pirate ships! Macrae's letter asserted that he immediately rowed over to *Greenwich*, which appeared to be preparing to meet the pirates. He, Kirby, and the *Stahremberg's* Capt. Richard Gargan, another Irishman, agreed to stand against them. Macrae rowed back to *Cassandra*, again unmoored and put two boats in the water to tow him beside *Greenwich* in the calm weather, "but [*Greenwich*] being open to a Valley and a Breeze, made the best of his Way from me."[87] Macrae had asserted that Kirby intended to betray him all along, but there is no evidence to support this from Barne's log.

Barnes' intelligence of these pirates noted "one a French built ship of 46 guns by name of victory Capt. England, The other a Dutch-built of 36 guns by name of Fancy Capt. Seager."[88] He then wrote that *Greenwich* "got all things in readiness for our defense."[89] Macrae's intelligence differed greatly, according to his letter. Newspaper reports also heavily inflated *Cassandra's* abilities and her dangerous circumstances, no doubt due again to the EIC's rising star Macrae and his letter. Macrae said that one of them mounted 34 guns and the other 30. He also implied that the larger of the two ships was the one that he had engaged from the start and who drove him

---

[86] Chief Mate John Barnes noted it as 7 a.m., Sunday, 7 August 1720; Macrae's letter passed through one or more transcriptions before being printed and may have been mis-transcribed as 17th August. Note also that Barnes mentioned nothing about plans to go after the pirates of *Indian Queen* on nearby Mayotte Island. Macrae may have made this up to impress the EIC.
[87] "Captain Mackra."
[88] "Greenwich: Journal, John Barnes, Chief Mate"; *Daily Post,* 18 Apr 1721; *Daily Post* reported *Cassandra* as 500 tons (actually 380), 30 guns (actually 26), and claimed that four pyrate vessels (actually two, but only one necessary to run her aground) attacked and took her.
[89] "Greenwich: Journal, John Barnes, Chief Mate."

aground – a 34-gun (36-gun) *Fancy*; but, 46-gun *Victory* was actually the larger and more powerful of the pirates.

Macrae's 380-ton vessel only mounted 26 guns, but *Greenwich*, the more powerful vessel, mounted 32 guns. It makes sense that the larger pirate, *Victory*, would chase after the more powerful *Greenwich* and her consort. Together, as Macrae asserted, with the 22-gun Ostender *Stahremberg* who had accompanied them, they stood a fair chance against these pirates – their 80 guns versus 64. Kirby's first mate, however, recorded the pirates' strength as a total of 82 guns – much more evenly matched. Yet, still, according to *Greenwich's* first mate John Barnes, they readied for a fight. Macrae may have downplayed the pirates' actual firepower in his letter – possibly to overstate his bravery and Kirby's betrayal.

Barnes' notes indicated that the battle began at 3 p.m. on the 8th of August, a full day after their discovery. *Cassandra* appeared to have been attacked first by Seager's *Fancy*:

> Att 3 P.Md. ye Cassandra being the Leewardmost Ship was ingaged by ye small Ship [*Fancy*, Seager, according to Barnes]. They fought under ye black flagg att ye main topmast head with death's head in itt/ ye Red flagg att the foretop mast head & St. George's Colours att ye Ensign Staff. We Tack'd and stood in for to assist him [;] in perceiving ye Cassandra aground Tack'd and stood off making the best of our way for Bombay.[90]

An important note in Barne's entry is that *Greenwich* apparently left only *after Cassandra's* grounding. Also in judgment of Macrae's condemnation, Barnes indicated that *Greenwich* yet had no wind and could make little progress in the calm. Still, Kirby put out their longboat with two men to help tow them: James Tate and William Prescott. *Victory* then came after them in the land breeze and almost got within range. *Greenwich* caught the same breeze. By nightfall, wrote Barnes, they had got clear of the action, having been chased all along by the larger pirate ship *Victory*, under Edward England.

Again, according to Barnes' journal, *Greenwich* waited until they saw *Cassandra* run aground *before* they finally decided to leave. Another important point was illustrated by Richard Lasinby, Macrae's 1st or 2nd mate, "That he understood by said

---

[90] "Greenwich: Journal, John Barnes, Chief Mate."

Pyrates discourse That one Seegar was Commander in Chief of both the aforesaid Ships and was in the Fancy during the Fight and one Taylor was Deputed by him to Command the Victoria [*Victory*]."[91] Note that Lasinby witnessed this discourse *after* the battle and assumed that Taylor, not England, had always been in command of *Victory,* though under Seager as Commodore. Lasinby clearly believed that the possibly elder Seager was in command of *both* pirate vessels.

Johanna Bay possessed a wide-mouthed entrance and a ship may easily slip away from an approaching danger, assuming they had breezes to propel them. As Macrae related, he felt surprised and referred to *Stahremberg*, the Ostender who also had promised to fight the pirates, but who he alleged to behave as *Greenwich*, "though the Captain had promised heartily to engage with us."[92] Macrae asserted ironically that Capt. Gargan wouldn't have left him without Kirby's first backing off from the fight – his angst certainly with Kirby. Still, Ostenders were heavily prejudiced by the English and he likely *avoided* helping them. After all, Kirby had the largest of their three vessels and both captains would have depended upon those guns. He said "I believe [Capt. Gargan] would have been as good as his Word, if Capt. Kirby had kept his."[93] Ostenders, however, were also viewed as pirates by the English and not unjustifiably, as many of their captains were Jacobite ex-English captains, having fled England. As he intimated in his letter to the EIC director, once he realized that Kirby probably intended to run, reducing his chances considerably, Macrae used his cannon to try and command them back into line:

> About half an Hour after Twelve [as Macrae recalled; note again that Barnes indicated the battle began at 3 p.m.], I called several times to the Greenwich to bear down to our Assistance, and fir'd Shot at him, but to no Purpose. For tho' we did not doubt but he would join us, because when he got about a League [three miles] from us, he brought his Ship to, and look'd on, yet both he and the Ostender [*Stahremberg*] basely deserted us, and left us engaged

---

[91] "Greenwich: Journal, John Barnes, Chief Mate."
[92] "Captain Mackra."
[93] "Captain Mackra;" "Mr. Lasinbys' Affidt. of his being taken by the Pyrates & of their proceedings," in British Library, India Office, IOR L/MAR/B/313A London Journal, ff. 175-179.

with barbarous and inhuman Enemies, with their black and bloody Flags hanging over us, without the least Appearance of escaping being cut to Pieces.[94]

Macrae's memory differed greatly with Barnes' journal. It may be that Macrae and Kirby had negotiated with the pirates at first, possibly hoping to do some trading – the EIC may have preferred this. Perhaps, negotiations fell through. This would explain how Barnes knew specific details about them. Macrae, in *Cassandra*, may have waited too long to run from the pirates. Was he too close and had no choice but face them alone, at first? It seems reasonable to assume that, once he realized that his consorts had left him to their mercy, he, too, would have made a run for it, if he could. Still, Barnes indicated that Macrae had already been run aground before *Greenwich* departed. Afterward, Macrae may have obfuscated his apparent foolishness to his superiors.

For whatever reason, Macrae wrote that he alone stood his ground against *Fancy* and *Victory*. He said that when the pirates came within range, he steeled himself and planned. Logically, he asserted that he targeted the larger (as he said – 34-gun) *Fancy* first and put "some Shot betwixt Wind and Water, which made her keep off a little to stop her Leaks."[95] *Victory*, again, as Macrae asserted, the smaller pirate (30 guns, not 46, as he said) tried her best to board him, using her oars to bring them within half a ship's length within the first hour. This must have followed *Victory's* disengaging with *Greenwich*, who Barnes declared faithful in the fight.[96]

Recap of Barnes' journal: Edward England, in *Victory*, chased after *Greenwich* and could not have been engaged with Macrae until late – Kirby was attacked also and probably did *not* abandon Macrae until it looked hopeless. Again, if Barnes was correct, *Cassandra* was engaged by the smaller ship, not the larger, as Macrae asserted, with 36 guns – *Fancy*, commanded by Jasper Seager. *Greenwich* would then have been chased away by the larger *Victory*, under Edward England, with 46 guns, who then assisted Seager, in *Fancy*, in capturing *Cassandra*.

---

[94] Letter from Captain Mackra.
[95] Letter from Captain Mackra.
[96] Letter from Captain Mackra.

Macrae put up quite the defense against *Fancy* - as he remembered it - and wrote "by good Fortune we shot all her Oars to Pieces, which prevented them, and by consequence saved our Lives."[97] As Macrae said, after his three hours of battle between both *Cassandra* and *Victory*, at about four in the afternoon (Barnes said it was about sunset), *Greenwich* and *Stahremberg* set sail for Bombay and disappeared below the horizon. Barnes, of course, disagreed. He assured that *Greenwich* had worked all day long to escape the larger *Victory* chasing them and parted after sunset - *only* after they were sure that they would not be able to aid *Cassandra*.

Kirby's political chastisement had been decided. Whether or not his first mate told the truth, the EIC director believed Capt. Macrae's story. Of course, Macrae's letter to the EIC director was published in the *Post Boy* newspaper several months later on 22 April. But, the news first appeared from presumably the same source as a brief synopsis the week before, on 15 April 1721. Surprisingly, this brief blurb contradicted Macrae, stating "the small Pyrate [*Fancy*] came up with and engaged" Macrae's *Cassandra*, "while the large [*Victory*] chas'd Capt. Kirby."[98] This article claimed that Macrae had "entirely" beat *Fancy*, but when the larger *Victory* joined in, Macrae lost. One should note, also, that no journal from Macrae's side of the story, from the captured *Cassandra*, yet existed to corroborate his story - only Macrae's letter to the director. His word would rule the narrative, reinforced by the newspaper account.

As far as the battle was concerned, we have only Macrae's word (agreed to by his mate Richard Lasinby) to tell the tale - and he told it as one might expect of a future politician - with great exaggeration! As he said, *Fancy* patched her leaks well enough to re-engage the battle with *Cassandra*. Macrae now faced both pirates; he saw no alternative but to escape inland. He related his disadvantage in that he "drew four Foot Water more than the Pyrate," and could easily run aground before they - even though *Cassandra* was the lighter vessel.[99] England,

---

[97] Letter from Captain Mackra.
[98] *Post Boy*, 15 Apr & 22 Apr 1721.
[99] Letter from Captain Mackra.

not Seager, he erroneously wrote, understanding Macrae's intent and sorely angry at having to lose so many men and resources, lunged *Victory* after *Cassandra* to prevent losing the opportunity to chastise her crew. *Victory* fired repeated broadsides as *Cassandra* neared the shore. When she ran aground, Macrae's men scrambled to man their boats and head for shore. But, as they did, *Fancy* also ran aground within shot of *Cassandra* whose broadside faced the pirate. Macrae rejoiced for another chance. He recalled that he told his men to lay broadsides into the pirate, taking another chance to jab at Richard Kirby:

> Here we had a more violent Engagement than before. All my Officers, and most of my Men, behaved with unexpected Courage; and as we had a considerable Advantage by having a Broadside to his Bow, we did him great Damage, so that had Capt. Kirby come in then, I believe we should have taken both, for we had one of them sure....[100]

Fancy was again in trouble. She could not fire the bulk of her cannon at *Cassandra* because her bow faced him – but Macrae, at a better angle, had the best opportunity to lay many volleys at *Fancy*, already greatly damaged. The pirate knew he had to board his enemy and sent his men in boats. *Victory*, as Macrae said, seeing her consort in such danger, put out three boatloads of her own, filled with men, to directly engage Macrae's crew. *Victory* approached *Cassandra* from astern and attempted to use her cannon on her, "by which time many of my Men being killed and wounded, and no Hopes left us from being all murdered by enraged barbarous Conquerors."[101] Again, according to Barnes, 46-gun *Victory* chased *Greenwich* until dark and could have been nowhere near the fight.

Macrae was again outnumbered. He allegedly ordered all the men that would fit in his longboat to make for shore. The ones who remained aboard would lay down cannon fire and cover their escape with smoke. Some of those dove in the water after firing the guns. Most of them were able to make it ashore.

---

[100] Letter from Captain Mackra.
[101] Letter from Captain Mackra.

When the pirates were finally able to board, at about seven that evening and after a full day's battle (if we believe Macrae; four hours, if we believe Barnes), they were so enraged; they sabered three wounded men still aboard *Cassandra*. Macrae and his men managed to escape and hiked twenty-five miles to the King's-Town of Johanna. Macrae wrote "I arrived next Day, almost dead with Fatigue and Loss of Blood, having been sorely wounded in the Head by a Musket Ball."[102] This all assumes that one can believe Macrae's narrative.

Johanna, or Anjouan (capital: Mustamudu), is one of the islands in the Comoros chain. Muslim rule had held supreme over these islands for centuries. Sultans thought Europeans good for business and the Portuguese made the Comoros an entrepôt for African slaves to be shipped to Malindi, Mombasa, Mogadishu, and Arabia. The Moheli Sultanate had ruled since around 1600 and it was still in power at the time of the arrival of *Cassandra*. As a captain with the East India Company, James Macrae might have ascertained that he could expect help from Sultan Salim (son of Alimah III) because the Sultanate welcomed their trade and offered protection since at least 1700.[103] Bethwell A. Ogot wrote in *Africa from the Sixteenth to the Eighteenth Century*:

> Nearly all the English ships bound for Mocha, Persia and Surat, put into port at Anjouan, thus forging a long-lasting Anglo-Anjouan link, a friendship on which the local sultans would call from time to time… The worst period was that of the pirates in the western Indian Ocean (1680–1720) when the sacking and destruction of Comorean towns became commonplace. It was precisely between 1700 and 1720 that British naval squadrons brought active aid to Anjouan and its sultan. This military assistance reflected the desire to extend Anjouan's effective

---

[102] Letter from Captain Mackra.
[103] Alimah III, also called Alimah, was the sovereign, Sultana regnant, of the Anjouan sultanate at Nzwani in the Comoro Islands from 1676 until 1711. She is the first recorded ruler on Anjouan, as well as the first female one.

control over the other Comoros and to obtain, in exchange, the sultan's refusal to shelter the pirates.[104]

Macrae's narrative continued with nursing his head wound. He then arrived in the King's Town to hear that the pirates had been looking for him and had offered a ransom for his return – a large one of 10,000 dollars, stll large despite the variable currency implied. Macrae worried that "many of them would have accepted, only they knew the King and all his chief People were in my Interest."[105] He said that he began a rumor that he had died of his wounds and was hopeful that this would abate their interest in him. Then, Macrae wrote a rather remarkable turn of events:

> About ten Days after, being pretty well recovered [from a gunshot head wound?], and hoping the Malice of our Enemies was nigh over, I began to consider the dismal Condition we were reduced to, being in a Place where we had no Hopes of getting a Passage home, all of us in a manner naked, not having had Time to get another Shirt, or a Pair of Shoes.[106]

Macrae claimed to have been in a "Place where we had no Hopes of getting a Passage home," but East India Company ships passed there all the time as well as others with whom he might have taken passage. Also, obtaining clothing should not have been a problem, either. The people of Anjouan were not dolts, but capable merchants. There was plenty to eat and wear. Clement Downing said that Anjouan offered "Fowls, Goats, and Bullocks at a very cheap Rate, with a Variety of Fruits and Roots for the Refreshment of those who have had a long and fatigueing Passage."[107]

Downing offered perhaps another explanation for this strange passage related by a "gallant" Macrae. He stated:

> But after a Day or two past, [the pirates] had a Consultation amongst themselves, and considering the gallant Behaviour of Capt.

---

[104] "Madagascar and the Islands of the Indian Ocean" in Bethwell A. Ogot, ed., *Africa from the Sixteenth to the Eighteenth Century* (Oxford: James Currey, Ltd., 1999), 437.
[105] Letter from Captain Mackra.
[106] "Substance of a letter from Captain Mackra, dated at Bombay, Nov. 16, 1720" in *The Post Boy*, 25 & 27 April, 1721.
[107] Downing, *History of the Indian Wars*, 43.

Mackray, and what a good Character he bore amongst his Men, they agreed to return him another Ship in the room of his own. They sent Messengers up into the Country to search for him, and Letters to assure him they would not hurt a Hair of his Head, but only satisfy him of their good Intentions towards him [even after killing 100 of them]. On which account he ventured down, and they entertained him in a very handsome manner on board his own Ship, with the best of his own Liquors and Provisions.[108]

This bit was rather questionable, but it had indeed impressed the many who had read it in print. It may be that Macrae invented most of the hardships under which he and his men suffered. He also may have invented the clever "exaggerated rumors of his death" story. Was he possibly embarrassed by the sound beating he sustained from these pirates? Was the East India Company unwilling to promote this message and perhaps added more to the "official" narrative? There are a number of possibilities.

Either way, Macrae met with Edward England and Jasper Seager. He apparently knew many of their men, having possibly served with them before. He claimed that the pirates threatened to kill him, but were held off by Edward England, who claimed to know him. Was this more rhetoric? Was he truly in that much danger or were these former merchants and military men more cognizant of military codes of honor? Evidence revealed on Edward "Blackbeard" Thache's never having killed anyone out of anger, the treatment of a Portuguese official by LeVasseur in Chapter Five, and Downing's heavily derogatory words seem to indicate that military and EIC officials, as opposed to civilians, were strongly biased against pirates – their victims, like Macrae, certainly. Because of Macrae's erroneous letter and its publication, the downcast Irishman Edward England developed an undeserved reputation on par with that of Bartholomew Roberts. It was reported in 1722 that Roberts had grown as "formidable" as "that of the Pirate England in the East Indies," remembered for taking the mighty East Indiaman *Cassandra!*[109]

Generally, pirates appeared more as maritime merchants working for themselves – yes, most of the time stealing – rather than a company – which stole more quietly. They were like

---

[108] Downing, *History of the Indian Wars*, 43.
[109] *Evening Post*, 19 Jun 1722.

modern American crony-capitalists on the water – even less ruthless, perhaps. Even though they robbed other merchants, they may not have been the "notorious" or "villainous" men by which they have been betrayed for centuries by authors and government officials. Even Edward Congdon lived as a reputable merchant in Lorient, France and married a wealthy woman from a good family (see Chapter Four). Also, pirates routinely gave a captured captain and crew one of their prizes to take them home. Conducting your pirate business did not mean that you had to behave like barbarians. Thinking along these lines, we read:

> They talked of burning one of their Ships, which we had so entirely disabled, as to be no farther useful to them, and to fit the Cassandra in her room; but in the End I managed my Tack so well, that they made me a Present of the said shattered Ship, which was Dutch built, called the Fancy, about three hundred Tons, and also a hundred and twenty nine Bales of the Company's Cloth, tho' they would not give me a Rag of my Cloathes.[110]

Macrae must have owned a fine set of clothes. Unfortunately for him, these pirates needed them to replace their own as they frayed from use. This was also common for pirates, not often available to freely shop at finer establishments in larger ports.

With torn sails, broken masts, and blood-soaked, sandy oak decks, Macrae would have to make the best of his way to Bombay in *Fancy*. All indications from Macrae's testimony and in Downing's version are that Edward England had been the magnanimous pirate – but, it came from the questionable Macrae. Still, he apparently paid a price for alleged civilized behavior with one pirate, confirmed by Richard Lasinby.

Richard Taylor, presumably quartermaster aboard *Victory*, but soon taking command of *Victory* from England, had not wanted to give *Fancy* to Macrae, but would rather burn her. Apparently, others agreed with Taylor. They immediately deposed England, putting Taylor in command of *Victory*. Clement Downing gave a contemporary account that he had presumably learned from Macrae upon his return to Bombay, understandably subject to Macrae's biases:

---

[110] "Substance of a letter from Captain Mackra, dated at Bombay, Nov. 16, 1720" in *The Post Boy*, 25 & 27 April, 1721.

The Pyrates had a great Demur amongst themselves about giving Capt. Mackray the "Fancy, in the room of the Cassandra; but Capt. England told them, that if they refused this, he would renounce his Command amongst them, and live a retired Life on some of those inhabited Islands. Capt. England being much beloved, they comply'd to this Proposal, tho' Taylor resented the same most bitterly, and vowed to be revenged on England for his Generosity.[111]

Richard Kirby, captain of *Greenwich*, suffered perhaps undeservedly. Downing chastised Kirby and added "that he was ashamed of the Meanness of it, and took the same so much to heart, that in his going a Voyage to Persia, he died before he got there."[112] Actually, John Barnes' account of their encounter with pirates at Johanna was quite different from Macrae's and Downing's, which apparently evolved from Macrae's. He wrote that Kirby died *after* reaching Persia on 29 August 1721 "after 3 or 4 days of sickness." This occurred before he might have adequately defended himself before the EIC director and Macrae's charges against him – perhaps a lucky break for Macrae. John Barnes took command afterward. Kirby and Barne's successor on *Greenwich* in November 1723 was Capt. Richard Lasinby who would command this ship for seven years – a posthumous blow to Kirby. Lasinby had been James Macrae's former 1st or 2nd mate on *Cassandra*, was captured by England/Taylor and Seager's pirates, and released by them on Île de Bourbon after their attack on the Viceroy of Goa's ship (see Chapter Five). The EIC's giving Lasinby this command was further proof of Macrae's political success over Kirby.[113]

---

[111] Downing, *History of the Indian Wars*, 44; "Mr. Lasinbys' Affidt. of his being taken by the Pyrates & of their proceedings," in British Library, India Office, IOR L/MAR/B/313A London Journal, ff. 175-179; "That [Lasinby] understood by said Pyrates discourse That one Seegar was Commander in Chief of both the aforesaid Ships and was in the Fancy during the Fight and one Taylor was Deputed by him to Command the Victoria."

[112] Downing, *History of the Indian Wars*, 44; "Greenwich: Journal, John Barnes, Chief Mate."; Capt. Richard Kirby died Tuesday, 29 Aug 1721, "of a feavor after 3 or 4 days of sickness."

[113] Journal of John Barnes, entry of 29 Aug 1721; British Library, India Office Records, website entry: Greenwich (1), Ship, Unspecified, http://searcharchives.bl.uk.

160   Sailing East

Seager, England, and Taylor also would continue their disputes all the way back to Madagascar. As Macrae told of the pirates, they left five days before him. They had taken about thirty-three of his crew, including Lasinby:

> They sailed the 3d of September; and with Jury-Masts, and such old Sails as they left me, I made shift to do the like on the 8th [October][114], together with forty three of my Ship's Crew, including two Passengers and twelve Soldiers, having but five Tons of Water aboard; and after a Passage of forty eight Days, I arrived here October 26, almost naked and starv'd, having been reduced to a Pint of Water a Day, and almost in despair of ever seeing Land, by Reason of the Calms we met with between the Coast of Arabia and Malabar [southwest India; Cochin is part of Dutch Malabar]. — We had in all thirteen Men killed and twenty four wounded; and we were told, that we had destroyed about ninety or a hundred of the Pyrates. When they left us, they were about three hundred Whites and eighty Blacks in both Ships.[115]

By chance, *Greenwich* anchored in Bombay road the same day the pirates left Johanna, 3rd of September, meeting *London* and *Chandos*, who had already arrived at the EIC port. The journal of John Barnes tells the story of *Greenwich* after their arrival there and offers a few clues as to the larger story of taking Macrae's *Cassandra*. It shows that on 23rd of October, Capt. Kirby, at Surat, met again with the 22-gun Ostender *Stahremberg* (see 146n79) that had been with him and Macrae at Johanna – she sailed the next day. Illustrating English disdain, Surat chief Jarvis Clarke was expelled for dealing with the Ostender's Irish Capt. Gargan. By 2nd of November, a gallivant arrived from Bombay in Surat to inform them that Capt. Macrae had recently arrived there in the tattered old pirate ship *Fancy*. On the 11th, *Greenwich* had returned to Bombay and five days later, Macrae had penned his original letter damning Kirby to the EIC director. Early that December, they weighed anchor for Cape Comorin. The 17th, they spied four ships that they thought were pirates, but who turned out to be merchants. Little did they know that *Victory* and *Cassandra* had indeed followed them to India. By Christmas 1720, while at Mangalore, they got word that the same pirates who had taken

---

[114] "Fort St. George, January 1720-1721," *Diary and Consultation Book, 1721* (Madras: Indian Government Press, 1930), 125.
[115] "Substance of a letter from Captain Mackra, dated at Bombay, Nov. 16, 1720" in *The Post Boy*, 25 & 27 April, 1721.

Cassandra had been spotted between Calicut and Tellicherry. Apparently unconcerned, *Greenwich* made Tellicherry by the 27th and Calicut the 29th, making another close call with them on the 31st. By the time *Greenwich* arrived at Cochin, the pirates had already sailed for Mauritius (next chapter) where they would repair *Victory's* damages and leaks. By the end of January, Capt. Kirby wrote a personal letter to Capt. Macrae, the substance of which is unknown. Presumably, Kirby had received word of Macrae's damning letter to the director, perhaps by way of their recent encounter with *London,* and Kirby offered a response. Achingly, nothing is known of the content of *that* letter – Macrae undoubtedly possessing more clout. By the end of April 1721, *Greenwich* left Bombay and sailed for Persia, after which Kirby would then die of fever.[116]

Plantain intimated through Downing that only the carpenter's mate of *Cassandra* had been kept by the pirates - "As to his Men, they suffered all of them to go with [Macrae], except his Carpenter's Mate, whom they compelled to remain with them."[117] Again, Macrae indicated about thirty-three crewmen while his former 1st or 2nd mate, Richard Lasinby insists through his deposition that he was taken as well and gives creditable account of his time with the pirates as the next chapter tells. Of course, Lasinby did not take that opportunity to dispute his former captain's narrative of the "Taking of *Cassandra*" at Johanna.

Soon after the pirates got under sail from Johanna on 3rd of September, they designed for India. But, first they made a detour for Madagascar (where he is later found) or possibly Mauritius to dispose of the overthrown Edward England and his men. Richard Taylor, then in command of *Cassandra,* certainly insisted, causing the majority of the rifts between them. Lasinby tells nothing of the dispute. Richard Moor only mentions that England was "turned out of command," but nothing about why or what happened to him afterward.[118]

The remaining details are hearsay mostly provided by Plantain and Downing. Downing relates the tale of Plantain when

---

[116] "Greenwich: Journal, John Barnes, Chief Mate."
[117] Downing, *History of Indian Wars*, 113.
[118] "The Examination of Richard Moor, 31 October 1724 (addenda 5 November 1724), HCA 1/55, ff. 94-97," in Fox, *Pirates in Their Own Words,* 209.

he told that Capt. England, with 60 or 70 Men had "dispersed themselves about the Island, and inhabited amongst the Negroes: but Capt. England being very poor, was obliged to be beholden to several of the white Men for his Subsistence."[119] The impression is that others had ignominiously ejected England, taking his cut of the profits. Jasper Seager remained in command of 46-gun *Victory* – Taylor in the prize *Cassandra* (probably augmented with Dutch guns from *Fancy*). Lasinby said they eventually reached India by 26 October.[120]

Capt. James Macrae made one more stab at the presumed faithless Richard Kirby. He blamed Kirby directly for the loss of *Cassandra* – a loss that the East India Company would take none too lightly. Macrae, on the other hand, was rewarded for his bringing 129 bales of cloth back to Bombay – no chastisement mentioned for other cargo lost. Downing gave an overview of the manifest: "75,000 l. in ready Cash on board of the Company's treasure, besides great Quantities of Bale Goods, with European Liquors of great Value."[121] Still, *Cassandra* had been taken. Why were the EIC officers not upset at Macrae for this loss? Perhaps Macrae's story of Kirby's near-criminal treachery and his heroic stance against these pirates – or some other administrative corruption persuaded them to ignore it? Governor Charles Boone accorded Macrae every courtesy:

> I am persuaded, had our Consort the *Greenwich* done his Duty, we had destroyed both of them, and got two hundred thousand Pounds for our Owners and selves; whereas to his deserting us, the Loss of the *Cassandra* may justly be imputed. I have delivered all the Bales that were given me into the Company's Warehouse, for which the Governor and Council have ordered me a Reward. Our Governor, Mr. [Charles] *Boon*, who is extreme kind and civil to me, has ordered me home with this Pacquet; but Captain *Harvey*, who had a prior Promise, being come in with the Fleet, goes in my room. The Governor hath promis'd me a Country Voyage, to help make me up

---

[119] Downing, *History of Indian Wars*, 116, Charles Johnson, *A General History of the Robberies and Murders of the Most Notorious Pyrates* (London: 1724), 124; Johnson offers an alternative and asserts that Edward England was marooned on Mauritius with three or four other men and then built a boat to go to Madagascar. In both versions, he ends up in Madagascar.
[120] "Richard Lasinby, a prisoner of Taylor," in E. T. Fox, *Pirates in Their Own Words* (Fox Historical, 2014), 277.
[121] Downing, *History of Indian Wars*, 45-46.

my Losses, and would have me stay to go home with him next Year.[122]

There are many parts of Macrae's narrative that seem self-congratulatory – human nature, assuredly. Still, Macrae may have had a point to his self-flattering account. Patrick Pringle assures that Macrae's account in his letter of 16 November 1720 worked to his advantage, alluding to massive corruption that would make any modern American politician jealous:

> ... as a reward for his valour he gained rapid promotion in the Company's service, eventually becoming Governor of Madras. The salary for this appointment was only £500 a year, but when Macrae retired after eight years he had amassed a fortune of £800,000.[123]

James Macrae disposed of the Dutch-built and wounded *Fancy* to a local merchant named William Wake. Wake was another corrupt president and governor of Bombay after Charles Boone, who died in 1751. Wake used the old *Fancy* to transport rice from Mangalore (north of Cochin) and "in whose service she was wrecked near Calicut in September 1723."[124]

Macrae composed his famed letter of 17 November 1720 in Bombay while visiting with "Gov." or Pres. Charles Boone (appointed 5 April 1715). He probably indeed commanded a special EIC task fleet to take the English pirates then raiding the Indian coast. Later, he conducted a special mission to the English settlement on the West Coast of Sumatra and finally sailed with William Mackett, Thomas Gilbert, and Richard Higginson for the trip back to England in June 1722. There, he then received his appointment to the presidency of Fort St. David, with reversion of the Governorship of Fort George.[125]

Macrae was afterwards appointed Governor of the Presidency of Madras, and began his duties on 15 January 1725.

---

[122] Downing, *History of Indian Wars*, 45-46.
[123] Patrick Pringle, *Jolly Roger: The Story of the Great Age of Piracy* (1953), Dover ed. (New York: Dover Publications, 2001), 228.
[124] Charles Grey, *Pirates of the Eastern Seas* (1618-1723), *a Lurid Page of History* (London: S. Low, Marston & co., ltd, 1933), 315.
[125] Downing, *History of the Indian Wars,* 45; "Fort St. George, January 1720-1721," *Diary and Consultation Book, 1721* (Madras: Indian Government Press, 1930), 12; "Fort St. George, August 1722," *Diary and Consultation Book, 1722* (Madras: Indian Government Press, 1930), 99.

He resigned the governorship on 14 May 1730, and on 21 January 1731, he bought several estates in the west of Scotland and eventually settled at Orangefield in Ayrshire. Macrae desired to at least possess land in his home place, something he could never do before his service to the East India Company. He also helped provide for his sister and her children. The former pauper became a burgess of Ayr on 21 July 1744 and died shortly thereafter. Did his experiences with these pirates help to elevate his position in the EIC? Were his self-flattering letter and his rhetoric against Richard Kirby, captain of *Greenwich*, simply politics and helpful to him in this regard?[126]

Olivier LeVasseur, later mentioned by Richard Lasinby, must have joined them before heading to the coast of India. He was probably Taylor's "quartermaster," as Lasinby referred to him. There is no mention of their returning to Madagascar to pick LeVasseur up before or after they took *Victory* in for repairs at Mauritius. They then sailed directly to Île de Bourbon, and captured the largest vessel yet – the Portuguese vessel carrying the Viceroy of Goa. LeVasseur almost magically appeared in command of *Victory* for that event, as told by eyewitnesses, with Taylor as *his* quartermaster! LeVasseur appeared to be the pirate leading that attack, then in command of *Cassandra*.[127]

London Journal of 22 April 1721 reported the news of *Cassandra*, received from an EIC advice boat sent by Gov. Boone. Macrae's news of the taking of *Cassandra* so alarmed the EIC Court of Directors, they petitioned the Crown to grant a Royal Navy Squadron of Men of War to suppress them. This effort would take time, of course. Meanwhile, the old pirate haven of Madagascar breathed new life! English pirates had once again made Île Saint-Marie their general rendezvous, "where they committed all manner of Enormities, and every one did as his own vicious Heart directed him," warned Royal Navy midshipman Clement Downing.[128] For the last few months of 1720, however, these newly successful pirates had grand visions of gold and diamonds, inspired by Henry Every *et al*, drawing them to the shores of India.

---

[126] Alexander Macrae, *History of the Clan Macrae* (Dingwall: Souter, 1910), 235-38; Thomas Seccombe, "Macrae, James" in Sidney Lee, *Dictionary of National Biography*, 35 (London: Smith, Elder & Co.), 720.
[127] *London Journal*, 22 April 1721.
[128] Downing, *History of Indian Wars*, 45-46.

Chapter 3: India

Pirating Bombay, Goa, and Cochin in the Arabian Sea

Richard Lasinby remained aboard *Victory* for the remainder of 1720, into spring of 1721. Much of what we know of these pirates in those years comes through his words. Two sources exist for this: one, told by Charles Grey in *Pirates of the Eastern Seas,* pages 316-325, and reprinted by E. T. Fox in *Pirates: in Their Own Words,* pages 276-285, with the nominalized spelling "Lazenby." The second and third narratives, one a draft and the polished version, titled "Mr. Lasinby's Narrative of the Proceedings of the Pyrates," taken 19 March 1722 and presented in court the following 22 March.[1] Both of these narratives of Richard Lasinby were found in the journal of the EIC ship *London*. These two *London* versions include quite a bit more detail than those given by Grey. This "official" depositon that was read in EIC Court of Directors on 22 March was signed "Richard Lasinby," therefore the assumption is that he himself spelled it that way. The basic story is covered in the cleaned up Fox version, but supplemental data from *London,* which includes abundant and phonetically difficult "y^e"s and "y:^{m}"s will be filled in at the

---

[1] British Library, India Office, IOR L/MAR/B/313A London Journal, ff. 165-178.

appropriate intervals. Another is a short abbreviated version of the first. All three versions are transcribed in the Appendix.

From these words, we gather that Richard Taylor took command after expulsion of a despised Edward England, which apparently occurred just after the battle. Lasinby, in fact, assumed that Taylor had always captained *Victory*, which probably indicates that the crew immediately removed England following the battle at Johanna, probably before Macrae's return from the interior. After leaving Edward England and his men with little but the cloths on their backs, Jasper Seager in *Victory* and Richard Taylor, with probably Olivier LeVasseur as quartermaster, in *Cassandra* sailed to India and arrived there by early-mid October 1720. They arrived ahead of James Macrae in the old tattered Dutch ship *Fancy*, having landed at Bombay on the 26th.

Richard Lasinby told how apprehensive he was made to feel when he first came aboard the pirate ship *Cassandra*:

> The first night I came on board & ye time came for these people to Sleep their was a watch ordered on my Acct: which made some of y:^{m} so angry as to say that if they saw me out on ye deck on any Acct: soever [they] would knock my brains out which did not a little concern me; some who were in ye Cabbin bad[e] me be of good Cheere but not to venture on ye deck for fear of ye worst, the Chief Surgeon in particular who took care to lay me down on ye Cabbin floor by him, more to prevent my Escape than any good nature in the Villain; which found afterwards when rose in ye night by his following me into ye Gallery and telling me if I offer'd att Escapeing they would oblidge Capt. Macrae to find me or else would take all from him again and burn ye ship.[2]

As the pirates prepared to leave on 3 September, Lasinby heard Macrae come aboard *Cassandra* to intercede for him, but to no avail. *Victory* and *Cassandra* then set sail.[3]

---

[2] "Mr. [Richard] Lasinby's Narrative of the Proceedings of the Pyrates," 19 Mar 1722, London: Journal, f. 165.
[3] London: Journal, f. 165.

Early sighting of two English ships before making land prompted Taylor to interrogate Lasinby about secret signals used by EIC ships, cruising on the Indian Coast, to alert them to the presence of pirates. Lasinby told him that he knew of none, had never had occasion to use any, and reported that Taylor, not accepting this, "abused me, calling me scurrilous names shook his broadsword at me, and said he would plague me like the dog I was."[4]

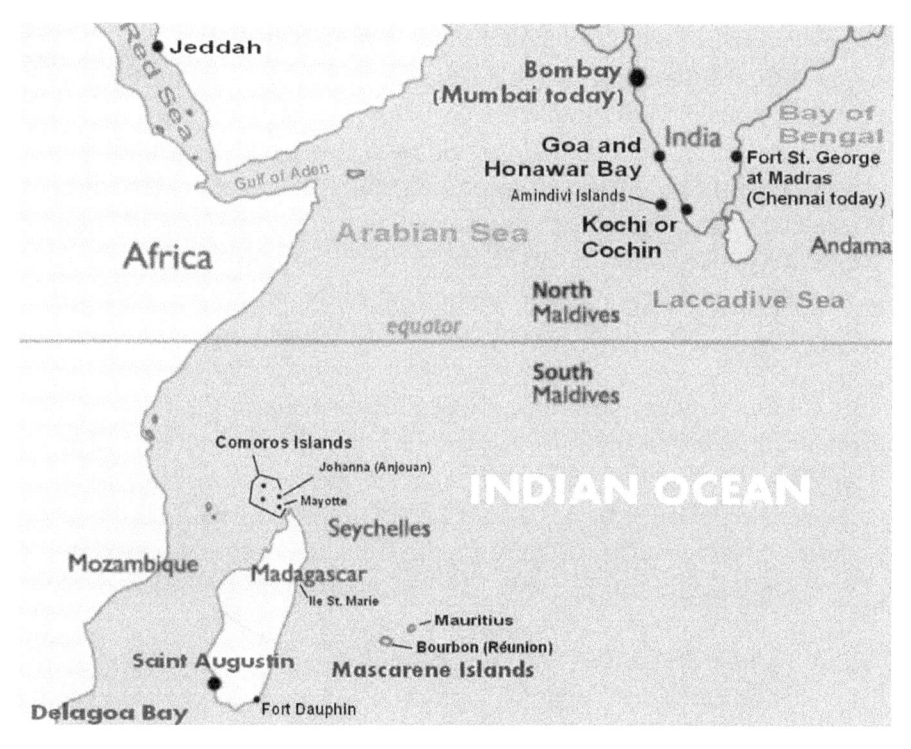

Taylor made this fuss prematurely. Indeed, many of his actions appear unorganized and tinged with paranoia as Lasinby saw them. The two ships that worried Taylor turned

---

[4] "Richard Lasinby, a prisoner of Taylor," in E. T. Fox, *Pirates in Their Own Words* (Fox Historical, 2014), 277; Downing told that they went again to the Red Sea and took another Moor ship, but he was probably confused by Plantain's tale of Edward England's first arrival on Madagascar. There simply was not enough time to have done this. He also seems to think that Edward England is still commanding *Cassandra*, but this is highly unlikely.

out not to be English, but Omani ships from Muscat with a cargo of horses.[5] Just as night fell, Taylor and Seager fired only a few shots before their quick surrender. Lasinby said "They brought aboard their captain and merchant and put them to torture to confess their money."[6] As Lasinby added in the *London* journal, the pirates originally believed or had hoped the Moor ships came from Mocha and had more riches than they professed. Taylor and Seager's men spent the night rummaging their ship and torturing the crew and when morning came, they realized they were in sight of the Indian shore.

Apparently, English ships were not far off – though these pirates feared that these vessels belonged to native Indian or Angrian forces, often called "pirates" by Englishmen. There was a fleet of ships sailing north just offshore, which also tended to extract more paranoia from these pirates. "They quickly debated about the disposition of the two Omani ships. They did not wish to be caught already entangled if they engaged a native fleet belonging to Konhoji Angrey.

Tim Travers in *Pirates: A History* gives an overview of the so-called Angrian "pirates." Several European companies vied for dominance in trade along the Indian coast. As a result, the English, Dutch, and Portuguese never held firm control over the region. The Portuguese had based themselves at Goa, West India, on the southern shore of the Mandavi estuary, and the English at Surat and Bombay. The Moghul Indian Empire, once a great power, was weakening because of Maratha incursions and internal strife. The Siddy, a naval force of Muslim Africans under the Sultan of Bijepur, occupied a fort at Murud-Janjira. Omanis, as well, from Muscat, the nationality of the two captured ships in Taylor and Seager's possession at the time, had raided Portuguese settlements on the Indian coast. Out of this power vacuum arose Konhoji Angrey (1669-1729), nominally allied with the emerging Maratha local power, centered in the state of Maharashtra. The British East India Company viewed Angrey as a "pirate," but the most proper interpretation, according to Travers, is that Angrey was a

---

[5] Muscat is a port on the west side of the Gulf of Omani, south of the entrance to the Persian Gulf, and across from modern Iran (former Persia).
[6] "Richard Lasinby, a prisoner of Taylor," in E. T. Fox, *Pirates in Their Own Words* (Fox Historical, 2014), 277.

Maratha privateer. Angrey extracted a fee for a "dastak," or a pass from foreign ships wishing to conduct trade on the Indian coast. To solidify his power, by 1703, Angrey established a string of forts from Bombay to Goa, and a strong naval force consisting of ten ghurabs or frigates of 16-30 cannon, with fifty gallivats of 4-10 cannon. Angrey's fleet tended to conceal themselves in "guerilla" fashion, waiting for foreign vessels to approach them. They became quite effective in their methods. By 1720, Angrian forces were quite feared by the EIC.[7]

Kanhoji Angré, Angrey or Conajee Angria or Sarkhel Angré was one of the first notable chief of the Maratha Navy in 18th century India. He fought against the British, Dutch and Portuguese naval interests on the coasts of India. As a result, his European enemies labeled him a pirate and sought to destroy him. Despite the attempts of the British and Portuguese to subdue Angrey, he remained undefeated until his death.

EIC officials had certainly been alerted to the *English* pirates' presence on the coast. Capt. James Macrae had arrived with his

---

[7] Tim Travers, *Pirates: A History* (Stroud, UK: Tim Travers, 2007), 245-247.

dilapidated pirate ship *Fancy* in Bombay on 26 October and they notified their directors by early December. In that same note, they indicated an active offensive against Angrey and their late success against Angrians "by burning two large ships, severall Galleys that were on the Stocks besides two of his Grabs."[8] They also mentioned "their intended Expedition Against the Pyrates," likely the southern-most Angrian strongholds of Gheriah and Deoghur.[9]

English newspapers reflected British prejudice and referred to Angrian forces as "pirates," such as an article in the *British Journal* of 15 June 1723. This article began with the EIC sending three ships "to cruise upon the Pirate Ships that infest [East Indian] seas," but then told that they were on the coast of "Angria."[10] The first impression of any westerner might be, of course, that these were *English* pirates. Similar references also appeared in official records. Newspapers often spoke the same way about *English* pirates in the Indian Ocean, confusing the issue for western readers.

James Macrae had been entertained by Gov. Charles Boone for some time after his arrival in Bombay, even passing up one opportunity to return home. Could it be that he planned to lead an expedition against the pirates who violated him personally? Had he sought to recover his ship? The pirates of *Victory* and *Cassandra* certainly believed it – as did Clement Downing.

Downing wrote that *London*, Capt. William Upton and *Chandos*, Capt. William Fazakerly, had earlier separated in April 1720 to repair their masts. They conducted their planned operations against Gheriah and Deoghur in September-October. Macrae made it to Bombay 26 October and most EIC references to a different fleet came *after* that date, around December. Macrae might easily have secured such a fleet, which probably headed south, in the direction the pirates would go. Still, the EIC fleet who first met *Victory* and *Cassandra* found them by accident on the 22nd of October, on their way back to Bombay, four days before Macrae's arrival on the 26th. This fleet sailed north after their recent debacle at Angrey's stronghold of Deoghur. Downing wrote:

---

[8] "Fort St. George, January 1720-1721," *Diary and Consultation Book, 1721* (Madras: Indian Government Press, 1930), 12.
[9] "Fort St. George, January 1720-1721."
[10] *British Journal*, 15 Jun 1723.

The whole naval Forces of Bombay were all mann'd, and our floating Engine or Machine [*Prahm*] along with us; and the *London*, Capt. Upton, was ordered to receive Mr. [Walter] Brown, one of the Council of Bombay, on board, in order to rectify all Affairs in behalf of the Company's Settlement at Anjango, and to hoist the Union Flag at their main Topmast-head. They were likewise to go in quest of the Pyrates, Taylor and England [Downing was unaware that England had been replaced by Taylor and also completely mistaken about the EIC fleet's intent – they were then after Angrians, not pirates].[11]

Again, this EIC fleet in October headed north back to Bombay and had not gone "in quest of the Pyrates." The EIC had learned of the pirates from Capt. Kirby in *Greenwich,* having arrived in Bombay from Johanna earlier with word of the taking of *Cassandra*. They were, however, otherwise occupied with Angrians at the time. Macrae may indeed have mounted his own run against these pirates to the south weeks or a month later– just not the battle-worn EIC fleet sailing northward to Bombay 22 Ocober.

Richard Taylor and Jasper Seager also had plenty of reason to worry about Angrian pirates – but they may have reasoned there was more to fear from the English EIC fleet. They were not aware, however, of the EIC's troubled offensive against Gheriah and Deoghur. EIC's mystery weapon, *Prahm*, had twice failed – proven itself an outright failure in the clashes earlier that month. The inexperienced Walter Brown's EIC fleet was drunk, wounded, and not looking for trouble.

The Indian seas in 1720 were filled with privateers and pirates of many nations, all struggling to establish dominance over each other. Adding to pirates' troubles, *Victory* had serious leaks, with four pumps going, including a borrowed pump from *Cassandra*. They were also in no shape for a fight and coming to the Indian coast in such condition must have been already an ill-conceived idea – a wounded tiger into the fray, so to speak.

Taylor and Seager's crews quickly held council to decide the fate of their captured Omani ships. Some argued to sink them, "horses and all," and be rid of the problem. Others, less ruthless, argued to throw their sails in the sea and disable their vessels to prevent them from alerting others to their presence. The decision fell on the latter,

---

[11] Downing, 46; Biddulph, *The Pirates of Malabar*, 150-152; *Prahm* was a floating battery with shot-proof sides and 48-pound cannon; designed by Walter Brown for the EIC to use against Angrian forces.

more humane approach, although the pirates did take their fresh water.[12]

While still debating the disposition of the Omani vessels, on 22nd of October, one of the distant fleet, including Walter Brown's wounded *Prahm*, spotted them, and tried desperately to ignore them, heading north. This confused the pirates. Still, if the distant fleet had decided to come after them, it would take some time before they came within firing range, so the pirates had time to complete their task with the Omanis.

They finished with the Omani ships as night fell and left them, moving away from the unknown fleet, whose course brought them nearer. Again, the pirates knew not whether the fleet was EIC or Angrian. If they approached, the pirates probably hoped that the fleet would at least stop to help the disabled Omanis first. Still, navigation at night was sketchy and the fleets drifted together, despite Brown's desire otherwise, remembering *Prahm's* earlier devastating debut against the Angrians.

Brown's EIC fleet flew British colors. The pirates raised red. The fleet finally came up to the Omanis at four in the morning, but, having the "land wind" then, could not stop, but appeared to keep closing on the pirates intentionally. The disorganized fleet ships came within range and began firing small arms and cannon and kept firing until daybreak, hoping for a lucky shot.

Taylor and Seager did not know what to do. They took the fleet chasing them for Angrian privateers, despite the British colors. Pirate ships often used flags of many nations to fool their victims – they assumed this was also true of Angrians. With only two leaky ships and 300 men (260 white and 40 black, which appeared to play a part in their thinking) they were grossly outnumbered. Eventually and "observing the indifferency of the fleet," or their avoidance of the disabled Omani ships, the pirates reasoned better that these vessels after them may not be Angrian ships, but EIC ships.[13] Still, something was wrong with them – they appeared disorganized. Downing identified them as "*London* [earlier sailed from Portsmouth with Macrae's *Cassandra*] with the *Victory* grab, the *Britannia*, the *Revenge*, the *Defiance* and the *Prahm*, a mighty big floating battery which the *Revenge* had in tow."[14] When the sea breeze rose and gave the pirate ships the best advantage, Seagar decided not to run, but rather engage them. In any other situation, this was perhaps unwise. But, not a spectator, Downing later interpreted, the dejected EIC fleet

---

[12] Lasinby, 278.
[13] Lasinby, 278.
[14] Downing, *Indian Wars*, 49.

captains showed great fear of the pirates and an inept response in battle:

> The *Victory* Pyrate discharged a Broad-side at the other [EIC] *Victory*, who never fired at her again, and the Pyrate told them at the same time, that the other Ship was the *Cassandra* [former consort of *London* - to instill fear]. There was such Confusion on board the *London*, that all the Ship was in an Uproar, and Capt. Upton frighted very much.[15]

From Lasinby's point-of-view, *Victory* and *Cassandra* came about and slipped amongst the EIC fleet guns blazing! As he said, this had the effect of making the EIC ships wrongly believe they were fireships intending a suicide run at them. Lasinby agreed with Downing that the fleet was worried about engaging with the pirates, but offered that the reverse was true as well. Both believed each other capable of using fire ships – and the fleet ultimately did – but for what reason? About sunset, after recovering from the alleged fright, the larger vessels or "Great Ships"gained upon them and kept with them all night, but then fell behind, no longer having the wind. Nothing happened until morning.

Downing said that the fleet ships had been too closely huddled until they got a land breeze to separate them and allowing them to maneuver. Downing's opinion was that the EIC crew focused too much attention on pecuniary details:

> In the mean time, the Pyrates got all things ready to engage. But Capt. Upton [captain of *London*], so soon as the Land breeze came off, was resolved not to fight, with out Mr. [Walter] Brown's Orders, who had a Commission from Governor [Charles] Boon[e] to hoist the Union Flag. Capt. Upton also required Mr. Brown to give him Security on the Company for all Damages the Ship might sustain. The Ship's Company was very eager to engage; Mr. Lyon... was then chief Mate of the *London*, and almost mad to see such ridiculous Proceedings. The Captain ordered a Man to the Mast-head to strike the [Union] Flag; the Fellow swore that he would send Flag-staff and all down with it. Accordingly he went up, and instead of striking the Flag, he drove the Fidd[16] out [essentially disengaging the topmast], and let the Flag-staff run down amain. This made the Pyrates laugh

---

[15] Downing, *Indian Wars*, 49; Downing had related details through the testimony of EIC fleet mariners after their return to Bombay.

[16] A "fid" or "fidd" is a square wooden or iron bar that takes the weight of a topmast stepped to a lower mast by being passed through holes in both masts.

in their Sleeve, tho' they did not well know how to venture to engage for they did not like the Looks of the Bombay Man of War.[17]

Lasinby saw "only some few Gallevats & a Small katch to Leeward."[18] He said that the fleet's crews were vacating one "Gallevat," but may have mistakenly referred to the ketch. Afterwards, the rest moved away. The pirates bore down on the ketch – "mighty big floating battery" *Prahm*, according to a possibly cheerleading Downing – and watched as the Company men vacated this "ketch" for a gallivat. Then, they set fire to *Prahm*, which quite annoyed Downing with this waste of resources. *Victory* and *Cassandra* managed to avoid the fireship, but could not keep up with the more nimble gallivat.[19]

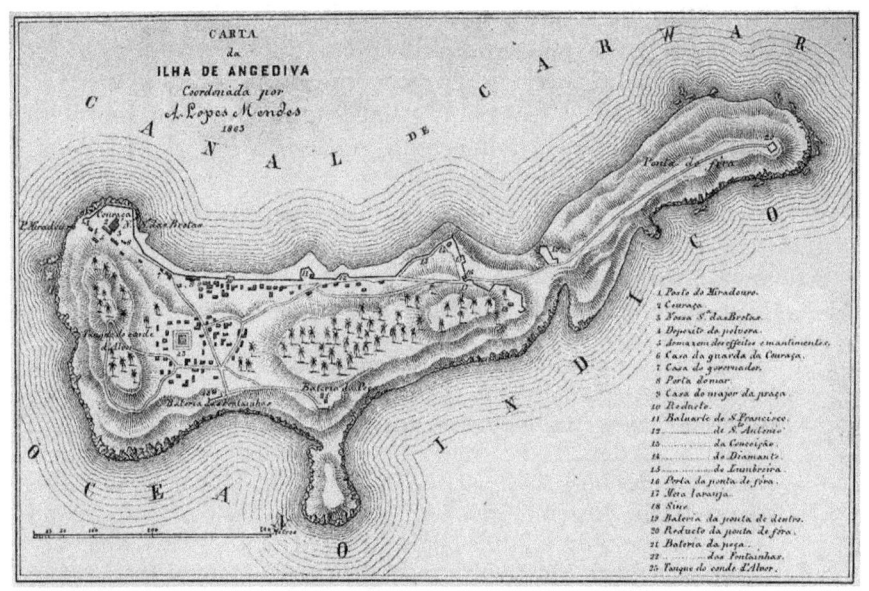

António Lopes Mendes, *Anjediva Island* (1886); source: A India portugueza; breve descripção das possessões portuguezas na Asia, dividida em dois volumes. Publicada por ordem do Ministerio da Marinha by Lopes Mendes, António, 1835-1894.

As Downing wrote, "After this the Pyrates made off, without any further Attempt on our Ships."[20] About an hour later, the

---

[17] Downing, *Indian Wars*, 49-50; *London* journal, f. 166.
[18] *London* journal, f. 166.
[19] Lasinby, 278-279; one possibility is that *Prahm*, or the "mighty big floating battery" that Downing referred to, was originally intended as a fireship and Downing misunderstood from tales he heard of the engagement.
[20] Downing, *Indian Wars*, 50.

pirates captured another gallivat that ran to their north. She was laden with bales of cotton intended for Calicut or Kozhikode. Taylor questioned the men of their captured vessel about the fleet they had just fought. These men, who had just left "Gogo," offered little to no information on them, even as the pirates tortured them by putting their limbs in a vise. They threw their cargo overboard and after a day, set the men free with a try sail and a little water. Afterward, they withdrew from sight of the shore.[21]

Cruising to southward along southwest India, the pirates ran along the Malabar Coast between Goa and Karwar (about 87 km), approaching Anjediva or Anjadip Island, just south of Karwar or southern Goa. They sent a boat to reconnoiter the islands for possible prizes. The boat sighted two grabs and returned at about two in the morning. Weighing anchor, *Victory* and *Cassandra* sought these grabs and when day broke, the grabs saw them. They hurried back to the island and nestled under the walls of Fort Anjediva.

Fort Anjediva off of Karwar (no date); source: http://www.supergoa.com/

The guns of the fort held off the pirates and protected the grabs. Disappointed, *Victory* and *Cassandra* held council on whether to leave or continue searching for prizes. They decided to forget the grabs, keep going, and sailed further south.

The next morning at Honawar Bay, they took an almost abandoned ship with "no one aboard but a Dutchman and two

---

[21] Lasinby, 279.

Portuguese, the captain being ashore with his officers."[22] The pirates recognized an opportunity to ransom the vessel and sent a letter ashore to inform their captain. He could have his ship back if he were to supply them with fresh water and provisions. The captain agreed and sent word that he would deliver it to them, but not over the bar – away from the bay. As Lasinby later told *London's* clerk:

> ... att night, [the captain of the ship] sent on board his Mate named Frank Harmless with a letter to y:m that if they would deliver the Ship into possession over ye Barr would Supply y:m with what water & provisions they wanted, and not before.[23]

The pirates did not trust Harmless and took this for a trap. So, they forced the Dutchman and Portuguese aboard their ship, burned their vessel, and headed for the Laccadives or Cannonore Islands, separated from the Amindivi Islands roughly by the 11th parallel north and from the atoll of Minicoy (Maliku).

The crews of *Victory* and *Cassandra*, by the East India Company man Richard Lasinby's interpretation, conducted themselves in an extraordinarily vile fashion. They also appeared incompetent to a trained officer like Lasinby. His description of their behavior concerning a small vessel from the island of Amindivi (probably Kadmat) and the natives of that island reflect sheer abhorrence. Still, the incompetence may explain the changes in command of *Cassandra* and the arguments between Richard Taylor and Olivier LeVasseur before they later returned to southern waters near Mauritius.

Immediately upon entering the Amindivi Islands three days later, the pirates captured a local "small Manchew, with the Govr of Carwar's[24] pass on."[25] Upon hearing of the island's offerings, they sent a boat ashore to investigate which returned an account of a large village with an abundance of fresh water. Having failed in their attempt to extort supplies at "Anjedivi" (Amini?) due to lack of anchorage, they again sought the

---

[22] Lasinby, 280.
[23] London: Journal, f. 167.
[24] Probably not "Karwar," but Cadamum or Kadmat Island; adjacent to Amini Island.
[25] London: Journal, f. 167.

desperately needed water at the island of "Melindra" (perhaps Kavaratti[26]).

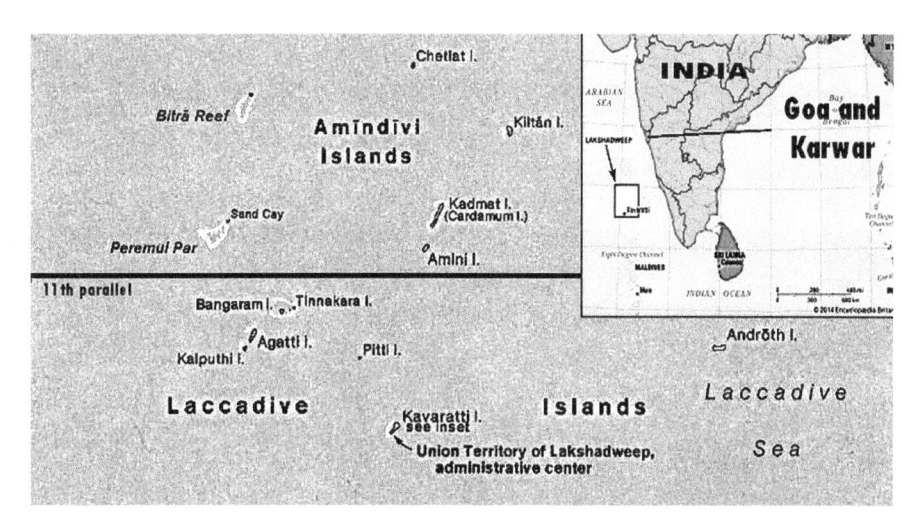

At the sight of *Victory* and *Cassandra*, the male inhabitants fled in boats to a nearby island. The pirates found the water they needed, but two days afterwards, Lasinby told:

> ... [the male islanders left] abundance of women and children hidden in the bushes, which the Pirates found and forced to their barbarous inclinations. Afterwards they destroyed all the coconut trees and everything else they met with and then burnt the houses and churches.[27]

James Horsburgh's *India Directory* tells that "in high latitudes, gales of wind, or storms, blow sometimes from one direction several days together, particularly during winter...

---

[26] Kavaratti is an island south of Amini, 218 miles off the shore of Kochi or Cochin on the mainland, with a long brackish pond in its center, surrounded by screwpine and coconut palms. It's inhabitants speak Malayalam and may have been erroneously identified as "Melindra." The island today has 190 ponds to collect monsoon waters and would be an obvious choice to collect water for the pirate ships if this reflects the geographic situation of nearly 300 years ago.
[27] Lasinby, 280.

prevailing from westward."[28] American missionary Rev. John Lowrie added "boats founder at once and all on board frequently perish."[29]

As if by divine retribution to smite these pirates nearing Christmas 1720, one such great gale arose. It easily surprised these West Indian pirates, unused as they were to East Indies' atmospheric phenomenon. The wind's force tore anchor cables, and propelled *Victory* and *Cassandra* west from the island and even threatened to drive them into the Indian shore. Seventy of their people and several casks of water had been stranded alone on the recently-razed island with burned houses and destroyed provisions for ten days until they were able to return for them.

Once they had retrieved their men and fresh water from the island, Taylor and Seager made for Cochin, or Kochi to seek provisions from the Dutch, supposed friends of pirates. In three days, as they headed to Cochin, they saw and took a small vessel owned by Gov. Robert Adams of Calicut. Its master John Tawke was drunk when they found him off nearby Tellicherry. His tongue may have been more loose than usual. Tawke inquired as to the health of their prisoner Richard Lasinby, having served with him in *Duke of Cambridge* on a voyage to Bengal. He also told them about an expedition against them of which he had probably heard about through Gov. Adams:

[Tawke] began presently to tell me y^t My Old Capt: Macrae was fitting out after y:^{m}, att which news ye QrMaster [LeVasseur] told me to prepare for the next Day Swore he would hang me like a Dog as I was.[30]

This news threw the pirates into a rage. They resented Edward England's civil treatment of Macrae by giving him

---

[28] James Horsburgh, *India Directory, or, Directions for Sailing to and from the East...*, Vol. 1 (London: W. H. Allen & Co., 1836), vii.
[29] John Cameron Lowrie, *Travels in North India: Containing Notices of the Hindus ; Journals of a Voyage on the Ganges and a Tour to Lahor ; Notes on the Himalaya Mountains and the Hill Tribes, Including a Sketch of Missionary Undertakings* (Philadelphia: Presbyterian Board of Education, 1842), 87.
[30] London: Journal, f. 167b.

Fancy and now they felt that this planned expedition against them was the result. Lasinby quoted Taylor's quartermaster, likely Olivier LeVasseur, as he shouted:

> The Villain that we treated so civilly as to give him a ship and other presents, and now to come armed against us? He ought to be hanged, and since we cannot shew our resentment on him, let us hang the dogs who wish him well if clear. Damn [Edward] England![31]

Calicut - Plate thirty-three from the first volume of James Forbes' "Oriental Memoirs", a work in the form of a series of letters richly illustrated, describing various aspects of nature, people, buildings and places he observed during his travels in India in the 1760s-70s. In 1772, Forbes (1749-1819) was appointed Warehousekeeper at the factory in Anjengo, Travancore in South India. His journey to the South of India took him through the coastal towns of Tellicherry, Calicut and Cochin. Forbes described the historic Calicut town in the erstwhile Malabar in this way: 'This humble fishing-town, scattered among the cocoa-nut woods on the coast of Malabar is all that remains of the grand emporium of Calicut, which was esteemed among the first commercial cities in India, when Vasco Da Gama, arrived there after his adventurous passage round the Cape of Good hope, at the end of the 16th Century.'

---

[31] Lasinby, 281.

180   Sailing East

Lasinby, as Macrae's former officer, immediately felt apprehensive. Lasinby asserted that he "would take the first opportunity to fight against them."[32] The pirates guessed that as well, but they would deal with him later and sent him below.

Letters from the Chief and Council of Anjengo (modern Anchuthengu) were sent to Madras on the 15th and 16th of December help to time this event. They enclosed copies of letters from Gov. Adams at Calicut concerning "two pirates near Cochin who had lately taken Capt. Tawke in a Ketch belong'g to that place."[33] Adams probably also increased the tone of urgency of Macrae's planned expedition against them.

Gov. Adams was the source of the intelligence on this intended action against the pirates and so, they angrily sailed directly for his home of Calicut. When they arrived, the two pirate ships endeavored to take a large Moor vessel coming from port, but were repelled by shore guns. The pirates feared that Macrae was personally hunting them and they may have been correct. Lasinby said "I was down below as usual thinking the story Cap^n Tawk told y:^{m} was forgot," but Richard Taylor and his quartermaster (LeVasseur?) ordered Lasinby, previously stashed below, to the deck.[34] They angrily ordered him to stand directly in the bow, in the hopes that the fort's guns might kill him. Lasinby refused and the quartermaster (LeVasseur) told him that if did not or left the deck afterwards, he would shoot him through the head. Lasinby told him to shoot him now so he could avoid such misery, and suggested that Capt. Taylor might be "lame of his hands." Taylor raged at this insult, "according to his Desire he fecht his Cane and began to Labour me unmercifully."[35] Some of the crew saw Taylor beating Lasinby with his cane and "hindered him and said he should be ashamed to so abuse [Lasinby], telling him they would have to put [Lasinby] ashore at Cochin" with Capt. Tawke.[36]

---

[32] Lasinby, 281.
[33] "Fort St. George, January 1720-1721," *Diary and Consultation Book, 1721* (Madras: Indian Government Press, 1930), 5.
[34] London: Journal, f. 168.
[35] London: Journal, f. 168.
[36] Lasinby, 281.

Taylor would not consent to that. Beaten and bruised, Richard Lasinby had been stashed below again. *Victory* and *Cassandra* moved out of range of the shore guns, another venture failed.

The next day, they came up with a Dutch galliot laden with limestone bound for Cochin. They put Capt. Tawke aboard her and Taylor's crew again urged their captain to release the battered Lasinby. Taylor again refused, saying that Lasinby knew all their plans for the next year, which was a weak excuse since their plans were rarely consistent. Still, many were inclined with Taylor's thinking. The men argued still, which so enraged Taylor that he swore to cut Lasinby's arm off before letting him go![37]

Again, the constant bickering between Taylor, his men, and his quartermaster's faction would eventually lead to yet another change. Part of the crew obviously supported LeVasseur's opinion and Taylor had demonstrated himself to be unusually harsh. They may have believed that they had put the wrong man in charge – the experienced and less brutish LeVasseur would seem to them a valid replacement. Lasinby rarely saw Jasper Seager, commanding *Victory* – thus, he never spoke of his opinion on these matters.

Victory and *Cassandra* again had sailed for Cochin and arrived in a day's time. They were fairly safe there, among Dutch friends, who had a habit of facilitating pirate activities and trading in illegal merchandise. When they arrived, they sent a letter by a canoe they encountered heading that way and slipped into the road. Saluting the fort with eleven shots each, the fort returned them. That night, "there Came on board a Large Boat Laden with fresh Provisions & Liquors with ye Serv:^{t} of an Inhabitant of y^t [that] place Vulgarly Called Jno: Trumpett He told them to unmoor and make a little further south where they could have everything they needed, including naval stores. The next day, much to their joy,

---

[37] Lasinby, 281-282.

182   Sailing East

Trumpett returned with about "90 Legors [lagers of arrack drink] and 60 bales of Sugarr."[38]

The next day, the pirates delivered by way of payment "a fine Table Clock... taken in our Ship [*Cassandra*] a Present to ye Gov:^{r} also a Large Gold Watch to his Daughter who in return sent y^m 10 Bales of Sugarr."[39] When the governor received his lavish gifts, all that the pirates needed and wanted was granted them. The wealthy pirates paid Trumpett £6,000 to £7,000 and "threw ducatoons in the boats by handfuls for the boatsmen to scramble for."[40]

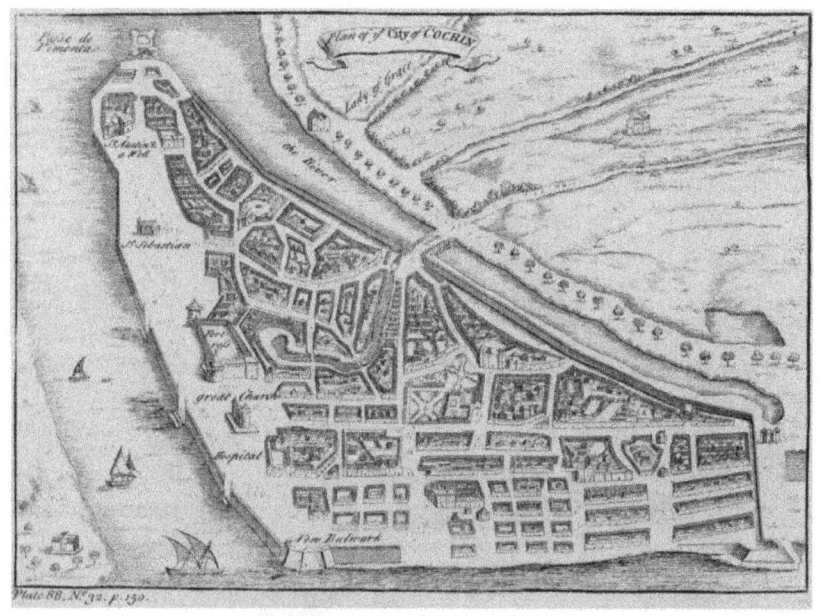

Baldeous, *City of Cochin* (1672)

Victory and *Cassandra* intended to weigh anchor that night, but there was little wind, so they remained another day. Trumpett again returned with "more arrack, piece goods and ready-made clothes," and "brought with him a person which

---

[38] *London*: Journal, f. 169; Lasinby, 281-282; Arrack is a distilled alcoholic drink typically produced in South Asia and Southeast Asia, made from either the fermented sap of coconut flowers, sugarcane, grain (e.g. red rice) or fruit, depending upon the country of origin; a lager is a small wooden barrel with a plug for dispensing liquid.
[39] *London*: Journal, f. 169.
[40] Lasinby, 282; Ducatoons were crown-sized silver coins of the 16th-18th centuries.

the said Trumpet assured them was the Fiscall of Cochin."[41] As Richard Lasinby told in his official narrative, that noon, they spotted another sail to the south:

> And this Deponent further saith That the said John Trumpet and the other person said to be the Fiscall were on board the Cassandra when she with her Consort first chased said Ship and continued on board till next day and that it was the Generall discourse among the Cassandra's Ships Company that said Two persons had assured their Captain he might take the said Ship from under the Fort without Molestation and at the same time desir'd she might not be carry'd away because they would give as much for her as any others Whereupon the Captain having desir'd the said Two persons to go into their Boat then along the Cassandra's side telling them it was time enough to talk of that matter when she was taken, he caused the Cassandra and Victoria to stand in Boldly into Cochin Road to board said Ship and they were within a Cables length or two of her but then the Fort Fir'd Two of their small Guns at them which this Deponent believes were not done with design to hurt either because he saw the Shot fall short of them[;] however both said Ships thereupon instantly bore out of the Road making an easy Sail to the Southward and Anchor'd at night at Mud Bay a place where the Dutch have a House and their Ships sometimes ly at[.] That Night a great Boat was sent to said pyrates at Mud Bay to get them Water and to acquaint them If they would stay there some few days longer they might expect a very Rich Ship to pass by Commanded by the General of Bombay's Brother whereupon the next morning the pyrates weigh'd and Cruiz'd to the Southward.[42]

This narrative of Lasinby's was more detailed on this event. Trumpett, as well as the Fiscal of Cochin, assured them that

---

[41] Lasinby, 282; *London*: Journal, f. 176; A "fiscal" was an admiralty officer whose duty it was to inspect cargos.
[42] *London*: Journal, f. 176b.

they may have this prize and that the Cochins would buy her from the pirates at a good price. It seemed that the officers of the fort, however, did not agree with Trumpett and the Fiscal. When they weighed after the vessel Fort Cochin fired her guns, forcing them back. The Dutch town appeared more pecuniary in their methods than most Europeans, which reflects a similar characteristic of Capetown, visited by Comm. Mathews in Chapter Six.[43]

Gov. Charles Boone's brother's ship might be a rich prize, but there were other considerations. Probably fearing a trap, the pirates held another council just off the Cochin Coast. Some of the men had wished to return to Madagascar, and some wanted to stay and search for another rich Mughal ship. Lasinby mentioned nothing else in regard to Boone's richly-laden vessel. Perhaps these paranoid pirates believed that it was led by their personal nemesis, Capt. James Macrae.[44]

They decided to keep going, but the first sail they chased got away, bringing *Victory* nine miles or three leagues away from *Cassandra*. Then, five sail appeared and bore down on them. *Victory* turned and headed back to *Cassandra* with all haste, certain that this was the expedition under Macrae. Happily for these paranoid pirates, they got clear of these ships, save one grab which came near, but finally turned away.

The pirates caroused and rejoiced their escape from the former captain of *Cassandra*, celebrating Christmas "in a most riotous manner, destroying most of the fresh provision [about two-thirds]."[45] After three days, the effects of the liquor wore off and they decided to make for Mauritius to repair the badly-leaking *Victory* and wait out the southern hemisphere's hurricane season of December to April. Lasinby regarded their poor condition:

> In their passage thither, they expected her to founder every day, and were several times going to quit her, were it not for scarcity of water and provisions, and that there was still a quantity of arrack aboard.[46]

---

[43] Lasinby, 282-283.
[44] Lasinby, 283.
[45] Lasinby, 284.
[46] Lasinby, 284.

They had only one bottle of water for each man per day, no more than two pounds of beef and a small quantity of rice for ten men per day. Lasinby believed that the arrack and sugar probably saved their lives.

By this time, the East India Company no longer saw these pirates as much of a threat. "A Gallivat in the fleet in quest of the Pyrates" reported the Council at Anjengo on 6th of January 1721, "that they had seen two of them at abt. Four leagues distant," but could not catch them.[47] Pres. or Gov. Boone asked whether it was expedient to bother with these pirates; that if they did, they may drive them to areas where they would interfere more with their trade, like Ceylon (Sri Lanka). The best advice that he had heard was to hire a small vessel to go up and down the coast carrying word of their latest position and to warn local shipping how to avoid them. He offered that Gunner Hugonin had offered his own vessel at a reasonable rate for that purpose.

The pirates of *Victory* and *Cassandra* had been done with them as well and left their shores. Truth be told, they were probably far too annoyed with running from their alleged nemesis Capt. James Macrae. A beaten and bruised Richard Lasinby, though still held captive by these men, might finally have some peace![48]

---

[47] "Fort St. George, January 1720-1721," *Diary and Consultation Book, 1721* (Madras: Indian Government Press, 1930), 17.
[48] "Fort St. George, January 1720-1721."

Chapter 4: Congdon

The Extraordinary Misunderstood Life Of One-Armed Edward Congdon

Capt. Vincent Pearse of HMS *Phoenix* sailed from his station at New York on the 8th of February 1718. Word of the king's Act for the Suppression of Piracy, enacted the previous 5th of September had spread around the fleet. It had time to reach the "pirate nest" of the Bahamas and the hundreds, if not thousands of pirates there. Pearse carried a formal copy of that pardon, but he still remained apprehensive of the reception that he was to receive upon his arrival.

Fifteen days later, on the 23rd of February, *Phoenix* slipped into Nassau Town Harbor at the island of New Providence. Pearse's worry proved unjustified. In only a week, by the time of his first letter to the Admiralty on the 4th of March, he had taken the surrenders of Capt. Francis Leslie, Thomas Nichols, Josiah Burgess, and even Benjamin Hornigold, along with 114 of their companies. Henry Jennings had already left for his family home of Bermuda to surrender. This portion of HMS *Phoenix's* log has been transcribed – it appears in the appendix.

The former mariners-turned-pirates had mostly lost interest in the sudden greedy passion that resulted from the massive Spanish treasure fleet wrecked on the Florida shores. Eleven treasure ships spilled over with 14,000,000 pesos worth of silver alone, plus gold and jewels spilled in the shallow depths of the East Florida shoreline. The hurricane that wrecked the fleet came on the 30th day of July 1715. It had been two-and-a-half years since that event and the tremendous appetite for treasure had faded – most of it already fished out of the waters by then. Most substantial, wealthier men looked forward to returning to their normal lives – preferably without the worry of avoiding the noose. The poorer lot of pirates would essentially return to their old patterns, perhaps more rebellious or desperate in their finances.

By the time that Capt. Pearse had taken this first grouping of surrenders, he had 209 in all, including Richard Taylor, John Augur, Leigh Ashworth and his sloop *Mary's* surgeon Jonathan Cockram, Palsgrave Williams, and Charles Vane. Some, like Taylor, Augur, Williams, and Vane, had returned to piracy, along with others who might have joined their crews. Some, however, responded as the king hoped and surrendered a second time to Gov. Robert Johnson of South Carolina just to make certain of their freedom from justice. Moreover, others on Pearse's list like Daniel Stillwell returned to legitimate maritime business, including the nominal stretch of that legitimacy into the more respectable smuggling business. The Jennings of Smith's Tribe, Bermuda had long engaged in that time-honored profession. Their son, the eager reform-minded pirate Henry Jennings had returned to his family's home with *Barsheba* to accept his pardon directly from Gov. Benjamin Bennett before Pearse's arrival at the Bahamas. Bennett's letter told:

> ... vessels that went lately out from Providence there were several others att sea (vizt.) one Tatch [Thache] with whom is Major Bonnett of Barbados in a ship [*QAR*] of 36 guns and 300 men, also in company with them a sloop [*Revenge*] of 12 guns and 115 men, and two other ships, in all which, it is computed there are 700 men or thereabt., one Coudon [Congdon] in a sloop of 12 guns, 6 pattireroes, 12 brass bases and 130 men, a French ship of 30 guns and 350 men most of that Nation [Bonadvis?], a French sloop [LeVasseur?} of 6 guns and 40 men, one Vaine in a sloop of 6 guns and 60 men,

and several others may be out that I have not been inform'd off.[1]

Some pirates like Edward "Blackbeard" Thache had been away for many months from New Providence Island. A few would surrender later there upon their return. And some, like Othenius or Othniel Davis, partner of Thomas Porter, would surrender to Gov. Woodes Rogers upon his eventual arrival, take a commission from him, and another from Johnson in July.[2] One such pirate, a "Sloop call'd the Dragon being gone out with Ninty Eight Men about eighteen Days before my arrival," under the command of Edward Congdon, had gone to Africa's Guinea Coast and had planned afterward to cruise Brazil.[3]

Congdon later declared himself a native of Plymouth, England. Newspapers generally told brief blurbs of his exploits in the West Indies. Still, newspaper information was greatly in error. He captured *Dauphin* with a shipment of wine for the Poulier brothers of Sainte-Crois, Tenerife in 1718. He took merchant ship *Alexander* of London on 18 March 1718, northwest of Cape Verde Islands. He sailed with two other pirates (one *Rover*, Capt. Butcher [La Buse?], and the other of 12 guns and 170 men). The three of them together allegedly took *Margaret* of London, Capt. Cassle, *Society*, Capt. Webley, and *Coulston*, Capt. Skinner in July 1718. Although, *Coulston* probably had not been taken by pirates and Capt. Skinner probably did not die being tortured – he died of natural causes

---

[1] "America and West Indies: May 1718," in *Calendar of State Papers Colonial, America and West Indies: Volume 30, 1717-1718*, ed. Cecil Headlam (London: His Majesty's Stationery Office, 1930), 242-264.

[2] Othniel Davis was "late Quartermaster of ye Sloop Egale"; received commission from Robert Johnson of South Carolina as privateer against Spain; became master of sloop *Mexico Cruizer;* part-owner with Thomas Porter (of Bahamas pirate Porter brothers, with Daniel), and sometime master of *Moville Trader*.

[3] National Archives, London, Pearse to Admiralty, 4 Mar 1718, ADM 1/2282; "James Phipps and John Stevenson to the Royal African Company," 12 Jan 1720, in Elizabeth Donnan, Documents illustrative of the history of the slave trade to America, Vol. II (Washington: Carnegie Institution of Washington, 1931), 242-243; "Pyrates design to range on the Coast to Windward till end of Febry, then for the Coast of Brazil, and thence to Madagascar."

a year later. Congdon eventually surrendered to Woodes Rogers in the Bahamas before January 1719 with two sloops.

> London, August 1. Letters from Barbadoes bring the unwelcome News, that Three Pirate Ships, viz. the Dragon, Capt. Conwel the Rover, Capt. Butcher, and a Sloop of twelve Guns and 170. Men, have taken the following Merchant Ships; namely, the Margaret of London, Capt. Caffle, the Society, Capt. Webley, and the Skinner, Capt. Coulston, both from Bristol, a Bristol Sloop, Capt. Wardner, a Dutch Ship, and another, whose Names was not known.

"London, August 1," *Boston News-Letter*, 17 Nov 1718, "Three Pirate Ships," with "Dragon, Capt. Conwel [Congdon]" specifically named.

Please note that the last half of the previous paragraph's detail from two newspaper articles convinced Charles Johnson to attribute this detail to Edward England. The article, however, *specifically* mentioned Congden's name and the name of his ship, though, yes, Edward England could have captained the unattributed 12-gun sloop. The explanation can be found in the opening of Chapter Two.[4]

Capt. Charles Johnson, Nathaniel Mist or the most likely author of *A General History of the Pyrates*, took great license with his facts. Still, this author certainly had at least a newspaper connection to *Le Mercure* in Paris. The details of Congdon's life in France and that he originated in the port of Plymouth, both mentioned by this author, may derive from that source. Still, he knew few other personal details and called him simply "Capt. Condent." This author also noted in his two-volume 4th edition that Congdon helped take the *Cassandra*, using his ship "*Flying Dragon,*" but both points are "fake news," to use a modern rhetorical epithet. Jasper Seager and Edward England , in their two ships alone took *Cassandra*. Likewise, Congdon's ship was 40-gun *Dragon*, according to a plethora of other primary

---

[4] "The Examination of Richard Moor, 31 October 1724 (and addendum, 5 November 1724), HCA 1/55, ff. 94-97," transcribed in E. T. Fox, ed., *Pirates in Their Own Words* (Fox Historical, 2014), 207-213; National Archives, London, Pearse to Admiralty, 3 Jun 1718, ADM 1/2282; Konstam, *Blackbeard*, 229; *Voyages: The Trans-Atlantic Slave Trade Database,* http://www.slavevoyages.org; *Weekly Packet*, 2 Aug 1718; *Boston News-Letter*, 17 Nov 1718, 1.

sources printed years before *A General History's* first publication in May 1724.

Most modern pirate authors, also misunderstand Congdon's true name, remarkably using the invention "Christopher Condent." Even professional historians and archaeologists still use this name in their work, but is there actual evidence for its use? The name "Christopher" never appeared in the French sources which told the most about this pirate. They repeatedly and ubiquitously refer to him as "Edward Congdon." One would have to wonder why Johnson, who at least had some connections to French newspapers, did not call him the same. Perhaps his connection was not direct, or in print, as in possession of an actual copy of *Le Mercure* itself – perhaps it was verbal or mere second-hand.

"Capt. Jerry Condent" in Evening Post (Charleston, South Carolina), August 6, 1927, 5.

Surname variations are abundant in pirate stories, partly due to eighteenth-century spellings relying typically upon phonetics. There are many Congdons, few Condents and none with the given name "Christopher" in records of the proper time on Ancestry.com, or in books older than 1953.[5] This "Christopher" phenomenon was not based on phonetic variations, but something else entirely. Nothing appeared earlier in a newspaper, record, or book suggesting that this pirate's name was ever Christopher!

An article in Washington, DC's *Evening Star*, 19 August 1906, Page 11, called "Stories of the Pirates, by John L. White, of course, strictly copies Johnson's 4th edition with "Captain Condent." Moreover, no newspaper articles in the Library of Congress collection ever printed a story about "Christopher Condent" and those newspapers date back to the 18th century. Same goes for Genealogy.com's database dating back to 1704. An article in the *Morning Star* (Rockford, Illinois), 2 April 1899, and Washington, DC's Evening Star, of 19 August 1906 again reprints *A General History's* "Capt. Condent" and never gives his first name. In fact, many ads for reprinting and selling copies of this book and its many nearly identical descendants attest to its great popularity. Still, no "Christophers" appeared in their pages. Finally, a story appearing in a South Carolina newspaper in 1926 called him "Jerry Condent." Again, *not* "Christopher."

Jerry? The question's muddy answer quickly becomes clear. The reason why there are so many names from which to choose is not because pirates were particularly fond of aliases – proudly arrogant pirates actually weren't – but because the general public, including professionals, liked to casually fantasize! The idea that pirates were fond of aliases may just be a convenient way for amateur historians to accept more of Johnson's mistakes. Pirates usually seemed too proud of their vocation to hide their name.

The author of that South Carolina article probably had a son or friend named Jerry and he added the name to please them – perhaps for their birthday or other special occasion. At the time, it may have been a joke or game, but, no one really remembers why these authors did what they did. The same happened with "Christopher," no doubt. The next generation was apt to accept this as gospel truth – and incorporated the name into "official"

---

[5] Patrick Pringle, *Jolly Roger: The Story of the Golden Age of Piracy* (1953), Dover ed. (New York: Dover Publications, 2001), 226; Pringle refers to him in *Jolly Roger* as "Christopher Condent," although no source is given.

pirate dogma! Massive digitization and digital access to this data has exposed these errors of our past historiography.

Illustrating the dangers of relying on faulty information is John De Bry's version of "Christopher Condent's *Fiery Dragon*," a tale which appears in the scholarly book *X Marks the Spot*. De Bry said that he received his information from Kenneth Kinkor at Mystic Seaport Museum, another known archaeologist on the Whydah expedtion. Fortunately, De Bry is superb at locating archival sources, but his inability to to accurately interpret them, his reliance on the secondary colorful hearsay and flamboyance from *A General History*, does not reflect the abilities of other archaeologists in this book. De Bry is excellent at combing foreign archives; however, his trusting reliance on Johnson's narrative of "Christopher Condent" was not so wise a decision. It potentially puts every effort he makes at risk.

Aside from flagrantly erroneous names in the title, the biases of Capt. Charles Johnson, or rather Nathaniel Mist, crept into and infected de Bry's scientific and archaeological analyses. De Bry included much of Johnson's flamboyant fiction in his historical preface, including the elaborate tale of how he lost his arm when an Eastern Indian (despite missing the arm well *before* he traveled to the East Indies) shot him and how the crew "hack'd him to Pieces, and the Gunner ripping up his Belly," tore out his heart and ate it! De Bry used Johnson's narrative of Condent's capture of *Prince Eugene* on 20 February 1720 [J: 9 Feb] to argue about artifact findings. This, however, is highly dangerous because *A General History* contains so many errors. Still, this detail just happened to be true – but Nathaniel Mist had sufficient evidence available to tell this tale.

Congdon had trade dealings with the captain of another *Prince Eugene*, Joseph Stratton just a few months later, only months after Congdon's arrival at Île Saint-Marie! Stratton was one of his first customers and clearly not taken by any pirate! He sailed this Bristolian *Prince Eugene* back to Virginia where he was arrested by Royal Navy personnel. In realty, there were actually two ships by the same name and Edward Congdon did capture the first earlier in 1720! This vessel was the Flemish one, a vessel of Ostend, although purchased from the English about 1715. This fact probably prevented de Bry from making a serious mistake!

The Ostend or Belgian *Prince Eugene* had been taken by a 38-gun, 280-man "Dragon pirate" in the same location, on its way home from China. James Naish's report detailed the Ostend *Dragon:* "She [Dragon] Sails Princely Well, Mounts forty Guns, & Twenty Brass Pieces upon Swiffles on their Gunnil, Two of them also, with one Chorn, in each Top & Small Arms for Twice her Complement, being Three hundred & Twenty Men when I left them on Feb:ry 16/27; they were compleately Stored with Ammunition, & Provision at full Allowance for fiveteen Months. We found them a Generous, tho' Common, Enemy, for Our Loss inconsiderable in the Ships Large & Valuable Cargoe"[6] It was coincident with the itineraries of both Edward England and Edward Congdon, causing much confusion between them. Nathaniel Mist or "Johnson" conflated much between these two pirates![7]

Most importantly, however, there is absolutely no quandary about this pirate's name. It was certainly Edward Congdon, *not* Christopher Condent and his ship is never mentioned in primary records, other than the assumed "primary," actually secondary, Johnson, as *"Fiery Dragon,"* just *"Dragon."* Imaginations run wild! There are far too many primary records that predate Johnson's 1724 book and 1726 second volume affirming this, including a large percentage of French origin. These will be explored throughout the chapter.

Too Dangerous to Retire
In the West Indies

Again, Capt. Vincent Pearse of HMS *Phoenix* came to New Providence Island of the Bahamas 23 February 1718. The king had recently issued his pardon and stipulations for its acceptance on 5 September 1717. Pearse intended to take surrenders from the pirates of that pirate nest in accordance with those provisions. In his letter to the Admiralty of 3 June from that location, Pearse sent a list of 209 pirates who had

---

[6] James Naish, "James Naish on board the House of Austria," IOR/E/1/11 ff. 226: 15 Jun 1720. *See* Appendix for a transcription of the entire report.
[7] *Daily Courant,* 28 Jun 1720; John de Bry, "Christopher Condent's *Fiery Dragon,"* *X Marks the Spot: The Archaeology of Piracy,* ed. by Russell Skowroneck and Charles R. Ewen (Gainesville: University Press of Florida), 100-130.

surrendered. He also wrote of the situation at the Bahamas concerning these pirates: number, ships, who was in, who was out and when expected. In that letter, he mentioned Congdon of *Dragon*, who had left New Providence with 98 men on about 5 February. Obviously, Congdon had been successful at picking up new recruits, for by March:

> One Mr. Ignatious Brown late Super Cargo of the Alexander of London Tho. Spencer Master but last from Madeira with wine for Boston, and one Capt. Ant. French a passenger, arriv'd here four days Since & Report that they Sail'd from Madera the 11 March last and that on the 18 following was taken in the Lat. of 26 0 28' & Longt from Madera 10 0 57' Wt by a Pirate Sloop Called the Dragon and Commanded by one Congdon (which I gave their Lordships an acct Sail'd from Providence before my arrival there) she had 130 Men 12 Six pounders & 12 Swivel Guns Mounted, that three days after they had taken her they put the said Browne & French onboard a London Pink from Lisbon for Maryland which they had 16 Days in possession, that the said Pirates had detain'd the said Spencer & Company but promis'd as soon as they should take a Ship fitter for their turn he and Company should have their own Ship againe the Pirates talk'd of going to the Cape de Verd Islands & thence to Guinea & Brasill and they have already Mounted 22 Guns onboard the sd Ship Alexander.[8]

Congdon, in *Dragon*, was alleged consort of Capt. Butscher in *Rover* in a London report of 1 August 1718 and repeated in the *Boston News-Letter* of 17 November 1718. This article, however, was one of the reports alleging the taking of *Coulston*, Capt. Peter Skinner, which Charles Johnson used in his error-packed tale of Edward England's deeds (see Chapter Two). Congdon had been a known pirate by early 1718, but few details have yet surfaced on his whereabouts at that time. Presumably, he pirated off the Portuguese coast of Brazil before taking a pardon early in 1719. Still, he had slaves aboard when he arrived in Madagascar and probably took these on the African coast or from a slave ship coming from there.

---

[8] National Archives, London, Vincent Pearse to Admiralty, 4 Mar 1718 and 3 Jun 1718, ADM 1/2282.

Edward Congdon[9] allegedly surrendered in early 1719. He may have made an honest attempt to retire, but no one apparently told the Portuguese. *American Weekly Mercury* reported that about September 1720 (1719; perhaps an old report?), he met two Portuguese Men-of-War (80 and 72 guns) twenty leagues off Terciera Island in the Azores, west of Spain and Portugal. Capt. Isaac Johnson of brigantine *Albany* left Amsterdam for Philadelphia, arriving there on the 27th of April. He departed from Philadelphia for Madeira, leaving that port on 15 October (1719?) and arrived in New York five weeks later. There, Johnson informed correspondents for the *American Weekly Mercury* of Philadelphia of a story he had heard on Madeira of this rather humorous incident of the pirate "with but one Hand," (*not* lost in the "East Indies" as *A General History* said). This pirate was also infamous for wreaking havoc off Brazil, a place also inhabited by Portuguese. This incident was rather humorous and probably told often on Madeira – about an event that occurred in late 1719 – they simply got the dates confused, as Congdon was on Madagascar by 1720.[10]

This pirate had augmented his armament. Thus, he was certainly not an amateur, but the Portuguese caught him at a rather bad moment. Nathaniel Mist, publisher of London's *Weekly Journal*, obviously read this report in his competitor's newspaper and made up elaborate detail to make his "Condent" character appear vile and notorious!

Congdon's 40-gun vessel, *Dragon,* needed to be cleaned badly and sailed slowly – it looked every bit as ragged as its commander, no doubt. The Portuguese ships, larger and supposedly slower, still easily caught up with *Dragon*. The Portuguese demanded to know what ship she was and where she was bound. Congdon answered them, trying not to mention the name, an "English Man of War from *Guinea* bound to Lisbon to careen."[11] They ordered Congdon to come aboard. Instead, he sent a lieutenant, who feigned to have forgotten his papers. Annoyed, they sent the lieutenant away, who returned to *Dragon* and informed Congdon that the men-of-war were prepared to engage

---

[9] "Connor" according to *Daily Post,* 28 Jan 1721 and *London Journal,* 4 Feb 1721.
[10] *American Weekly Mercury* (Philadelphia, Pennsylvania), June 2, 1720, 2, and November 24, 1720, 3.
[11] *American Weekly Mercury* (Philadelphia, Pennsylvania), Sunday, November 24, 1720, 3; It was sheer idiocy that he would careen in Lisbon, having angered the Portuguese. Still, he was just off their coast in the Azores.

them. Much to the pirates' happiness, however, the Portuguese moved off, probably laughing. This incident undoubtedly made Congdon desire to search for other opportunities in the East Indies. Still, *Dragon* probably received its careening first – though perhaps not in the capital of Portugal![12]

Edward Congdon meets the Portuguese Men of War ca. Sep 1720

Ex-pirate Congdon immediately decided to semi-retire in Madagascar, taking 60 to 80 slaves from Guinea to begin this trade, illegally obtained, no doubt. Slave dealing and smuggling became Congdon's primary vocation there, although he alternated occasionally between these and supplemental piracy – less risky in the East Indies. In 1720, he captured Ostenders, a rich vessel of Surat departed from Jeddah, and traded weapons (through a Bristol connection) and Spanish dollars on Île Saint-Marie, Madagascar. One of these vessels was *Prince Eugene,* captured above Cape of Good Hope with *House of Austria* in February 1720 (see pages 132-134 for details). Still, these were Ostenders and not necessarily included in the list of *legitimate* traders, as viewed by the English – thought no better than pirates themselves! Congdon may have viewed this incident as "legitimate" in English eyes. It is worthy to note that the EIC ceased their profuse discussion of the

---

[12] *American Weekly Mercury* (Philadelphia, Pennsylvania), Sunday, November 24, 1720, 3.

intrusion of Ostenders immediately after this incident in which Congdon captured two of them.[13]

At Madagascar, he encountered a second vessel named *Prince Eugene* – this one, of Bristol! In September 1719, the Lord Mayor and Aldermen of the City of Bristol petitioned the EIC for a pass allowing *Prince Eugene* to trade for slaves from Madagascar. The next February, several members of the House of Commons and the owners of the vessel also made the same request. All requests had been denied; nevertheless, *Prince Eugene* set sail May 1720, regardless of the restrictions of the East India Company.

Thirty-two-year-old Joseph Stratton of Bristol, captain of *Prince Eugene* transported slaves from Madagascar, contrary to the EIC monopoly. Stratton also carried back Spanish gold that he received for "Arms and other Stores of War" delivered to pirate Edward Congdon.[14] In the case of *The King v. Joseph Stratton*, 13-14 November 1721, Stratton faced many accusers for operating a smuggling circuit from Bristol to Madagascar and Virginia. Royal authorities picked him up in York Town, Virginia. In September, Capt. Thomas Whorwood of HMS *Rye* transported him and key witnesses back to England for trial. As he was a substantial gentleman, related perhaps to the Strattons of Virginia, husband and father in Bristol, even though he was obviously guilty, he was yet acquitted of all charges. Five years later, he was back at sea, transporting 300 slaves for Thomas Freke & Co. in *Susanna* galley.[15]

The trial itself told a great deal about Edward Congdon and the trade he conducted from Madagascar. It also tells about the corruption of the court system of the day that set many a wealthy and/or gentlemanly pirate free, along with their many substantial

---

[13] Henri-Francois Buffet, "The End of the Pirate Edward Congdon," *Recueil de documents et travaux inédits pour servir à l'histoire de La Réunion*: (ancienne Ile Bourbon), Volume 4 (Saint-Denis: Archives départementales de La Réunion, 1960), 131.

[14] Spotswood to Secretary Craggs, 28 Jul 1721, Virginia Historical Society, *Collections*, II: 351.

[15] National Archives, London, Lords' Letters: Orders and Instructions, 22 Sep 1721, ADM 2/50; *England, Marriages, 1538–1973*. Salt Lake City, Utah: FamilySearch, 2013; David Richardson, *Bristol, Africa, and the Eighteenth-century Slave Trade to America*, Vol. 38 (Bristol: Bristol Record Society, 1986), 126; Joseph Stratton married 3 Oct 1703 to Martha Cables, in Christ Church, Bristol, Gloucester, England; his son Joseph Stratton, Jr. was baptized Saint Mary's Redcliffe, Bristol, Gloucester, England on 28 May 1713; Stratton captains *Susanna Galley*, delivering 300 slaves for Thomas Freke & Co. to Jamaica.

accomplices. The evidence against Stratton, however, was certainly substantial and begged for justice. It also assures all serious researchers that this *Prince Eugene* indeed survived meeting *Dragon,* assuming its commander's drinking and carousing with Edward Congdon at Île Saint-Marie caused no debilitating physiological affects.

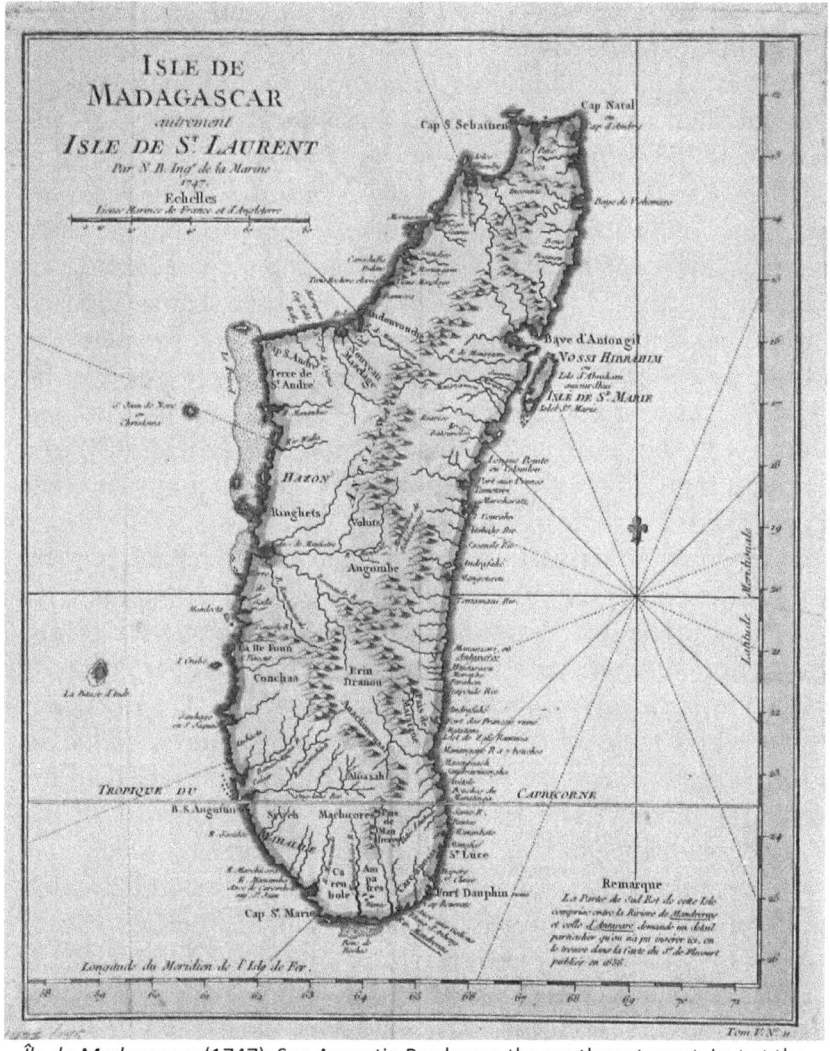

Île de Madagascar (1747); San Augustin Bay lay on the southwest coast, just at the line representing the Tropic of Capricorn. Public Domain.

In May 1720, Capt. Joseph Stratton of Bristol, Robert Dunwich of Devon, Morgan Miles of Swansea, Glamorgan, William Doale of Bristol, Joseph Hollat and William Voisy, also both of Devon, set sail in *Prince Eugene* for Ireland, then to Madagascar, and finally to Virginia. The men listed above would all be witnesses at Stratton's trial. In Ireland, Stratton took on brandy, wine, and provisions and from thence proceeded to Madagascar.

That summer, Stratton's *Prince Eugene* and their consort *Rebecca* sailed into Port or Fort Dauphin (Tolagnaro) on the coast of the Merina Kingdom (c.1540–1897) of southeast Madagascar for a two-week stay. Stratton's purpose for stopping in Fort Dauphin is not known, but while in port there he met the captain of another merchant ship, *Henrietta* of London, Capt. Richard Herbert. Herbert came aboard Stratton's ship several times and they spoke privately in Stratton's cabin. He informed Stratton of a trader based in Île Saint-Marie who could offer him good deals and that he had done well by him. Weighing anchor for Île Saint-Marie, Stratton found there the Congdon's ship *Dragon* and two other vessels recently captured by her.[16]

Upon the arrival of this unknown merchant vessel, Congdon sent natives or slaves by canoe to *Prince Eugene* with a note of invitation. Stratton, agreeing with Congdon's terms, then ordered two hogsheads of brandy and a hamper of liquor placed into the canoe. They rowed back to shore. The next day, three white men with ten blacks came in another canoe to *Prince Eugene* and were well-received by Capt. Stratton in his cabin for privacy. The white men spent the better part of the day negotiating with Stratton and then they left.

The following day, Capt. Stratton ordered Robert Dunwich and William Voisy to take 100 hogsheads of brandy, several chests of weapons, 70-80 barrels of gunpowder, as well as

---

[16] National Archives, London, Information of Robert Dunwich, 13 Nov 1721, HCA 1/55; Note: the Merina Kingdom, in the 1720s controlled the Southeast portion of Madagascar, but they would later conquer the whole of the island by the 19th century. The French settlement at Fort Dauphin had failed in the 17th century, but the French maintained a nominal presence until their return in the 19th century. In 1896, the Merina Kingdom was put under French protection as the Malagasy Protectorate and in 1897 the French Parliament voted to annex the island as a colony, effectively ending Merina sovereignty.

several sundry provisions that belonged to Stratton's creditors back in Bristol, to Capt, Congdon. One can only assume that he planned to share the profits with his creditors – assuming that he had not already been instructed by them to make such an illegal trade. In return, Congdon sent aboard "a great quantity of Spanish dollars in cases, each reported to be of the value of £1000."[17]

Morgan Miles of Swansea also testified that Stratton held many meetings with Edward Congdon and "the two were used to drink together under a tree." The day before sailing, Capt. Stratton dined ashore with Congdon. They then returned to Port Dauphin to take in more wood and water. After staying there three weeks they went to Port St. Clare (Ytapore; southern tip at Cape Saint-Marie), long popular for Antandroy slave-trading on Madagascar, to purchase 100 slaves before he sailed, which may have satisfied the original intent to this particular voyage.[18]

Once *Prince Eugene* sailed from Madagascar, rounded the Cape, and traversed the Atlantic on their way to Virginia, Morgan Miles explained events from that point. Apparently while avoiding customs, Stratton anchored in York River on 21 July 1721. Three days later, the money was put into the longboat and yawl, at night. They carried six chests (or £6,000) of it upriver to the home of Col. Phipps, and buried them in the sand. There were also six bags stowed in the stern sheets, i.e., of the long boat, hidden from customs officers or tidewaiters, and towed to York Town. Dunwich believed that the Spanish dollars "were concealed there for some time and then sent to Bristol by reason that several Bristol ships then lay there."[19] The Virginia Council directed Cole Diggs, Esq. to instruct the Collector and Naval Officer of York

---

[17] Information of Robert Dunwich.

[18] Information of Robert Dunwich.; *The King v. Joseph Stratton* in Peter Wilson Coldham, "Examinations in Criminal Cases," *English Adventurers and Emigrants, 1661-1733* (Baltimore: Genealogical Publishing Co., 1985), 189-190; Francis Cauché of Roan, *A Voyage to Madagascar, the Adjacent Islands, and the Coast of Africk* (1711), 11-12,`17, 59; the isolated and nomadic Antandroy of the Tandroy region, meaning "people of the thorns," from spiny thickets of endemic plants in the arid southwestern region of Madagascar.

[19] National Archives, London, Information of Morgan Miles, age 20, of Swansea; William Doale, age 21, of Bristol; Joseph Hollet, age 21, of Devon, William Voisy, age 21, of Devon; all mariners, 13 Nov 1721, HCA 1/55, 9-13; Information of Robert Dunwich.

River to "Seal up the bags & Chest" and give him a receipt for the goods therein until the results of Stratton's trial could be determined.[20] Robert Carter of Virginia also had 120 hogsheads of tobacco consigned to Joseph Stratton on that voyage that may have wound up in the wrong hands. The important detail was that Stratton was arrested *not* for dealing with pirates, but for having stolen East India Goods on his ship and illegally trading slaves without permission of the EIC! Stealing from others was not nearly as illegal as stealing from the company.[21]

John Walker at York River, Virginia officially informed the EIC Court of Directors in Aril 1722 of these transgressions. Negotiations continued throughout the year. By February 1723, *Prince Eugene's* owners John Duckingfield and Abraham Hooke offered to pay the Company £600 for infringing their monopoly – i.e., for pirating their slaves. Undoubtedly, they still made quite a profit![22]

Congdon dealt with as many as four vessels at that time, *Prince Eugene,* Capt. Joseph Stratton, *Gascoigne,* Capt. Chalonce Williams, and *Rebecca* snow, Capt. Timothy Tyzack, and *Henrietta* of London, Capt. Richard Herbert, all independent traders from Bristol (except one), and all transporting slaves and other merchandize into Virginia in spring-summer of 1721. Only Stratton was shipped back to England for trial, as the evidence in his case appeared sufficient. His mate, Evan Morgan was instructed to follow them back in *Prince Eugene.*

Shortly after these dealings, Congdon took a rich prize off the back of Bombay, near Surat, having recently come from Jeddah, that netted nearly £900 per man (137 crew average) – worth "12 lakhs of rupees" or £123,000.[23] John Biddulph told the pirate put

---

[20] H. R. McIllwaine, ed., *Executive Journals of the Council of Colonial Virginia*, Vol. 3: 1705-1721 (Richmond: Virginia State Library, 1928), 550.

[21] "Letter from Robert Carter to John King, 1720 July 13," *Diary, Correspondence, and Papers of Robert "King" Carter, 1701-1732*, transcribed by Edmund Berkeley, Jr., http://carter.lib.virginia.edu/html/C20g13h.html (accessed 22 Feb 2018).

[22] British Library, India Office, Letter 184: John Walker at York River, Virginia to the Court concerning the Prince Eugene sailing to Madagascar, 22 Aug 1722, IOR/E/1/13 ff. 438-439v; British Library, India Office, Letter 44 John Duckinfield and Abraham Hooke to the Court acknowledging that the Prince Eugene sailed to Madagascar illegally and offering to pay the Company £600 for infringing their monopoly, 1 Feb 1723, IOR/E/1/14 ff. 78-78v.

[23] Charles R. Ewen and Russel K. Skowronek, *Pieces of Eight: More Archaeology of Piracy* (Gainesville: Univ. Press of Florida, 2016), 60; Archaeologist John de Bry claims this ship to be a "Hajji ship belonging to the son-in-law of Abdul Ghafur [d. 1718] of Surat, ... [with "diamomds, rubies, and emeralds,"] gold, drugs, spices and

the crew ashore at the affluent district of "Malabar Hill" - essentially gave them a ride home. Richard Moor called it "Riches enough (by pirating) to maintain them handsomely as long as they lived," and Congdon decided to break up and stop pirating.[24] He pondered retirement on Île de Bourbon, or today's Réunion Island. A lot happened to him, however, before he could accept pardon and retire: two-thirds of his crew was poisoned, his ship wrecked, and a violent storm threatened to kill his remaining crew before they reached Île de Bourbon.

Le Mercure of Paris, France published on a monthly basis as a news and society gazette. This publication included many details from the French Colonies of both Indies. The issue of May 1722 read by way of introduction:

> From the Île of Bourbon:
>
> This Île formerly called Mascaragne, named after a Captain or Chief of the Portuguese, who discovered it, is situated by Africa in the Ethiopian Ocean [western Indian Ocean?]. It is on the east of the Île of St. Lawrence or Madagascar, about five leagues long and fourteen miles wide. The Portuguese had formerly settled there, but it passed under the dominion of the French, who gave her the name she bears today. It is said that there is a mountain which throws fire [volcano]: the country is fertile, the waters are healthy, and there are almost all the conveniences of the Île of Madagascar, with the Ports of St. Paul, Assumption, where the dwellings of the French are made.[25]

Thus began *Le Mercure's* tale of Edward Congdon's trials to be a free man. Congdon would soon settle briefly on Bourbon after taking a pardon from the French governor. Bourbon was, however, only the first leg in a long journey to

---

silk [worth] £150,000"; Note that Col. John Biddulph, with ready access to East India Company records in 1907, thought the pirate was Edward England, but wasn't sure – so, the name of the pirate had probably never been known to EIC officials. Many of this period gave England more credit than he actually deserved because of the *Cassandra* incident.

[24] "The Examination of Richard Moor, 31 October 1724 (and addendum, 5 November 1724), HCA 1/55, ff. 94-97," transcribed in E. T. Fox, ed., *Pirates in Their Own Words* (Fox Historical, 2014), 213.

[25] G. Cavelier, ed., *Le Mercure*, May 1722, p 152-156; Joan DeJean, The Essence of Style: *How the French Invented Fashion, Fine Food, Chic Cafés, Style, Sophistication, and Glamour* (New York: Free Press, 2005), 47.

retirement for this one-armed pirate. Contrary to the ends of most pirates, he married and lived, for all the records tell, a happy and complete life as a wealthy merchant. The road to retirement, however, was paved with disaster!

The 22nd of May [J: 10 May] issue of *Le Mercure* then told of a letter dated November 1721 that arrived from Bourbon. This letter contained details of Congdon's experiences after taking the West African ship full of rubies, diamonds, and specie that made them rich men. Soon arriving back at Madagascar 1 October 1720 [J: 19 Sep], Edward Congdon, "who has an arm cut off," met a Mr. Henry Beker, master of *Cooker*, seeking slaves from Madagascar.

Similar to Capt. Stratton, Beker and Congdon had transacted some business for wine and liquors at Île Saint-Marie. Unlike Stratton's pleasant business with the pirate, however, Congdon then took by force Beker's captain, surgeon, and carpenter, and two sailors, as well as some of his cargo. Congdon, however, had no intention of keeping these people and items. Congdon wanted to insure that the now surprised Beker sailed *Cooker* to Île de Bourbon to deliver a message. He needed the governor there to know that Congdon and his crew wished to surrender and beg for a pardon. He sent three surgeons, one a Parisian named Du Vernet, a Flemish man, and one English, the latter two taken off vessels of Ostend (*House of Austria* and *Prince Eugene*), as a measure of good faith.[26]

Beker agreed to his terms – not as if he had a choice. He sailed from Madagascar and arrived at the port of Saint-Denis on Bourbon on 15 November 1720 [J: 4 Nov]. Beker and the three surgeons made depositions before Gov. Joseph de Beauvoilier de Courchant, who had orders from the French East Indies Company, based in L'Orient, France, to employ all means of attracting pirates to surrender themselves and settle there. All those who would hand over their vessels to them and abandon piracy would receive full pardons. The rich pirates were expected to be quite helpful for the island's economy.[27]

Congdon drove a hard bargain, but so did Courchant. Congdon had ordered Beker to tell the governor that in case

---

[26] *Le Mercure*, May 1722.
[27] *Le Mercure*, May 1722.

there was no amnesty for them that his men would fortify in four months, and would do the most harm and injury, till an amnesty of Europe had been sent. Courchant offered "that the Pirates had to assure them that if they were granted an Amnesty, they would come to the Île de Bourbon to deliver their ship, arms and ammunition to the Governor, to submit to his orders, Good & faithful Subjects of the King of France."[28] They were to bring with them only peaceable and mild-mannered slaves. For each of these slaves (and each white man could retain only one), they were to pay twenty piasters to the French *Compagnie des Indies* in L'Orient, in compensation for the loss to their commerce.[29]

Gov. de Courchant assembled the Provincial Council of the island. After maturely examining the details, they granted Congdon's wishes, for the benefit of all nations which traded in India, for the French CDI, and for their own local economy. Beker returned to Madagascar with an approved and signed pardon, dated 25 November 1720 [J: 14 Nov], for 135 men, accompanied by a letter for Capt. Congdon.[30]

By the end of December, Congdon returned Beker in Cooker to tell him that they happily accepted the pardon and were preparing to burn *Dragon* and proceed to Bourbon in *Cooker*. Some of the pirates had already died, of what is unknown, but they were increasingly anxious to leave Madagascar. They set fire to two other of their ships, after spiking their cannon. It took twenty-seven days to finish preparations and Beker returned on 3 January 1721 [J: 22 Dec 1720] to pick them up.[31]

In the meantime, a plot was brewing amongst the Betsimisaraka of Île Saint-Marie. King Ramaromanompō (1694-1754) and his people had happily traded through Congdon for a year. They enjoyed the relationship, particularly the merchandise of *Dragon* and its crew. Sudden news of his departure was quite unwelcome.

---

[28] *Le Mercure*, May 1722.
[29] *Le Mercure*, May 1722.
[30] *Le Mercure*, May 1722.
[31] *Le Mercure*, May 1722.

Mostly female natives poisoned Congdon's crew, probably in food that they prepared for them in a farewell feast. Many of *Dragon's* crew took suddenly ill and Congdon soon realized what they had done. He ordered his crew to get aboard *Cooker* as fast as they could, but "several of them having dragged themselves to the shores of the sea to escape, were falling dead before they could set foot in the shallop" or a canoe.[32] On the 30th of January 1721 [J: 19 Jan], 42 out of 135 set sail while some of their brethren were left still dying on the beach. The fleeing 42 were in little better shape, "nearly all in very bad condition by the poison given them by the blacks of Madagascar."[33] In the crossing four of their comrades died, leaving a miserable 38 sickly remainder for conveyance to Bourbon.

Their misery, however, was not quite over. On 2 February 1721 [J: 22 Jan], before landing at Saint-Denis, the sea grew wild, with all the signs of a monsoon. At first, a large gust of wind came from the southeast, after having passed from north to east. Then, the winter storm became steady and tossed them in every direction for two days. Congdon and what remained of his poisoned, wet crew finally landed at Bourbon on the 6th of February 1721 [J: 26 Jan].

The storm had done great damage to Île de Bourbon. It ravaged all the mountains and destroyed crops of rice, coffee, cocoa, and bananas. Whole trees of cocoa were broken or uprooted. The article stated:

> The inhabitants of the Île of Bourbon will feel this year the loss of their banana-trees, whose fruit is of great help to their food. It had been bad weather for almost the whole month of January, but there had always been more rain than wind. Since the monsoon had ruined nearly all the

---

[32] *Le Mercure*, May 1722; Alfred Grandidier, (19031907), *Collection des Ouvrages Anciens concernant Madagascar*, Vol. 5: 1718-1800 (Paris: Comité de Madagascar, 1907), 104 n1; Translated: In a manuscript of the Deposit of Maps and Plans of the Marine of Paris, volume 84 ', Sea of India, Exhibit 17, at the bottom of page 7, it says: "In 1722, Mangaely [Mamoko Islands, of Ampasindava] was repaired by pirates, and it is said that there was a massacre of pirates made there by the blacks of the country, and that the king of Massailly [Bombetoke Bay], named Ratocaffe [Ratoakafo] sent his soldiers there to cover all the black men, women and children, even the dogs, and pillaged all the cattle, and since that time the place has been deserted."

[33] *Le Mercure*, May 1722.

trees of Moka, in all the districts of the Île, only 215 were fruitful, out of 3,595 which have not yet produced. In spite of the quantity of seeds which the hurricane has destroyed; so that whatever may be the presumption many of these seeds in the earth will perish, and that several of them will be eaten by the insects.[34]

The establishment of pirates at Bourbon was not clandestine, as many have supposed. It took place under the protection and supervision of the government. The following regulation was enacted by Gov. de Beauvollier de Courchant on 10 January 1721 [J: 30 Dec 1720], following the council's decision on 25 November 1720 [J: 14 Nov] to offer amnesty to Edward Congdon, and the hundred and thirty-five men, at that time, forming the total complement of his crew. The requirements were somewhat specific:

10 January 1721 [J: 30 Dec 1720]

Regulations for the food and shelter of the pirates to whom the amnesty has been granted:

Let every pirate pay for his board and lodging, to the inhabitant who will lodge and feed him, the sum of 15 piastres a month ...

The inhabitant who lodges one or several pirates furnishes each with a suitable bed, furnished at least with a good mattress, a pillow with its case, and a blanket. These beds ought to be in a hut, or of which a bangar or ajoupa was added, and which the insults of time could not penetrate it.

He will be obliged to give them twice a day meat, that is to say, to have dinner and supper, except nevertheless every

---

[34] G. Cavelier, ed., *Le Mercure*, May 1722, 152-156; Farchi (Jean): Petite histoire de l'île Bourbon. Paris, Presses Universitaires 1937, in-8°, 62 in Henri-Francois Buffet, "The End of the Pirate Edward Congdon," *Recueil de documents et travaux inédits pour servir à l'histoire de La Réunion*: (ancienne Ile Bourbon), Volume 4 (Saint-Denis: Archives départementales de La Réunion, 1960), 131-133; the Company of Madagascar was founded at L'Orient, France, undoubtedly a reason that Congdon came there.

day in spite of the year without exception, that they are very closely defended, of their without giving any consideration to the difference of religion, unless it be by some urgent and indispensable necessity, in which case the inhabitant shall address the parish leader for permission.

The ordinary dinner must be composed of a soup, a boiled, or, failing that, a roast and an entry, in such quantity in the whole that there is enough to eat, joining the bread or at least the rice for those who will be unable to give bread.

The supper must be made of meat with bread or rice in the same way that it is explained for dinner, except always on lean days.

With regard to drinking, it is regulated to a half-bottle of *frangourin*[35] to each man to have lunch without meat or anything else cooked; but only to the said breakfast of bread or rice and the said *frangourin*, as it follows and is said, unless the inhabitant does not wish to add some fruits, which will be without consequence. If, in the settlement, the pirates lodged in the inhabitants, want the extraordinary, they must pay for them according to custom and their confidence.[36]

M. I. Guët, in his *Les Origines de l'ile Bourbon* asserted that while Capt. Congdon's companions admitted to having hidden booty in Madagascar before coming to Bourbon, they yet possessed 4,000 crowns each in ready cash to spend. For the governor, it "would have been unbecoming to refuse the 'extraordinary,' provided they consented to pay well."[37] M. de

---

[35] A Fangourin is a type of mill for grinding sugar cane formerly used on the island of Réunion, as well as in Mauritius. "Frangourin" here is presumably a type of fermented sugary fruit drink; similar to brandy.

[36] M. I. Guët, *Les Origines de l'ile Bourbon et de la Colonisation Française à Madagascar* (1888), 221.

[37] *Les Origines de l'ile Bourbon,* 222 ; Guët quote in Grandidier, *Collection des Ouvrages Anciens Concernant Madagascar*, Vol. 5, 220n1a1 ; "According to the Colonial Archives of Bourbon, the pirates, who numbered 2 in 1687, 9 in 1695, and 3 in 1702 (out of 308 inhabitants) and 11 in 1705, 7 in 1706 and 135 [only 42 of Congdon's 135 crew actually made it to Bourbon] in 1720 [1721] out of 734 inhabitants, a total of 167 [actually 74] in thirty-three years, but it is probable that the 135 pirates who came in 1720, who belonged to the same ship, have not all remained [many of the 42 had sailed to France within two years]."

Courchant followed the example of 1696, when his officers expressed certain contempt for the "newly-fledged filibusters [pirates]" that visited their island. They saw that these pirates liked to waste their money in "frenzied manner to the sailors of his vessels, who tended to overcharge them." Guët added:

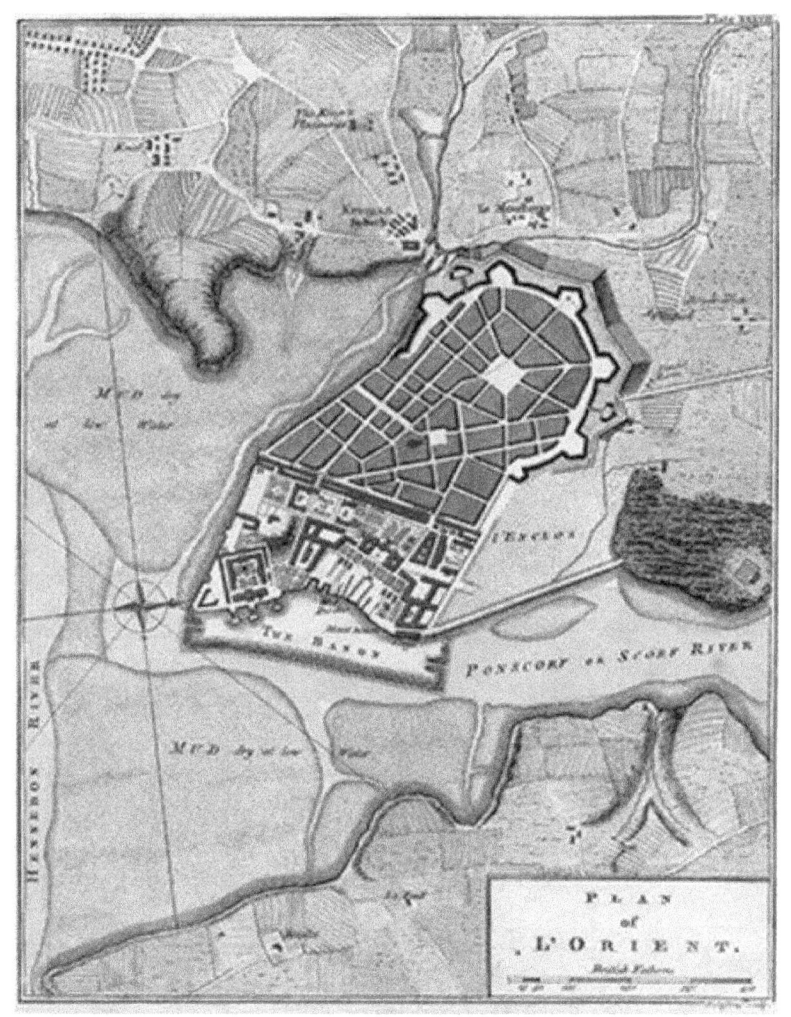

Plan of L'Orient, Brittany, France, home of the Company of Madagascar. Source: Archives départementales du Morbihan.

From all that precedes the pirates, it follows, that if their action in the Indian Ocean has been fatal to ships traveling unaccompanied with rich cargoes, this act, by a singular fortune, has not been without profit for Mascarene [Bourbon], their captors, fatigued their exploits, came to rest, spending their last share of booty. For, it must be emphasized, to be received and treated in the colony, they had to solemnly renounce their former profession. It is necessary to add that those who were born in the "heresy of the Reformation" could not marry at Bourbon until they had converted to the Catholic religion.[38]

While most of the pirates remained in Bourbon and devoted themselves to agriculture, it was not the same for Edward Congdon. Henri Buffet, archivist at Île de Réunion, found that former pirate Edward Congdon had asked to be established in France. Congdon would there marry and establish himself as a wealthy merchant in the founding city of the French CDI, L'Orient, Brittany.

On the 23rd of February 1723 [J: 12 Feb], he landed at L'Orient, in a ship of the Company of the Indies, *Vierges de Grâce* [*Virgin of Grace*], commanded by Joncheé de la Goletérie, and immediately settled at Port Louis of Brittany. François Burin de Ricquebourg then served as the King's lieutenant there.[39]

A month later, on 25 March 1723 [J: 14 Mar], Edward Congdon, who at that time declared himself a native of Plymouth, signed his marriage contract with Marie-Catherine Ancré, in the presence of de Ricquebourg and one Major Simon de la Vergne de Villeneuve, native of Saint-Omer and residing at the citadel of Port Louis. Ancré proved to be a powerful woman of strong financial talent and resources.[40] Four days later, the couple celebrated their marriage at the Church of Our

---

[38] *Les Origines de l'ile Bourbon*, 222.
[39] Farchi, op. cit., 84 from Buffet, *End of Pirate Edward Congdon*, 131; Gabriel O'Gilvy, *Nobiliaire de Guienne et de Gascogne*, Vol. 4 (Paris: Champion Librarie, 1883), 446-447; FRANÇOIS II DE BURIN, knight, born in 1681, count of Ricquebourg, obtained under this name a thousand arpents of earth, erected in fief of honor, by letters patentes given to Fontainebleau on October 1, 1742 [J: 18 Sep], recorded in execution of May 18, 1743 [J: 6 Mar], at the États de Bretagne. Lieutenant, then brigade major; aide-de-camp of Marshal Bouliers at the siege of Lille, received knight of Saint-Louis February 4, 1709 [J: 25 Jan] by King Louis XIY in person, finally lieutenant of the king and commander of the forts of Blavet, Port-Louis, Lorient, etc., he marries the 23 February 1732 [J: 11 Feb], MARIE-LOUISE DU PARC, daughter of a captain of the ship.
[40] Arch. not. Port-Louis, minutes Kersal, 25-3-1723 [J: 13 Mar] from Buffet, *End of Pirate Edward Congdon*, 132.

Lady of the Assumption, with a certain solemnity, since the assistants included the King's Lieutenant, Francois Burin of Ricquebourg and the widow of one of his predecessors, Constance Poulain, lady of Montgogue. The ceremony likely legitimized a contract of convenience for Congdon and Ancré - Ancré needed a man's legitimacy in a male-dominated society to conduct her business. Congdon, on the other hand, benefitted from her powerful family connections.[41]

On 7 October 1723 [J: 26 Sep], Congdon purchased the brigantine *Marie*, which he baptized *Catherine* or *Sainte-Catherine* in honor of his wife, from Philippe Lucy, merchant of Guernsey. Catherine Ancré Congdon, from her own finances, on the following 1st of November, fitted out this small vessel of 40 tons at Port Louis. She sent it to Le Croisic and to Ireland, under Irish master J. Kelly. She refitted *Sainte-Catherine* for Nantes on 27 April [J: 16 Apr], and again on 6 June 1724 [J: 26 May], and finally for Le Croisic, on the following 12th of November [J: 1 Nov]. The masters to whom she entrusted *Sainte-Catherine* for these successive sorties were Pièrre Mollo, J. Aguevisse, and J. Le Douarin.[42]

Catherine Ancré Congdon's husband did not take charge of the management of this vessel. What was he doing then? It seems that he was still in Port Louis and that he oversaw her business' commercial operations.

The slave whom Beauvollier de Courchant had authorized Congdon to keep back on Reunion had come to France with him. He was baptized at Our Lady of the Assumption on September 10, 1724 [J: 30 Aug], and the priest noted that he belonged to "M. de Congdon," affording the former pirate some gentility.[43]

Edward Congdon, on 25 September 1725 [J: 14 Sep], purchased for 2,400 livres from Thomas Joeans and André Lind, based at L'Orient, the remaining two thirds of the barque *Trois Amis* [*Three Friends*], of Nantes (70 tons). Now, he possessed 100

---

[41] Arch. mun. Port-Louis, reg. Catholicité. from Buffet, *End of Pirate Edward Congdon*, 132.
[42] Beauchesne (Geneviève): Répertoire de la sous-série 2 P des Archives de l'arrondissement maritime de Lorient from Buffet, *End of Pirate Edward Congdon*, 132.
[43] Arch. mun. Port-Louis, registres dè Catholicité from Buffet, *End of Pirate Edward Congdon*, 132.

212   Sailing East

percent of that vessel. Sometime later, however, on 19 November [J: 9 Nov], he sold a third interest of *Trois Amis* to César Gence. They negotiated the terms of that agreement at Port Louis.[44]

Congdon indeed called himself "a negociant of Port Louis," and under this flattering *nom de plume* he sold on 7 December 1725 [J: 27 Nov], to Sir John Allen of London, a third of the brigantine *Catherine*, for the price of 1,666 livres 13 sols 4 deniers. This indicates his continuing ties to English affairs. Indeed, L'Orient, Brittany lay less than 200 miles from Plymouth, England, across the English Channel.[45]

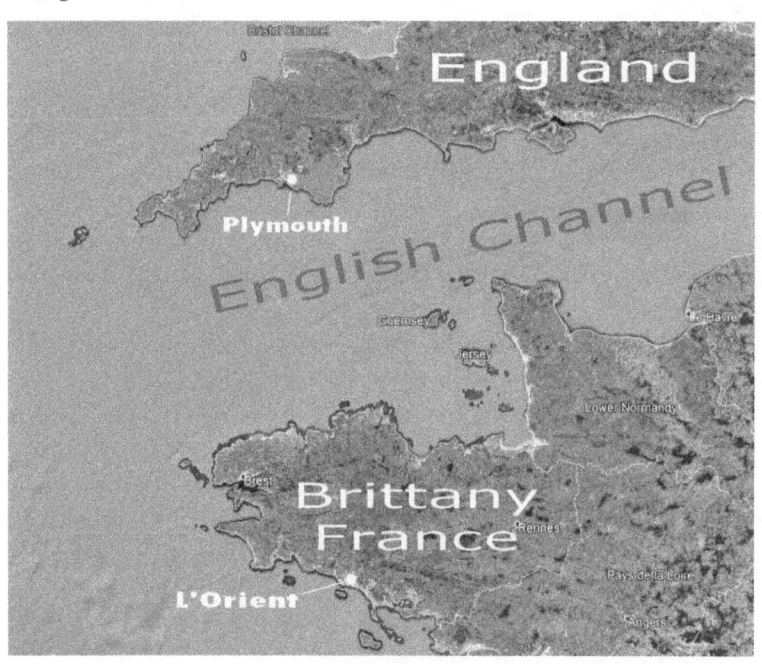

Perhaps it had been awhile since Congdon "wet his feet." In 1726, Edward Congdon twice made a voyage to La Rochelle as a master, on the brigantine *François-Louis* (40 tons), belonging to the Port Louisian François de Lards (8 July-4 September and 8 September-10 November) [J: 27 Jun-24 Jul and

---

[44] Arch. not. Port-Louis, minutes Kersal, 25-9-1725 [J: 14 Sep] et 19-11-1725 [J: 8 Nov], from Buffet, *End of Pirate Edward Congdon*, 132.
[45] Arch. not. Port-Louis, minutes Kersal, 7-12-1725 [J: 26 Nov], from Buffet, *End of Pirate Edward Congdon*, 132; for perspective, L'Orient lay 185 miles from Plymouth, as the crow flies; Madagascar is the world's fourth largest island and is 945 miles long.

29 Aug-30 Oct]. Meanwhile, his own ship, 60-ton *Saint-René* was traveling in the same seas under its master Piérre Forbin.[46]

Henri Buffet found evidence that Congdon's eventual arrival in L'Orient had its roots in his refuge on Île de Bourbon. Pierre Forbin was the near relative of and, perhaps, Renée le Gouzronc's own brother-in-law. Renée was the first wife of Antoine Boucher des Forges, who had countersigned, as a member of the Provincial Council of Bourbon, the pirate amnesty of Edward Congdon and his companions in 1721. Des Forges also served as governor after de Courchant.

Piérre Forbin returned *Saint-René* to Edward Congdon on November 10, 1726 [J: 30 Oct], making him the sole master of his late, but legitimate destiny. He concentrated his voyages between Port Louis and Nantes, but he also managed to sail this vessel to Bordeaux and even to Spain. He even traded as far north as Honfleur and Rouen.[47]

According to the records of Mlle. Genevieve Beauchesne, Edward Congdon filled his remaining six years on the sea. The list of armaments or "fitting outs" of *Saint-René* show the pattern: on 12 December 1726 [J: 1 Dec], he fitted out at Port Louis for Nantes; on 8 April 1727 [J: 27 Mar], for Marennes; on 10 July [J: 30 Jun] and 11 November 1727 [J: 31 Oct], for Nantes; 3 January 1728, for Nantes and Rouen; the 5th of May, 1728 [J: 24 Apr], for Nantes and Le Havre; 2 November 1728 [J: 22 Oct], January, 19 May [J: 8 May] and 8 October 1729 [J: 27 Sep], February 1730, for Nantes; on 7 July 1730 [J: 26 Jun], for La Seudre, Marennes, Bordeaux and Honfleur; the 3 February 1731 [J: 23 Jan], for Nantes, Le Croisic and Spain; the 1st of April, 1732 [J: 20 Mar], and the 8th of January, 1733 [J: 28 Dec 1732], for Nantes.[48]

On 2 May 1734 [J: 27 Apr] Edward Congdon died in his bed, a perhaps seemingly strange end for a pirate. His widow Catherine Ancré Congdon married again at Notre-Dame de

---

[46] Beauchesne (Geneviève), op. cit., from Buffet, *End of Pirate Edward Congdon*, 133.
[47] *Ibid.*
[48] Arch. not. Port-Louis, minutes Kersal, 27-11-1730 [J: 16 Nov], from Buffet, *End of Pirate Edward Congdon*, 133.

l'Assomption to Jean Foynard, surgeon-major of the city and citadel of Port Louis. Buffet writes:

> Congdon's widow had quickly forgotten him. We, at least, retain the memory of this man who had so well been able to renounce the mad and fascinating adventures of piracy, to live the obscure and laborious existence of the mariners of Brittany.[49]

Edward Congdon, moreover, still remains virtually forgotten today. Whereas Capt. Charles Johnson's *A General History* began the process that led to this, it cannot be blamed for the result. That blame must belong to those who have focused so intently upon Johnson and other uncited, badly-sourced, and often questionable texts as absolute historical evidence when they were most certainly not.

Denis Piat's *Pirates & Privateers of Mauritius* is a well-researched book. He has included information on pages 42-43 that include details that had to have come from these French records in *Le Mercure* and he had access to records from Île de Réunion. Piat has to know that what he sees in *A General History* is compromised. Still, he titles his section "Christopher Condent (?-1734)." and its first line, as well as "Condent's" early history, comes straight from *A General History*. Piat absolutely ignores the man's true name of Edward Congdon, choosing instead to use the name conjured from pirate folklore.

Furthermore, John de Bry, the archaeologist in search of William Kidd's *Adventure Galley* was led to question the dating of his rich watery find in the bay at Saint-Marie Island with gold coins and porcelain. He suspected it came from the period 1720-1721. Upon this discovery, the scholarly De Bry performed excellent historical pre-study on this new pirate and his ship, with the help of Barry Clifford who helped excavate the *Whydah* in New England. De Bry also obviously knew about French records in *Le Mercure*. Still, bowing to pirate folklore devotees, Clifford suggested to him that it may be the "*Fiery Dragon* of Christopher Condent!" All of his reports include this persistent error. Thankfully, we now understand

---

[49] Buffet, *End of Pirate Edward Congdon*, 133.

that "Christopher" is not historical and *Fiery Dragon* is merely an invention.

Edward Congdon was a solitary merchant sort, but had certainly known Richard Taylor, Edward England, John Plantain, Olivier LeVasseur, Jasper Seager, and many other West-Indian pirates who sailed east from his days as a pirate, slave trader, and smuggler on the Island of Madagascar and afterward, on La Bourbon. They never appeared to have sailed together, as far as we can determine. Still, there will always be many missing fragments throughout the historical body of knowledge – for perhaps as long as we keep searching!

Now, we go back to the story of *Victory* and *Cassandra* as they descend from the Indian Coast to Île de France or Mauritius and then to Île de Bourbon to capture the ultimate prize in the bay at St. Denis. They and their captives, like Richard Moor, would also find the opportunity to say goodbye to one of the residents of St. Paul's Parish on Île de Bourbon – a man quite well-known now, thanks to the efforts of archivists on the island like Henri Buffet in particular– former pirate Edward Congdon.

Chapter 5: Bourbon

Nossa Senhora do Cabo &
The Viceroy of Goa at Bourbon

Unlike Edward England, Edward Congdon definitely experienced Henry Every's legendary results when he captured a rich "Moor" or Mughal ship in the Arabian Sea-Indian Coast area – enough to make him and his crew rich men and retired in luxury. His experience was the most successful of this later group of West Indian pirates who came east in the 1720s. Richard Taylor, his probable quartermaster Olivier Levasseur, and Jasper Seager also ventured to that locale to seek the same prize – after first stranding Edward England, shipless and penniless, with most of his men – about 60-70 according to Clement Downing. As this narrative shows, pirates entertained little bias and often pirated pirates.

Congdon's luck had not exactly been shared, however, by Taylor, LeVasseur, and Seager. Through quite comical antics and overtly paranoid reactions, augmented by a seriously leaky vessel, they almost purposely evaded their eagerly sought and coveted rich prize. This may have encouraged Richard Taylor's horrid behavior, especially toward *Cassandra's* former mate, Richard Lasinby. Of course, the time they spent with their friends, the Dutch at Cochin, had been hazily glorious – with all the brandy and arrack fit for a King's Christmas! This and the not-insubstantial riches of *Cassandra* might have defused their desire to pirate the Malabar Coast and to give up on their hard-won treasures.

Cochin, furthest south on the Malabar or Indian Coast had fittingly been the final stop on that particular pleasure cruise. They then limped back to familiar waters – the muddiness of which was easily visible coursing through *Victory's* many busy pumps. Their vessel must have staggered, "three sheets to the wind" (a maritime reference, of course), much like the injured *Victory*, hung over and hungry from a raucous Christmas holiday. It reminds one of a wild spring break in Daytona Beach and later having to explain to parents about why the car had a smashed fender and a foul stench in the cab.

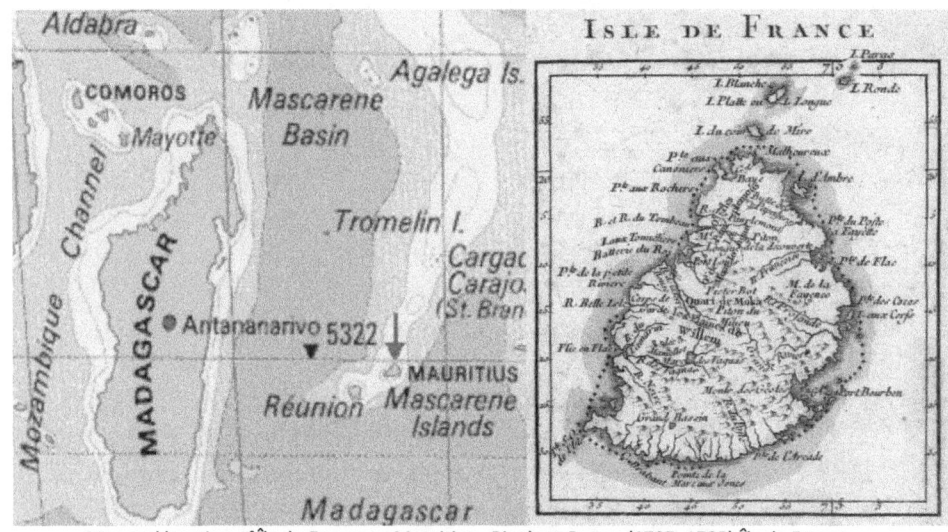

Map and location of Île de France or Mauritius - Rigobert Bonne (1727–1795) *Île de France*, Nebenkarte aus: Partie de la cote orientale d'Afrique avec l' Île de Madagascar et les cartes particulieres des Îles de France et de Bourbon. Projette et assujetie aux observations astronomiques, Paris 1791

As they sailed back toward a more familiar and receptive French pirate haven, Lady Luck would surprisingly and ironically bestow these plodding pirates with the greatest treasure of them all, *Nossa Senhora do Cabo*, a massive vessel holed for seventy-two guns! Of course, when they found her, she had barely twenty left; moreover, her crew was sick from days soaking in yet another East Indian springtime monsoon – an event to which Edward Congdon could well relate. The entire population of Saint-Denis Harbor on Île de Bourbon watched in utter amazement as these petty pirates captured the massive vessel in their harbor with the Viceroy of Goa, leader of the Portuguese East Indies, aboard. They nabbed two more ships and spent a couple of weeks lavishing their ill-gotten profits on that island. Their luck, it seemed, had changed when they arrived in April 1721 at Île de Bourbon.

Mauritius, Bourbon, *et al*, or the Mascarene Islands appear with the Portuguese name *Cirne* on early Portuguese maps, dating to 1507. Portuguese sailor, Dom Pedro Mascarenhas, gave the name "Mascarenes" to the Archipelago to which they belong. Two of the most important islands in this chain were Mauritius with its capital at a port later called Port Louis (northwestern shore) and Bourbon and its primary port of St. Denis also on the northwest shore.

Map of Mauritius by Jacques-Nicholas Bellin (1764), Hydrographer at the Depot de la Marine.

Mauritius, and its sister island of Île de Bourbon, or today's Réunion, are best known for their beaches, lagoons, reefs, typically mountainous interior, rainforests, and waterfalls – literally both paradises. This is, however, a recent impression. In 1598, a Dutch squadron under Admiral Wybrand van Warwyck landed at Grand Port (southeast shore) and named the island Mauritius, in honor of Prince Maurice van Nassau, stadholder of the Dutch Republic. They abandoned the disease-ridden island by 1710 and the French claimed it in 1715, rechristening the island Île de France. Warwyck bay was renamed Port Bourbon. Its old Dutch-era deep-water port (since 1606) on the flatter and rocky northwest coast, or "Rade des Tortues" ("Harbor of the Tortoises") would later be named Port Louis in 1735 by Gov. Mahé de La Bourdonnais. He established the old Dutch shipyard officially as a naval base and a shipbuilding center. By 1721 French settlers from Île de Bourbon began to repopulate the island – which still possessed a creole and maroon population. The first Bourbon colonists landed at Warwyck Bay (Mahebourg) in 1722, an event then commented upon by Richard Lasinby.

Arab traders called Mauritius' sister island Dina Morgabin. This island was officially claimed by Jacques Pronis of France in 1642, when he deported a dozen French mutineers to the island from Madagascar. The convicts were returned to France several years later, and in 1649, the island was named Île de Bourbon after the French Royal House of Bourbon. Colonization started in 1665, when the French East India Company or CDI sent the first French national settlers to the Mascarenes as well as Madagascar or Île St. Laurent or St. Lawrence. Megan Vaughan, in "Slavery and Colonial Identity in Eighteenth-Century Mauritius," tells that while Île de France or Mauritius had been settled directly from France, Île de Bourbon had been settled by French from their failed settlement of Fort Dauphin (later Port Dauphin) on Madagascar. Many of these settlers had native Madagascar roots and favored pirates a bit more than their provincially-elite neighbors lately arrived on Mauritius in 1722, just *after* the pirate vessel *Victory* had need of the shipyard. "Some commentators admired the 'simplicity' of the Bourbon Creoles," writes Vaughan, "their rustic ways and their established family lives, and though their origins in the French possessions and piratic communities of Madagascar meant they all were of 'sang melé' [mixed blood], yet they were apparently eager to profess their loyalty to France."[1] Still, for many decades, Île de Bourbon, with more of a settled French Creole population had outgrown its sister Mauritius or Île de France.

Piracy flourished under Dutch rule, which initially had attracted this latest band of brigands, but the Dutch literally abandoned these islands, giving pirates, some from Bourbon, a general self-rule over the Mascarenes until the French sent settlers. Piracy waned somewhat after the first two decades of the eighteenth century under proper French rule. Illustrating the increasing fiscal control of the French East Indies Company in L'Orient, in 1723, the year Edward Congdon left for L'Orient, the *Code Noir* or "Black Code" (compare to the same type codes in early Virginia, or "Jim Crow" laws in the United States) was established. These laws categorized one group of human beings as "goods," or produce to make it possible for the owner of these goods to obtain insurance money and compensation in case of loss of his so-called "goods." This, of course, increased control, profit, and capitalization. Essentially capitalism, or legalized piracy, with its sister institution of slavery, then reigned supreme.[2]

---

[1] Megan Vaughan, "Slavery and Colonial Identity in Eighteenth-Century Mauritius," *Transactions of the Royal Historical Society* Vol. 8 (1998), 195; Another excellent and more contemporary account on all aspects of these locales is Bernardin de Saint-Pierre, *A Voyage to the Isle of Mauritius, (or, Isle of France), the Isle of Bourbon, and the Cape of Good Hope, &c. With observations and reflections upon nature and mankind, By a French officer, Tr. from the French by John Parish* (London: W. Griffin, 1775).

[2] De la Barbinais le Gentil, *Nouveau Voyage Autour du Monde* (Paris: 1727), 137-138; "This Îsle having thus become more populated, the inhabitants could maintain one or two large boats to traffic the slaves in Madagascar from Mascarin in the season proper to this navigation. Not only can they procure through this trade the Slaves necessary for the maintenance of their dwellings, but they could also withdraw a great deal of gold from Madagascar in exchange for the goods which might be seen from France or India, by the vessels of the [French East India] Company. I have seen in this Îsle a Spaniard who has been established there a short time, and who, having lived a long time in Madagascar, brought back a pound of very fine gold which he had taken in a stream of this Îsle, so that there is reason to hope that it would be easy

Pirates generally relied on Bourbon's discretion, which became codified just for them in 1721, as illustrated in Chapter Four. Both islands briefly became popular resorts for pirates at this time. Still, the arrival of engineer de Nyon 5 April 1722 would begin Île de France's development into a mature coffee island, much like Bourbon, and an island whose future industry would heavily depend on slavery. Piracy would then wane in importance to the inhabitants. On both islands, however, agriculture had been hampered by cyclones, droughts, and pests. It would take great effort until either of them became the grand coffee producers that they had hoped to be.[3]

Marcellin's Map of La Reunion (1802)

Salisbury's Midshipman Clement Downing referred to the Mascarenes as "Domascaicus," his confusing reference specifically for La Bourbon. He told that pirates often went

---

to trade with the Indians of this country, by giving them gold in exchange for other goods."
[3] Vaughan, "Slavery and Colonial Identity in Eighteenth-Century Mauritius," 22.

there and had "clandestine Dealing with the French, who inhabit that Island, and are suspected of trading with such Pyrates."[4] Of course, the French were British competitors in the lucrative slave and spice trade and Downing probably held a bit of bias in this regard. Still, there definitely was some truth to the notion and he assumed that *Victory* and *Cassandra* "intended to winter there, under Pretence of being English East-India-Men."[5]

The pirates, however, most likely followed *Nossa Senhora do Cabo* from Mauritius. They spent the better part of two-and-a-half months (the majority of the hurricane season, from February to April) repairing *Victory* at Île de France or Mauritius' old Dutch shipyard at Port Louis. The mangrove trees, or *paletuvier*, growing on the flat, rocky shores would provide a useful oak-like repair material. They probably continued carousing as well, drinking whatever the islanders had to offer. Moreover, they apparently continued their arguments. Richard Lasinby spent the winter there with these irate drunken pirates. He told that before they arrived:

> They were reduced to one bottle of water per man, and two pounds of beef, and a small quantity of rice for each man for ten days... had it not been for the arrack and sugar, most of them would have perished of hunger and thirst. In this condition they arrived at Mauritius in the middle of February 1721, finding there good provision of all sorts, and materials with which to repair and re-sheath their leaky ship.[6]

When they departed on the 13th of April and came roughly 120 miles to Bourbon, Seager was then captain of *Cassandra*, but Taylor had again been demoted, then serving as Olivier LeVasseur's quartermaster on the newly-repaired *Victory*. He had been demoted and replaced by LeVasseur. This is assumed

---

[4] Downing, *History of the Indian Wars*, 47.
[5] *Ibid.*
[6] Lasinby, 284; *see note 11 about dates*.

to be so because De Menezes, Viceroy of Goa, in his account, called Taylor "Englishman and Quartermaster of the Pirates."⁷

Luís Carlos Inácio Xavier de Menezes (1689-1742), 5th Count of Ericeira and 1st Marquis of Louriçal, Administrator of the Portuguese East Indies at Goa, India

Luís Carlos Inácio Xavier de Menezes (1689-1742) - 5th Count of Ericeira and 1st Marquis of Louriçal, was Administrator of the East Indies at Goa, on the Indian Coast. Having obtained permission from the King to return to Portugal, he departed from Goa on the 25th of January 1721 [J: 14 Jan] in the vessel called variously *Guelderland, Vierge du Cap*, or *Nossa Senhora do Cabo*.⁸ A massive war vessel, she was yet

---

[7] *Ibid.*; "Relation of the Voyage of His Excellency the Count of Ericeira, Grand of Portugal, to Viceroy & Captain General of the East Indies for His Portuguese Majesty," G. Cavelier, *Le Mercure*, May 1722, 54-68.
[8] Research conducted by Baneto and Verazzone at Les Archives Nationales Portugaises de la Torre do Tombo. LISBOA – Portugal, http://ybphoto.free.fr/diamants_goa_ch2.html; this royal frigate was named after the DNS *Zeelandia*, DNS *Gelderland* and DNS *Galderland*. It was a second-class

handicapped for her present diplomatic mission. Though she was pierced for seventy-two cannon, she carried only thirty. A skeleton crew of 130 operated the vessel, which also carried a great number of "Ecclesiastical Passengers" and "People of Justice" who were returning to Europe, southward from Goa, approaching Mauritius from north.[9]

Winds failed her and the trip became laborious. Still, her relatively slow, wind-deprived travels to Portugal changed radically on 9 March 1721 [J: 26 Feb]. As the pirates' *Victory* and *Cassandra* repaired and cleaned at "Rade des Tortues" on Mauritius, they and *Nossa Senhora do Cabo* experienced a hurricane, natural for the southern hemisphere at this time, about 700 miles from Bourbon. *Do Cabo* necessarily reduced sail and tried to weather the storm.[10]

Comte d'Ericyera and his ship's master narrated events, day by day, through the storm. The master recalled that on the 10th [J: 27 Feb], "we ran with the Mizzen only: the wind made the compass turn, and the sea became frightful."[11] The storm intensified the next day:

> In less than one hour the ship was dismantled all but the bowsprit. It was opened by the flanks and other places, to the point of placing seven feet of water in the hull. The flow of water increased; the roll which was furious, threatened the shrouds being cut, which yet fastened the masts, some at the stern, and others on that of starboard. At sight of so great a danger the crew lost courage... the Count of Ericeira took charge and shouted orders, but not before the ship was entirely deprived of its three masts. The whirlwind always continued, and the shocks of the ship were more violent, for lack of sails to hold it. At daybreak it became apparent that the rudder was split from top to bottom, which discouraged even more of the

---

warship and was bought and renamed the *Nossa Senhora do Cabo* ("Our Lady of the Cape" called *Vierge de Cap* in Dutch or "Celebrate the Cape," *Nossa Senhora do Cabo* in Portuguese by Comte d'Ericiera) by Portugal in 1717.

[9] "Relation of the Voyage."
[10] "Relation of the Voyage."
[11] "Relation of the Voyage."

crew, who thought themselves lost without resources… [still] they were enabled to apply iron bars, and to tie the rudder with ropes.[12]

On the 12th [J: 28 Feb], they threw nine cannon into the sea, a quantity of merchandise, "and all that was in the Viceroy's room [stores]."[13] The magnitude of the storm sustained itself through the 13th, without even a spritsail. In this state, they focused upon blocking the water-tanks, for all the pumps not being sufficient to keep out the salt water. The storm weakened a bit on the 14th [J: 1 Mar] and 15th [J: 2 Mar], but the damaged ship was still at the mercy of the turbulent sea.

The weather had subsided enough that the crew was able to mount a small parrot sail in place of the little topsail, and a little topsail in place of the mizzen. They then steered towards Île de Bourbon, about 480 miles away, as it was the nearest land to their position. The next day, they were able to jury-rig masts and add more sail and over the next three days, until the 20th [J: 9 Mar], enough sail had been added to ensure their delivery to Bourbon.

More than a week passed and another wave threatened to undo their swiftly-rigged repairs. This tempest increased in strength until the 1st of April [J: 20 Mar]. Finally, by the 3rd [J: 22 Mar], Mauritius was visible on their port, or eastern, horizon.

As fate would have it, *Victory* had been repaired and in only two days, she would depart Port Louis for Île de Bourbon, under her new captain, Olivier LeVasseur, accompanied by Jasper Seager in *Cassandra*. Perhaps they spied *Nossa Senhora do Cabo* limping past them, heading south. It's hard to imagine that they did not, given she was only a league away. They probably recognized *Do Cabo* as a large Portuguese ship, with jewels and gold, most likely, so they were definitely interested. Moreover, the hurricane season ended by March-April. Good sailing weather now afforded these pirates even better opportunities.

On the 4th [J: 26 Mar], the Viceroy's sickly crewmen spotted Île de Bourbon, where they anchored on the 6th [J: 28 Mar] at daybreak at six o'clock. There, *Nossa Senhora do Cabo* anchored

---

[12] "Relation of the Voyage."
[13] "Relation of the Voyage."

in St. Denis harbor. M. Joseph de Beauvoilier de Courchant, "Governor of the Île for His Most Christian Majesty, received the Comte d'Ericeira with all the honors due to a Lord of a birth so distinguished."[14]

[Map: Isle de Bourbon (Réunion), showing Nossa Senhora do Cabo taken here, Saint-Denis, La Possession, Saint-Paul where Edward Congdon and his crew were settled, Dos d'Ane, Arrondissement of Saint-Paul, Saint-Gilles, Le Bernica]

Seven cannon shots were fired in salute. A throng of people appeared and a double retinue of militia saluted him as well with three volleys of fire. Because of his exertions in the storm, the Viceroy of Goa, however, could not leave his own ship, being in no condition to walk. He had to be carried to the house prepared for him, which was a good distance from the harbor where they landed. The Governor came to receive him on the same day with inhabitants carrying arms, in honorable fashion. As there were several sick men on the ship, the Comte d'Ericeira requested a house prepared for them as well.[15] Ten

---

[14] "Relation of the Voyage."
[15] *Ibid.*; Richard Moor declared that the capture of *Nossa Senhora do Cabo* had occurred on Easter Sunday (mod. calc. 13th of April, 1721 [Eng. Julian: 2 Apr (11 days diff.)]). Richard Lasinby deposed that it was the 8th of April (or six days *after* Easter Sunday). The Viceroy of Goa's account stated the 16th [J: 5 Apr, three days after English Easter Sunday for 1721]. The Viceroy's opinion in this matter is assumed correct because he appears to have taken details of his travels directly from the ship's log (already using the Gregorian calendar, with an 11-day diff.). Lasinby asserted that the pirates left Mauritius on the 5th, 3 days after Easter Sunday, adjusted

days barely afforded time for recovery – many had not by the time trouble arrived.

Three days after Easter Sunday, on the 16th of April [J: 5 Apr], as the sun rose, appeared two ships approaching Saint-Denis from the direction of Mauritius. They both flew English flags. Having recovered well enough from fatigue and ague, the Viceroy, or Count of Ericeyra came out of his house and proceeded to the harbor, followed by the Captain of the Guards in the Indies, and his *valet de chambre*. Gov. M. de Courchant followed with his soldiers, trying to stop him from exposing himself to the guns of possibly dangerous unknown vessels in the harbor. Ericeyra told him that "he thought it his duty to run the same risks as the Master's Ship, which had been entrusted to him."[16] He then went aboard his ship to secure her and better observe the English vessels:

> His Excellency having only 21 pieces of cannon, 34 rifles, no sabers, no pikes, no grenades; And at last lacking all that was necessary to prevent boarding, on account of the fact that some boxes full of these arms had been thrown into the sea with a portion of the cannon and the merchandise; [the author said] "we must not be surprised if we find ourselves in a great embarrassment," but as the greatest perils are not capable of frightening this Lord, he prepared as best he could to defend himself.[17]

The coast of the island being devoid of cannon, fortresses, and troops, it was not possible to prevent the approach of any two ships - even in the case they were hostile. Neither did the harbor then have enough boats to make an escape. There were a few piraguas made of a single piece of wood, which the inhabitants seldom even used.

When *Victory* and *Cassandra* were within range, they drew down the English colors and raised black pavilions with "skulls and bones." They began to abruptly discharge their small arms. Ericeyra, resolved to fight these pirates, attempted to return the

---

for the Julian calendar, indicating that the pirates' voyage from Mauritius to La Bourbon took them three days.
[16] "Relation of the Voyage."
[17] "Relation of the Voyage."

same, but his resources being weak, the volley was largely ineffective.

Victory, mounted with thirty-six cannon and 200 men, commanded by "La Bousse," or Olivier LeVasseur, "Frenchman," approached first came under *Do Cabo's* bowsprit. At the same time, "the other pirate named *Fantasy* [*Cassandra*], commanded by Siger [Seager] An Englishman of 58 guns and 280 men of crew came by the deck on the starboard side but the Portuguese fire made him miss the boardingAfter being so vigorously repulsed, Seager turned astern of *Nossa Senhora do Cabo* and continued his fire till he had cleared the quarterdeck. ."[18] *Cassandra* circled past and came back on the other side.

The fire continued on all sides. Seven cannon of the Portuguese vessel were in sorry condition, one having been fouled by seawater, and six, having been dismantled from their carriages, were tossed by the roll of the vessel. Rolling cannon on the deck distracted the Vicceroy's men, giving the pirates a second chance to board. They came along the Viceroy's port.

Seager's men entered with nearly a hundred men, who overwhelmed the weakened Portuguese. LeVasseur's men joined them over the bow. Many had been killed or wounded – some surprisingly had "taken part with the Pirates."[19] Others of the crew went over the side, swimming for land. Count of Ericeyra found himself on the abandoned bridge all alone save twenty men, "including his three Domestics, and those who remained in the inter-bridge, guarding the place where they were placed."[20] The author of this passage wrote:

> As His Excellency had the goodness to communicate to us this Relation written in his own hand, and that his modesty has imposed silence on an infinite number of heroic actions which he did during this rough battle, of which the Governor of the Île de Bourbon Has sent an exact and circumstantial detail to the Company of the Indies, we are compelled, in spite of ourselves, to suppress

---

[18] "Relation of the Voyage;" 58 guns may have been a slight exaggeration.
[19] "Relation of the Voyage."
[20] "Relation of the Voyage."

that which fame will not fail to publish, And we shall content ourselves with obeying M. le Comte d'Ericeira, merely to say that he remained firm on the deck from behind, where he sustained a terrible and continual fire at the head of his little troop, composed of eleven persons, Where he was all the more exposed, because he alone possessed a scarlet coat... the two Pirates had always drawn upon him, choosing him at each blow, so that it was a kind of a miracle that he was not killed, having been obliged to point several cannon himself with pieces of wood, for lack of necessary instruments, which so much irritated the Pirates....[21]

Ericeyra had been exposed and overwhelmed. He would have been killed, if not for Richard Taylor "Englishman and Quartermaster of the Pirates" shouting to his people to cease and desist. They then accepted the sword from Comte d'Ericeyra and took him into custody aboard Seager's *Cassandra*. The pirates treated him well – indeed like civilized gentlemen. They even gave back his gold and diamond-encrusted sword. Then, negotiations began.

Meanwhile, on 21 April [J: 10 Apr], 24-gun, 400-ton *Stadt Oostende, La Ville d'Ostend,* or *City of Ostend,* a vessel owned by Jacques Maelcamp, had been filling with water nearby. Having learned of a commotion at Saint-Denis, she moved that way and approached a bit too closely just as the action had ended – she had been spotted by the pirates. LeVasseur sent *Victory's* shallop after the Ostend ship, which had 24 guns and 60 crewmen. She surrendered, however, without firing a single shot. It seems that the crew had mutinied against their captain, Erderik-Andrik (first: André Flanderin). She was then towed into harbor to join the captive *Do Cabo*.

Nossa Senhora do Cabo and *City of Ostend* were then towed as far as the roadstead of St. Paul by *Victory*, the best sailor, at a distance of seven or eight miles from the harbor of St. Denis.[22] The pirates decided to use *City of Ostend,* found to be "formerly Greyhound Galley of London," to repair the large Portuguese ship. They fitted her with yards and a makeshift rudder from

---

[21] "Relation of the Voyage."
[22] "Relation of the Voyage."

the Ostender.[23] She had been sent to St. Paul's in a boat loaded with prisoners taken by the pirates from the Portuguese crew, guarded by the Portuguese pirates who had sworn fealty to LeVasseur *et al*.

Much work had to be done if the pirates were to make use of their crippled new prize warship – dismasted as she remained. The pirate Portuguese, with an English prize crew, no doubt, also would guide the warship and *City of Ostend* or *Greyhound* back to San Augustin to negotiate with timber merchants for new masts. LeVasseur *et al* planned to use the Ostender and 200 Mozambique slaves of the Viceroy's as payment for those masts. Unfortunately, their Portuguese allies were still sick, perhaps from their recent miserable travails in the storm. *City of Ostend* and *Do Cabo* then launched for San Augustin.[24]

Meanwhile, Gov. M. de Courchant, who had left St. Denis, had gone ashore at St. Paul's, where he feared some dissent from the former pirates living there. Contrary to his fears, ex-pirate and new resident of Bourbon, Capt. Edward Congdon offered to help. At eight o'clock that night, Comte d'Ericeyra met with Capt. Congdon aboard *Cassandra*. He seemed an able negotiator, a skill shown in his earlier elaborate dealings on Madagascar, yet:

> He made compliments from the Governor to his Excellency, and endeavored to persuade the Pirate Officers to allow the Count of Ericeira to go ashore, but he did not succeed in obtaining any of his entreaties.[25]

Capt. Jasper Seager did not like Ericeyra and he did not afford his guest on *Cassandra* the proper courtesy - or so thought Ericeyra. So, the next day Ericeyra spoke to French Captain Levasseur, "who promised to make every effort

---

[23] London: Journal, f. 169b ; *Greyhound Galley*, a slaver formerly captained by Alexander Selkirk in 1715 and owned by Lawrence Hollister of Bristol?.
[24] Yannick Benaben, "Chapitre II - Dans le sillage de la Nossa Senhora do Cabo," Les Diamants de Goa, http://ybphoto.free.fr/diamants_goa_ch2.html.
[25] Benaben.

imaginable to obtain his liberty, but it was impossible for him to overcome the obstinacy of the [older veteran pirate] English Captain Siger."[26] A dialogue ensued:

> The Count being at a table with these unfortunates, said to them, laughing, "That he was a very useless piece of furniture in a Pirate Ship, that he only served to make their provisions rarer, and that they ought to let him go to the Île of Bourbon." On which [the obstinate] Siger asked him if his Excellency could find as much as 2,000 piastres for his Ransom. [Ericiera] replied, "That after having lost all he had, it might be enough." He requested permission to write to the Governor by one of his Gentlemen; which was granted him, and the next day La Bousse offered to carry the Letter himself. The 2,000 piastres arrived at noon, and the Pirates [LeVasseur's men, most likely] magnificently carpeted their finest canoe, which they offered to the Count to take him ashore. The officers accompanied him, each ship, as well as the prisoners saluted him with 21 cannon shots, and eleven cries of "Long Live the King."[27]

The governor, always attentive to heads of state, awaited Comte d'Ericeyra on the shore, with a proper retinue, armed, of course. He led the Viceroy of Goa to dinner that night at M. des Forges-Boucher's, King's Lieutenant (previously referred to in the chapter on Edward Congdon).[28]

Pirates went ashore unarmed and no violence resulted. The nominal truce reached by payment of the ransom eased tensions and allowed the pirates' crews to move about unmolested on the island. The mediation of Edward Congdon may have helped after all. LeVasseur, probably to the objections of Taylor, even allowed Richard Lasinby to go free.[29] They were treated like guests, received refreshments, and paid the current price, without argument. This congeniality, however, soon faded.

---

[26] Benaben.
[27] Benaben.
[28] Benaben.
[29] Fittingly, Richard Lasinby made it back to England and was later placed in command of *Greenwich* by the British EIC, casting even more shade on the dishonored and deceased Richard Kirby.

While the pirate captains were ashore, *La Duchesse de Noailles*, a ship of the French East Indian Company, 180 tons, 16 guns, commanded by the Sieur Grave of Saint Malo (piloted by a Capt. Plattel), and previously armed at L'Orient, approached Saint-Denis to resupply the colony with slaves from Madagascar. Thanks to the *Duchess's* "betrayal of an unhappy man," LeVasseur and Seager discovered this vessel and went back aboard their respective ships to capture her. A passenger of *Duchess*, who may have been Lt. L. Robert, an officer originally stationed at Fort Dauphin on Madagascar, wrote:

> The ship was ruthlessly pillaged but with great disappointment, since the cargo consisted [apart from slaves] mainly of food destined for the island of Bourbon and did not satisfy the pirates' appetite for gold; they burned our ship [later, at Île Saint-Marie], taking some fresh food to fight scurvy... the rest thrown into the sea soon after.[30]

Earlier depredations of these pirates had greatly annoyed the government of Bourbon. They make visiting ships shy away from the island, fearing that it was in the hands of the

---

[30] Benaben ; L. Robert, "Description, in general and in detail, of the island of Madagascar, made on the best memoirs of the old officers who lived in this island [at] the Port Dauphin; all checked exactly on the spot by the sieur ROBERT; Part 1. The discovery of the island. - 2nd part. The detail of each kingdom or provinces. - 3rd part. The Dauphin Port. - 4th part. The rancidity of the pirates; the great advantages that there would be in forming colonies there." (1730), No. 196, Manuscript 3755, *Manuscrits de la Bibliothèque du Service Historique de la Défense, Bibliothèques de la Marine* (Vincennes, Val-de-Marne, France), 4th part, ff. 109-117; We read on the leaflet: "Bought in the inventory of the Duke de Chaulnes, with a map in the hand of the island of Madagascar, made by the same author in December 1729." - "Given to the Library of the General Depot of Maps and Plans of the Navy, February 14, 1812, by Mr. Rochon, member of the Legion of Honor, the Imperial Institute of France, etc., etc. Buache."; "[Robert] awaited, while his ship [*La Duchess de Noaillles*] was at anchor, the return of a king of the country who had gone to war to make him slaves. This accident happened by the bad faith and betrayal of an unhappy man who commanded a boat, which the author sent to the Isle of Bourbon, to carry a few negroes [Malgaches], who, having met with the pirate ships he might have avoided, giving themselves up to them, took part in their unworthy company, declared to them where the ship of the author [Robert], *The Duchess La Noailles* was anchored, and led them there."

pirates – that La Bourbon was no longer safe. Still, it was a trifling event of little note to them. The inhabitants could hide some amusement at the spectacle of the first two catches – they were foreign vessels and of little concern to Frenchmen.

The audacious (and quite rude) capture and burning of *La Duchesse de Noailles*, however, supremely irritated the agents of the French Indies Company at Bourbon. Furthermore, the loss of *Duchess'* cargo had been eagerly awaited by many merchants and upset the inhabitants, desperate for resupply. They promised to avenge this crime dearly, if the opportunity should arise. For LeVasseur, that opportunity came a bit late, but certain, because the *Duchess* was clearly one of the piracies that condemned "The Buzzard" at his later trial on that island. Not quite a decade following these events, he was hanged for precisely these crimes at Saint-Denis.[31]

Two days after capturing her, the pirates put a prize crew aboard the captured *Duchess*. *Victory*, *Cassandra*, and their prize then departed Bourbon for Madagascar to rendezvous with *City of Ostend* at San Augustin to re-mast their grand prize, leaving behind an island full of angry residents. John Freeman, 2nd mate of *City of Ostend* or "*Ostend Galley*," as he called it, deposed that "the Dutchmen and Portuguese on board, finding themselves with only two [English] pirates, [revolted and] put the latter ashore and escaped with the ship."[32]

Most authors and researchers believe the Ostender, or the former *Greyhound*, had been lost to the pirates. Did this happen and how? Researcher Yannick Benaben explored travel accounts of the *City of Ostend* in Lisbon archives trying to answer this question. The deposition of Gyles Neal, confirmed by Freeman, both captives of the pirates, said the pirates proceeded to Île St. Marie and there split their booty. Benaben found that they sailed to San Augustin afterward to meet up with *City of Ostend*:

---

[31] M. I. Guët, *Les Origines de l'île Bourbon et de la Colonisation Française à Madagascar* (1888), 219.

[32] Lasinby, 285; Deposition of John Freeman (Mar 1723), quoted in S. Charles Hill, "Episodes of Piracy in the Eastern Seas, 1519 to 1851" *Indian Antiquary*, v. 49 (April 1920), 61-62; Freeman apparently remained with the pirates throughout 1722, to Delagoa Bay, and back to Madagascar. He there witnessed the capture of a French ship at "Tullear Bay" (mouth of Timerly River – Bombetoke Bay) and the slaughter of LeVasseur's crew (as he says "80 men").

City of Ostend was sent to Madagascar with [13 sick] Portuguese pirates [those who had joined with LeVasseur and Seager] and Portuguese military prisoners [taken from] the Viceroy of Goa in order to have masts prepared for the *Nossa Senhora do Cabo*.[33] Two hundred [Mozambique] slaves[34] and the *City of Ostend* would serve as exchange money [for the Eastern White Pine timber merchants from America who must have had an outpost at San Augustin, Madagascar]. The journey of the *City of Ostend* did not end as planned – [on 22 July,] the [two] sick pirates were overthrown by the Portuguese prisoners [and their repatriated pirates] and escaped in the Bay of Saint Augustin in the Southwest of Madagascar. [*City of Ostend* fled the island under the repatriated Portuguese prisoners.] Meanwhile, Taylor [Seagar?] and Levasseur set sail for the bay of Saint Augustin to join the *City of Ostend* [but, of course, did not find her].[35]

---

[33] "The King's Broad Arrow and Eastern White Pine," *Northeastern Lumber Manufacturers Association* (website: lagniappe), http://www.nelma.org/lagniappe/kings-broad-arrow-and-ewp/ ; [Early American] colonists immediately discovered that the tall, straight Eastern White Pine was the perfect material for shipbuilding, particularly as masts for large vessels. English explorer Captain George Waymouth brought his ship, Archangel, into Pentecost Harbor (Maine), near the St. George River in 1605, where he recorded having "found notable high timber trees, (that would make) masts for ships of four hundred tons." Twenty years following the Pilgrim's landing at Plymouth Rock, "Masting" became New England's first major industry as Eastern White Pine quickly became a popular item for export to shipbuilding ports in the Caribbean, England, and as far away as Madagascar; San Augustin on Madagascar may have been a site to store this lumber for the preparation and replacement of masts – and the reason why the pirates would send a ship there to obtain them.

[34] Lasinby, 285; Lasinby told that 200 Mozambique slaves were aboard *Nossa Senhora do Cabo* when the pirates took her. He also said that the pirates took the Portuguese prisoners as well. Moreover, he asserted that the governor of Bourbon believed the pirates would leave them a vessel to return Ericeyra to Portugal, but lied.

[35] Yannick Benaben, "Chapitre II - Dans le sillage de la Nossa Senhora do Cabo," Les Diamants de Goa, http://ybphoto.free.fr/diamants_goa_ch2.html; *La Gazette de Paris*, 25 Apr 1722 – "The merchants of Ostend, having received notice, that one of their vessels returning from the East Indies had taken possession of [by] the pirates of Madagascar, had the cargo and provisions sold, of a ship which they had still resolved to send this year to India"; may also be another reference to *City of Ostend*, captured by Taylor [LeVasseur] and Seager in April 1721. This is concurrent with the

This was confirmed by the *Weekly Journal and British Gazette* of 2 June 1722. The article states that *City of Ostend* was "retaken by its own Crew, consisting of English, Flanderkins, and Portuguese, who courageously attack'd the Pyrate's Men that were put on board, and having got the better, carry'd the said ship afterwards to Mozambique...."[36] *Daily Courant* reported a possible exaggeration – that 50 pirates were killed in retaking the vessel.[37] The owners then sold the vessel and cargo on 27 July to Portuguese merchants. At the same time, Comm. Thomas Mathews visited St. Augustin with his fleet and left a letter for these pirates!

His Excellency Comte d'Ericeyra, Viceroy of Goa, remained the better part of that year at Bourbon Island until the 15th of November [J: 4 Nov]. By then, M. de Fougeray-Garnier de Saint-Malo in the brigantine *Triton*, a ship of the French East India Company or CDI, came from Mocha. Ericeyra was immediately welcomed aboard. The ship arrived at Port Louis, France on the 22nd of March 1722 [J: 11 Mar] and transferred Ericeyra to the French vessel ironically named *Île de Bourbon* for the remainder of his journey to Lisbon.[38]

The day after his arrival in France, *La Gazette de Paris* reported the incident. The same paper reported again, bestowing honors, on 12 September [J: 1 Sep]:

> His Majesty has just given the honorary marks of the Order of Christ to Sieur Fougeray-Garnier, in recognition of the care which this Captain Francois has taken for the Count of Ericeyra Viceroy of Goa, bringing him home on

---

news of the Count of Ericeyra, a passenger on *Nossa Senhora do Cabo – Guelderland -Vierge de Cap*, captured at the same time, also appearing in April 1722 in the French newspaper; another ship that may have been taken by these pirates appears also in the same issue, titled from London 2 Apr 1722: "That *Josseline* had arrived on the 23rd of November last at Calabar, having remained for nearly two months in the hands of the pirates, who gave him liberty only after having plundered the greater part of the merchandise, of which this vessel was loaded"; the travel time from Madagascar to England, France, Spain, Holland, or Portugal may have been two-three months or more; l'Abbé Norbert Laude, *La Compagnie D'ostende et son Activité Coloniale au Bengale: 1725 – 1730* (Brussels: 1944), 20, 230.

[36] *Weekly Journal and British Gazette*, 2 June 1722.
[37] *Daily Courant*, 31 May 1722.
[38] "Relation of the Voyage."

board *Île de Bourbon*.... It has been received from Surat, that the ship for that place with the new archbishop of Goa, has fortunately arrived there, as well as an Ostendois ship [*City of Ostend*], which had had the good fortune to escape from the Pirates.[39]

Another eyewitness account of the taking of *Do Cabo* comes from manuscript of D. João Fernandes de Almeida, passenger on *Guelderland-Vierge de Cap* or *Nossa Senhora do Cabo*:

"I noted the great disorder of the attack, thirteen Portuguese sailors turned against their camp during the attack and participated with the pirates in the plundering of their ship, some Portuguese sailors threw themselves into the sea, others sought to take refuge in the bottom of the hold. Besieged without further defense (the bulk of the armaments having been lost during the storm), the Count strove to defend his ship until his sword was broken. The two pirates, in admiration before so much bravery, wished to restore the sword to the Viceroy, whose handle was encrusted with gold and diamonds. As the latter refused preferential treatment over the rest of the crew, the pirates kept all the booty and plundered the *Nossa Senhora do Cabo*... The pirates destroyed one of the most valuable possessions for history: the collection of books and writings by Count Ericeira. The paper of the books was used by the pirates as rings for their muskets."[40]

A further narrative of Richard Lasinby's time spent on the island of Bourbon appears in one *London* version of his deposition. He believed that the pirates worried that the EIC fleet would continue hunting for them and talked about escaping into the Eastern Seas or China. The following had not

---

[39] "From Lisbon, 6 August 1722," *La Gazette de Paris*, Bureau d'adresse (Paris), 12 Sep 1722.
[40] "Manuscript of D. João Fernandes de Almeida," from Museu Nacional do Azulejo, http://www.marinha.pt .

appeared in any previously published version. To complete his tale, it is presented here:

> Dureing my Stay on ye Island there arrived in May two Ships from france bound for Madegascar for Slaves & from thence to Misisippi, the beginning of June Arriv'd Another from St. Maloe for China. And in her way to Settle the Island of Pullecondore [Pescadores in the Taiwan Strait?], having on board her A. Gov:^r 2 Engineers & about 100 Soldiers & Officers. They made butt very little Stay, when they Sail'd I took Care to write to China to acquaint your Hon:^s Ships of What is herein Mentioned. On ye first of Nov:^br Last Arriv'd the Triton, French Ship from Mocha, last from ye Island Mauitius Where had Stay'd 40 days dureing Which time had taken Possesion of ye said Island; by Erecting a Large Cross & leaving A French flagg flying. The Governour of this Place had Some time before been in Expectation of Ships for y^t [this] Purpose, but none Comeing [the Bourbonias] had began to Build A Small Vessel to send up there with People to Settle itt, much fearing that the Ostenders would do it before y:^m which he had on Acct. they intended_ Having now an Opertunity Embarqu't with ye Vice Roy & Several Others for France but luckeyly touching att ye Isle of St. Hellena mett Capt. [William] Hutchinson [of EIC's *Sunderland*], who was so Oblidging to take me on Board, being almost Starv'd in ye French Ship.
>
> Rich: Lasinby[41]

Afterward, Richard Lasinby found himself closer to home aboard *London* and gave his deposition to William Upton's clerk on 19 March 1722. Capt. James Macrae's officer's long trial with the pirates was over.

LeVasseur, Taylor, and Seager soon had a 60-70-gun vessel in their pirate fleet – at least it was desgined for that many, even if it only possessed 21 when they captured her – and those not in the best shape. Together with the "maybe" 58-gun *Cassandra*, they were indeed formidable. Compare this to the

---

[41] London: Journal, ff. 171-171b.

420-ton *Stanhope*, the ship that brought "President of the Castle and Island of Bombay; Governor and Commander in Chief of all the United Company's Forces, on the Coast of India, Persia and Arabia," Charles Boone to Bombay in 1715, which carried only 30 guns.[42] This was the typical rating of most British EIC vessels.

The pirates' sheer audacity with taking *Cassandra* made them visible to the British EIC as well as the Admiralty. With the firepower they now possessed, however, they could take any vessel or group of vessels they met, including those of the Honorable British Company of the Indies. One exception might have been the Royal Navy Squadron sent to hunt down and destroy these pirates:

> The repeated insults and the great depredations of the Pirates on the Indian and English ships in the end caused the Court of Directors of the East India Company to make application to the King and Council to send out a squadron to destroy the Pirate settlements at Madagascar, and to take their ships wherever found. Accordingly, a squadron of four ships, consisting of the Lion, the Salisbury, the Exeter, and the Shoreham, were sent out under command of Commodore [Thomas] Mathews, to suppress all such Pirates and sea-robbers as should interrupt trade in and to the Indian seas.[43]

Still, the Admiralty's best intentions did not go as they planned. Comm. Mathews had his own corrupt plans for the pirates' treasures at Madagascar.

---

[42] Downing, *History of the Indian Wars*, 1; British Library (website), ship statistics, *Stanhope*.

[43] Clement Downing, quoted in Charles Grey, *Pirates of the Eastern Seas* (1618-1723), *a Lurid Page of History* (London: S. Low, Marston & co., ltd, 1933), 326.

Chapter 6: The Fleet

Commodore Thomas Mathews, The "Anti-Pirate" Squadron & Dutch Engineer Jacob de Bucquoy

After negotiating with timber merchants at San Augustin, the pirates sailed *Nossa Senhora do Cabo* from that port on the southwest quadrant of Madagascar to exactly the opposite quadrant at Île Saint-Marie. They arrived there presumably by late May-June 1721 to refit. One of the French officers at Fort (or Port) Dauphin, captured by the pirates in *La Duchess de Noaillles* at La Bourbon, stated they "do not all live in the same township [most at Antongil Bay], being at some distance from one another; the land they occupy between all may contain twenty leagues of coast."[1] He also asserted in 1730 that they remained there as much as "ten or twelve years."[2] Pirate captive Gyles Neal later deposed that all four pirate ships (*Victory, Cassandra, Nossa Senhora do Cabo,* and *Duchess de Noaillles*) were at Île Saint-Marie where they were "refitting a great ship which they had taken from the Portuguese Vice Roy."[3] Lt. Robert, the French officer estimated they remained at

---

[1] Robert, *Bibliothèques* (1730).
[2] Robert, *Bibliothèques* (1730).
[3] National Archives, London, HCA 1/55, Information of Gyles Neal, 28 Oct 1724, ff. 93-94.

Île Saint-Marie for about ten months (April 1722); "the provisions which they were obliged to purchase, caused them a great expense, having paid for all they needed in money and in books twenty times more than the value."[4] Robert detailed their activity there and the lives of the Malagasy they befriended. His deposition, taken in 1730 in reference to Olivier LeVasseur's trial (see Chapter Eight) that year, also alluded to Edward Congdon's difficulties when the women of the village poisoned him and his crew:

> When they arrived there, they each made a box on the ground to lodge in particular, and on all these huts they wore a colored silk banderolle and, besides, their special mark to know them. A negro [Malagasy] to serve them, the wife, and there during the long stay there they live a life of bandits and villains, many of these species of women were given considerable presents; others inherited from some who gave them good will by dying; others in greater numbers. Having been mistreated and threatened with being sent away to take others in their stead, used poison through jealousy or revenge, caused them to die, and carried away all that belonged to these unfortunates, escaping with canoes on the island of Madagascar, so that the misconduct of these pirates in this place was the only reason for the loss of more than 80 of their best men. All this, together with other pirates who had already passed in this place to shelter themselves in the hurricane season, and to make various provisions, has rendered this place and its environs very rich; also, there are the negresses [Malagasy] covered with the finest Indian stuffs with embroideries of gold and silver, and many carry chains, buckles, rings and shackles of gold, even diamonds of a considerable price, which would make it a very good trade, for the natives would exchange everything they had for little, unable to dispense with arms, powder, or other goods that they need and that hackers cannot provide them.[5]

---

[4] Robert, *Bibliothèques* (1730)
[5] Robert, *Bibliothèques* (1730)

Nossa Senhora do Cabo received provisions, other supplies, and additional guns taken probably from *Victory* and *Duchess*, for the pirates intended to burn them. *Duchess* and the old French *Le Victorieux* of Nantes were set ablaze in the small bay of Île aux Forbans, on the southwest side of Île Saint-Marie. The two ships were likely part of the burned ships later observed in the harbor there by Comm. Thomas Mathews and his men.

Jasper Seager probably died there at the old pirate settlement about this time and LeVasseur replaced him as captain of *Cassandra*, the largest vessel available until the refit of *Nossa* was complete.[6] During their refit, they received word perhaps through passing merchants that a squadron of Royal Navy vessels came to Madagascar in pursuit of them. "They had made all the Dispatch they possibly could to fit her [*Do Cabo*] and get her away," reported captive Gyles Neal.[7] Still, they appeared not to have fully completed their task. Neal said they left for Port Dauphin, and then proceeded to San Augustin to investigate, finding possibly good news:

> ... [and] there [they] found amongst the Natives a Letter which had been left with them by Comodore Matthews for Capt. Cockburn ye Comander of the Salisbury & that the sd Letter was publickly read by the sd Quarterma^r Taylor before all the Company of the sd pirate Ship & that he ye sd Taylor then declared before all the sd Ships Company that he knew what Strength the sd Men of War were of & that he knew that they did not come there to seek for the Pirates but to force a Trade.[8]

Downing commented that the pirates had found the Commodore's letter. So, the pirates intercepted this letter between the time that Mathews left it for them, 12 July 1721, and when HMS *Salisbury* arrived at San Augustin, 2 August, a relatively narrow window of time – surrounding the time of the Portuguese rebellion aboard *City of Ostend* on 22 July. They

---

[6] Moor, 210.
[7] Moor, 210; Information of Gyles Neal, f. 93.
[8] Moor, 210.

must have been hopeful, by Taylor's opinion, of Mathews intending to trade, but they could not be certain.

Richard Moor testified that the pirates immediately fled to Delagoa Bay, but he literally passed over a year of detail in his deposition. The pirates indeed fled to Delagoa Bay, but in April 1722, nearly ten months after this incident. While Neal offers nothing further, the pirates probably returned to Île Saint-Marie after finding the letter to complete the interrupted refit. When finished, demoted captain, then quartermaster for the pirates, Richard Taylor assumed command of *Nossa Senhora do Cabo*, the most powerful vessel ever yet possessed by these pirates. Taylor rechristened her *Defense*.

Nearly an entire year passed since these pirates read the letter written by Comm. Thomas Mathews, intended for his other ships or consorts belonging to his "anti-pirate" squadron – or, might it have been intended *for* the pirates? All evidence suggests that pirates partied and caroused at their usual rendezvous at Île aux Forbans, in a southwestern bay of Île Saint-Marie, or the "Pirate Town," established decades earlier by their seventeenth-century pirate predecessors. They seemed little concerned for the Royal Navy fleet sent for them.

Yet, the wait must have, at times, been maddening – good or evil, profit or death, riches or a noose hung in the balance. Taylor and LeVasseur probably debated Mathews' intentions at every opportunity. What exactly were those goals: capture them or perhaps trade with them? Leaving that letter at San Augustin seemed at best reckless for a Royal Navy "pirate hunter" who knew that it could easily fall into his quarry's hands. This had to be why some pirates thought Mathews intended to trade with them – but, what if they were wrong? LeVasseur probably erred on the side of caution and recommended staying clear of the squadron – after all, that much firepower could easily be their undoing, even with 64-gun *Defense*, and there were no second chances with death.

Afterwards, the squadron that had allegedly been sent *after them* rendezvoused at Bombay, as planned – presumably to plan an operation for early in 1722. The pirates felt that the fleet had sailed away and, after some time, perhaps had forgotten about them. Comm. Mathews, however, had not forgotten about these pirates. In January 1722, the fleet indeed launched again and sailed from Bombay in search of them. Mathews stopped at Mauritius, Bourbon, and finally lighted upon Charnock Point of Madagascar just nine miles from where *Cassandra* and *Defense* lay at anchor at Île aux Forbans (Pirate Island). The pirates appeared surprised at this turn of events, perhaps a bit shaken, and decided to go with Olivier LeVasseur's more cautious plan – to just get out of the squadron's way. The interesting thing is what Comm. Mathews did when he arrived at Madagascar. The Taylor faction had been correct about him wanting to trade rather than fight; in fact, Clement Downing, midshipman aboard *Salisbury*, was able to interview John, James, or William Plantain, so-called "King of Ranter's Bay," whom the Commodore appeared delighted to meet!

Comm. Thomas Mathews

Born at Llandaff Court, Thomas Mathews was the son of Col. Edward Mathews and maternal grandson of Sir Thomas Armstrong, executed in 1684, for his part in the Rye House Plot. He joined the navy in 1690, serving aboard HMS *Albemarle*, which was then under the command of his uncle, Sir Francis Wheler. Mathews served during the Nine Years' War aboard HMS *Portland*, HMS *Boyne*, and HMS *Deale Castle*. He was finally promoted to command of HMS *Yarmouth* in 1703. After this first command, Mathews then took several years off from the service.[9]

Mathews returned to active duty in January 1718, for the impending outbreak of another war with Spain. He took command of HMS *Kent* on 31 March, and joined Sir George Byng's fleet in the Mediterranean, commanding a squadron to blockade Messina and hopefully intercept Vice-Admiral George Camocke. Camocke was the infamous Jacobite British national who committed treason and had gone over to the

---

[9] "Mathews, Thomas (1676-1751)," *Dictionary of National Biography (DoNB)*. Vol. 37, 43-44.

Spanish navy. Because of his Jacobite politics, he had been courted politically by pirate Charles Vane *et al.* Camocke managed to evade Byng's fleet and escape in a small boat. In autumn 1720, Mathews returned to Britain with Byng and took command of a squadron outfitted for service of the British East India Company.[10]

Claude Arnulphy (1697–1786), *Admiral Thomas Mathews* (1676-1751) - Description: Painted while Vice-Admiral of the Red and Commander-in-Chief of the English Mediterranean fleet, 1742-44. In the background is Hyères Bay, Toulon, with Mathews' second in command, Richard Lestock's flagship the 90-gun 'Neptune', and units of his squadron on the right; the stern of Mathews' flagship the 90-gun 'Namur', is on the extreme left of the picture.

Thomas Mathews and Richard Taylor may have had some personality quirks in common. In his later years, many claimed

---

[10] "Mathews, Thomas (1676-1751)," *DoNB*; Baylus C. Brooks, *Quest for Blackbeard: The True Story of Edward Thache and His World* (Lake City: Baylus C. Brooks, 2016), 239-240; Colin Woodard, *Republic of Pirates* (New York: Harcourt, 2007), 230-231.

that Mathews was "hot-headed, [and] intemperate." Horace Walpole became a vociferous opponent and noted that "Mathews believes that Providence lives upon beef and pudding, loves prize-fighting and bull-baiting, and drinks fog to the health of Old England." He also declared "Mathews remains in the light of a hot, brave, imperious, dull, confused fellow." Horace Mann declared "Tis wonderful how void Admiral Mathews is of common sense, good manners, or knowledge of the world. He understands nothing but Yes or No, and knows no medium." They even gave Mathews the derogatory epithet of "Il Furibondo," or "Madman."[11]

Most of this criticism came as his rank increased and with it, his attendance among "polite" society. That society thoroughly rejected him. Of course, the "Madman" was fresh back in service when he received orders to head to the East Indies in 1720. His most turbulent days and courts-martials would begin in the near future.

On 9 November 1720, while *Victory* and *Cassandra* still frolicked along the Malabar Coast with the "pirate-loving" Dutch at Cochin, Admiralty Secretary Josiah Burchett wrote to Thomas Woolley, secretary at the India-House Offices, reporting that the Lords Commissioners of the Admiralty gave orders for fitting out and preparing a fleet to sail to the East Indies in the East India Company's service. In two months, an EIC storeship, 36-gun *Grantham*, Capt. Timothy Field was ordered from the Downs 31 January 1721 and joined with others waiting at Plymouth. Then, they departed 8 February from that port. The main body of the fleet consisted of: Capt. Covill Mayne of newly-refitted 24-gun HMS *Shoreham*, Sir Robert Johnson of 60-gun HMS *Exeter*, Capt. John Cockburn of 50-gun HMS *Salisbury* and Capt. Edward Reddish of 60-gun HMS *Lion*. Thomas Mathews served as commodore of the fleet and HMS *Lion* was made his flagship.[12]

---

[11] "Mathews, Thomas (1676-1751)," *Dictionary of National Biography*, vol. 37, 46; Any resemblance to Republican Senator Mitch McConnell is purely significant, I assure you.

[12] British Library, India Office Records, Letter 228, Secretary Josiah Burchett at the Admiralty Office to Thomas Woolley reporting that the Lords Commissioners of the

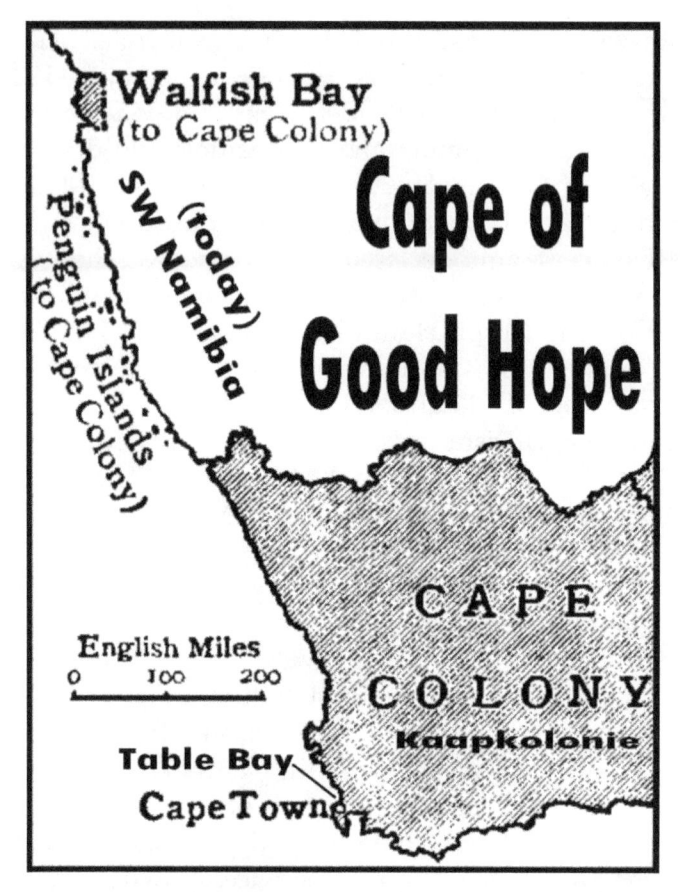

They reached Madeira by early March and São Jago by the end of that month, anchoring in Pryor Bay (Dakar, Senegal) on the 27th. They remained until 7 April to allow the fleet to regroup. Apparently, *Exeter* and *Salisbury* encountered rough weather and had to turn back to re-mast at Lisbon, Portugal. The log states that by late May, *Lion* anchored at the Penguin Island group, about 525 miles from Cape Town. Here, *Lion* watered and resupplied, waiting on *Exeter* and *Salisbury*. *Salisbury* was long delayed and only *Exeter* showed.

On 26 April 1721, their orders had been issued. Mathews received them 60 miles north of Capetown, in Table Bay, probably 27 May. After provisioning and watering for 17 days,

---

Admiralty have given orders for HMS Lion, Salisbury, Exeter and the Shoreham to..., IOR/E/1/11 ff. 392-393v : 9 Nov 1720; Secretary Thomas Woolley to Captain Main of HMS *Shoreham*, Sir Robert Johnson of HMS *Exeter*, Captain Cockburn of HMS *Salisbury* and Captain Reddish of HMS *Lyon*, IOR/E/3/100 f. 317v (4) : 26 Apr 1721.

they made for Capetown to meet *Shoreham, Exeter,* and *Grantham* already there on 13 June. The Dutch administrators of Capetown, however, claim that *Lion* arrived there with *Shoreham* on 27 May [J: 6 Jun], perhaps referring to when Mathews entered Table Bay and *Shoreham,* at Capetown.[13]

At this point, pirates Seager, LeVasseur, and Taylor had already captured *Nossa Senhora do Cabo* at St. Denis, Île de Bourbon. They had taken her to San Augustin negotiating for masts with American merchants there and should have returned to Île Saint-Marie, refitting the Portuguese ship for their purposes. Seager died and they burned *Victory* in the bay. They had just about prepared to meet any challenge – but, perhaps not one like Mathews' squadron. That fleet would soon sail to San Augustin from the Cape only a couple of weeks behind the pirates' visit there to negotiate for masts.

Hunting English pirates was only a part of Mathews' orders – and not the largest part, or even the most serious objective, as it would appear. Capture of *Cassandra* supremely annoyed important people of a most important company in Bombay with tendrils of annoyance stretching back to England. While this may have angered some EIC investors, a great deal of commerce yet passed those waters without interruption from small-time pirates. Therefore, the Admiralty did not so much focus upon this matter. There was also the pirate-like Dutch company's expansion into the same territory.

Still, the problem of defeating Konhoji Angrey's forces in India ranked even higher with important EIC officials – the British would get more bang for their buck, in other words. The two sets of "pirates," as termed by English communiques simply existed coincident to one another. Commodore Mathews had left England at the head of a squadron of Royal Navy vessels, with the stated mission of destroying "pirates" of the Indian Ocean – but not so much *Victory* and *Cassandra.* Most likely while at Table Bay, near the Cape of Good Hope, he received a letter from the governor of Madras, warning him

---

[13] Moor, 210; National Archives, London, ADM 52-436, Log of HMS *Lion,* 9 Jan 1721 – 12 Oct 1722.

that Angrey's forces "were foaming [cruising] the Indian Ocean with eleven ships and 1,500 men." *They* posed a much greater problem for the EIC and probably figured more prominently in Matthew's orders.[14]

Moreover, Mathews' reception at the Cape by the Dutch administrators was nothing close to cordial. At 11 am on the 4th of May, *Shoreham* had been ordered by the flagship *Lion* to chase a distant sail. She unmoored and moved ahead of the fleet. Therefore, *Shoreham* arrived at Capetown first near the end of May while *Lion* caught up to her, having just left Penguin Islands, 525 miles behind to Table Bay, only 60 miles from *Shoreham* by 26 May, according to the log. *Lion* witnessed eleven "Great Dutch Ships all outer bound for India" in Table Bay.[15] She would soon be joined by *Exeter;* still, *Shoreham,* alone at first, instantly received a bad reception from the Dutch authorities at Capetown. Capt. Covill Mayne penned a letter to Mathews (aboard *Lion*) concerning their harassment by the Dutch at the Cape of Good Hope:

> Last Saturday [27th May; Greg.: 6 June] I sent an hawser on board the next Dutch ship to you for enabling me to get into a better Birth [berth] and they detained the Boat some time before they would let it be made fast, the Company calling my People in the Boat Pirates. On Sunday [28th; G: 7th June] the Yawl went on shoar for a Barecco of Water, and some Necessaries the former was refused, and as the Boats' Crew was bringing some Bottles and Cags over one of the Dutch Longboats they took them from them, and drank to one another out of each: Last Night at my coming off [as Mayne was leaving,] as the Boat was under one of their Water Cocks they turned it, and let the Water on my self, and Company with me in the Stern Sheets...."[16]

---

[14] Downing, 15.

[15] Log of HMS *Lion*, 26-27 May 1721; an average of 70 large vessels each year traded at Table Bay. Portions of the log are available in *Philosophical Transactions: Giving Some Account of the Present Undertakings, Studies and Labours of the Ingenious, in Many Considerable Parts of the World.* (S. Smith and B. Walford, printers to the Royal Society, 1776).

[16] National Archives of London, Covill Mayne, "From C Mayne to Thomas Mathews concerning his ill-treatment by the Dutch at the Cape of Good Hope. Including accusations of piracy and the turning of water cocks on his crewmen.," 1 Nov 1721 Report (dated 30 May), SP 42/17/112.; Leibbrandt, *Precis of the archives of the Cape of Good Hope*, 283-284; Note that Dutch records show that *Lion* and *Shoreham* arrived at the Cape district simultaneously: *Lion* remained in the bay while *Shoreham* went ahead to Capetown: June 6, 1721 [J: May 27]; Liliana Mosca, "Slaving in Madagascar: English and Colonial Voyages in the Second Half of the 17th Century

The Dutch demonstrated an overall disrespect for British naval officers and men. It came from all their people, including their naval personnel – perhaps not without reason. As Dutch records inform, Mathews arrived at the Cape District in *Lion,* with *Shoreham,* on 27th of May. Moreover, the English did not "salute the Castle according to the usual custom."[17] *Exeter* was the only vessel that did salute the Dutch, after it had arrived 22 June [J: 11 June], although it was "presumed that the salute was intended for its consorts."[18]

Lion's log records show Mathews's arrival at Capetown, joining *Shoreham,* on 13 June, he said that he sent his lieutenant ashore on the morning of the 14th, who allegedly brought back a letter from the Dutch governor "Harison," actually named Maurits Pasques de Chavonnes (VOC governor there from 1714 to 1724). That letter snubbed Mathews and "insisted that [Mathews] should Salute him, and Send [his] Comission on Shore, before [he] should have the liberty of the Port, for Water or any other Refreshments."[19] Mathews' 2nd Lt. Caldecot asserted that they simply should leave and not trade with them. Mathews alleged that an officer came aboard *Lion* at about 4 pm demanding to know why Mathews did not immediately salute them, saying that *Lenox* and *St. Albans* had done so in 1712. The officer demanded that Mathews come ashore with his commission. Mathews touted arrogantly "as he did not belong to the States [not an official government], but a Governor elected by a [Dutch] Company of Merchants [VOC (*Verenigde Oostindische Compagnie;* founded 1602)], I expected he should pay the respect due to his Majties. Colours."[20] Still, Comm. Mathews probably lied in his letter.

The Dutch Cape Colony or *Kaapkolonie* was, between 1691 and 1795, a Governorate of the VOC, established by Jan van

---

A.D.," *TADIA, the African Diaspora in Asia: Explorations on a Less Known Fact* (2008),597; It should be noted here that English pirates in the mid-1680s had supplied the Dutch at the Cape with Madgascar slaves. Note also that The Dutch were equally as rude to Ostenders.

[17] Leibbrandt, *Precis of the archives,* 283.

[18] Leibbrandt, *Precis of the archives,* 284.

[19] National Archives of London, Thomas Mathews, "Extract of a letter (dated 13 June) from Commodore Mathews at the Cape of Good Hope to Burchett," 1 Nov 1721 Report (dated 13 June), SP 42/17/111.

[20] Mathews to Burchett, 1 Nov 1721.

Riebeeck at the old town of *Tafelbaai* as a re-supply and layover port for VOC vessels trading in East Africa, India, and other parts of Asia. Owing to its strategic location, the British had long coveted the Cape Colony to re-supply its own ships, but would not gain control until 1795, and then only briefly. It was after 1803 when the Dutch regained control that the VOC colony firmly came under Dutch government control at The Hague. So, Mathews' assertion that the Cape Colony was not under a legitimate sovereign nation may have held merit. At the time of Mathews' brief visit, Dutch farmer or Boer conflicts with the normally pastoral native San people, or *Khoikhoi*, and smallpox epidemics were decimating their numbers, leading to firmer Dutch control. Dutch Burghers lived much like wealthy English plantation owners in Carolina and Jamaica, with residences in Capetown to conduct financial affairs or government, leaving trusted slaves in charge of their Holland-style homesteads, or "Cape Dutch." The VOC, however, maintained strict control of trade through their port to maximize profit, often leading to adversarial situations much like the one Mathews alleged to have encountered.[21]

Mathews insisted that he did not officially recognize the Dutch VOC administration at the bustling cosmopolitan Capetown. He asserted that they possessed no sovereign legitimacy, thus, he refused to produce his commission or to salute them, as he would with more sovereign political entities. All of this information Mathews wrote to Secretary of the Admiralty Josiah Burchett in a report dated 1 November 1721, though he dated this specific letter 13th of June, two days before occurrence of most of the events which he included in that letter. Most of this seems rather improbable.[22]

The next part of the letter described events that occurred well after the *Lion's* log declared the ship to have already left the Cape. Mathews said that he attempted to send a boat ashore the next morning (the 15th), which was refused, the centinel saying he had orders to refuse any English boat attempting to land. Mathews then sent Capt. Edward Reddish, the captain of Mathews' flagship HMS *Lion* to demand to know the reason. Mathews then said that the centinal apologized for his orders from the Council of

---

[21] Solomon Daniel Newmark, *The South African Frontier: Economic Influences 1652-1836* (Stanford: Stanford University Press, 1957), 10-11; for an excellent cultural introduction, see www.capetown.at.co.za.
[22] Mathews to Burchett, 1 Nov 1721; Owing to its multi-cultural, frontier reputation, Capetown resembled "Sin City," or Port Royal, Jamaica, of the same time period.

Burghers and admitted that he knew that Mathews' men were from the Royal Navy. It took him some effort, Mathews wrote to Secretary Burchett, but soon they had liberty to water the fleet. The matter that seriously bothered Mathews was why the Dutch called his men "pirates." Also, he wanted to know why they were treated so uncivilly. His impressions offer insight into the political circumstances between the English and Dutch efforts in Africa as well as the nature of Mathews' mission, which did not exactly focus on pirates:

> All that I can find out, is, that they are jealous We are not come in quest of the Pirates, but to act in some manner contrary to their Interest in these Seas, but their cheif Jealousy is, that We are to molest them in the New Settlement [at Maputo in Delagoa Bay] they are making, somewhere on the Main in the Channel of Mozambique, but I cannot learn exactly whereabouts.[23]

Mathews' words here have enormous implications, even if the events that spawned his musings may not have actually occured. Did Mathews ponder a possible corporate espionage mission for the EIC to discover the VOC efforts at Fort Lijdzaamheid (Fort Agility) at Delagoa Bay? This is the very same fort in Mozambique which Olivier LeVasseur and Richard Taylor would attack and occupy the next year when Mathews approached their hideout at Île Saint-Marie! Whether intentionally or not, did these pirates actually aid Mathews' efforts?

Again, the oddest inconsistency was that Mathews spent less time at Capetown, according to *Lion's* log, than he intimated in his letter. For instance, the log states that he arrived at Capetown at noon on the 14th, and his fleet left "Cape Bonne Esperance" or the Cape of Good Hope at 6 pm on the *same day*, not what he told Secretary Burchett – that he was at Capetown at least two nights (after moving south through Table Bay to the town proper). The 15th was the day in which he allegedly and boldly confronted Dutch officials who supposedly cowed to his authority. The log stated that, at noon on that day, they had been at sea since the evening before and were 260 miles east of Capetown, on their way to Madagascar. *Lion's* log revealed that Mathews remained at Capetown only a total of six hours. The log simply did not

---

[23] Mathews to Burchett, 1 Nov 1721.

support the timing required by his letter's self-aggrandizing erroneous assertions. Instead, Comm. Mathews made it appear that he defiantly departed the Cape almost immediately after his brief contact with the allegedly intractable Dutch. He allowed Capt. Mayne to bear the Dutch insults while he sat far out in the bay for 17 days!

Dutch records indicate that the three English warships left the Cape 24 June [J: 13 June], in agreement with *Lion's* log. According to the log, *Lion* met squally, rainy weather with high wind and seas. By evening on the 14th, *Lion et al* made 85 miles on their journey eastward to the Island of Madagascar and then, 260 miles by noon the 15th. Halfway through the voyage, after sailing more than 900 miles towards San Augustin, and on 23 June, *Exeter* and *Shoreham* suffered further damage in another of many storms. This storm also caused the fleet to drift off their intended course and made them believe they were near land. They spent days dead-reckoning from their last known position and taking numerous observations of the stars, difficult with such frequent bouts of weather. By the 26th, they determined themselves to be 20 miles north of where they should have been and were able to recover their course after dealing with another storm. Monday, 3rd of July, they finally spotted land eight degrees north of east at 7 leagues or 21 miles. They had arrived at the southern-most point of Madagascar, Cap Saint-Marie (modern Cap Vohimena).[24]

After 538 leagues or 1614 miles of indifferent seas, HMS *Lion* first made Cap St. Marie, then hugged the coast west and anchored in San Augustin Bay (Ianantsony; Malagasy: Anantsoño) in 36 fathoms of water on 5th of July 1721. The anchorage was located on the south side of the bay, just under steep cliffs that extended all the way east to the bar at the mouth of Dartmouth River (see map on page 136). *Exeter* and *Shoreham* anchored beside them. The log indicates a great variance in the depth of the bay – from 5 to 100 fathoms. After going on shore, they found "Extraordinary larg fatt Oxen" with "Great humps upon their shoulders." They noted also sheep, goats, lemons, potatoes, as well as an abundance of fish from the bay. Capt. Reddish of *Lion* deployed longboats to fetch water from the so-called "Three Rivers" area, where the mouths of those rivers emptied into the bay, and cattle for their consumption. There is no mention in his log of the letter that Mathews left for Capt. John Cockburn of

---

[24] Log of HMS *Lion*.

Salisbury with natives there explaining the fleet's rendezvous at Bombay.[25]

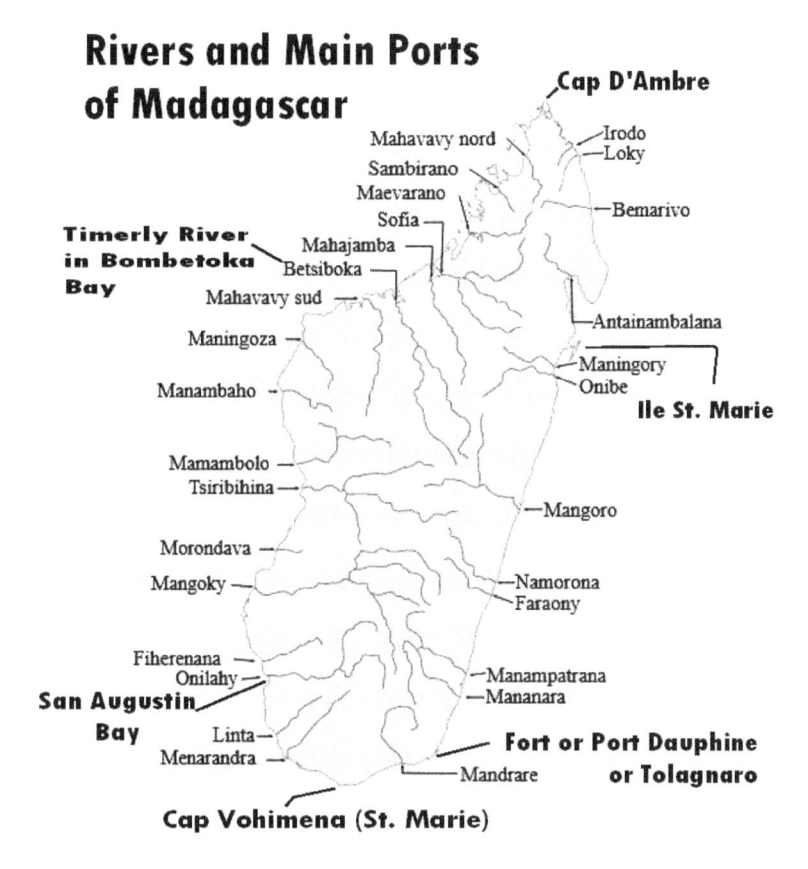

Rivers and Main Ports of Madagascar

Cap D'Ambre
Mahavavy nord
Irodo
Loky
Sambirano
Maevarano
Sofia
Bemarivo
Timerly River in Bombetoka Bay
Mahajamba
Betsiboka
Mahavavy sud
Antainambalana
Maningoza
Maningory
Manambaho
Onibe
Ile St. Marie
Mamambolo
Tsiribihina
Mangoro
Morondava
Mangoky
Namorona
Faraony
Fiherenana
Onilahy
Manampatrana
San Augustin Bay
Mananara
Linta
Fort or Port Dauphine
Menarandra
Mandrare
or Tolagnaro
Cap Vohimena (St. Marie)

Like most ships, the fleet planned to take on supplies and provisions at San Augustin before proceeding elsewhere in the Indian Ocean. They remained a week at San Augustin taking on these supplies, and then weighed anchor on 12 July. Afterward, *Lion* followed the western shore of Madagascar, heading north, landing at Timerly River ("Betsiboka" today; a river which emptied into Bombétoke Bay) the 17th, remaining there until the 19th. Then, she set sail for the islands of Mayotte, Johanna, and Comorros, meeting with the "King of Johanna" and taking aboard more potatoes, yams, fowls, goats, bananas, rice, limes, etc. The

---

[25] Log of HMS *Lion*.

256   Sailing East

pirates that Mathews supposedly hunted sat safely on the other side of the huge island at Île Saint-Marie, the traditional refuge of pirates. It was almost as if the fleet avoided contact – perhaps until the pirates had opportunity to read the letter Mathews left behind at San Augustin Bay.[26]

Downing told that the remainder of the fleet, *Salisbury* (on which Downing was then stationed) and *Grantham,* had lagged behind the commodore's ship, *Lion*. They arrived later than the fleet, both at Capetown and Madagascar. After receiving new masts in Lisbon, he reported, *Exeter* and *Salisbury* made São Jago in April, a month behind *Lion*. They watered and departed on the 22nd. While at the Cape Verde Islands, *Exeter* was sailing better and Sir Robert Johnson pulled *Exeter* alongside *Salisbury* to tell her they would go ahead, making Capetown in time to join Mathews. This left *Salisbury* to arrive so late at Capetown (27 June [J: 8 Jul]), two weeks after Mathews. They also departed 8 July and were joined by *Grantham* 9 July, just 50 miles out of Table Bay. They finally arrived at Madagascar by 2 August. They landed in the bay of San Augustin, twenty-one days after *Lion* departed. Downing and his captain learned that the pirates had found the commodore's letter sometime within those twenty-one days - between 12 July and 2 August 1721, after HMS *Lion* left and HMS *Salisbury* anchored there.[27]

This prompted quite the reaction from Downing, who was certain that Comm. Mathews never needed to leave such a letter and put them all in danger. They knew the rendezvous point of Bombay, even without the orders Mathews received at Table Bay. Downing wrote:

> [Mathews in *Lyon*] had not been gone long, before the Pyrates in the *Victory* [*Defense*] and *Cassandra* arrived there, to whom the Blacks delivered his Letters, who at that time did not know of any Men of War coming in quest of them. They took the Letters and brought them on board the *Victory* [*Defense*], where Capt. Taylor [of *Defense*] was pleased to have them read at the Mast, by which they were satisfied of the Strength of the Squadron, the Names of every Ship, the Commanders Names, and the Number of Guns and Men. This looked as if they were left with an intent to fall into the

---

[26] Log of HMS *Lion*.
[27] Downing, 52; Log of HMS *Salisbury*.

Hands of the Pyrates; for as Capt. Cockburn [of *Salisbury*] was the Senior Captain next the Commodore, he must certainly have known the Place of Rendezvous... For had not these Letters fell into their Hands, the *Salisbury* would probably have fell in with these Pyrates; but they finding these Letters left for her, did not think proper to stay there, but directly weighed and run for Port Dolphin [Dauphin; opposite side of the island]. The Inhabitants of St. Augustine did not know what was right or wrong, and being an ignorant People, they gave the Letter to the first Ships that came.[28]

It is interesting to note here that Downing assumed the natives of Madagascar too innocent and ignorant to understand the difference between pirates and the Royal Navy. This shows the outright prejudice of the early eighteenth century English/Europeans. Natives there had decades of experience with the English and particularly with the Royal Navy, who often landed there to resupply like most ships did after rounding the Cape. The native peoples of Madagascar knew exactly who they were. Pirates had even more experience with these natives who were well acquainted with *them*. The natives suffered little by fooling these navy officers and simply relied on that prejudice to escape condemnation for helping their pirate friends – the source of their good fortunes.

As to the imprudence of Mathews leaving the letter, Downing condemned the action and explained that it was customary, "for fear of losing Company by Distress of Weather, for every Captain to have his sailing Instructions, and an Account of Places appointed for Rendezvous." He went so far as to explain that all ships of war have their signals, with a list of a line of battle, "So that every Fore-mast Man may look up and see the Ship's Name, Captain, and Compliment of Men and Guns, as they steer the Ship." This list, he said, was always "hung up at the Mizen Mast for the better Instruction of the

---

[28] Downing, 52; Downing refers to the pirates' largest vessel as "*Victory*," however Jacob du Bucquoy called it *Defense* and since he actually sailed on that ship with Taylor from Delagoa Bay, he probably learned her name.

petty Officers on the Quarter-Deck."[29] There was no reason for the letter!

Why would Mathews have risked leaving it, then? Downing believed that he put *Salisbury* and *Grantham* at risk of attack by the pirates, as they were separated and weaker alone. But, if this were true, then why did the pirates not keep the letter and attack them by surprise? One may attribute this action of Mathews as simply ill-considered, but Downing (as well as Richard Taylor) felt that there was more to it. A pirate captive deposed that Taylor exclaimed upon seeing the letter, "he knew that [the fleet] did not come to seek for the Pirates but to force a Trade."[30] In Mathews' defense, and presuming faithful intent, he did not yet know the strength of the pirates' vessels – that they had refitted *Defense* with 60-70 guns (Lt. Robert, in *Bibliothèques,* stated she was reduced "from three bridges to two and a half bridges and reduced to 60 guns"; Dutch reports said 64). This might have changed his decision. Still, the letter served no relevant purpose according to Downing and events proved that Taylor may have been absolutely correct about Mathews![31]

Mathews' fleet finally regrouped at their long-planned rendezvous. "*Lyon* and *Shoreham* arrived at Bombay in the beginning of September 1721, and the *Exeter* in about a fortnight after," wrote Downing. *Salisbury* and *Grantham* followed on "the Second or Third of October."[32] There, they camped on Bombay Island, commissioned officers to lead expeditions, and amassed an army of 5,000 troops to go after Konhoji Angrey's forces. By far, this had been their primary mission. The fleet would not return to Madagascar for several months. John Barnes, then acting-captain of *Greenwich* following Kirby's death, noted their presence in Bombay Road upon his return from Persia, Saturday, 21 October 1721.[33]

Richard Moor's narrative seems quite confusing on this point. He had a problem with dates, confusing the years of

---

[29] Downing, 52-53.
[30] Information of Gyles Neal, f. 94.
[31] Robert, *Bibliothèques* (1730).
[32] Downing, 53.
[33] British Library, "Greenwich: Journal, John Barnes, Chief Mate," India Office Records, IOR L/MAR/B/488A, 6 Oct 1719-13 Jul 1722.

1720 and 1721. He also gets ship names wrong on occasion or confused their times of capture and appearance with that of the pirates. For instance, Moor asserted that the pirates went to Delagoa in April 1721 briefly, but it was April 1722 - the pirates were at Île de Bourbon in April 1721. He also skipped over large spans of time. As he had been with pirates for almost four years, he may have lost track of time. Moreover, his interviewers had specific goals (prob. Mathews' trial) in mind and may have asked specific questions, answers to which formed his official deposition.

In essence, Moor cannot be helpful in determining the pirates' activities for the better part of summer 1721 to spring 1722, after the fleet left. The fleet's sudden appearance and just as sudden departure may have lulled pirates into a false sense of security. Certainly, it made them more comfortable. The letter and the fact that Mathews avoided Île Saint-Marie when they first arrived no doubt added to their confidence. They remained at Île Saint-Marie to lay low, parked *Cassandra* and *Defense* in the harbor there and drank and caroused with their friends. Why not leave Madagascar altogether? There was nothing more they could do on the island but trade with the occasional merchant who dropped by. Perhaps they planned to live there or awaited Mathews' arrival to trade. They certainly had goods to sell, but also much of it they wasted and allowed to spoil on the beaches of their island. The carelessness of these slothful pirates cannot be understated.

Douglas R. Burgess Jr. looked for the reason that pirate Henry Every vacated the East Indies after gaining his fortune. He assumed in *The Pirate's Pact* that Madagascar "was a fine place to revictual and satisfy one's lusts but little more."[34] These pirates, probably infused with the great exploits of Every at Madagascar, possessed even less ambition than their venerated icon, it would appear. They probably remained there and simply enjoyed booze and lust for the better part of that

---

[34] Douglas R. Burgess, Jr., *The Pirate's Pact: The Secret Alliances Between History's Most Notorious Buccaneers and Colonial America* (New York: McGraw-Hill, 2008), 139.

year. Psychologically, they did not really compare with "King" Adam Baldridge, of Every's day, an ex-pirate who lived on the island then, but also a successful entrepreneur. Moor deposed that he and his later captors met with Baldridge's alleged successor, "King of Ranter's Bay," John Plantain at Île Saint-Marie "who appeared to be and was intimately acquainted with many of the Pirates and eat and drank and caroused with them."[35] Most certainly, they had!

Comm. Mathews Again Visits Madagascar

After witnessing Gov. Boone's retirement and the succession of John Pitts as governor of Bombay for the EIC, and after removing Sir Robert Johnson as captain of HMS *Exeter* for violating orders, the fleet departed Bombay in February 1722 – *Exeter*, then under Capt. Samuel Braithwaite. They followed the Indian west coast or Malabar in the south. They were bound for Madagascar and, so then branched off and made for Mauritius, as Downing wrote:

> In February 1721-2 we left the Coast of Malabar, and took our Departure from Cape Commeron [Comorin] in the Latitude of 7 Deg. 10. M. Northerly, and shaped our Course for the Island of Moroslas [Mauritius], but made no Stay there; tho' we here found writ on Capt. Carpenter's Tomb with a Piece of Charcoal, ["]We were here in the *Cassandra* and *Victory* [not *Defense?* Was this written when the pirates repaired *Victory* Feb-April 1721?], expecting your Coming; we left this Place on the 28th of February [confusing; if 1721, they arrived about that date – did they leave this message for Macrae?], and are now on our Voyage for Port Dolphin [Dauphin], on the Island of Madagascar.[" Was this misdirection for Macrae?][36]

The Commodore and his men, however, almost missed the pirates' message, which appears to have been written instead for James Macrae, who they believed followed them as they fled the Malabar Coast. As *Lion's* log recorded, the fleet made sail on 15 March for Bourbon, "where some of our People disposed of

---

[35] Moor, 212.
[36] Downing, 62.

several Casks of Arrack, and Madera Wine, &c. for very good Profit."[37]

The fleet then left Bourbon for Madagascar. *Lion's* log told, however, that weather alternated for weeks between fair, rainy, and contrary winds– *Lion*, *Exeter*, and *Salisbury* made little headway. There came a strong lightning storm thirty miles northwest of Round Island, a small island about fourteen miles north of Mauritius. The storm separated *Lion* from her consorts and split her mizzen topsail "from head to foot."[38]

Blown six leagues back southeast, *Lion's* crew made sight of Round Island four leagues away. They knew they were close to Mauritius and decided at nightfall to return to that destination for resupply and to make repairs. The next afternoon, 28 March at 3 pm, *Lion* anchored in the northwest harbor of Mauritius, where the pirates had made their repairs to *Victory* the year before. *Salisbury* and *Exeter* had landed there as well. On 29 March, the fleet made for the next bay north, or Carpenter's Bay ["Baye de Tombeau" or "Bay of Tombs"], to "wood and water." This bay is apparently where they found the message written on Capt. Carpenter's tomb by the pirates, which the Navy men believed was a taunt written for *their* benefit, not Macrae, urging them to find them at Port Dauphin.[39] As HMS *Salisbury's* log makes clear,

---

[37] Downing, 62.

[38] National Archives, London, ADM 52-436, Log of HMS *Lion*, 9 Jan 1721 – 12 Oct 1722.

[39] Log of HMS *Lion*; "The Manuscripts of P. Edward Tillard, Esq., of the Holme, Godmanchester," *Fifteenth Report, Appendix, Part X* (London: Her Majesty's Stationary Office, 1899), 79; Cemetery location and fauna detail from the observations of William Tillard, 17 May 1699 at Carpenter's Bay, Mauritius: ""There is verry good fresh water about half-a-mile up ye river from Carpenters bay w[h]ere we lay with our ship, so y^t we made 3 turns with fresh water every day, & y^t with ease. There is a tomb built at ye entrance of ye river [Terre Rouge or Rivière du Tombeau], a little way from ye shore, where lyes one Welden, who died on this Isl^d ab^t 2 y^{rs} since, returning home in ye Benj^a from Bombay. Here are also sharks and manatees about this Isl^d but we took no notice of either, to strike them. Here is also a great many sea turtle, but we were too soon in ye year to find any of them. Here is abundance of ebony wood, wch we saw going up to ye freemens houses, wch lay 3 mile fr^m Carpenters bay. As for birds, we did not see many, ye most plentifull are hawks and turtle-doves wch will suffer you to come verry nigh them before they fly away, the grey hawk is verry good food. Here is also a very large batt, at least a yard distance fr^m ye tip of one wing to ye tip of ye other, there (*sic*) body as large [as] a midle sized monkey, & there (*sic*) head just like y^m, the inhabitants eat y^m, & say they

Carpenter's tomb was large and obvious enough so as to function as a navigational feature, seen from aboard ship. *Salisbury's* log mentions "wee finde here 2 french Ships that brought people to Settle this place" to join with English pirates already there.[40] They mounted forty and thirty-six guns. Mathews informed the Admiralty that they brought twelve shore guns, but were "in a very bad condition, and no way provided with Men sufficient, or Provisions, or, indeed, with any necessaries to preserve them from the attempts of the Pirates."[41] After nearly a week at Mauritius, the fleet resupplied and weighed anchor on 4 April to resume her voyage, now for Port Dauphin, following the misunderstood message of the pirates, to find them at Madagascar, not at Île Saint-Marie, but at the location to which they hoped to misdirect Macrae.

First, however, Mathews would divert to Île de Bourbon. Mathews' fleet anchored in St. Paul's Bay off western Île de Bourbon on the 9th to resupply. There, at the pirate settlement, Mathews learned of an English pirate named Kendall and his thirty-two men, settled there from Île Saint-Marie. Kendall, George Wilkins, carpenter Joseph Foot, and a caulker named "Jemmy" were still on the island. Mathews negotiated with Gov. Beauvollier de Courchant about these pirates before setting sail for Madagascar. De Courchant wrote back to him 21 April, while Mathews was at anchor at Madagascar, with the expected refusal. The French governor told him that their king had offered amnesty to these men and they accepted. Therefore, he intimated that without further orders from his king, he would not release these men to Mathews. Mathews, of course, later complained of this to the Admiralty – probably because the pirates were likely broke.

---

are very good food, I see one of them cut open on the breast, & 'twas nothing butt fatt."
[40] National Archives, London, ADM 52-294, Log of HMS *Salisbury*, 3 Feb 1718 – 10 May 1724; Letter (28 June) and order (21 January) concerning the petition of the United East India Company for the despatch of His Majesty's [war]ships to supress the (mostly English) pirates in the Indian Sea [Ocean], SP 42/17/9, 28 Jun 1720..
[41] National Archives of London, Thomas Mathews, SP 42/17/282, Concerning the letter (dated 13 January) from Mathews about intelligence of French warships in Mauritius, the poor condition of the French defences on Cooper's Island (against the Pirates), and news of the pirate Kendall and 30 of his men on Don Mascareen, 17 Sep 1723.

Baylus C. Brooks 263

All of these negotiations appeared to be useless but nominal diplomatic parley.[42]

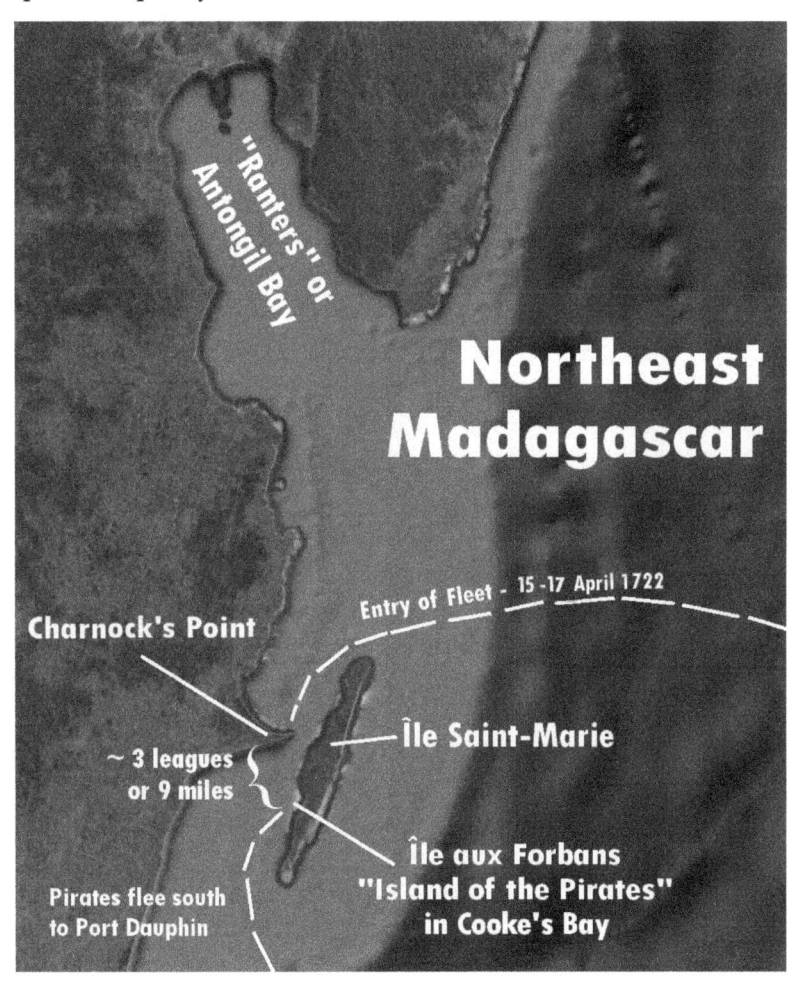

Northeast Madagascar

"Ranters" or Antongil Bay

Charnock's Point

Entry of Fleet - 15-17 April 1722

~ 3 leagues or 9 miles

Île Saint-Marie

Île aux Forbans "Island of the Pirates" in Cooke's Bay

Pirates flee south to Port Dauphin

---

[42] National Archives, London, SP 42/17/284, Copy of the letter [9 April 1722] from Admiral [Comm. Thomas] Mathews to Monsieur Beaurollier [Beauvollier] de Couchant Governor of the Island of Bourbon, 17 Sep 1723; SP 43/17/283, Letter (in French dated 21 April 1722) from Monsieur Beaurollier de Couchant Governor of the Isle Bourbon to Admiral Mathews commander in the Indies, concerning the release of 32 pirates of Kendall's crew, 23 Sep 1723; SP 78/179/84, Folio 151: Crawfurd to Delafaye. Has complained about Governor of [Réunion] who gave refuge to pirates, 13 Oct 1723; SP 42/17/284, Copy of the letter from Admiral [Comm. Thomas] Mathews to Monsieur Beaurollier [Beauvollier] de Couchant Governor of the Island of Bourbon, 17 Sep 1723.

Mathews weighed anchor from Bourbon on the 11th to make for Port Dauphin, as LeVasseur and Taylor's message had mis-instructed them, via tombstone scribble. Again, on this attempt, still squally weather forced the fleet to change course on 14 April for Île Saint-Marie rather than Port Dauphin where the pirates had scrawled on the tombstone – again, likely for Macrae's eyes – about where they would be. Unless Mathews had been uncharacteristically shrewd, they surprisingly landed quite near *Cassandra* and *Defense,* which lay *not* at Port Dauphin, hundreds of miles south of them, but at the very destination for which they now sailed – Île Saint-Marie. It rained from noon until six that night – reducing visibilty. They might have completely surprised the unsuspecting pirates, who may have forgotten about any possible trade with Mathews, but the weather may have had other ideas.

On the 15th at noon, the fleet rounded the north end of Île Saint-Marie, and then by 6 pm turned south to go between that island and Madagascar. HMS *Lion* had trouble with the weather and anchored for two nights at the north end of Île Saint-Marie, while *Salisbury* and *Exeter* continued all night to Charnock's Point. *Lion* set out again at 6 am, still in squally weather. At 5 pm on the 17th, they joined *Salisbury* and *Exeter* already anchored in Tintingue Bay formed by "Charnock Point which is a low point full of trees [which] shoots out within six miles of St. Marys." They sat more like three leagues or nine miles northwest of Île aux Forbans, or "Pirate Island," in modern Bay of Ambodifotatra of southwest Île Saint-Marie.[43]

Firing their guns at Charnock's Point in salute alerted the pirates, in easy earshot nine miles away at Île Saint-Marie. Richard Moor deposed that they heard the guns. Possibly fearing that Macrae found them, they undoubtedly scrambled and quickly fled for the coast of Mozambique, first stopping at Port Dauphin. They may also have supposed the fleet intended to hunt them instead of trade with them – still a possibility. Of course, Mathews still wanted to trade with these wealthy pirates – but the weather simply derailed his plans.

Two hours later, HMS *Salisbury* weighed for "Pirate Island" to reconnoiter for the Commodore and contact these

---

[43] Log of HMS *Lion;* Log of HMS *Salisbury.*

men. *Lion* remained at Charnock's Point to water, but sent their barge with two lieutenants and a flag of truce with *Salisbury*. Downing's book version stated:

> The Commodore sent the *Salisbury*, and his Second Lieutenant [Crawford with another], with his six-oar'd Boat [barge], up to the Island, to make Discoveries; where we found the Wrecks of several Ships which the Pyrates had demolished, with their Cargo's of China Ware, rich Drugs, and all sorts of Spices, lying in great heaps on the Beach of the said Island: there were also several Guns.[44]

HMS *Lion's* barge returned that night and this log entry appeared on 18th April:

> "… in the Evening our barge Return:d from Saint-Maries [and] bro^t: word that Capt. [Edward] England and all the Rest of the White Men was fled up the Countrey for fear of us [and] that the piratts Ships Saild home 5 Months [*Salisbury's* log stated 3] ago but Where wee Cannot find out."[45]

Mathews must have been sorely disappointed. The next day, the 19th, at 4 pm, *Salisbury* had also returned from Île Saint-Marie to water at Charnock's Point. Then, *Lion* and *Exeter* weighed for "Pirate's Island" to further investigate, having left a contingent of men at the point. Squally weather again slowed their progress. At 3 pm, *Exeter* lost another "topsail yard" and they did not make Île Saint-Marie, only nine miles away, until the next morning. That morning, on the 20th, they had difficulty navigating their approach without a native pilot. West of Île aux Cailles (Îlot Madame after 1820), the large island at the entrance of the bay, illustrated in maps, the channel sounded at only 3 fathoms, but on the east side, there appeared a navigable channel of 5-6 fathoms. Finally they "turned up nearer the Harbour of the Land at Noon… [called] Cockey [Cooke's] Bay," now called the Bay of Ambodifotatra.[46]

---

[44] Log of HMS *Lion;* Downing, 63; National Archives, London, HCA 1/55, Information of Clement Downing, ff. 78-80, 26 Oct 1724; This deposition of two contains almost the same information as Downing's book, with slightly different wording.
[45] Log of HMS *Lion;* Log of HMS *Salisbury.*
[46] Log of HMS *Lion;* Cooke's Bay is now called the Bay of Ambodifotatra.

On the 21st, the Commodore's men made a full survey of Cooke's Bay, finding two more islands, with Île aux Forbans nestled strategically in the center of the bay. They regarded it as a fine harbor, but it was obvious that pirates had made it their chief resort for many years. There were four burnt hulls of sunken ships from Ilôt Madame to Île aux Forbans. Mathews salvaged cannon from one.[47] There was another halfway between this island and the third, a smaller island to west, within the harbor, about a quarter of mile in circumference and known as "Redwood Island," for the trees upon it. "Pirate's Town" sat "two Ships Lengths" inland of Île aux Forbans. There were houses on both islands, the majority on Île aux Forbans at the town. They were all about two feet off the ground and then inhabited by natives. The natives proved friendly, helping HMS *Exeter* with a new topsail yard, fashioned from the abundance of wooded forest around them.[48]

Fenerive, ö. Madagaskar. Risbod och hönshus hos betsinuisaraka. Fenerive - SMVK - 001653 - Betsimisaraka people – Wikipedia

As Midshipman Clement Downing later related in his book, the pirates obviously celebrated their good fortune on Île Saint-Marie, making a huge mess and wasting tons of valuable cargo. Items of great value, like fine china and cloth, useless to pirates uninterested in such items, were left strewn on the beaches.

---

[47] Log of HMS *Lion;* Ewen and Skowronek, *Pieces of Eight*,, 59-62; Archaeologist John de Bry claims this wreck to be that of "*Fiery Dragon*," or Edward Congdon's *Dragon.*
[48] Log of HMS *Lion.*

Plan du Port de l'Isle de Saint Mary's de Madagascar (FM DFC XVII/28PFA/2), by Reynaud (1733) in Archives de l'Outre Mers, Aix en Province, France and Google Map of same area. Reynaud (1733) was borrowed from *X Marks the Spot: The Archaeology of Piracy*, 111. Highlighted "Z"s indicates known shipwrecks of the time.

By the evening of the 23rd, a boat from *Salisbury* entered Cooke's bay, *Lion* hoisted a white flag to be visible to the boat as she came through darkness. The boat brought word to the Commodore that "One of the White men who had been a pirating [had] Come Down to the Water Side with a Strong Guard of Armed Negros," at Charnock's Point. Comm. Mathews must have been relieved. *Lion* then returned to Charnock's Point to meet this man. Meanwhile, *Exeter* continued her repairs in "Cooke's Bay" until the 26th.[49]

How this pirate contacted these navy men is a tale in itself. *Salisbury's* first mate, one Mr. Henry Davies, Midshipmen Frost and Clement Downing, as well as a carpenter from *Exeter* had earlier on the 23rd gone ashore at Charnock's Point to cut a fresh jib boom. While ashore in such reduced numbers, they saw "a white man coming down towards the shore with 20 to 30 black men armed."[50] The white man asked who they were and first mate Davies lied to him, as they were outnumbered, saying they were merchants. The man responded, obviously aware of Mathews' letter, "No. No. I know better. You are the Squadron of Men of War come to look for us."[51] Davies was worried then that he and his men might be in trouble.

John Plantain, reputed "King of Ranter's Bay," or Antongil Bay, however, appeared rather friendly to them and officially presented himself to Lt. Davies.[52] It seems that Plantain had once been part of *Dragon's* crew the year before when his poisoned mates were left behind and their captain Edward Congdon quickly fled from angry natives for the island of Bourbon. Some were also apparently spared by the natives and may have made a deal with them for their survival. Since this initial fright, Plantain had done quite well for himself.

Moor deposed that Plantain *et al* "had got Riches enough (by pirating) to maintain them hansomly as long as they

---

[49] Log of HMS *Lion*.
[50] Information of Clement Downing, f. 79.
[51] Information of Clement Downing, f. 79.
[52] Information of Clement Downing, f. 79.; Downing, in his later book, had elaborated on Plantain's long voyage to the East Indies with Edward England. Plantain then told them that he was "born at Chocolate Hole in Jamaica [Port Royal]," and that he belonged to Edward Congdon's pirate ship *Dragon*, but that he was also present at Bourbon when they took the Viceroy's ship, just a year earlier; note that Downing stated that Plantain's first name was "William" in the deposition; see Chapter 2 for details.

lived."[53] He further asserted that Plantain had "left off pirating." If Plantain had joined LeVasseur, Seager and Taylor at Bourbon, then he had also joined them on the Malabar Coast and at Mauritius when they repaired *Victory* in the old Dutch-new French shipyard at the later Port Louis. Still, he may have stretched his tale quite a bit.

Salisbury's midshipman Clement Downing was utterly fascinated by Plantain and interviewed him at length. Downing's assertions of Plantain being a "King of Ranter's Bay"[54] and having a native retinue are reasonably supported by the local population of that locale who were probably inclined to support his spending habits. Many of them already possessed European genes from their parents' earlier contacts and had some affinity for the pirates. This chapter's section on Bucquoy and Chapter Eight will explore more of the anthropological makeup of Madagascar.[55]

Plantain willingly informed Lt. Davis that the pirates of 40-gun *Cassandra* and the 60 or 70-gun (64, according to Dutch reports) Portuguese ship, named *Defense* by them, "had gone out with the sd. Ships."[56] Contrary to the earlier assertion made by the natives at Île aux Forbans of "Five months," or "3 months" in *Salisbury's* log, which was simply a lie to protect their pirate friends, Plantain unabashedly told them the truth, perhaps desiring to secure any trade that might take place for himself. Plantain probably drank and caroused with LeVasseur and Taylor at "Pirate's Town" often. He might have been

---

[53] Moor, 213.
[54] Antongil Bay; northeast Madagascar, north of Saint-Marie Island – "Ranter's Bay" refers to modern Rantabe - a town and commune (Malagasy: kaominina) in Madagascar. It belongs to the district of Maroantsetra, which is a part of Analanjirofo Region. The population of the commune was estimated to be approximately 20,000 Betsimisaraka in 2001 commune census.
[55] Clement Downing, *A Compendious History of the Indian Wars... with Account of the Notorious Pirate John Plantain at Madagascar...* (London: Printed for T. Cooper, 1737), 105-114; note that Richard Moor, in his deposition, also claimed that Plantain served as well on the *Dragon* under pirate captain Edward Congdon, who was then (after Jan 1721) a resident of Réunion Island; Downing also mentioned that Plantain claimed to be "a part" of *Cassandra's* crew, but he probably meant that he was part of taking her on England's ship, *Fancy*.
[56] Information of Clement Downing, f. 79.

within sight of Île Saint-Marie when the fleet's guns fired nine miles away and saw their ships leave. Startled, Taylor and LeVasseur hurriedly fled in the cover of the rain from Madagascar, leaving the reputed "King of Ranter's Bay" to boldly meet and trade with the Royal Navy alone. Drawn by the cannon sound, he then headed toward Charnock's Point with his retinue of armed natives to prepare for trade his goods with these navy men.

Downing wrote in his book that his commander, Capt. John Cockburn, wanted to arrest Plantain, but the large number of native defenders, more than 1,000 most likely Betsimisaraka of East Madagascar, at his side prevented this. Still, Downing doth protest too much. His official deposition stated nothing about anyone wanting to arrest this wealthy pirate trader – but, then Comm. Mathews' first courts-martial was already over by the time he published his book (1737). Mathews was only a few years away from being promoted to Vice Admiral by then. Downing's deposition declared there were *only* 20 to 30 men total, not 1,000, though he may have referred to the total force of fighting men seen later at Plantain's town.

Plantain offered trade to the navy officers, which they accepted willingly and sent word to the Commodore. Richard Taylor had certainly been correct about Mathews' actual intentions. Too bad he and LeVasseur had fled to Mozambique![57]

On the morning of the 24th, *Lion* waited at Charnock's Point for word of this pirate Plantain while his men scrubbed decks. Then, two of the white pirates came with five armed native guards to meet the Commodore, but refused to go aboard the ships. Instead, they invited the Commodore and his men to come with them twenty miles (6 or 7 in Downing's book) inland to Plantain's base, southward of the mouth of Ranters' or Antongil Bay, possibly near modern Manompana.[58]

---

[57] Information of Clement Downing, f. 80.
[58] This Manompana, at about 9 miles from Chantock's Point agrees best with Clement Downing's book. Antanmabe, or the next town north is about 20 miles further away. Both appear to have good small bays, but Manompana has grown significantly since 1722, now with 10,000 people, exporting cloves and vanilla. The Cascade de Manompana provides an excellent source of fresh water.

Mathews had been quite eager to meet this "King of Ranter's Bay" and agreed to follow. On April 27th, they arrived at Plantain's chief town on the lusher eastern coast protected by the large mountainous spine of Madagascar. There, they met three more white men: one English, one Scot, and a Dane. Gyles Neal and Clement Downing's deposition tell that the Englishman was James "Jimmy" Deer or Deering. The Dane was probably Hans Burgen. All four of them had been part of *Dragon's* crew. They all flew flags of their respective nations beside their homes, with retinues of native soldiers, and all claimed to be wealthy beyond one's wildest imaginations, stoked with money and jewels from a "Rich Mocho Man and the Great Portuguese Ship." They carried a presumed air much like rich colonists of Port Royal, Jamaica, or Charles Town, South Carolina. Moor's testimony confirmed the rumors.[59]

Downing's deposition clearly shows that Richard Taylor was right about Comm. Mathews, who readily dealt with Plantain and his fellow former crewmates. As Plantain was backed by the bulk of the Betsimisaraka of Northeast Madagascar, he probably had a formidable army at his disposal, reputed to number 1,000. Still, Mathews had no interest in fighting them. Downing deposed that "there were afterwards carryed on Shoar from ye Lyon in the Salisbury's long boat several baskets and hampers of glass bottles & some small Casks of Arrack."[60] Downing described the illicit trade in detail:

> And then the sd. Comodore & Capt. Cockburn & the Men returned on board & ye Casks Baskets or hampers with a pint silver Mug a Case of Silvers knives & forks a firken of Butter a parcel of Sugar Candy & other Goods were kept in the Boat all night & the next Day the sd. Comodore[,] Capt. Cockburn[,] the informant [Downing] & others went on Shoar again & then ye aforesaid Goods were delivered out of the Boat on Shoar[.] And he the informt. saw the same

---
[59] "Entry: 27 April" in Log of HMS *Lion*; Information of Gyles Neal, f. 94; Moor, 212-213..
[60] Information of Clement Downing, f. 80.

delivered to the Servants or Agents of the aforesd. Plantin by the sd. Mr. Davis & Mr. Bassett & he the informant heard ye Comodore order ye sd. Mr. Bassett to go to ye sd. Plantins house [log entry 27th: 20 miles inland on Madagascar] & to see ye sd. Goods safely delivered & to be very carefull in his Accounts & the next day about four in the afternoon… Mr. Bassett told [Downing] that he had paid the sd. Comodore the money for the aforesd. Goods & that he had reced. of the sd Plantin & delivered to ye sd Comodore five Barrs or Wedges of Gold & several Diamonds and then showed [Downing] a Diamond about the bigness of a large Pea which (As he told [Downing]) he ye sd Mr. Bassett had for himself… there were carryed on Shoar from the Lyon several large Puncheons of Arrack & a Butt of Madera Wine… ye Comodore feasted with ye sd Plantin & 2 other white Men (to wit) James Deering [Deer?] a Scotch Man and the other a Dane [Hans Burgen of Copenhagen] the greatest part of the Day.[61]

Of course, ship's master Robert Douglass recorded in *Lion's* log the many riches from the rich Mocha-man captured by the pirates, but *nothing* of any portion of that traded wealth being loaded aboard the *Lion* and *Salisbury*. Douglass only referred to "continuous victualing," the loading of fresh beef and other meat.[62] Neither did *Salisbury's* log mention any details beyond the vagaries of the weather and brief ship movements. Everything loaded aboard the Navy vessels from Plantain's town was done in secret.

---

[61] Information of Clement Downing, ff. 81-82, 92-93; Log of HMS *Lion*; Capt. John Dolling, then Thomas Creed, masters of 45-ton, 2-gun *Coward*, w/16 crew, captured by pirates in summer 1719 – CO 390/7: The National Archives (Kew, UK) Colonial Office; page 115: "HANS BURGEN, the Dane, was born at Copenhagen, and had been brought up a Cooper; but coming to London, he entered himself with Capt. Creed for Guinea - the Ship being taken by the Pyrates, he agreed to go with them, and became a Comerade to King Plantain;" pirates burned Creed's *Coward,* 27 May 1719..
[62] Log of HMS *Lion;* Log of HMS *Salisbury.*

Ile aux Forbans in Bay of Ambodifotatra

Downing also deposed that, on the 29th, Mathews had been told by Deering and Plantain that they had intel of rival natives who planned an attack on their town. Notes made by an unknown officer in Admiralty records later show that these pirates departed that day "w:th so much Precipitancy that they left there the two Puncheons of Arrack."[63] *Salisbury's* men took a boat ashore under crewman Bassett to *retrieve* these liquors. Junior officers then carried them aboard *Lion* by the order of Capt. Cockburn along with a stolen bag of gold containing four or five hundred pounds Sterling. These illegal events were

---

[63] National Archives, London, Observations on the Lyon at Charnock Point on the Island of Madagascar, Being the Place where the Pyrates are said to Rendezvous (notes for 27-29 April 1722), no date, ff. 138-139.

backed up by depositions of crewman James Holmes and another captive of the pirates, Gyles Neal. It might have been difficult to tell who the real pirates were: Olivier LeVasseur and Richard Taylor or the Royal Navy men under Comm. Thomas Mathews![64]

The fleet weighed anchor on 30 April to round Madagascar on its north point, Cap d'Amber. They found quite a few small rocky islands – thirteen in all. The fleet eventually landed at the cape to water. They cruised northward of Madagascar and along the coast of Mozambique, north of Delagoa Bay, for a couple of months. Once again, they had just missed *Cassandra* and *Defense* at the Fort there. But, then, Royal Navy Comm. Thomas Mathews and his fellow captains had enough gold and diamonds to satisfy them for quite a while. *Lion* parted from *Salisbury* and *Exeter* in Johanna Bay to return to Bombay in June. *Salisbury* and *Exeter* cruised northward from the Comorros along the shores of Ethiopia, finally returning to Bombay in early September. Again, they never caught sight of Richard Taylor and Olivier LeVasseur. Where had they gone?

Fort Lijdzaamheid (Fort Agility) at Delagoa Bay

LeVasseur and Taylor had left Île Saint-Marie in quite the hurry on the evening of 17 April 1722. They sailed south from Île aux Forbans, or "Pirate's Island," away from Charnock's Point and the Royal Navy squadron anchored there. Landing at Port Dauphin, they held brief conference. They decided to visit their "friends" the Dutch, who had been building a fort near current Maputo in coordination with the African Kingdom of Delagoa (on southern coast of Mozambique) on the east coast of Africa and directly across the Mozambique Channel from Madagascar. This Dutch fort may have been the one objective sought by Comm. Mathews – and the pirates knew precisely where it sat. Hopefully, they must have thought, the Dutch would have a large supply of brandy and arrack for their next fete. They arrived there late in April 1722 and found that the

---

[64] Information of Clement Downing, ff. 92-93.

Dutch had almost competed their new fort, but were drastically undermanned – an open invitation to these men. They realized that taking control of the fort from the Dutch would be an easy matter; and, the fort would provide them a better defense against Mathew's fleet, just in case Taylor had indeed been wrong about Mathews. They took another Dutch vessel upon entering Delagoa Bay, 30-gun *Comptoir Holland*, a ship these pirates later called *Greyhound* (not to be confused with the English ship *Greyhound*, renamed *City of Ostend*). They proceeded to occupy Fort Lijdzaamheid. There, they found Jacob de Bucquoy, a Dutch scientist, mapmaker, and engineer to whom Richard Taylor took definite interest.

Delagoa Bay was located on the coast of Mozambique. Portuguese navigator António de Campo, one of Vasco da Gama's captains, found it in 1502. In 1544 the merchant trader Lourenço Marques explored the region. Portuguese King John III named the region Baia de Lourenço Marques in his honor. Lourenço Marques himself is reputed to have renamed it Baía da Lagoa or "Bay of the lagoon," thus "De Lagoa."[65]

About the time that Mathew's fleet left England, by 14 February 1721 the Dutch East India Company or VOC (*Verenigde Oostindische Compagnie*; founded 1602) had established a fort and factory called Lijdzaamheid on the northern coast of Lourenço Marques' Baía da Lagoa (Delagoa and now Maputo Bay). This is the establishment that the Dutch at Capetown feared Mathews may be after. After April 1721, the fort was governed by a chief factor or Opperhoofd, under authority of the Dutch Cape Colony. Jean Michel served as acting-Opperhoofd when, a year later, pirates Richard Taylor in *Defense* and Olivier LeVasseur in *Cassandra* surprised the fort's weakened forces and occupied the new citadel for five months, from late April-28 June 1722. The Dutch venture at the bay did not last long; they eventually abandoned the fort by December 1730.[66]

---

[65] Hugh Chisholm, ed., "Delagoa Bay," *Encyclopædia Britannica*, 7 (11th ed.) (Cambridge University Press, 1911), 942.
[66] "Delagoa Bay," *Encyclopædia*, 942.

Marinus Lodewijk Deventer, in *La Hollande et la Baie-Delagoa*, describes that the VOC lacked in their administration of the fort, "to the point of putting its existence in danger."[67] Administrators of the nascent colony had little faith in its future. He wrote that "they were charged, first of all, with supplying new personnel… reinforcing the incomplete troops and crews in the Bay, decimated from the beginning by diseases."[68] Incompetent, administrators rarely authorized the officers at the Bay of Delagoa to these positions, so that the fort was wholly neglected.[69]

JACOB DE BUCQUOY,
Geb: te Amst: 26 Octb: 1693;
BUCQUOY des Zeemans Gids, in Wiskonst wel bedreeven die's Waerelds kusten en zyn Reistocht heeft beschreeven.

Early in 1722, a malaria epidemic wiped out, with the governor and the commander-in-chief, most of the garrison.

---

[67] Marinus Lodewijk Deventer, *La Hollande et la Baie-Delagoa* (Amsterdam: C. I. Brinkman, 1883), 9.
[68] Deventer, *La Hollande et la Baie-Delagoa*, 9.
[69] Deventer, *La Hollande et la Baie-Delagoa*, 9.

The fort was then unable to resist an attack of any kind. Still, administrators at the Cape waited on orders from the Hague before acting. When they finally received those orders, it was already too late to preserve the Dutch establishment from being seriously compromised.

Thus, when pirate ships, armed with over a hundred cannon between two ships attacked the fort in this condition in late April 1722, it surrendered quickly. They also seized the only Dutch lugger [hooker], or hulk, *Comptoir Hollande*, which was at that moment in the Bay. The guns of the fort, scarcely finished, were effortlessly silenced, and the garrison surrendered quite easily. Deventer blamed the fort's surrender on the untrustworthy foreign acting-commander or Opperhoofd, Jean Michael. "After having beaten the surrounding country," he wrote, "these pirates carried away the provisions, and took away some of the Dutch personnel [22 in number], with the cartographer (de Bucquoy), forced to serve as their pilot on their expedition to Madagascar."[70]

Jacob de Bucquoy, born 26 October 1693, was a hydrographer and cartographer of the Netherlands. He began his career as a cartographer in Europe and then from 1721, he worked for the Dutch East India Company or VOC. During his first overseas excursion to Dutch Fort Lijdzaamheid at Delagoa on the southeast coast of Africa to map the river there, however, he was interrupted in this work and captured by pirates. He had produced remarkable works of cartography and, even if by consequence of his capture, ethnology of Madagascar. His natural curiosity about all things made him an excellent emergency field anthropologist.

In 1735, he returned to the Netherlands where he taught geography. He later penned, in 1744, the tale of his captive anthropological opportunities and his unique personal experiences with pirates and natives of Madagascar. More importantly for this work, he afforded a detailed look at the

---

[70] Deventer, *La Hollande et la Baie-Delagoa*, 9 ; Note : Archives of the Dutch East India Company (VOC), 1602-1796, at http://www.tanap.net, is the most complete and extensive source on early modern World History anywhere.

apparent narcissistic psychosis of Richard Taylor from the vantage point of a scientist. Still, a singular criticism of his efforts would be that Bucquoy may have been overwhelmed by "hero worship" associated with Taylor's vain, self-important fantasies. Furthermore, Taylor's deep-seated paranoia probably fueled the many arguments between him and his French colleague, Olivier LeVasseur de la Buse or the "Buzzard."

One detail about Bucquoy's narrative that may have affected its veracity was its late date. He published this tale more than two decades after the events had occurred. Being a scientist, though, he may have attempted to record or note his observations at the time. Certainly, writing of the book began well before publication – how early is the question. Perhaps we could easily be unnecessarily harsh on Bucquoy. Being in a wilderness environment was difficult, especially for a scientist such as himself. It is difficult to know whether he had pen and paper to make *in situ* records of his observations. Modern anthropologists, of course, use recording media, but that obviously was unavailable to Bucquoy. Still, as a scientist, used to observing great detail that others would easily dismiss, he perhaps served as the best witness of whom we researchers might have requested.

Bucquoy's narrative begins as the pirates left Delagoa Bay still on the hunt. He wrote "On leaving Delagoa Bay [28 June], pirates Taylor and La Bouze [LeVasseur] crossed in front of Mozambique [looking for prizes], but without success." On the night of 17 August, however, LeVasseur and several of his officers plotted to abandon Taylor and go to the West Indies. The crew of the *Defense*, however, rejected this mutinous plan. They fired cannon, "and displayed the black flag, signal of distress." They again held council concerning LeVasseur and afterward, degraded and deposed him, chaining the French "Buzzard" to the mainmast and confiscating his possessions as they made for Sofala, just north of Delagoa on the coast of (then) Mozambique.[71]

In his capacity as observer, Bucquoy found that Richard Taylor had served as a lieutenant in the Royal Navy and probably turned Jacobite at the accession of German-speaking

---

[71] Bucquoy, 103.

King George I. He also clearly respected Taylor's ability to command his men. Taylor had, however, become highly paranoid, the probable reason for his many fights with Olivier LeVasseur. Bucquoy observed:

> As long as I had been forced to travel with the pirates, I had always slept in Captain Taylor's cabin. It often happened that he would awaken with a start, as if seized with terror, and, uttering some horrible blasphemies, he extended his hand towards his pistols, which were hanging within his reach... Thus awakened, he rose to his feet, looked on all sides, and seeing that no danger threatened him, lay again; if he did not fall asleep, he would gladly talk with me.

> It was on these occasions that we often spoke of the kind of life and the habits of the pirates. He had, he said, a horror of that life which was only good for the rabble. He then told me his adventures. How, being an officer in the English Royal Navy, he was disgraced during the reign of Queen Anne after a change of ministry [Hanoverian George I; probable Jacobite]; how he had succeeded in enrolling himself among the pirates who soon elected him for their captain... His disappointed ambition inspired him with the desire to avenge himself, and compelled him to pay for his misfortunes, especially to the English nation, against whom he cherished a bitter resentment.[72]

Taylor's narcissicism, in particular, was all too apparent. He had convinced Bucquoy that he, personally, took *Cassandra* from James Macrae – *not* Edward England and *not* Jasper Seager. He also told his avid listener that he, foremost, *not* LeVasseur or Seager, led the fight to take *Nossa Senhora do Cabo* at St. Denis, la Bourbon. For example, he said it was he who first opened fire. *Taylor*, not LeVasseur, he asserted, stood forth and demanded the Viceroy's surrender, despite the viceroy's personal account that told of the French pirate having done

---

[72] Bucquoy, 107.

this. Likewise, it was *Taylor* who took Portuguese prisoners and treated with the "reluctant" viceroy. *Taylor*, not LeVasseur, he said again, magnanimously handed back his jewel-studded sword, saying "Keep it; I present it to you in memory of your unhappy fate." It was *Taylor* who…

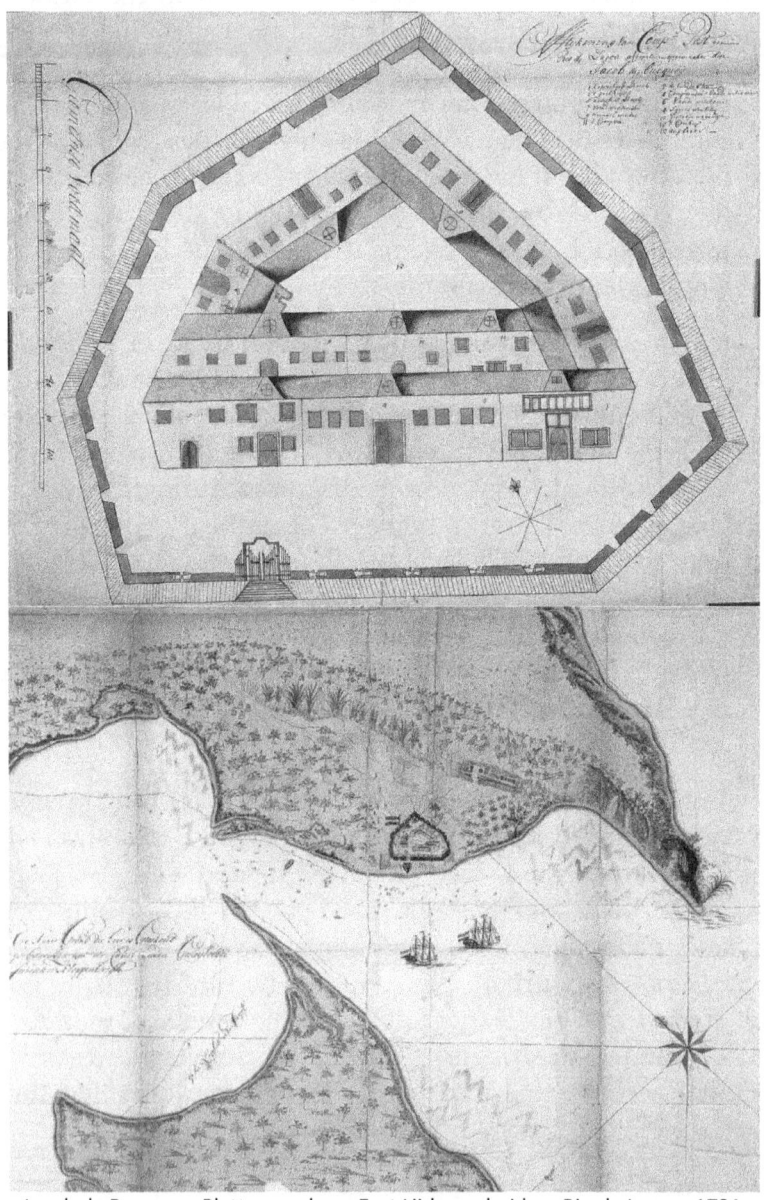

Jacob de Bucquoy, Plattegrond van Fort Lijdzaamheid on Rio de Lagoa, 1721.

... conducted him with his two companions to his cabin, where he endeavored to amuse them by a playful conversation and music in his own way. He took them back to the shore, and the Portuguese sailors were re-embarked on board the ships, with the exception of a few who remained on shore to serve the pirates when they went down there.[73]

Taylor took credit for all things pirate – it seemed that he alone ruled the East Indies! The man was dripping with narcissism – a characteristic well-known to American political pundits of the Trump era. Bucquoy must have seen and understood this blustery self-absorption as a human failing, but it seems that Taylor somehow still impressed the scientist with his captivating tales of "alternative facts," resulting in what we would probably call "fake news."

One day, probably while leaving Sofala and while trying to decide whether to keep pirating on this cruise, Taylor proposed to his crew to go back to where they had just left and raid the "city of Mozambique," or Maputo, "where it was assured to make at one stroke as much booty as on one hundred ships." Hard to imagine that, in the four months they stayed at the fort at Delagoa, they did not already raid the town surrounding it! The French crew, Bucquoy wrote, or of LeVasseur's crew that they, "found themselves sufficiently rich to oppose this project, which would have required at least six times as many ships and men [forts provided them substantial protection from an enemy – generally a 3-1 advantage]." Taylor exclaimed, "If we could ascend to heaven, I would fire my first gun at God," and, recounting some of his audacious deeds, he added, "Why are you pirates, is it not because you are not afraid of the danger and you want to take booty" and that there were riches in Mozambique (referring again to Maputo)? Seeing their inclinations to return home, Taylor taunted his men, "but I see that I am dealing with cowardly people, too cowardly to embark on viable ventures, so let us win the

---

[73] Bucquoy, 110-111.

nearest land, and let every one seek to make his fortune as he pleases." His speech did not affect these men. They voted to return to Madagascar – by then, they were certain, the squadron would have stopped looking for them. Perhaps still cautious, they dropped anchor 1 September 1722 on the west side of Madagascar (other side of the island, but in the same latitude as Île Saint-Marie) in the river Masaliet (Bay of Boeny, Old Mathelage, Mahajamba or Bombétoke). This was the site of the old Arab settlements at the mouth of Timerly River, the location where Comm. Mathews stayed an entire week the year before.[74]

The pirates fired cannon and hoisted the black flag to the top of the mainmast. Immediately, a signal fire appeared and others followed from the interior of Madagascar, "in less than an hour in the harbor, the king knew that a ship had arrived." The excellent ethnographer Bucquoy noted:

> No sooner is a ship wet [arrived] than one or two natives come on board to see where it comes from and to what nationality it belongs. Three or four sailors then went ashore with them, carrying gifts destined for the king, with whom they went to ask him, in the name of the whole crew, permission to land and buy provisions in his own country; Without this permission no one can set foot on the shore, and no native has the right to approach foreigners or sell them anything. The king, after granting the permission requested, sends his general-in-chief with a troop of men to carry a gift of food to the people of the ship, who then descend on shore in groups, erect tents, and each takes a wife; It is a real fair where each one leads a joyous life. Nobody, however, ought to act brutally

---

[74] Bucquoy, 103-104; Grandidier note: In a manuscript of the Deposit of Maps and Plans of the Marine of Paris, volume 84 ', Sea of India, Exhibit 17, at the bottom of page 7, it says: "In 1722, Mangaely [Mamoko Islands, or Ampasindava] was repaired by pirates, and it is said that there was a massacre of pirates made there by the blacks of the country, and that the king of Massailly [Bombetoke Bay], named Ratocaffe [Ratoakafo] Sent his soldiers there to cover all the black men, women and children, even the dogs, and pillaged all the cattle, and since that time the place has been deserted"; Arab slave traders or *Antalaotra* influenced Malagasy language, science, and religion through 600 years, from early 10th-16th centuries.

towards the natives, otherwise the general would apprehend and carry on board the culprits.[75]

On 4 September, Ratocaffe, the king of the Massailly, came with 2,000 armed men to summon the captain, his men, and the twenty-two Dutch prisoners. The traditional show of respect for the king, father, or Salamanga was to kiss his hand, a habit which they probably learned from earlier Europeans. The Salamanga then asked who these prisoners were. The pirates told him and the Dutchmen begged to be allowed to remain on their shores while they built a boat to return to Delagoa. Bucquoy described the response of these men and the festivities afterward:

> He promised to give us satisfaction on condition that we live in peace and do not harm the natives. With that we kissed His Majesty's hand again, thanking him. The king then made us sit in a circle with the pirates behind us and brought a liquor called *Thook* [Toaka], a kind of mead, each one of which he drank as much as he wanted, but which did not take long to effect most of us; some began to sing, others jumped like actors who play drunken roles. This little party lasted till evening. Then those who could walk went to sleep with them in huts, others fell to the ground where they fell asleep.[76]

On the 5th, Bucquoy went to the pirates and asked them, as they were planning to leave, if they would return the hulk *Comptoir Hollande* to them as promised. They also requested provisions for the journey. The pirate council rejected his proposal and they "left us in Madagascar in complete destitution." Moreover, the pirates forced the Dutch to help them refit *Comptoir Hollande* into their newly-named *Greyhound*, perhaps to replace the vessel of the same name lost to Portuguese revolt the year before. During the effort, the clever Bucquoy mentioned that "while helping them, we did not

---

[75] Bucquoy, 105.
[76] Bucquoy, 105-106.

make a mistake and hid as many objects as we could to use when we built our boat."[77]

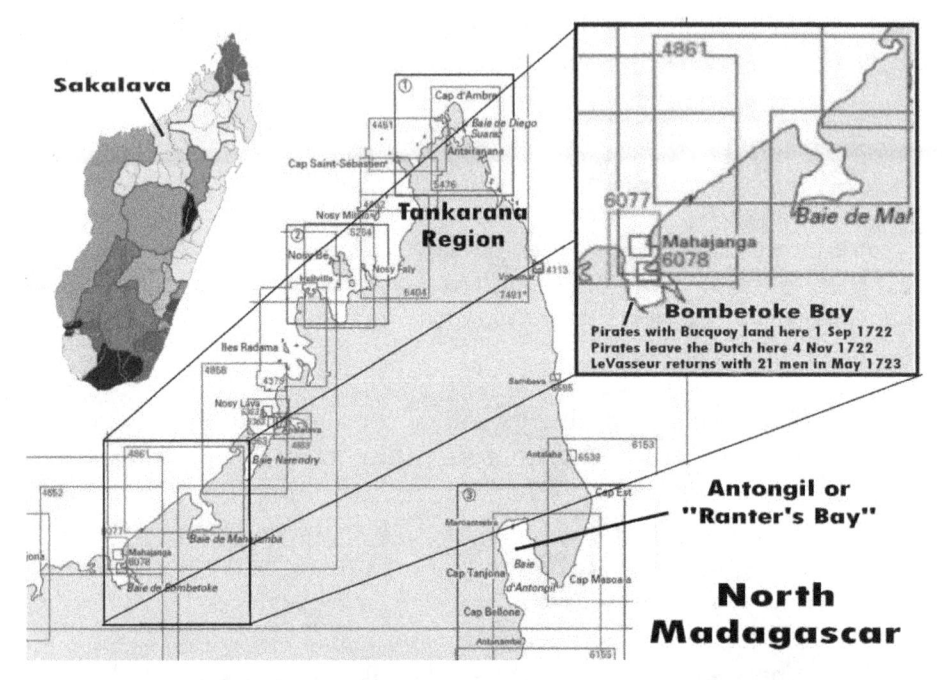

North Madagascar map with inset showing Bombetoke Bay:
Pirates with Bucquoy land here 1 Sep 1722
Pirates leave the Dutch here 4 Nov 1722
LeVasseur returns with 21 men in May 1723
Antongil or "Ranter's Bay"

The pirates had plans for the hulk. It was to be fitted as a pirate and given to Capt. Elk, a Scotsman. The *Cassandra* was then given to Capt. Taylor, who now wished to go to the West Indies, and the "great ship" or *Defense* was then placed in LeVasseur's charge, "who had been lately degraded, and who was disposed to cross the Indian Sea" and continue the game. This decision to split LeVasseur and Taylor was certainly for the best.

Constant arguments between Taylor and LeVasseur undoubtedly led to Taylor's abrupt decision to leave for the West Indies. Bucquoy observed their blustery argument aboard *Cassandra*, then still under LeVasseur:

> The two captains and a master pilot who had been dismissed were in the cabin of La Bouze [LeVasseur] to bid farewell; they quarreled while drinking and made such animosity that La Bouze succeeded in provoking Taylor

---
[77] Bucquoy, 111.

and offering him a fight between their ships. The latter [Taylor], who was easily angry, told him that his proposal was absurd and disgraceful, and he asked him if, by chance, he did it out of resentment of [being] formerly condemned, [and because] he and his accomplices, to serve the [men for] punish[ing]... "It is I," said [LeVasseur], "who punished you; so it's not up to my crew to pay for me. Is it because your ship is now bigger than mine and you think you're crushing me? You are only a coward who do not dare to trust your personal courage."[78]

Taylor's fury blinded him more and more. He began cursing "with his usual seasonings of swearing and blasphemy," at bystanders. Referring to them, "If you are like him," Taylor blurted, "I am ready, go ahead and I will give you satisfaction with the pistol or Saber, as you please!" Of course, Bucquoy said, no one challenged him, "for they knew [Taylor] well enough not to dare venture into a singular combat with him." Taylor was then determined to seek a pardon, away from LeVasseur. The crews likely decided that he should take command of the smaller *Cassandra*. Probably in a huff, Taylor weighed anchor and set sail for the West Indies. *Defense* and *Greyhound* sailed in the opposite direction, for India. This all occurred the 4th of November 1722.[79]

Jacob de Bucquoy had become fascinated and a bit enamored with Richard Taylor. It developed almost into hero worship. He commented:

> In the ordinary course of life, Captain Taylor was easily fed up, and his fury made him out of his power. But as soon as an imminent danger in combat, as in the struggle against the sea, he was no longer the same man; His calmness, his presence of mind, and his personal courage in grave circumstances had won him the admiration of his companions. I have witnessed the skill with which he

---

[78] Bucquoy, 112.
[79] Bucquoy, 106-107; Bucquoy here gets the pirate vessels switched; Hill, "Episodes of Piracy," *Indian Antiquary*, 61; John Freeman deposed "December."

knew how to appease his displeased crew, when he feared a revolt, and the audacity and courage with which he quenched and repressed the revolt, when it burst forth, boldly throwing In the midst of the insurgent pirates, which he struck to the right and left, as if he were dealing with poultry birds; in spite of his severity, which he deemed indispensable, he was much loved by his people, his affability and his adroitly familiar manners, often forgetting his captain's prerogatives to come into the bridge, to chat, play, eat, and drink with the common cauldron.

He had, moreover, a clever policy; thus, in order to establish his authority, he distributed his men by squads of seven men, grouping together, for example, a Frenchman, a Swiss, a Portuguese, and three or four Englishmen, so that the English, Were always in majority, and warned of all that was passing or said on board.

He was polite to the prisoners [to Bucquoy, yes], and received the officers at his table, advising them to resign themselves to their fate, and at times entreating them not to converse together, so as not to arouse the mistrust of the crew.[80]

A little more than three weeks after the pirates left Madagascar, the Dutchman placed in charge of building their boat died. Through repeated nightly attacks by natives and disease, they lost "two-thirds of [their] men, including the captain, Pilot and chief carpenter, so that [they] remained eight, mostly sick and without strength." The last death occurred 23 February 1723.

The following May, "we heard loud cries of people coming to us; when they were very near, we were astonished to see that it was the English pirates who had left here with the great ship [*Defense*]." They arrived at the Dutch camp, almost naked and half starved. They told Bucquoy that their ship had been torn to pieces on the north tip of Madagascar at Cap d'Amber. While building a bark from the debris, natives, presumably the

---

[80] Bucquoy, 117-118.

Antankarana (or "Antakarana"), fishermen from Ampasindav or Mamoko Islands in the Tankarana region north of the Tsaratanana Mountains, had surprised them sleeping. They massacred all but twenty-one of LeVasseur's 123 men. "Many had saved their diamonds," remarked Bucquoy, "which they always wore on them, but others had no riches."[81] King Ratocaffe sent his men to retaliate, wiping out the Ampasindav who had apparently committed the act.

The Dutch then saw their advantage and began to elicit trade with LeVasseur and his remaining men, "like great merchants," for old clothes "of which they had great need, and which we had in abundance." The pirates desperately paid in their diamonds, "without looking at one or two carats more or less; Clothes and breeches reached very high prices." A few days later, another bark arrived, bringing Portuguese and Frenchmen, more of LeVasseur's old crew.

The Dutchmen watched in amazement as the French drove the Portuguese from the bark, "who all swam to the coast." This act of paranoid suspicion was shocking to witness from a group of men who were once as confident and powerful as these pirates. "Desperate times...," Bucquoy must have thought. He also noted with astonishment that:

---

[81] Bucquoy, 128-129; In a manuscript of the Deposit of Maps and Plans of the Marine of Paris, vol. 84, Indian Ocean, Exhibit 17, at the bottom of page 7, it says: "In 1722, Mangaely [Mamoko Islands, of Ampasindava] was landed upon by pirates, and it is said that there was a massacre of pirates [LeVasseur in *Defense?*] made there by the blacks of the country, and that the king of Massailly [Bombetoke Bay], named Ratocaffe [Ratoakafo] sent his soldiers there to take vengeance upon all the black men, women and children, even the dogs, and pillaged all the cattle, and since that time the place has been deserted"; Robert, *Bibliothèques* (1730), L. Robert described these diamonds as "one that is said to weigh 64 karats, many between 30 and 40, between 20 and 30, between 10 and 20 and from 3 to 10;" and "The author [Robert] knows a place on the coast of Madagascar where 60 pieces of iron guns [possibly *Defense*] of different calibers, namely 18 pounds of bullets, 12 and smaller, are to be found at the seashore; During the work of the reconstruction of Fort Dauphin, which Robert advocates, he should send a frigate to take them; They would cost little or nothing, because they came from a large pirate vessel which was purposely grounded in 1722 [1723?], and that they were of no use to the islanders of that country," (Ms. 755), pp. 104, Copy of the Bibliotheque Grandidier, p. 204.

288   Sailing East

TANKARANA HOMELAND

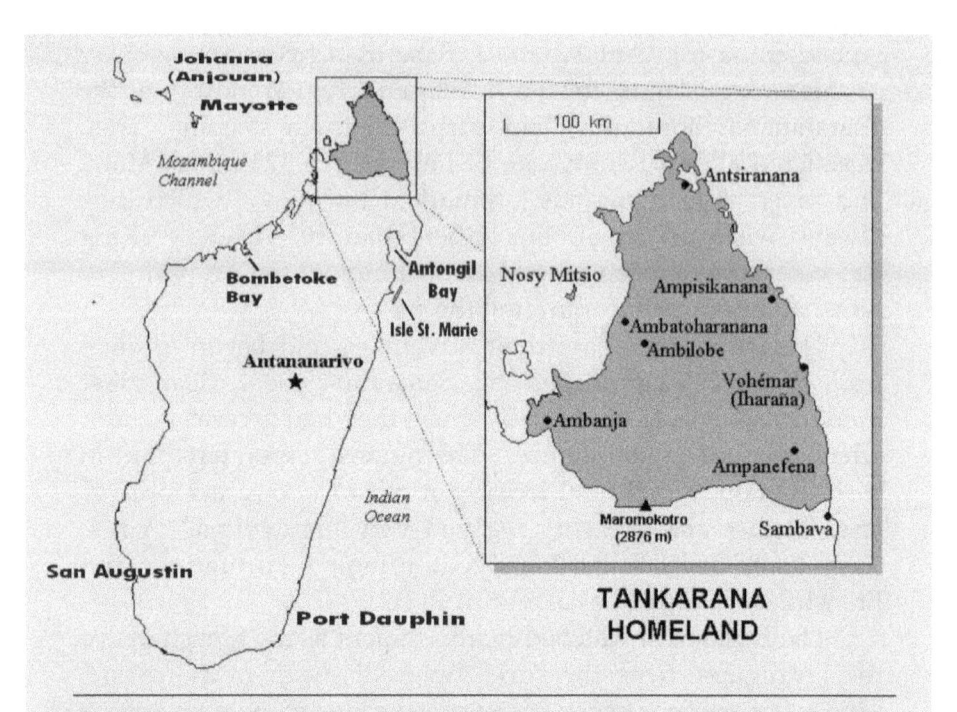

The Tankarana (literally 'people of the rocks') occupy the far northern part of Madagascar where they are geographically cut off from the southern regions of Madagascar by the Tsaratanana mountain range.

In spite of their geographic isolation, the Antakarana were conquered during the eighteenth and nineteenth centuries by the Sakalava, the Merina and the French. Some believe that the Antakarana language and ethnography would reflect the strong Sakalava influence in the area, but the Tankarana historically had closer bonds to the Betsimisaraka of the north. They are mostly fishermen, although those in the interior raise cattle.

As the English had stretched out their sail to dry it, and we went with our canoe to their boat, the French, thinking that we intended to chase them, became frightened and surrendered without further reflection; we had no intention, however, of attacking them. [Nevertheless, the Dutch happily accepted the bark and] It was on this boat that we were hoping to leave the island.[82]

They happily accepted the better-built bark of the pirates and prepared it for their voyage. After seven or eight weeks, the work was completed on refitting the bark "and we prepared to go to sea and to go to Mozambique to deposit the

---

[82] Bucquoy, 129.

Portuguese there, and then to continue our journey towards the Rio de la Goa [Delagoa Bay] or towards Cape Town."[83]

After learning of their imminent departure with the diamonds, LeVasseur's men surprised and attacked them, took back the diamonds, and all the Dutchmen's provisions as well. Then, they compelled them to "embark and take the sea at once, lest we should complain of [LeVasseur's behavior] to the [Salamanka]," or chief. Bucquoy said:

> We were in all twenty-two. Having stretched out our little sail [in their unfinished boat], we descended the river as far as the sea, and made our way to a port further south to take water, firewood, and provisions, and also to caulk our poor boat, in pitiful state, and store water, for we were going to undertake a sea voyage of 160 miles.
>
> We had in all a bad little sail and an old compass, and we had no cables, no anchor, no cabin to shelter us, so that it would have been impossible for us to resist a tempest, and for all Provisions, a little fire-dried meat and a few handfuls of old rice.
>
> The enterprise was certainly a challenge, for it was a very perilous journey through chance, but necessity forced us not to let ourselves be stopped by danger and to do the impossible to save ourselves...
>
> We arrived in Mozambique twenty days later (after leaving Madagascar) and found Portuguese [there] who had been taken by the pirates about two years ago at the harbor of Don Mascarin Island and who recommended to the authorities to welcome us.[84]

Olivier LeVasseur had fallen on bad luck, indeed. Twenty of his men were left of a large crew. They had only a small bark of no real threat value. Moreover, they may have been worn out and dejected. In only a few months, these pirates made a

---

[83] Bucquoy, 129.
[84] Bucquoy, 129-131.

request of the governor of Île de Bourbon to grant them a pardon under the same authority as the one given to Edward Congdon and his men. By September 1724, it had been approved and most of the men left for Bourbon. Still, LeVasseur remained on Madagascar at Île Marotte of Antongil Bay and became a pilot there, hiring himself out to passing merchants trading with other factors and natives of Madagascar. This, however, would not be the end of his story. Chapter Eight tells of this reputedly retired pirate's betrayal and eventual death at the proverbial end of a rope, despite a full pardon!

White Hart Public-House, Wapping, London

As to the perceived piratical nature of Royal Navy men so far away from authority, former midshipman Clement Downing's depositions provided damning testimony against Comm. Thomas Mathews. These depositions originated as the result of complaints from the East India Company's director, Thomas Wooley, one of which involved, as Adm. Secretary Josiah Burchett saw it, "one more especially of the highest Nature, vizt. his Trading with Pirates in his outward bound Voyage to India."[85] Burchett determined that Wooley provided enough evidence to convene a court martial. He then directed John Andrew, Doctor of Laws, one of the commissioners of Oyer and Terminer and Gaol Delivery for the Admiralty to take depositions of several men in preparation of the trial, to be held aboard HMS *Sandwich* in the River Medway the Saturday following Christmas 1724. From 26-28 October 1724, Clement Downing, James Holmes, Gyles Neal, John Thurston, and Richard Moor gathered at the White Hart Tavern run by Mr. Stoney in Wapping, London to officially be interviewed by

---

[85] British Library, Secretary Josiah Burchett at the Admiralty Office to Thomas Woolley concerning the Court's accusations that Captain Thomas Matthews had been trading with pirates, IOR/E/1/15 Letter 143, 19 Sep 1724 ff. 290-270v.

Andrew. His office was in Doctor's Commons, also on the Thames River, just west of Wapping.[86]

Richard Moor had been living with a Mr. Rose at the King's Head, also in Wapping on the north bank of the Thames River. Moor, perhaps over a few pints with his fellow mariners, reflected upon his ordeal with pirates at Madagascar and in the Indian Ocean – an ordeal that lasted for three or four years with Andrew. Moor and Neal, the captives, told Andrew that the pirates suspected that Mathews was, indeed, more interested in treasure than in capturing them. Downing, in particular, detailed the merchandise taken aboard *Lion, Salisbury,* and *Exeter* in late April 1722 at Plantain's town on Madagascar.

James Holmes and Gyles Neal made statements then as well – that confirmed the others. Interestingly, Neal lived in a house owned by prominent butcher and London wine merchant William Braund of Market Lane in St. James Market. Braund was made a director of the East India Company in April 1747. These depositions of the Admiralty condemned Mathews' actions at Madagascar. He suffered four months loss of pay, mainly for allowing "disallowed merchandise on board a navy ship."[87] Also, the EIC directors successfully sued him in 1728 for compensation of the goods traded with pirates.

Still, there is little evidence that Comm. Thomas Mathews' career or the careers of any of his fellow officers, complicit in the illegal activities, suffered unduly from his profiting off pirates. Indeed, Mathews made the rank of Vice-Admiral of the Red and Commander-in-Chief of the English Mediterranean Fleet, 1742-44. He then commanded 90-gun HMS *Namur* in Richard Lestock's squadron.

---

[86] British Library, Judge Advocate John Coupland at Chatham reporting the date of Captain Thomas Matthews's Court Martial for trading with pirates on board HMS Sandwich, IOR/E/1/15 Letter 209, 24 Dec 1724 ff. 390-391v.

[87] William Stewart, *Admirals of the World: A Biographical Dictionary – 1500 to the Present* (London: McFarland and Company, 2009), 213; Further Information of Clement Downing, 93; *The Gentleman's and London Magazine, or Monthly Chronologer,* 1741-1744 (April 1747), 185.

By every sign, the Admiralty simply slapped Mathews on the hand for this pirate profiteering indiscretion in 1724. It was an actual battlefield transgression, "disorderly" conduct in taking the field, which eventually fixed him in 1746. Mathews was court martialed again beginning that October, in a lengthy trial that lasted four months! This time, for *this* disobedience, the Admiralty finally cashiered him. Sideline profits were of minor consequence.[88]

Richard Taylor's return to the West Indies resulted in his greatest notoriety yet. His attempt to elicit a pardon from the governor of Jamaica, parley with the Royal Navy, and play one governor against another, eventually joining the Spanish at Portobello made him something of a legendary nuisance. The British EIC never recovered their property – *Cassandra* – and was forced to face the continuing possibility of meeting her as an enemy at sea!

---

[88] Stewart, *Admirals of the World*.

Chapter 7: Surrender

Richard Taylor Takes Up with the Spanish at Portobello

Henry Bentinck, 1st duke of Portland (1682-1726), having just recovered from illness, sent a letter to Lord Carteret. Portland asserted that he had just heard that *African Packet* and *Fellowship*, two ships "by which I had sent several letters to England [a year earlier], and particularly, answers to things recommended to me by your Lord^p., had fallen into the hands of pirates, and all the letters flung into the sea."[1] These letters described every activity alleged by Portland to have occurred since he took office as governor of Jamaica, replacing long-time resident Sir Nicholas Lawes. Could this have been rather fortuitous for Lawes?

Lawes had taken over from the acting-governor, Peter Heywood, who had, with many members of the Assembly, booted Lord Archibald Hamilton from that position on the charge of dealing with pirates (like Heywood was innocent) and also accused him of Jacobitism. The Prince of Wales, or future King George II, who had well-regarded Hamilton as his personal friend, welcomed him home and regarded the charge of Jacobitism as wholly absurd. The king felt that Hamilton's

---

[1] "America and West Indies: March 1724, 1-10," in *Calendar of State Papers Colonial, America and West Indies: Volume 34, 1724-1725*, ed. Cecil Headlam and Arthur Percival Newton (London: His Majesty's Stationery Office, 1936), 37-56.

brother George, personal servant to his majesty, as well as Archibald, although Scottish, were quite loyal to the new German regent of the British crown. Heywood's men had likely forced Hamilton out because he was an outsider who took advantage of prize money from hunting Spanish and French pirates. Still, when Jamaica's own gentlemen began taking great sums of silver from the recent and quite lucrative wrecks on the Florida shore, twice raiding on land, Heywood took that opportunity to blame and oust Hamilton.[2]

By the time the wrecks had pretty much been fished out, Lawes, then a wealthy merchant of Port Royal with five warehouses in the reputed "Sin City," and a multitude of plantations across the island, including Temple Hall, was appointed by the Board of Trade and king. Replacing Heywood was viewed as a rather expedient necessity and Lawes was easily available.

By October 1721, however, the Board found the financially-ailing Portland and sent him to Jamaica against his better hopes. Portland was the son of Hans Willem Bentinck, Earl of Portland, who had come with Dutch William III of Nassau in 1688, at the ousting of James III (or Jacobus in Latin; known from that time forward as the "Pretender" and a source of Jacobite resentment for decades). Jamaica had not been considered a very prestigious post. Still, as the son of a highly resented Dutchman in England, Portland accepted it eagerly. He also lost a large amount of money in the South Sea Bubble the previous year. His orders came 16 March 1722.[3]

---

[2] Brooks, *Quest,* 274-284.
[3] Thomas Bayly Howell, ed., *A Complete Collection of State Trials and Proceedings for High Treason and other Crimes and Misdemeanors ... : with notes and other illustrations,* vol. 14 (1700-1708) (London : printed by T.C. Hansard for Longman, Hurst, Rees, Orme, and Brown [etc.], 1816), 233-349; Hans Willem Bentinck, Earl of Portland, as a fellow countryman, had been loaded with gifts upon accession of Dutchman William III of Orange, including large land grants in Ireland. Parliament fought against William's further attempted gifts of land in Wales. The jealousy felt for him as a Dutch foreigner, made him very unpopular in England. As ambassador to Paris in 1698, he opened negotiations with Louis XIV for a partition of the Spanish monarchy, signing two partition treaties for William III (Treaty of The Hague, 1698). For his share in drawing up the partition treaties he was impeached, but the case against him did not proceed. The trial for "High Crimes and Misdemeanors," however, lasted from Apr-Jun 1701.

Henry Bentinck, 1st Duke of Portland (17 March 1682 – 4 July 1726) and Lady Elizabeth Bentinck (Noel), Duchess of Portland (1685 - 1737). Bentinck was a British politician and colonial statesman styled Viscount Woodstock from 1689 until 1709. In 1721, Portland accepted the post of Governor of Jamaica, which was a not a very prestigious post, but accepted by him nonetheless after losing a huge amount of money in the South Sea Bubble the previous year. He died in office in 1726 at Spanish Town and his body was returned to England for burial.

Not surprisingly, Portland seldom appeared to enjoy his job and officials with the Board recognized this. In this letter to the Board, he assured them that he did his duty:

> The accounts will shew that there has been received and paid more money since I have been here, than what has been for some considerable time before, and the inclosed paper concerning credit will shew your Lordp., what a tedious and troublesome piece of busyness this has been; As to my delay of Justice, I hope nobody can be uneasy since my arrival, having dispatched some time ago, all matters depending in Chancery before me, where I commonly sit every fortnight, and continue sitting day

after day, till the Council at the Bar tell me they have no more busyness to offer.[4]

Portland, like many saddled with a tedious and unprestigious position in a faraway land, took his time arriving in Jamaica. He assured Jamaicans in a ostentatious speech that he was still working for their interests. He promised to renew expiring laws, but he also cautioned the Council and Assembly there, renowned for their divisiveness, that "private Piques, or publick Party wants Honour or Wisdom, and very often Both."[5] Portland also mentioned the "scourge" of piracy that continued to infest their island. Truthfully, common residents of Jamaica, and indeed, all of America, quite enjoyed the material and pecuniary benefits of piracy.

Portland and his wife Lady Elizabeth Noel Bentinck and their seven children finally ventured into that miserably hot and humid maritime wilderness of the "Wild West" Indies, "beyond the lines of amity." Hopefully, they would catch no incurable diseases. A gentleman in Barbados noted his arrival there on 28 November 1722 in 64-gun HMS *Kingston*. "President Cox leading the Dutchess from the Wharff to the Broad Street," wrote the Barbadian gentleman, "and placing her in his Coach, walk'd on the Left of the Duke to his House, being attended with a vast Cavalcade of Gentry."[6] The gentleman continued for the benefit of his gentile London readers that the streets were lined with Musketeers, twelve regiments of foot-guards, the Life-Guard, all armed and accompanied by the cheers of "Ladies of the Best Fashion."[7]

The *Boston News-Letter* noted after they left Barbados 8th of December and arrived in Jamaica, that they were received "with all the Marks of Joy imaginable."[8] Capt. Chaloner Ogle of HMS *Swallow*, later famous for his killing pirate Bartholomew

---

[4] "America and West Indies: March 1724, 1-10," in *Calendar of State Papers Colonial, America and West Indies: Volume 34, 1724-1725*, ed. Cecil Headlam and Arthur Percival Newton (London: His Majesty's Stationery Office, 1936), 37-56.
[5] *American Weekly Mercury*, Sunday, April 18, 1723, 1.
[6] *New-England Courant* (Boston, Massachusetts), Thursday, April 1, 1723, 1-2.
[7] *Ibid.*
[8] *Boston News-Letter* (Boston, Massachusetts), Sunday, February 21, 1723, 2.

Roberts off Africa, confirmed to the citizens of New York that Portland had indeed arrived in Jamaica.[9]

A squadron of warships based in Port Royal, Jamaica under Comm. Barrow Harris on 50-gun HMS *Falkland,* included freshly-sheathed 36-gun HMS *Mermaid,* Capt. Joseph Laws.[10] Another ship in that squadron was 40-gun HMS *Launceston,* Capt. Bartholomew Candler, who had lately died (October 1722) and succeeded by acting Capt. Digby Dent. The next month, they began searching for a wrecked pirate ship of 24 guns and any of her crew still alive in the Grand Caymans. The previous year, *Launceton* encountered two ships taken by Thomas Anstis and/or John Fenn. One, *Portland* of London, Anstis or Fenn took immediately after Anstis and crew submitted a petition for pardon on 28 April – and pirated her at Samana Bay, Hispaniola almost the next day.[11]

Comm. Harris served in Queen Anne's War at Jamaica as part of Commodore Charles Wager's squadron. He commanded 50-gun HMS *Assistance,* aside Capt. Tudor Trevor of 60-gun HMS *Windsor,* on which served the future Blackbeard, Edward Thache. Comm. Harris took the next turn at *Windsor* after Trevor, and then the 60-gun HMS *Bredah.* He was involved in the Battle of Cape Passaro in 1718. He took command of *Falkland* as Commodore and was later lost in a hurricane in March 1726, although *Falkland* survived until disassembly at Portsmouth Navy Yard in 1743.[12]

Since the recent reorganization of the Spanish territories in northwest South America and Panama as "New Granada," the essentially-exiled West-Indian British found a closer relationship with Portobello. José Manuel Serrano Álvarez, in *Fortificaciones y Tropas,* sees a Portobello at this time that evolved a unique method of "well-differentiated military

---

[9] *Boston Gazette* (Boston, Massachusetts), Thursday, April 1, 1723, 2.
[10] It is unknown if he was related to former governor Sir Nicholas Lawes.
[11] National Archives, London, ADM 52/436, Master's Log of HMS *Launceton,* entry 8 May 1722; Abel Boyer, *The History of the Reign of Queen Anne*: digested into annals, Volume 7 (London: M. Coggan, 1709), 194; threedecks.org.
[12] Boyer, *The History of the Reign of Queen Anne*; threedecks.org.

financing."[13] Although this city held vital strategic and commercial importance, it "did not have full autonomy in the military field."[14] Portobello began with a notable disadvantage compared to other military enclaves of the region, such as Cartagena or Panama. These cities held direct control over their defenses and their funding resources, but Portobello had necessarily remote operational independence and, yet an almost absolute financial dependence on Panama.[15]

A report of 1716, indicated that between 1708 and that date, the 44 men who had served in the fort of Santiago de Portobello, made 22,941 pesos, or 58 pesos per soldier per year. This came to a third of their regular wages. Álvarez found another report of 12 August 1718 that supplies "are consumed in the extraordinary provisions that occur with the accidents of war, subjection of rebellious Indians, repairs, construction of barracks, dressing of carriages, and projectiles for the artillery."[16]

The new British-friendly Governor and Captain General of Panama, J. Gerónimo Badillo hoped to supplement the funds coming through Panama by seeking other, unconventional sources of revenue. In the West Indies, these types of revenue invariably included illicit sources. As expected, part of Badillo's plans included illegal trading with the French and British. The area of the "Grout" behind Monkey Key, on the Coast seven miles Southwest of Portobello functioned as a loading-offloading point for these illegal goods. Ships that carried these goods were unmolested by the Royal Navy who happened to dispatch vessels there from time to time and used the location as an unofficial rendezvous near the capital of Portobello.

---

[13] José Manuel Serrano Álvarez, *Fortificaciones y Tropas: el Gasto Militar en Tierra Firme*, 1700-1788 (Seville: University of Seville, 2004), 109.
[14] *Ibid.*
[15] *Ibid.*
[16] *Ibid.*, 113.

"Monkey Key" is a long, thin land bar across the mouth of the "Grout" or "Navy Bay," a general rendezvous for many vessels of all nations, but especially the Royal Navy, thus "Navy Bay." "Monkey Hill" is the small islet whereon the 19th century town of Aspinwall, later Colon is established. This location is approx. seven miles from Portobello.

Richard Taylor
Sails *Cassandra* to Panama

After returning from the Dutch fort at Delagoa, the pirates of the *Cassandra* and *Defense* or the Viceroy of Goa's old Portuguese *Nossa Senhora do Cabo* gathered aboard *Defense* and took a vote. Richard Moor, still with the pirates on *Cassandra*, deposed as to the events that followed. "Which of the Men," he said, regarding the vote, "would continue to go a pirating and which of them would go to the West Indies to endeavor to get a Pardon."[17] Richard Taylor, with 112 white men and forty black had voted to return to the West Indies. Taylor's men gave up the larger *Defense* and boarded *Cassandra* for the return voyage. Richard Moor came with Taylor and said that he and two surgeons, Thomas Arnett and the Dutch Mr. Snear, joined them to sail the Panamanian coast.

Daily Post of 14 February 1722 reported the reappearnce of *Cassandra* in the West Indies. But, of course, Comm. Thomas Mathews had yet to visit Madagascar, running off both Olivier

---

[17] Richard Moor deposition, 211.

LeVasseur in *Cassandra* and Richard Taylor in their new 70-gun *Defense*. How could *Cassandra* be in two places at once? This article referred to a battle between HMS *Falkland*, Comm. Harris and the EIC ship *Cassandra*, resulting in 350 men lost on her as well as 100 from *Falkland*. This article seems prescient in that it paired *Falkland* and *Cassandra*, as though *Cassandra* might naturally return to the Caribbean to face her final days. "Some letters," repeated the same report in the next issue of 15 February, "but," as it stated, "some others speak doubtfully of that Matter."[18]

The answer probably owed much to the pirate activity humming quite loudly in the Caribbean. There was the 24-gun pirate ship that had wrecked and of whom HMS *Launceston* searched. Consistent reports of the piracies of *Morning Star* and *Good Fortune*, of Thomas Anstis and John Fenn, came almost weekly to the attention of Capt. Bartholomew Candler of *Launceston* while he searched. *Morning Star* and *Good Fortune* would by April 1722 submit a request for pardon to Gov. Nicholas Lawes of Jamaica, but the seas remained quite active. Bartholomew Roberts had just recently been killed on the coast of Africa. *William & James* had just brought word of that capture to Barbados on 27 September 1722. Pirate captains Edward Low, truly notorious for his cruelties, and George Lowther had become quite active from north to south. There were pirates off Africa, Virginia, Carolina, Rhode Island, Newfoundland, as well as in the Caribbean; indeed, they were all around the Atlantic Ocean. A more accurate *Daily Post* report appeared on 24 March about the Viceroy of Goa's capture "with a vast Treasure" by *Victory* and *Cassandra* nearly a year before at Bourbon Island in the Indian Ocean. So, news from the East Indies was expectantly much later than from the West Indies.[19]

News arrived no faster than the ships to carry that news. Richard Taylor had taken *Cassandra* and parted from Olivier LeVasseur in *Defense* 4 November 1722. He had arrived back in the West Indies, perhaps with some diversion, by spring 1723 and headed for Panama. Once they had anchored at the Isle of

---

[18] *Daily Post*, 14 & 15 Feb 1722.
[19] *Daily Post*, 24 Mar and 27 Sep 1722.

Pines in the old failed Scots settlement of "Darien," or New Caledonia, they fitted out two Periaguas with fifteen men each. Taylor was in one and Moor, the other. Their objective involved traveling to the "Grout" at Monkey Key, just northwest of Portobello to meet with the naval ships that usually anchored there. If a pardon was available, they would be able to parley with the Jamaican governor for them.

En route to the Grout, the two periaguas met with a small Spanish sloop with four men. The Spaniards told them that their own governor Badillo would issue them a pardon. Taylor altered his plan somewhat, perhaps by way of demonstrating to the British that they were intimately acquainted with alternative Spanish proposals. He hired the Spanish sloop for 50 Crowns to deliver Richard Moor as an emissary for them to the Grout. After his long ordeal, Moor would finally be able to return home by this opportunity.[20]

HMS *Mermaid*, part of Comm. Harris' squadron, at the "Grout" in early spring 1723, received a visit from the Spanish sloop with Richard Moor carrying the petition. He told Capt. Joseph Laws that he represented the pirate Richard Taylor, captain of the pirate ship *Cassandra*, recently arrived from Madagascar. They wished to surrender and take a pardon. Capt. Laws asked where Taylor was then and if would come aboard *Mermaid*. Moor confirmed that they were nearby, about fifteen leagues away, and would come aboard if Laws would send a hostage to trade for him. Eager to secure *Cassandra* for the benefit of his majesty, Laws sent his own brother with a copy of a sample pardon for Taylor *et al* to review. Realizing Laws' good faith, Taylor returned on the Spanish sloop the next morning, with Laws' brother remaining with the pirates for security.

They negotiated for five days. Laws suspected that Taylor preferred to make this offer to surrender to his own British king. Still, if the terms were not to their liking, they would make another offer to the Spanish at Portobello, with whom they apparently already engaged in negotiations. They would

---

[20] Richard Moor deposition, 211-112.

302   Sailing East

then serve Gov. Badillo as a privateer in the Spanish fleet. Badillo had every reason to welcome the prize money that a powerful ship like *Cassandra* could bring to his ailing finances.

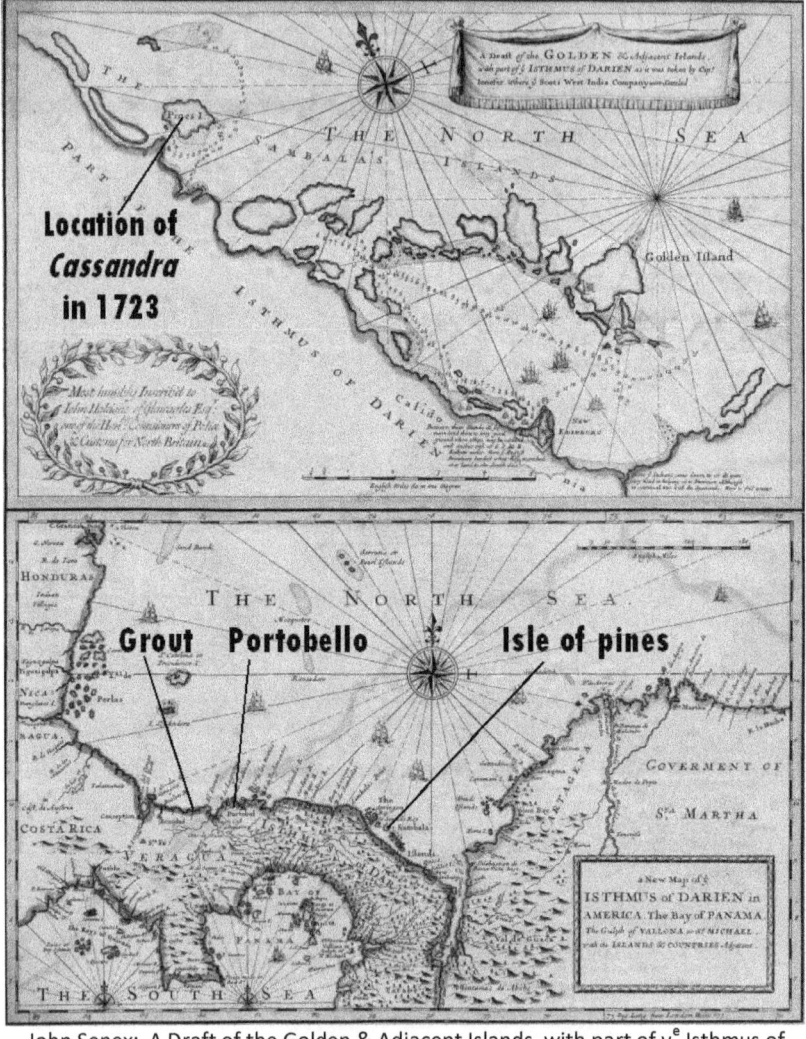

John Senex: A Draft of the Golden & Adjacent Islands, with part of y^e Isthmus of Darien as it was taken by Capt. Ieneser. Where y^e Scots West-India Company were Setteled [and] a New Map of y^e Isthmus of Darien in America, The Bay of Panama, The Gulf of Vallona or "A Map of the Isthmus of Darien in America; The Bay of Panama" (1721).

The sloop returned Taylor and brought back the captain's brother. This event ended Richard Moor's nearly four year ordeal with pirates. He eventually returned to England on *Mermaid* with Capt. Laws.[21]

Laws and Taylor and two of his men, William Fox and William Bates, signed as witnesses to the petition to Gov. the duke of Portland at Jamaica. This occurred 16 April and was dispatched by Capt. Laws in his squadron's snow to Jamaica's new governor, duke of Portand. A second petition was sent 26 April 1723 by his brother, the date of the first communication in the National Archives "Colonial Office" document CO 137/52.

The documents in this file form the subsequent communication that followed the silence from Portland after he should have received the original petition. These copies were later studied by the Board in London. The first line is probably misleading: "Petition of the pirates from on board the Cassandra at Pines near Caledonia the 26th April 1723."[22] The first impression that results is that this is the original petition. This was not the first petition, however, but a second request for consideration by the reticent Gov. Portland:

> To his Grace the Duke of Portland Captain General and Governor of his Majesties Island of Jamaica
>
> May it please your Grace -
>
> It being our misfortune not to know, to whom we directed our first petition, this comes to implore your Pardon for not dictating as we ought, and that our ignorance may not prejudice us in your Grace's favour. We

---

[21] Moor settled in at the home of Mr. Rose at the King's Head public house in Wapping and gave several depositions to John Andrew, Dr. of Laws, for the Admiralty. Clement Downing, Gyles Neal and John Thurston had joined him there. They also gave their statements as well in October 1724.

[22] National Archives, London, Petition of the pirates from on board the *Cassandra*, 26 Apr 1723 – 5 Oct 1723, CO 137/52; "Pines" refers to the Isla de la Pinos, or "Isle of Pines," located at the former location of a defunct Scottish colony called "New Caledonia," or "Darien." This location was opposite the "Grout" or south of Portobello, near the mouth of a river in the Province of Darien. *London Journal* of 3 Aug 1723 reported the location as the "Rocks" or the "Keys of Jamaica," obviously an erroneous reference. Their later issue of 28 Sep 1723 reports more correctly that *Cassandra* was then in "Porto Bello," having surrendered to the Spanish.

have lately had the honour of a letter from Captn: Laws Commander of his Majesties Ship Mermaid, with a coppy of your Grace's pardon to some that have already apeal'd to your Grace, and found mercy. We humbly solicite & x x x with all humility implore for your Grace's pardon, that we may once more Serve our King and Country. We had Surrendred our Selves to Captn: Laws upon the receipt of his letters to us, but knowing our Selves to have been a longer time under these circumstances, tho against our inclinations, than those persons that received your Grace's Clemency was the only obstacle, therefore We humbly beg, and with all submission wait for your Grace's answer, and tho it should be our misfortune not to Obtain your Grace's act of indemnity, the which , would be the greatest calamity that can befall us, We will never more molest nor commit any acts of hostility against any nation, but content our Selves to live here amongst the indians destitute of all hopes & bid farewell to all relations, & what is more dear our liberty to live in our native country.

May he that is the giver of all good, Shower down, on your Grace all happiness & prosperity in this life, & eternal felicity in the next, is the Sincere prayers of Your Grace's most humble & most Obedt: Servts: to command -

Richd: Taylor Wm: Fox Wm: Bates[23]

Meanwhile, Capt. Laws, fully respectful of the process, did not interfere with the pirates at the island until arrival of Portland's answer. As expected, however, the Spanish of Portobello made inroads to convince *Cassandra* to negotiate with them. On the 5th of May, Laws wrote to Gerónimo Badillo, governor of Portobello, "I can't help taking notice how officious you have been in Sending a Sloop with officers to treat & invite

---

[23] Petition of the pirates from on board the *Cassandra*, 26 Apr 1723 – 5 Oct 1723; Note that Richard Taylor's name, as transcribed in the Calendar of State Papers collection, printed and bound in 1936, is given erroneously as "William Taylor." It is also repeated on the online version at http://www.british-history.ac.uk . The actual documents in CO 137/52, however, show "Richard Taylor."

the abovementioned pirates into your port."[24] Badillo had hoped to bring *Cassandra* closer to him and under "protection" from the British men-of-war, under the guns at Fort Santiago. Laws understood perfectly well Badillo's intentions. He reminded the governor that *Cassandra* belonged to the East India Company. He reminded Badillo also of the number of ships taken by them, including the Viceroy of Goa's ship and treasures. Laws also noted that they never took anything of Spain's and had no Spaniards aboard, so "by what authority [do] you assume to pardon those people?"[25] He accused Badillo of acting in private interest – for profit's sake. Still, in that case, was it wise to have reminded Badillo of the treasures that must be aboard *Cassandra*? Did Laws not understand the political situation? Laws then made an open threat:

> ... in case I meet any boat, bark, or vessell, going to or from the pirate, that is treating, corresponding, or trading with the said pirates, [I] shall endeavor to take them, & carry them to Jamaica, to be tryed as the Act directs, and for your better information, I send the Act of Piracy for you to peruse I am,
>
> Sr. Your humble Servant Jos. Laws.
>
> Postscript: Sr, I am no stranger to your Sending the two armed Sloops to protect the said Pirates. J Laws –[26]

Richard Taylor and his crew certainly enjoyed being courted by both sides. It gave them a perfect bargaining advantage.

Capt. Laws wrote to Portland the day after, explaining to him that Gov. Badillo was "all mad to get the Pirates into their port."[27] Laws sent his brother to Jamaica with the message, which somehow did not sit well with Portland. He suggested

---

[24] Petition of the pirates from on board the *Cassandra*, 26 Apr 1723 – 5 Oct 1723, "Captn: Laws Letter to the Governor of Porto Bello dated the 5th of May 1723."
[25] "Captn: Laws Letter to the Governor of Porto Bello dated the 5th of May 1723."
[26] "Captn: Laws Letter to the Governor of Porto Bello dated the 5th of May 1723."
[27] "Captn: Laws Letter to the Governor of Porto Bello dated the 5th of May 1723"; "Capt. Laws Letter from the Grout Dated ye 6th May 1723."

that they attempted to undermine his own authority. Still, undermining the London aristocrat Portland would mean that the governor planned to negotiate with the pirates, but there was yet no evidence of this. He later wrote Lord Carteret:

> ... what is most remarkable, is, that a brother of the Captain of the man of war, who was not any chief Officer on board, was the person entrusted with the negotiation, and always told the pirates, that nobody here could shew mercy, and that it was only the Captain of the man of war who was his brother that had it in his power.[28]

How would Portland know that Laws' brother undermined their negotiations with the pirates – unless Laws' brother simply admitted it to Portland? Chances are that Portland just assumed betrayal from the Royal Navy men. He never had the best relationship with them.

Portland, perhaps petulantly, ignored the first and second petitions from the pirates. By 8th of May, Taylor and his crew began to consider Spain's proposals and eventually accepted them. Laws told the pirates to give it two or three more weeks. He pleaded with them not to forsake their own nation, "in Short turning Banditoes as long as you live, & [likely] to come to an untimely death."[29] He offered, as before, that they would take none of their money or goods. Laws also told them to look closely at their situation with Portobello, that "they have not the liberty to speak to any of the factory, so you may judge what is to be expected when full in their power."[30] Laws' plea temporarily worked. Still, his brother may have expected Portland's lackluster reaction, and suggested to the pirates that they ignore him. This occurred at the same time as the Spanish made an offer too good for Taylor *et al* to refuse:

---

[28] "America and West Indies: March 1724, 1-10," in *Calendar of State Papers Colonial, America and West Indies: Volume 34, 1724-1725*, ed. Cecil Headlam and Arthur Percival Newton (London: His Majesty's Stationery Office, 1936), 37-56.
[29] CO 137/52., "Captn: Laws's Letter to the Pirates on board the Cassandra Dated the 8th of May 1723."
[30] "Captn: Laws's Letter to the Pirates on board the Cassandra Dated the 8th of May 1723."

Sr   Your's we reced, & are much obliged to you for your great care & trouble in taking so much pains to get us to our native Country again. Sir, We do assure you, it was a fault of Mr. Laws, when he on board us, by questioning whether the Petitions should go to Jamaica or not, which put us into a Stranger amusement; & it was to be questioned had not the Portabell Sloop arrived the day after Mr. Laws departure but we should aquitted the ship & a gone headlong we know not whether but Sir, Since you have taken so much trouble beyond our deserts we Shall content ourselves to wait for his Grace the Duke of Portland's answer. Sir all from us unfortunate people who are Cassandra May 14th 1723. Sr. Your most obedient & hble Servants

Richard Taylor[31]

By this, it appears the captain's brother had committed an error – or had purposely undermined the negotiations. He surprised Taylor's men when he asked them whether or not they would continue negotiation with Portland at Jamaica. They told Capt. Laws that, if he had not done this, they may have accepted Portland's offer, assuming it ever came. Still, they were willing to give Portland another chance. Gov. Badillo, on the other hand, assured Laws of a fair proposal to Taylor and his crew. He wrote to HMS *Mermaid's* captain the same day:

This Morning returned the Sloop from the pirates, & brought two of their officers, with two other hands, who wait here for their pardon, & to return to the rest With it, who are all inclined to accept on it; some body [Laws' brother] having told them, it would not be granted at Jamaica, & that there were Ships of war coming from thence to attack them [Taylor made no mention of this, neither did he seem concerned about an attack], they

---

[31] "Captn: Laws's Letter to the Pirates on board the Cassandra Dated the 8th of May 1723."

likewise complain, that as your brother did not give them any hopes, but to the contrary assured them, there would be no pardon granted, they have accepted of the Spaniards with the follg. Articles Vizt:

- ➢ That there are but some of them Roman Catholicks, they desired those that were not Should not be forced so.
- ➢ That their Jewels, gold, plate; & merchandize should not be molested or taken from them, but remains with them, as subjects of ye King of Spain.
- ➢ That they should have liberty to go to Europe, or any place they desired.
- ➢ That they shall have liberty to Sell their Slaves merchandise & without being any ways molested.[32]

Negotiations with the British quickly disintegrated and were superseded by those with the Spanish. Badillo intimated that the pirates felt apprehensive about HMS *Mermaid* in their vicinity, and they expected "more coming from Jamaica." He said they desired of him, the Spanish governor, to send two sloops with soldiers to defend her coming down to Portobello and to defend *Cassandra*. If they met with a man of war, Badillo assured Laws that the pirates told him that they would:

… burn the Ship, & make their escapes in Small craft, but if the said Ship comes safe into Post it is with all the rigging, powder, Balls, & victuals to be delivered up to the Governor, but if any of them will Serve the King of Spain as a Sailor or Soldier, they are to make use of their own arms, every man having a gun, pistol, & Cutlace.[33]

Obviously, the negotiations had gone badly awry for Portland, Laws, and the British Crown. What did Capt. Laws' brother actually tell Portland when he was in Jamaica? Did

---

[32] "Captn: Laws's Letter to the Pirates on board the Cassandra Dated the 8th of May 1723;" "Coppy of a paper Sent by Captn: Laws which he received; Portabell May the 14th 1723."

[33] "Coppy of a paper Sent by Captn: Laws which he received; Portabell May the 14th 1723."

Portland simply ignore the petitions of these men and pretend that they were vagabonds unworthy of his notice in his letter to Carteret? Did Capt. Laws understand the governor's biases clearly? Was Portland seriously planning to petulantly blow the negotiations all to hell by sending warships!?

Portland apparently treated these negotiations with complete indifference. For the first time since sending the pirates' two petitions on 16th and 26th April, and sending two letters in early May, Capt. Laws finally received his first response from Gov. Portland. He had just arrived for a brief stay in Kingston when he received his grace's letter 21 May 1723. Portland casually told him he had the four documents, that he "duely weighed & considered the nature of Such an affair as being wholly inconsistent with the honour of the English nation, & my own Character & therefore have thought fitt, to take no notice of their application to me."[34] This was an incredibly childish response. Portland left the decisions up to Capt. Laws and Capt. Digby Dent of 40-gun HMS *Launceston*, returning with *Mermaid* to the Grout. He insinuated that Comm. Barrow Harris on HMS *Falkland* had previously provided them with instructions to sufficiently handle this affair. Portland flippantly regarded the "flattered Securety [Taylor et al] may think them selves in" and told Laws to tell them all about it when they returned![35]

Joseph Laws had word that *Cassandra* had entered Portobello on the 23rd. Having been undercut by Portland, he knew that the Spanish were going to win over Taylor and his crew. On the 31st, he changed tack from negotiator to that of a commander. He demanded that the Spanish turn over *Cassandra* to their forces to meet justice:

> I can't but remonstrate to your Excellencie, how hainous it will appear in all Courts of Europe that an English pirate

---

[34] "Coppy of a paper Sent by Captn: Laws which he received; Portabell May the 14th 1723;" "Letter to Captn: Laws on board the Mermaid Man of War, Kingston May 21st: 1723."

[35] "Letter to Captn: Laws on board the Mermaid Man of War," Kingston May 21st: 1723."

who has plundered the Subjects of most Princes except his Catholick Majesty, should only have protection and Shelter from the Governors of Panama & Portabell, & that without even the formality of a tryall, but by expressed Articles, that are in themselves contrary to equity & the known Laws of nations, when at the Same time your Excell:cie very well knew for this two months last past, the said pirates have been petitioning to his Grace the Duke of Portland for mercy who in these parts represents the King my Royal Master, whose subjects they were, and as the Ship belongs to the English East India Company Subjets of my Royall Master, in whose name I'm obliged to demand her & all the men that Surrendred; as to their effects & treasure belonging to the Subjects of so many Princes, I can't doubt but your Excell:cie will Secure; so in expectation of your Excellencie's complying with my request, or your reasons to the contrary I am

Your Excell:cie's humble Servant

Jos: Laws[36]

Capt. Laws wrote Badillo again three days later to inform him that he needed an answer. Portland, eyeing perhaps the possible chance to capture treasure, seconded the claim to *Cassandra* "and & to any part or parcell of the cargo, that shall be found to be the property of any of the Subjects of Great Brittain."[37] He sent the letter by way of Capt. Candler of *Launceston* and demanded that *Cassandra* and her cargo be handed over to him. Again, he mentioned her being owned by the British East India Company. It was a long letter, full of all the imperious and regal-sounding words befitting a gentleman of high station. It was all that was necessary in the usual game of West Indian brigandage and asset recovery.

---

[36] "Letter to Captn: Laws on board the Mermaid Man of War, Kingston May 21st: 1723;" "Captn: Laws Letter to the Governor of Panama, dated the 31st May 1723."

[37] "Captn: Laws Letter to the Governor of Panama, dated the 31st May 1723;" "Capt. Laws Letter to the Governour of Panama Dated the 3d of June 1723;" "His Grace the Duke of Portland's Letter to the President of Panama, concerning the pirates of the Cassandra, n.d."

Baylus C. Brooks   311

By this time, however, HMS *Mermaid* had been blown off-station by "westerly winds and Easting currents." Laws was likewise unable to maintain contact with *Cassandra*. Finally, he was able to get a letter off the Portland concerning the loss of *Cassandra*. He undoubtedly bit his tongue when he wrote, perhaps admonishing the governor only a little for his laziness. He insinuated that he would have been able to make a success of the negotiations if it had not been for "other" factors:

My Lord.

> I… am very Sorry, not to give your Grace a better account of the Cassandra then she arrived at Portabell the 23rd of last month… & shall be very sorry should they be disappointed of; I must confess to your Grace, the Letters to the pirates were too candid, not but I would have performed them to a tittle had they Surrendred & brought them to Jamaica; what would have been determined on their tryall am not a Judge.[38]

Laws also warned Portland of about seventy odd French pirates living with the Indians on the coast, about 160 men altogether. Laws complained that "my boat with the purser which I sent to the pirate Ship last was taken by them." Laws worried perhaps that Taylor and others might join with these Frenchmen. Laws signed off, warning:

> I don't See what Sloop would lay on this coast [that might not be taken by the now-Spanish *Cassandra*] no doubt but it is a detriment to the trade; their going into the Spaniards, for the Governor of Portabell have publickly declared, that he will encourage the Villains, & then See what Sloop will lay on the coast. for these reasons before mentioned induced me to give them some encouragement [to come to

---

[38] "His Grace the Duke of Portland's Letter to the President of Panama, concerning the pirates of the Cassandra, n.d.;" "Capt. Laws Letter from the Grout, dated the 4th June 1723, To his Grace the Duke of Portland."

Jamaica], & indeed when it was not in my power to Suppress them. Your Grace may assure your Self, what I have done design'd for the best, & this Satisfaction without any view of private interest; I have no answers from the Governors to my Letters Yesterday inclos'd coppys & Sent to the factory who has promised to deliver them; if answered before Captn: Dent Sails, they shall likewise be inclosed I am &c:

Jos: Laws[39]

Portland had no experience with the wilder ways of West Indian politics and he certainly did not want to be there. Perhaps as a matter of retribution against Britain for posting him on the edge of this squalid, destitute West Indian frontier, the duke of Portland had persistently engaged in a running feud with Royal Navy officers stationed at or near Jamaica. Then again, Portland assured that the officers also probably possessed lofty ambitions. He wrote to Lord Carteret:

The behaviour of all the Capts. of men of war, from the first to the last, if strictly inquired into, is not to be justified. They put the Government at home to a vast unnecessary charge... and if one seems to take the least notice of what they do, tho' it be the most irregular thing in the world, their answer is, that they are independant, equal to the King's Governours, and above the Council... [At] Court of Admiralty, [they insist] to take [the] place of everybody, which occasions great inconveniencies, and which the Council is not inclined to give up... I would say more, but that it might look as if I had some private ends in representing this, but do declare upon all that is valuable that nothing but my regard for the publick service, obliges me not to conceal what one may venture to call so gross an abuse which will, and must be attended with many ill consequences. I don't pretend to say, how it should be rectified, but as it is now, it is not to be look'd at with any tollerable patience.[40]

HMS *Mermaid* arrived back in Kingston Harbor in June 1723, just after the failed efforts with *Cassandra* at Portobello. Two other merchant vessels were in port when he arrived: *John*, Capt. James Pearce, and the snow *Ruby*, Capt. Jeremy Pearce. Both of these captains worked for London merchant Humphrey Morice, owner of William Snelgrave's *Bird* galley and other vessels captured by these pirates. The first to write to Morice, James Pearce on 12 May, informed him of the particulars as he had heard it through Capt. David Greenhill. Capt. Greenhill, sailing a South Sea Company vessel had just come back to Jamaica on 17 July, then from Portobello and brought word that the East India Company's *Cassandra* had just secured themselves 30 leagues to windward of Portobello. He also wrote that the pirate captain was named Taylor and that he had sent his doctor (Richard Moor) with a message to HMS *Mermaid* asking about the pardon. Greenhill stated that the pirates had "got the ship *Cassandra* into so Crooked a place that all the Navy of England cannot hunt them... [they] had Lightned their ship three foot to get her over the Shoales."[41] Taylor indeed protected himself from any British or Royal Navy retaliation.

The Pearces kept up correspondence with Morice over the course of the negotiations, as William Snelgrave arrived there also with 426 slaves in *Henry* from West Africa, by way of Barbados. He still sailed for Humphrey Morice and probably coordinated with the Pearce's on their correspondence. Jeremy Pearce wrote to Morice next on 19 June, which arrived in Morice's hand the next month. Closely following this letter was James Pearce's of 4 July. Both informed Morice of the

---

[40] "America and West Indies: March 1724, 1-10," in *Calendar of State Papers Colonial, America and West Indies: Volume 34, 1724-1725*, ed. Cecil Headlam and Arthur Percival Newton (London: His Majesty's Stationery Office, 1936), 37-56.
[41] British Library, India Office, "Copy of a Letter from Capt. James Pearce to Humphrey Morice, Esq.," 12 May 1723, IOR E-1-14, f. 298; *Bristol Journal*, 24 Aug 1723.

conclusion and failure of the negotiations with Portland. Pearce wrote "they had a free pardon for themselves & Goods, only paying the [Spanish] King's Duty." He added that "they were selling their Diamonds & India Goods there when he came away; They have taken to the Ship for the [Spanish] King, & Christened her with great ceremony."[42] Morice had investments in the East India Company, worth £500 at the time of his death in 1731. This was paltry by comparison to his South Sea Company investments, worth three times as much. Still, many of his friends and he were intently interested in *Cassandra's* possible return. Undoubtedly, Morice was then quite annoyed with the duke of Portland's handling of that affair.

These events also infected normally cordial relations of governors with their Royal Navy officers. On Sunday, 19 July, Capt. Laws spoke with Gov. Portland at Edward "Blackbeard" Thache's family church of St. Catherine's after services. The conversation heated and grew into an argument. The governor impugned the captain's honor slightly by his heated response suggesting he should throw the navy officers all in jail. This incident, however, must have passed, for the next day, Laws, the governor, and Mr. John Fielding dined together, apparently amicably.

Afterward, Laws asked if he might borrow the governor's coach for the ride back to his ship. The governor agreed and offered a "gentleman" to attend him. Upon the captain's discovery that the "gentleman" loaned him by Portland was his Gentleman of the Horse, not his usual house servant, Capt. Laws took offense. In Laws' way of thinking, Portland had the audacity to inflict a smelly equine servant upon him. Portland intended this odorous man to ride beside him in a carriage all the way to the docks! Obviously, Laws' pride would not allow it and he said so. Fielding deposed that Capt. Laws responded indignantly "What," said Capt. Laws, "do's the Duke think I will sit by any one in his coach, that he do's not permit to sitt

---

[42] British Library, India Office, "Extract of a Letter from Capt. James Pearce to Humphrey Morice, Esq.," 4 Jul 1723, IOR E-1-14, f. 299.

down with him at his table."[43] His Grace answered that anyone of quality in England would take it as a complement. Fielding explained the rest of the argument leading up to the arrest of Capt. Joseph Laws, of which Walter Lake was also witness. He said the earlier insult had added fuel as well:

> As to confineing Capts. of War he durst not do it, nor had he it in his power *etc.*. repeating, you dare not confine me, in a very angry and threatning manner *etc.*, which obliged my Lord Duke to say I'le try that, and sent the officer of his guard Lt. [Daniel?] Plowman to make Capt. Laws his prisoner.[44]

Capt. Laws refused Portland's offer to return to his ship with an officer of the guard, or to submit to the duke's authority. Instead, he insisted upon being imprisoned in the guardhouse, refusing other lodgings offered to him. Portland asked the advice of the Council who advised that Laws was guilty of assault upon the governor, to arrest him, and prosecute the crime. Afterward, the governor wrote to the Earl of Berkeley and complained about the insolence of all the officers, but especially Comm. Harris. Portland also felt that the Royal Navy, and not him, failed in the matter of the pirate ship *Cassandra* as well. He also mentioned this to Berkeley.[45]

Portland wrote a note to Comm. Harris on *Falklamd* describing what had transpired in Laws' arrest and asked what Harris wanted done. Harris wrote back the next day asking him to release Laws, that "there's Such a vast Disproportion between Words & a Prison that I cannot undertake to Determine anything in the matter." "If what he says affected your Grace's honour," Harris added that, "your making him a

---

[43] "America and West Indies: July 1723," in *Calendar of State Papers Colonial, America and West Indies: Volume 33, 1722-1723*, ed. Cecil Headlam (London: His Majesty's Stationery Office, 1934), 301-318.
[44] "America and West Indies: July 1723," in *Calendar*.
[45] "America and West Indies: July 1723," in *Calendar*.

prisoner affected the honour of his office as Capt. of one of H.M. ships much more."[46]

Portland regarded Capt. Harris' response as imperious. He insinuated that he would get no further help from the navy and that he would have to handle the Spanish himself – which he had already done quite badly. Again, Portland wrote to Gerónimo Badillo on 5 August, demanding recompense for the East India Company vessel.

After all had been said and done – meaning *Cassandra* had been lost to the mismanagement of Portland – the duke issued an official order on the subject of the lost EIC ship, pointing the blame-finger at the pirates, of course. "To the Marshall of the Admiralty and his Deputies Port Officers," issued the decree by Portland in August 1723, "and other hs Majesty's executive Officers of Justice, whom it may concern, importing,"

> That whereas a notorious Pyrate has come into those Parts, in a Ship formerly called the *Cassandra*; and having on board Effects consisting chiefly of Diamonds, rich *East-India* Silks, Quilts, Pepper, Elephant's Teeth, China, and Gold Dust: And whereas the said Pyrates, (who had been guilty of the most flagrant Outrages against the Subjects of the most Christian King, the King of *Portugal*, and the States of *Holland*, the good Allies of his most sacred Majesty, as well as his Majesty's Subjects) purposed and intended secretly to disperse, and covertly to shelter themselves and their unjust Acquisitions, in such Place as they could best find Means of being concealed in, and passing undiscover'd: They were therefore required to direct their respective Deputies and Under-Officers, to take strict Care that all Vessels arriving from suspected Places might be searched, and that all such Effects abovementioned, of which they had not a satisfactory Account, might be seized in his Majesty's Name, and an Account thereof transmitted to the Court of Admiralty, that Right might be done to the Persons concerned; and that all strange Sea-faring People, who could give no good

---

[46] National Archives, London, Capt. Harris of HMS Falkland to Duke of Portland, 25 July 1723, SP 47/17/292, f. 625.

Account of themselves, should be taken into Custody, and carried before Commissioners for trying Pyracies, in order to their being examined relating to the Matters aforesaid.[47]

That Portland blamed the Royal Navy for *Cassandra's* loss, he made quite obvious and made certain that the public knew as well. Information was released to *Evening Post* concerning Capt. Joseph Laws arrest, "variously reported; some say it was for letting the Pyrate-Ship Cassandra escape to Porto Bello; and others, that it was for trading with the Pyrates."[48] Either way, Portland made certain that no one blamed *him*.

Rather, some blamed the Spanish governor Badillo. *London Journal* of 31 August told that they had received more than one letter affirming intel that *Cassandra* had been offered a pardon by the Spanish governor, who then betrayed Richard Taylor and his men, taking the treasure onboard. "All who know anything of Trade," wrote this "gentleman," "must certainly condemn the Spanish Governor for the Steps he has taken in this affair."[49] This gentleman supported Portland's decision, saying that the Crown did not have standing orders to pardon any and every pirate who came asking for one. He also averred that "If the Spanish Nation do not resent this Step in their Governour, by calling him to a strict Account for it, they ought never hereafter to complain, if Pirates rob and plunder them, and are immediately pardoned for it by any other Government."[50]

Still, this report may have been false. Gov. Badillo let Portland stew, but finally answered him on 5 October 1723, saying rather joyously "the only motive that could induce me [to take *Cassandra*], is to advance the Securety of commerce which I take to be an indispensable part of the duty of my Station... kiss your hands, and am your most Obliged Servant -

---

[47] A. Boyer, *The Political State of Great Britain*, Vol. 26 (1723), 234-233.
[48] *Evening Post*, 17 Sep 1723.
[49] *London Journal*, 31 Aug 1723.
[50] *London Journal*, 31 Aug 1723.

J. Ger:mo Badillo."[51] Badillo had won and he rubbed it in. Certainly a sore point with the EIC, the goods "amounted to one Million Sterling; one fourth Part of which the Pyrates agreed to give to the *Spanish* Governor," whose cut amounted to £216,000.[52] The rest was shared by the 144 pirates of *Cassandra*.[53]

Needless to say, officials like Henry Bentinck, duke of Portland, Comm. Barrow Harris, Capt. Joseph Laws, and others did not readily concern themselves with pardoning pirates so far from London. Other nominal characteristics of life in the eighteenth-century Caribbean included the casual piracy of states, as long as they could get away with it. In the West Indies – far from authority – the game was simpler and cruder. English raided Spanish as they had intended when they first came to the West Indies. Spanish, in turn, preyed on English shipping. It was far from civilized.

Nationality though, had blurred lines in the crude pirate-capitalistic atmosphere. Spanish hired vessels as *guarda-costas* to take English vessels especially who cut logwood from the Bays of Honduras and Campeche. *Cassandra* was most likely employed as a *guarda-costa*. She then preyed upon English and Dutch vessels. As a former pirate, it seemed reasonable to her crew - simply part of the West Indian frontier game.

Full Circle

No further sighting of *Cassandra* has yet been found buried in the dusty roomfuls of archived records. Yet, two of her crew had appeared in the 16 July 1724 issue of the *Boston News-Letter*. This article suggested that at least they had made a full circle back to the African Coast almost five years from the time they left in 1719.

---

[51] CO 137/52, "The President of Panama's answer to his Grace the Duke of Portland, Panama 5th October 1723."
[52] Boyer, *The Political State of Great Britain*, Vol. 26, 233.
[53] *Weekly Journal and Saturday Evening Post*, 31 Aug 1723; *British Journal*, 31 Aug 1723.

In early summer 1724, HMS *Enterprize,* Capt. John Yeo, patrolled the formerly turbulent waters off Africa. Just two years before, Capt. Chaloner Ogle captured famed pirate Bartholomew Roberts off that same locale. The presence of the Royal Navy ship intended to calm the nerves of the slave merchants, like Humphrey Morice of London, who had suffered so terribly so recently.

John and Mary, one of those merchant ships loaded her cargo of 158 slaves (*BNL* reported 175), anchored two leagues from Cape Charles on the Windward Coast. Capt. John Jones[54] had been contracted to take these slaves to the York River in Virginia. They spoke with HMS *Enterprize,* who assured Jones that there was "No Enemy on the Coast."[55]

Then, on 5th of June, a large vessel appeared flying British colors. With no reason not to trust the word of Capt. Yeo of the *Enterprize,* Capt. Jones "took the pirate to be a friend" and mounted no defensive posture.[56] Jones and his crew were totally taken by surprise when they were ordered to stand to and seventy men appeared over the rails and took aim at Jones' crew with small arms. This Spanish privateer, or *guarda-costa,* and former prize vessel of Bristol, had captured them without a fight. Capt. Jones and four of his men went aboard and were confined.[57]

The Spanish captain introduced himself as "Signior Don Benito, a Knight of the Spanish Orders." The crew consisted of 60 Spaniards, white and slave, 14 English or Irish, and 18 French. Capt. Jones learned that two Irishmen, John Moore and John Smith, "were of Pirate Taylor's Crew at his taking the Cassandra in the East Indies."[58] These men had pirated the

---

[54] Donnan, III, 50n3; John Jones was probably the husband of Mary and brother-in-law of Peter Fanueil. He would also have been part owner in *Jolly Batchelor* and one-time captain of *Duke of London.* Jones had a long career as a mariner trading on the York River since 1705 and possibly until 1740.
[55] *Boston News-Letter,* 16 Jul 1725, 2; *Voyages* database.
[56] *Boston News-Letter,* 16 Jul 1725, 2.
[57] *Boston News-Letter,* 16 Jul 1725, 2.
[58] *Boston News-Letter,* 16 Jul 1725, 2.

African Coast in 1719 and had returned – they had come full circle in their not-so-distinguished careers.[59]

The same day, after securing *John and Mary* to travel, they came up on a brigantine, *Prudent Hannah,* Capt. Thomas Mousell. They had also been going to Virginia. Seignior Benito had secured Capt. Mousell and his "boy," then put six Spaniards aboard to sail the brigantine to an unknown Spanish port. His losses amounted to £1,200.[60]

The next day, Benito sighted another sail. As they came near, she was reckoned as *Godolphin* of Topsham, Capt. Thomas Bane. The Spaniards took her as well, ordering Bane aboard and taking £3,000 worth of cargo.[61]

Capt. John Jones' "good behavior with the English & French" impressed the Spanish and they decided to let him go with his vessel and slaves. He arrived at York River to tell this story with 135 who had survived. The *Boston News-Letter* reported his losses on 15 July as "*l*. 350 Ster. in gold Dust, 1000 Gal. of Rum, about *l*. 200 Remains of Guinea Cargo, 38 of his Slaves [actually, he only lost 23, some probably to disease – overstated here probably to pad the insurance payout]; his whole loss tho't to be *l*. 1600."[62]

Other infamous English men in Seignior Don Benito's crew included Rich Holland, Irishman, "formerly of St. Augustines [whether Florida or Madagascar, the article did not say]." Holland had been wanted for taking vessels off Virginia before. There was their mate Benjamin Evans, formerly mate of a New England vessel. Another man named Smith was their pilot. Fifteen of the eighteen French were said to be pressed and probably came from a recent capture. This Spanish privateer did not discriminate. Though the article had not indicated so, likely more than two of Richard Taylor's old crew of *Cassandra* served aboard this Spanish privateer.[63]

James Macrae, captain of *Cassandra* when she was taken by Jasper Seager and Edward England at the island of Johanna, mattered to British East India Company presidents and

---

[59] *Boston News-Letter*, 16 Jul 1725, 2.
[60] *Boston News-Letter*, 16 Jul 1725, 2.
[61] *Boston News-Letter*, 16 Jul 1725, 2.
[62] *Boston News-Letter*, 16 Jul 1725, 2; *Voyages* database.
[63] *Boston News-Letter*, 16 Jul 1725, 2.

governors like Charles Boone in Bombay. They mattered to investors like Humphrey Morice. They made quite the noise about this vessel, mostly because Macrae was being groomed for higher political office. Farther away, in the West Indies, *Cassandra's* projected import mattered only in the few months surrounding the Spanish intrigue and to satisfy the honors of haughty self-important men. Two or three years down the road? Not so much in the West Indies wilderness. The Spanish capture of *Cassandra* was a novelty outside of British EIC influence – an acceptable loss to these casual state brigands "beyond the lines of amity."

Chapter 8: Trial

Trial of the "Buzzard" Olivier LeVasseur de la Buse

M. Isidore Guët, in *Les Origines de l'ile Bourbon et de la Colonisation Française à Madagascar* told the usual tale familiar to most of us about Olivier LeVasseur's capture, trial, and execution. Guët's first paragraph reads:

> Nevertheless, it was a weakness (it seemed at least) to pass the sponge on the pirate's conduct and to grant him and forty of his friends an amnesty at Bourbon by a deliberation of the Higher Council of Europe, dated January 26, 1724 [J: 15 Jan] [actually, 23 September [J: 12 Sep]] – LeVasseur probably requested the pardon in January]; but on the condition "that the said John Cleyton and his own, or that the said captain La Buse [LeVasseur] and his own, shall commit no act of hostility, on pain of nullification of this present deliberation, and be punished as pirates, if they were caught."[1]

---

[1] M. Isidore Guët, *Les Origines de l'ile Bourbon et de la Colonisation Française à Madagascar* (1888), 218-219 ; Guët noted that, "on 4 November 1724, amnesty was granted to several pirates who embarked on the *Royal Philip* to return to France."

Guët expressed his feelings that Île de Bourbon should never have allowed this "notorious" pirate to run free on Madagascar. According to the date, January 1724, this request would have closely followed LeVasseur's wrecking of *Defense* and the slaughter of over a hundred of his crew by Madagascar natives at the north end of the huge island. There was only twenty-two of Levasseur's crew left after that disaster. The other eighteen may have come from other pirate crews on Madagascar desiring to surrender, perhaps some of Edward England's men. Only a half-year separated the wreck of *Defense* and LeVasseur's giving up piracy. He and most other pirates on that island appeared to be finally defeated men so late in the game.

Guët's second paragraph represents – and repeats – the almost universal illogic used by nearly all writers to complete his historical trail to the gallows:

> Le Vasseur, mistrusting himself, perhaps not without reason [note: anti-pirate bias], preferred not to profit by the amnesty. He continued the fruitful trade in which he had acquired so great a reputation... But in order to continue his exploits, he had not counted on a French ship, *La Méduse*, who came to the station in these parts, in order to ensure the navigation between Bourbon and the coasts of Madagascar, where they were then actively working for the benefit of our colony.

Ah, the strong and stalwart champion of the seas, *La Méduse* – a 280-ton slave ship! Certainly, *she* would stop this villainous pirate and promote commerce! *La Méduse* belonged to the French East India Company, based in L'Orient, France. Guët called her captain, M. Hyacinthe d'Hermitte, "a sailor as bold and skillful as an officer of the king, to whom Le Vasseur was a pirate."[2] This phrase carried a bit of national pride – and some disgust at pirates who interfered with the business – which increasingly involved slavery – of that nation (er... company). One problem: there's no evidence that LeVasseur practiced piracy since accepting the pardon six years earlier.

---

[2] *Ibid.*

Coat of arms of the French East India Company or "Armoiries de la Compagnie des Indes Orientales" (1664). In public domain for both France and the United States.

La Méduse had been "cruising on the coasts of Madagascar," as the usual tale goes, when d'Hermitte heard, "that La Buse was in the quarries of Fort Dauphin, secured [in] his place of retreat."[3] If it sounds like a cat hunting a mouse, that's exactly the analogy that Guët uses. Moreover, the usual story is that LeVasseur was working as a pilot, a somewhat restricted occupation, and d'Hermitte requested his services. This seems rather odd considering he was supposed to be a known, notorious, villainous, and still active pirate. Guët cheerfully wrote that the French *Compagnie des Indes* (CDI) captain "succeeded in surprising him, took possession of his person, and brought him in his ship at [or to] Bourbon."[4]

---

[3] *Ibid.*; "La Réunion et les Pirates," Libertalia, http://libertalia.re/1315-2/ ; Another online source gives the location as Antongil Bay, near Îsle Saint-Marie.
[4] *Ibid.*

Many details simply do not ring true. How was it that LeVasseur, the pilot, interfered with that *company's* business? He simply piloted merchant ships through Madagascar's waters. Why did d'Hermitte arrest LeVasseur – for what crimes? He supposedly had received a pardon from the CDI-run island of Bourbon for the piracies he had committed there, but had done nothing known to violate that pardon. He had been working as a pilot on Madagascar for the last five or six years without incident. We know this because of his trial documents and the dates of the crimes for which he had been indicted. Those documents only show piracies that occurred at Bourbon, all in the same two weeks in 1721, three years before his pardon was even granted. Guët said the d'Hermitte "knew La Buse by reputation," and that he knew "the last three actions he had committed with aggravating circumstances."[5] Weren't these "last" crimes, however, already adjudicated in 1724?

Levasseur's trial documents specified: capture of *Nossa Senhora do Cabo* (aka, *Guelderland*), *La Ville d'Ostend* or *City of Ostend* [former *Greyhound* of London], and the vessel of the French CDI, *La Duchess de Noailles*. These violations were his *last* three actions. Agreed, one of them was a vessel of the CDI and LeVasseur had burned it, but he had already been pardoned for all of these crimes six years before d'Hermitte "captured" him. What else did he do – what other criminal act did he perform – that caused d'Hermitte to become so angrilly judicious and drag him back to Bourbon, chained in his hold? Did LeVasseur steal something from him? Did he cheat him on the price of his services? Did he personally insult the man? What?[6]

Guët described an act of almost gleeful revenge on behalf of the whole island, which, truthfully, the burning of *La Duchess de Noailles* earlier encouraged in 1721. Guët reflected rather colorfully:

> ... from the moment when he had put into practice his pirate trade after the signing of the act of grace, he had at the same time begun to twist the hemp, which was to

---
[5] *Ibid.*
[6] Archives Colonials – Bourbon, carton 2 – Letter de M. Dumas, 29 December 1730.

separate him from the earth by bringing him nearer to heaven. In fact, he had to admit the day when he was hanged on the beach of Saint-Denis, to the applause of the Boubonnais population, happy to show, once, by [Bourbon's] avengers' acclamations, that it did not like pirates[,] badly brought up to oblige them to fail[,] in the duties of hospitality.[7]

So now, Guët insulted LeVasseur's parents, too! Agreed that LeVasseur was a thief, but he was probably not overly ruthless or murderous, assuming a great deal of the usual hyperbole in reports of his piracies. Moreover, his parents probably had little to do with his later choices – that was just rude. LeVasseur would simply leave his victims to fickle fate once he took their valuables and set them free, like de Bucquoy, in a small raft with few provisions. Still, the hardship had not killed de Bucquoy and LeVasseur probably knew that it probably (admittedly, there is some uncertainty) would not. Between the two pirate brethren, Richard Taylor was perhaps the more ruthless character. Moreover, LeVasseur continuously argued with him until they finally separated. More than a little bias probably crept into Guët's narrative. Again, why was LeVasseur *actually* arrested, tried, and hanged?

Assuredly without meaning to, the *Libertalia* website offers a suggestion. It reads "The new governor wanted to turn a page of history by killing the last great living figure of piracy."[8] That new governor, since July 1727, was Pierre Benoît Dumas. Dumas conducted his job conservatively, more businesslike and probably despised the more liberal government of his predecessor de Courchant. He established the City of Réunion in 1730. He increased French national migration to the island under a plan originally conceived of by his predecessor – not the mixed-race migrants from Madagascar. He also had begun a period of infrastructure expansion and, on 16 June 1730, while LeVasseur sat in his prison cell since 26 April [J: 15 Apr] (yes, Piat also found the document showing LeVasseur's date

---

[7] *Ibid.*
[8] "La Réunion et les Pirates," Libertalia, http://libertalia.re/1315-2/

of incarceration: 26 April 1730 [J: 15 Apr]), initiated construction of a new 30-km passage from Saint-Denis to the neighboring commune of La Possession. Perhaps ridding the French CDI of the "last great living figure of piracy" had, indeed, been a part of the "improvements." Denis Piat writes, in *Pirates and Privateers of Mauritius* that "piracy was on the wane in the Indian Ocean, and the new governor had no love for the remaining pirates."[9]

Perhaps LeVasseur had simply become an unknown factor, a "wild card," if you will, in Dumas' mercantile visions for Bourbon and the French seas around Madagascar. Or, was there more? Piat also argues that LeVasseur had refused the pardon because one stipulation of that amnesty, as outlined by Beauvollier de Courchant in 1721 when Edward Congdon was pardoned, was that the individual absolved would have to reside on Bourbon – and they hated LeVasseur! More specifically, of course, they would be forced to spend their fortunes *there*. He tells that four members of LeVasseur's crew: John Clayton, Joseph Pascal of La Rochelle, Adam Johnson, and Guillame Planter, had accepted the pardon and were then living on Bourbon. And, here's the clicker: Piat argues that Dumas took the initiative and actually *ordered* d'Hermitte to go to Madagascar in *La Méduse* and capture LeVasseur. D'Hermitte did not just stroll by Madagascar and say "Aha! Found me a pirate!"[10]

Still, LeVasseur had been minding his own business on Madagascar and had committed no piracies from there since his crew was pardoned. He was no apparent threat to Dumas' capitalist scheme. Also, how was d'Hermitte tied into it – simply as a captain for the French CDI? Was there more?

Zero-sum economics was fading fast in the advancing eighteenth century. The new economics, of course, had much to do with the sugar and coffee trade and the slaves required to engage in it. Indeed, it appears that the company feared "loose

---

[9] Auguste Toussainte, *History of Mauritius* (Macmillan, 1977), 29; Denis Piat, *Pirates and Privateers of Mauritius*, English ed. (Singapore: Dider Milet, 2014), 60.
[10] *Ibid.*

ends," like LeVasseur, that may interfere with their increased business *out* of Madagascar – the business of slavery.[11]

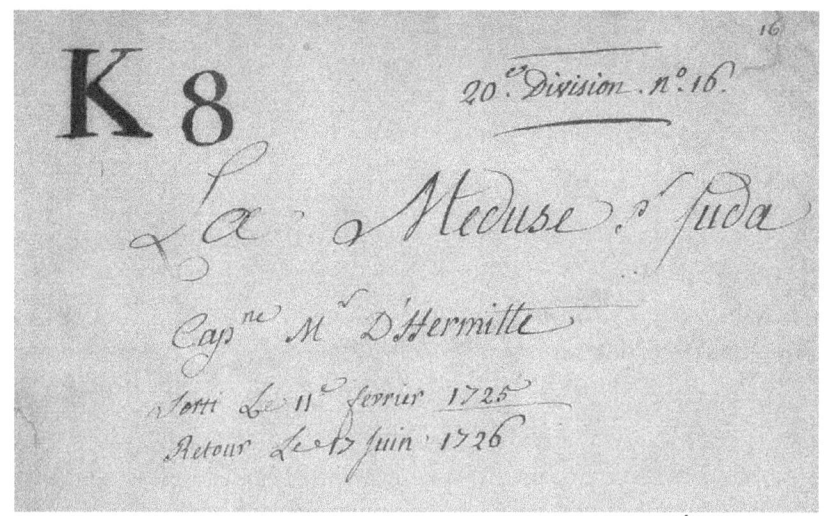

Campagne de la Méduse (1725-1726). - MAR/4JJ/69/16 - Logbook of Étienne Michel Orceau, pilot (original). Campaign of the Medusa, armed by the East India Company, Captain Hyacinth d'Hermitte. Road: Lorient, Goree, Guinea (Judah), Prince Island, Santo Domingo (Cape Town), Lorient.

La Méduse, fitted out by the French *Compagnie des Indes* (CDI), and captained by Hyacinthe d'Hermitte, later captain of *La Diane*, had been a career slave trader. Her captain first sought slaves from the West African port of "Juda," "Ouidah," or "Whydah," for the French CDI in 1725. Certainly, this West African source of slaves lay far from Bourbon (Réunion) and Île de France (Mauritius). This put a strain on the Company's finances. Historian J. Verguin tells of an alternate source employed by the Company:

> ... judging clearly of the risks [money] of bringing blacks from so far, [the Company] reconsiders the idea of the slave trade in Mozambique [East Africa, directly across from Madagascar]... In August 1728, however, the ship *La Méduse*, captain d'Hermitte, had to pass to Jude (Judah - or

---

[11] Jean-Claude Félix Fontaine, *Deux siècles et demi de l'histoire d'une famille réunionnaise (deuxième volume): L'aventure du sucre ou la volonté d'émergence, 1730-1915* (L'Harmattan, Sep 1, 2005), 16.

Ouiddah) to get a cargo of blacks, bring them to the islands of Bourbon and France and then make the trade of Madagascar.[12]

The ships of the French CDI took slaves from West Africa, traveled back to Madagascar for other goods, and then returned those goods and the slaves to Bourbon and Île de France, or Mauritius. The Company felt that this long route wasted their money. Moreover, Mozambique slaves coast too much. The Royal African Company in Britain received the better deal from the African Kingdom of Delagoa in 1721, diverting their imports from Madagascar, and cut out the French CDI.[13] The CDI then ordered the passage of slaves from Senegal, India, and Madagascar, but not from Mozambique:

> It should be noted that, despite the report of 1711, the slave trade does not seem to have been practiced regularly on the coast of the Cafres [Mozambique]; no black contingents from this region are reported. That is because, in 1722, three ships, commanded by the Sieur de Marquaisac, had been sent to Mozambique with the Sieur Robert, embarked with merchants, but the trade proved unsatisfactory, the blacks having cost 200 piastres and sold for only 180 at Bourbon.[14]

There were perfectly good slaves in Mozambique *and* on Madagascar, and CDI already regularly visited Madagascar, as English pirate-merchants had since the late 17th century.[15] Thanks to the RAC, slaves in Mozambique, however, offered them only a financial deficit, but Madagascar had its problems,

---

[12] J. Verguin, "La Politique De La Compagnie Des Indes Dans La Traite Des Noirs A L'ile Bourbon (1662-1762)," *Revue Historique*, T. 216, Fasc. 1 (1956), 49-50.
[13] Elizabeth Donnan, *Documents illustrative of the history of the slave trade to America*, Vol. II (Washington: Carnegie Institution of Washington, 1930-35), 262-264.
[14] Verguin, "La Politique."
[15] Liliana Mosca, "Slaving in Madagascar: English and Colonial Voyages in the Second Half of the 17th Century A.D.," *TADIA, the African Diaspora in Asia: Explorations on a Less Known Fact* (2008), 606-607n32; "A census in Barbados at the end of the seventeenth century counted 32,473 slaves, half of them from Madagascar. Some of these Madagascans were surely transhipped from Barbados to Carolina, accompanied masters who were relocating there, or arrived directly on voyages of the many English and American pirates actively trading for slaves in Madagascar between 1688 and1724."

too. Verguin suggests that the Bourbonnais were not immediately pleased with Madagascar slaves:

> On December 8, 1728, *l'Akion* brought back 120 blacks, negresses and Negroes from Madagascar. The Company seemed to make some efforts to help the inhabitants of the islands of Bourbon and Île de France. However, a letter of the same December 8, 1728, addressed to the Company, reveals the discontent of the colonists. "If the Company does not care to send black Guineans [West Africans] into this Île, let them send warships to patrol here and at Île de France, for with a good number of blacks, whether from Madagascar or Mozambique, she will not see the crop of Île de France anytime soon and she will lose considerably in it [for] the coffee that the inhabitants cannot pick up and what they are obliged to leave on the trees, for want of slaves to pick it, each having planted on the hope that the Company had given, that it would not leave black men lacking."[16]

The French CDI, as well as the RAC, may have considered Madagascar slaves lazy. More specific to the needs of the CDI, perhaps they feared that Madagascar lay much too close to Bourbon and Mauritius. Slaves from there might try their best to revolt and return home. The Company made excellent profits from the coffee of Bourbon. This remonstrance by their colonists probably gave them pause, so the Company looked elsewhere. In 1729, the Company sent ships to the coast of Sofala and, "if it succeeded, it would focus on drawing them from there for the use of the two islands."[17] That attempt also failed. The capitalization of the Company's investment would not be denied and Verguin accounted for the people then transported from Madagascar by d'Hermitte:

---

[16] Verguin, "La Politique"; *Malagasy*, the official language of Madagascar, has a written literature going back presumably to the 15th century. When the French established Fort-Dauphin in the 17th century, they found an Arabico-Malagasy script in use, known as *Sorabe* ("large writings"). This Arabic Ajami script was mainly used for astrological and magical texts. The oldest known manuscript in that *Sorabe* is a short Malagasy-Dutch vocabulary from the early 17th century.

[17] Verguin, "La Politique," 51.

The Company orders "The same year [1729], *La Méduse* will be trading on the west of Madagascar [Seclave people]; and we also give the order to trade blacks to Judah. The vessel *Syrène* must, before returning to France with more than 1,500 bales of coffee, go at the end of the year to take the blacks of Madagascar." D'Hermitte actually makes two trips and brings back 630 blacks at the beginning of 1730.[18]

In 1729, *La Méduse* brought back 318 blacks from Madagascar, but increased his load in 1730: 430 on 26 April [J: 15 Apr] and 249 on 19 October [J: 8 Oct]. A ship is then assigned to trade in Madagascar exclusively for one year, by order of the Company on 24 September 1730 [J: 13 Sep]. On 23 December [J: 12 Dec] of the same year, the Company also ordered that the vessel destined for the slaving at Madagascar also trade as much as they could from India. At least the company did not discriminate between various shades of brown – still, they clearly desired a white French national population in control of the island.

Note that *La Méduse*'s largest single haul of Madagascar slaves – 430 destined for Bourbon – arrived on 26 April 1730 [French Julian]. This is precisely the date found in local records by Denis Piat for the incarceration of Olivier LeVasseur, brought to Bourbon by Capt. d'Hermitte in *La Méduse,* and then loaded with 430 slaves from Madagascar. Alfred Grandidier later contradicted the work of M. I. Guët and wrote that d'Hermitte was said to have "surprised La Buse in the neighborhood of Fort-Dauphin," but then "On the other hand, [Gov. de] Valgny, who had so long resided in Madagascar, said: 'I notice that an officer [d'Hermitte] was rewarded for having arrested under the veil of friendship and good faith the pirate La Buse, who was removed alone and defenseless from Marosy Island (Île d'Anjou, Île Marotte, or Nosy Mangabe; at the mouth of the river in Antongil Bay).'"[19] It may be that

---

[18] Verguin, "La Politique," 51-52.
[19] De Valgny, Papiers de De Valgny, gouverneur de l'Etablissement français de Madagascar pour la Compagnie des Indes, MS 887 (1741), 54, quoted in Alfred Grandidier, *L'Origine des Malgaches* (Hachette, 1901), 179n1a ; Nosy Mangabe (also called Marosy) is a small island tropical rainforest reserve located in Antongil Bay about 2 km offshore from the town of Maroantsetra. It is part of the larger Masoala National Park complex.

Dumas had given the order to take LeVasseur by force in the midst of this flurry of slave-trading action from Madagascar. D'Hermitte made that arrest on 26 March [J: 15 Mar] and returned LeVasseur to Bourbon 26 April [J: 15 Apr], with the pilot and former pirate chained in his hold.

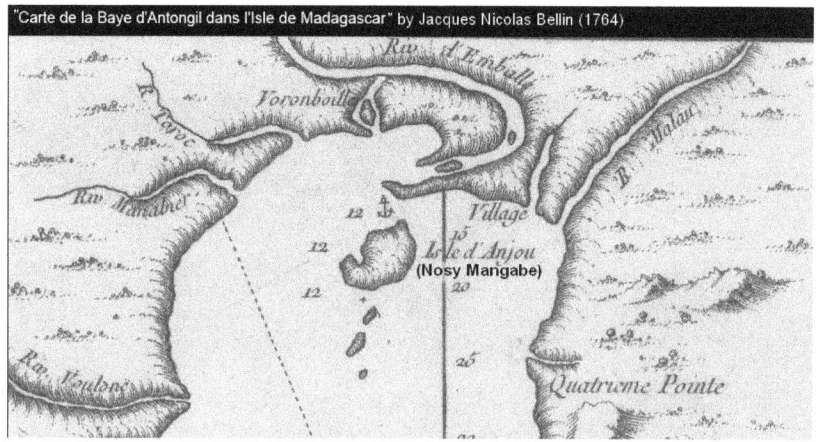

"Carte de la Baye d'Antongil dans l'Isle de Madagascar" by Jacques Nicolas Bellin (1764)

Source: University of Illinois at Urbana-Champaign. University Library.

Another theory involves examination of a later court case which revealed that d'Hermitte had re-established a base on "L'Île Anjou" or Nosy Mangabe to trade for slaves – possibly usurping LeVasseur's former business operations. This is probably the same location as the 1642-1646 Dutch entrepôt intended to supply Mauritius' timber operations with Madagascar slaves. The transcript of the trial indicated a "letter from Sr. Morphy written from Île Marotte [Another French name of Nosy Mangabe], the twenty-nine of the said month, to Mr. Dumas, governor of this island [La Bourbon], which justifies the inhabitants of Antongil Bay were very angry with the said Sr. d'Hermitte."[20] D'Hermitte apparently operated tyrannically, according to his own surgeon. The added part concerning "conduct on the subject of the acquisition of L'Île Anjou" may refer more directly to LeVasseur's stolen business operation.

---

[20] Archives Colonials – Bourbon, carton 2 – Letter de M. Dumas, 29 December 1730 ; "Judgment condemning Sr. Hermitte, captain of the ship *La Diane*," 3 April 1734, f° 49° - 50°, online pdf (accessed 5-17-2018), http://www.reunion-esclavage-traite-noirs-neg-marron.com/IMG/pdf/rec-3-2519-06.pdf..

334 Sailing East

Home of Olivier LeVasseur?

Fourà

L'Isle d'Anjou, Ile Marotte, or Nosy Mangabe - 18th cent. - showing habitation on mainland side of the island in Antongil Bay near anchorage.

A = Camp of King Roy Baltriche

Bananes

A

"d'Hermitte's Trust"

Was this the former home of Olivier LeVasseur, later the base of King Roy Baltriche, native trading partner of Capt. D'Hermitte? *Vüe de la partie de l'isle d'Anjou qui fait face à la grande terre du fond de la baye d'Anton-Gil* - Source: Bibliothèque nationale de France, département Cartes et plans, GE SH 18 PF 217 DIV 5 P 5 D and *Vüe de l'ance d'hermitte* [D'Hermitte's Trust] 18th cent. - Source: Bibliothèque nationale de France, département Cartes et plans, GE SH 18 PF 217 DIV 5 P 6 D. Public Domain.

LeVasseur possibly resented their efforts in "Massaly, Antongil Bay, and at Foulpointe" to take slaves, many who may have been his offspring.[21] Also, LeVasseur saw d'"Hermitte a competitor trying to "muscle-in" on his business. Even if not family-related, he had established a rapport with the natives at least for his safety and the safety of other whites doing business on the island. LeVasseur had undoubtedly remembered that Adam Baldridge and Edward Congdon once betrayed these people, with disastrous consequences.[22] The island base functioned as a fortress with a large moat. Still, he may have hoped to continue his trade in peace with them – which they, in turn, respected the former pirate and allowed his residence then on Nosy Mangabe, or l'Îsle Marote. He probably had established a rather comfortable base on that island – a base that might aid the plans of d'Hermitte and Gov. Dumas to personally profit from CDI operations. The trial notes of April 1734 show d'Hermitte was:

> … convicted of deception and embezzlement... ordered [by Dumas?] to go and treat in the eastern part [of Madagascar – Nosy Mangabe], by particular views and for his personal interests, and to have made a particular and fraudulent trade against the orders of the Company [amounting to 8,000 livres damages].[23]

Furthermore, Megan Vaughan quoted a piece from 1764 that may have applied to a possible growing discrimination on

---

[21] Verguin, "La Politique De La Compagnie Des Indes Dans La Traite Des Noirs A L'ile Bourbon (1662-1762)," 52.

[22] John Franklin Jameson, *Privateering and Piracy in the Colonial Period: Illustrative Documents* (New York: MacMillan Company, 1923), 187n19; William Kidd reported to Gov. Bellomont of New York that Adam Baldridge caused a massive slaughter of white pirates on Ile Saint-Marie by capturing local natives and delivering them to Mauritius. Kidd said "Baldridge was the occasion of that Insurrection of the Natives and the death of the pirates, for that having inveigled a great number of the natives of St. Maries, men, women and children, on board a ship or ships he carryed and sold them for slaves to a French Island called Mascarine or Mascaron, which treachery of Baldridges the Natives on the Island revenged on those pirates by cutting their throats;" leader of the Betsimisaraka in 1733 was King Roy Baldriche Mulâtre, possible mixed race, or *zana-malata*, son of Adam Baldridge.

[23] "Judgment condemning Sr. Hermitte," (3 April 1734 [J: 23 Mar]).

Mauritius, an ethnic-cleansing that may have been strictly enforced on more creole Bourbon by Dumas and his administration. She writes:

> It causes great disorder on Isle de France to see men of a certain rank publicly associating themselves with negresses whom they treat as wives and with whom they have children who will one day become a bastardised and dangerous race. This shameful mélange has been introduced by the séjours of troops and sailors ... In this respect it is not so much the established residents who were the most guilty but a vice once introduced by outsiders, does not leave with them, but stays and grows larger.[24]

LeVasseur most certainly would not have minded men, women, and even children of the northern Antankarana (or "Antakarana") group who had slaughtered his crew in 1723, taken as slaves and probably at war with his wives' Betsimisaraka. He probably still harbored a strong resentment for the Antankarana. Still, those from Antongil Bay or Plantain's "Ranter's Bay" and southward, or the Betsimisaraka and their mixed pirate offspring of *zana-malata*, were probably closer to "family," may indeed have included his wife (wives?) and children, or at the very least those upon whom he relied for support as he resided there as a pilot.[25]

---

[24] Congregation de la Mission, Receuil 1504, ff. 189, Teste, 1764 quoted in Megan Vaughan, "Slavery and Colonial Identity in Eighteenth-Century Mauritius," 196.

[25] Betsimisaraka have a long history of extensive interaction with European seafarers and traders, including pirates of Saint-Marie Island, that produced a significant subset with mixed European-Malagasy origins, called the *zana-malata*; there is also the possibility that d'Hermitte may have tried to take members of LeVasseur's own family – assuming he attempted to settle on the island since 1723, married and had children amongst the Betsimisaraka. Slaves for purposes of trade would have normally been taken from other nations currently at war with the Betsimisaraka. LeVasseur would most likely have continued a similar smuggling business at Île Marotte, much like Adam Baldridge had from Île Saint-Marie in the 1690s, trading in the usual silks, pearls, gold, and other treasures of the East.

Betsimisarakas women drawing water, 1900/1910. Wikipedia.

Did LeVasseur express his reservations and concerns to d'Hermitte on his earlier voyage in 1729 – perhaps violently? Did d'Hermitte also express his worries of a possible problem with LeVasseur to Gov. Dumas, who gave the order for his arrest? It could have been an easy decision for Dumas. After all, LeVasseur had insisted upon living in Madagascar, violating the stipulations of the amnesty granted to him and his crew. *Technically*, he had never *truly* accepted the pardon offered in 1724 – no matter that he had committed no crime for six years. Furthermore, Guët suggested that Olivier LeVasseur was not a foreigner, but a French national, a native of Calais – "No international difficulty was to be feared" in capturing and executing him.[26] The stricter nationalist Dumas most likely felt him a constant mercantile threat, a possible threat to his personal plans, if not then an actual pirate. LeVasseur had *been* a pirate after all, Dumas may have argued; he had damaged CDI property – certainly, he would never reform – right? According to the deliberation of the Superior Council of Bourbon on 7 July 1730 [J: 26 Jun]:

> By advice, the criminal proceedings extraordinarily made and instructed at the request and diligence of the Attorney General of the King [illegible] and accusation against Olivier Levasseur nicknamed "La Bouse" accused of the crime of piracy, prisoner in our prisons, defendant in the affirmation made the 26 of March [J: 15 Mar] and 19 of May [J: 8 May] last at the declaration of Sieur d'Hermitte captain of the ship *La Méduse*, [showing as evidence] the letter of said Levasseur dated March 25, 1724 [J: 14 Mar] addressed to Monsieur Desforges and signed Olivier La Buse, by him recognized and initialed, nor variation.
>
> [Also offered to the court, the] Letter from the Superior Council to Sieur La Buse for response dated 23 September of the same year granting Amnesty and Surety, [and supported in the] interrogation suffered by the accused on 15 May [J: 4 May] and 20 May 1730 [J: 9 May] and 03 [J: 22 Jun] of this month. First general conclusion of the king of the 04 [July] [J: 23 Jun], [and] preparatory judgment of the same day which orders that it will proceed to the final judgment [to be] awaited [by] the public notoriety.
>
> Final conclusion of the Attorney General of the King of the 06 [July; J: 25 Jun], sudden interrogation in the room of the council [illegible] and all considered the council declared and [illegible] the name "Olivier Levasseur dit la Buse,"

---

[26] Guët, *Les Origines de l'île Bourbon*, 219.

native of Calais, hard hit of the knowledge of the crime of the piracy for several years, for having ordered several pirate ships to be taken and brought to the roadstead of Bourbon Island, a vessel belonging to king of Portugal and another named the *City of Ostend* belonging to the company of the same city, but equally participated in the capture, plunder, and firing of the vessel *La Duchess de Noailles* belonging to the company of France and other [illegible], for repair of which the council condemned him and condemned to make amends in front of the principal door of the church of this parish, naked in a shirt, the rope at his collar, in hand, a torch of two pounds of pitch for there, to say and declare with high and intelligible voice, that For a long time, he was a reckless and reckless man who became a filibuster [pirate] and asked for forgiveness from God, the king and justice.

This sentence will be carried out in a public place to be hanged and strangled until death ensues on a gallows erected for this purpose. (He) will be hanged in the usual place his dead body will remain there 24 hours and then exposed to the waters' edge… his belongings are confiscated for the benefit of the king, and he must also pay a fine of one hundred pounds for the offense done to "the Lord King." Done and declared in the council chamber on July 17, 1730 [J: 6 Jul]. Dumas.[27]

The new economic and quite personal system of capitalism probably condemned Olivier LeVasseur "dit la Buse" – known best and not-so affectionately as the "Buzzard!" The assumption is that his fine was paid *before* the actual hanging at 5 p.m. – alternatively, they could have just raided his purse afterward. Moreover, his body was exposed to sea vermin that

---

[27] Archives Colonials – Bourbon, carton 2 – Letter de M. Dumas, 29 December 1730; also Mr. Dumas, Governor of Bourbon, to Minister de Maurepas, December 29, 1730, *Centre des Archives dOutre Mer, Aix en Provence*, Correspondance générale de Bourbon, t. V, 1727-1731.

would clean the bones of flesh. Most likely, they simply left the bones to be quietly scattered by the waves afterward.

LeVasseur, in essence, was tried twice for the same crime. He was offered no procedural defense of "double jeopardy." Then again, this was most likely a political and pecuniary expediency to secure the seizure and sale of slaves to the new French residents of the island. Profit certainly figured into LeVasseur's death, as one source states, "in 1733, the governors decided to found a small colony on the small island of Île Marotte [LeVasseur's recent former home]… an island that was previously uninhabited…."[28] It certainly was not inhabited by CDI personelle until they established "d'Hermitte's Trust" after 7 July 1730 [English Julian]! The same source also indicates that this colony failed in 1733 as a result of the agency of the Betsimisaraka, LeVasseur's own presumed people who got the final word.

Certainly, Gov. Dumas would also have approved of the financial tourist boon that the death of the "Buzzard" would later bring the island. Today, tourists flock to see Olivier LeVasseur's grave (probably with no body inside or at least not LeVasseur's) in Saint-Paul's. The locals encourage legends, rumors, and wild stories about the "last great pirate of the Indian Ocean." One of them entails a large piece of parchment, or animal skin, on which was drawn a cypher that the "Buzzard" allegedly assures will lead to his treasure. He supposedly "throws the crowd a parchment that he had kept tight in his hand and yells 'To whoever solves this, discover my treasures!'" Of course, he was naked except for a linen nightshirt when brought to the gallows, with a torch in one hand, so where he hid this large animal skin until that moment is anyone's guess.

That alleged parchment of the "Buzzard" has driven locals on different islands of the region to destroy their yards, blast boulders with dynamite, dig holes on other's private property, and other wild behavior. As with pirates of the West Indies, legends of vast treasures of gold, diamonds, rubies, and the treasure-hunters searching for them, have also driven pirate

---

[28] Jane Hooper, *Feeding Globalization: Madagascar and the Provisioning Trade, 1600–1800* (Athens: Ohio University Press, 2017).

enthusiasts of the East Indies to similar extremes. Pirates of the west, however, generally wasted their fortunes on booze and women or other similar extravagances. They probably never buried anything. Still, pirates who sailed east may have affected others similarly!

An artist's conception (by Michael Fauré) of and sign at the alleged gravesite of "Olivier LeVasseur dit La Buse," or the "Buzzard" on Île de Reunion. Below is the parchment with the cypher. Fauré is a renowned comic artist and author born in France. He lived for a time on Madagascar and currently lives on La Reunion. His brief comic-novel "Le Fin de la Buse," or "The End of the Buzzard" depicts the story of the trial and hanging.

342   Sailing East

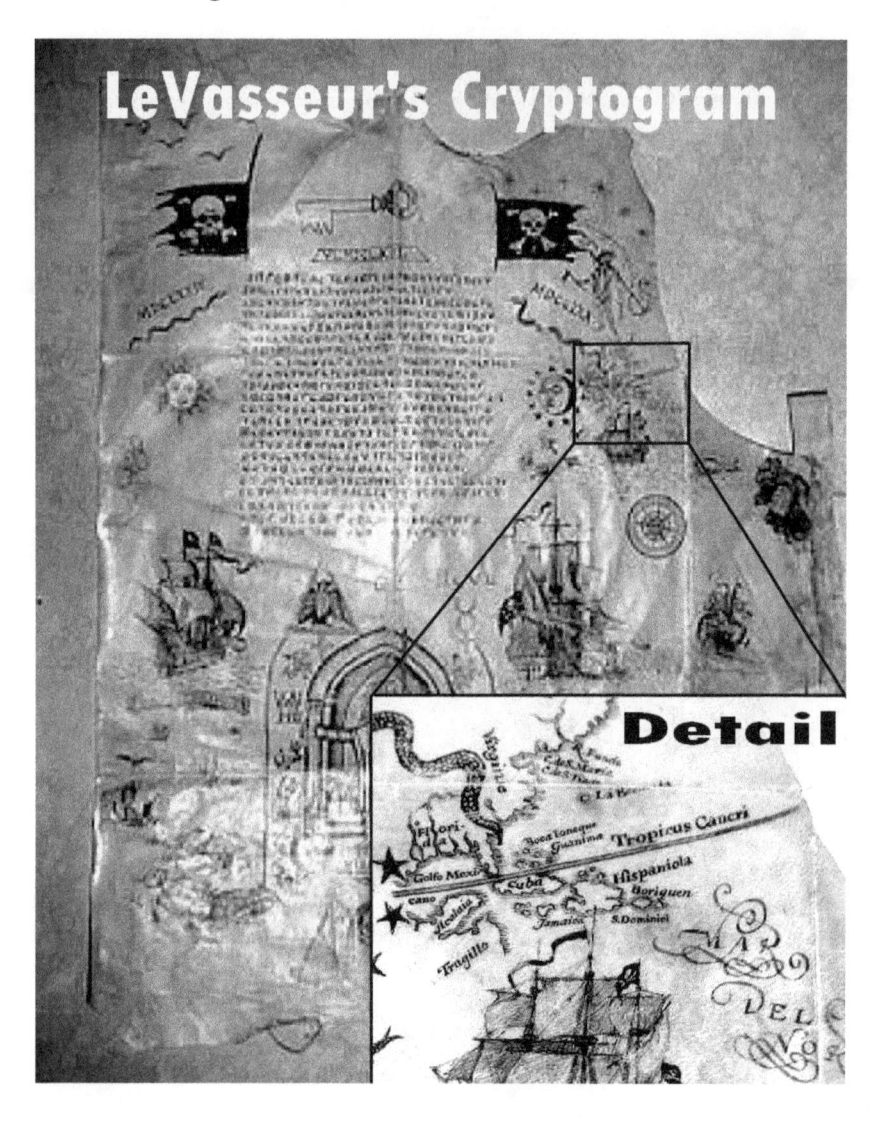

Appendices (Some Primary Sources)

A list of ships allegedly taken by pirates on the African Coast in spring-summer 1719

Quoted from page 115-117 of Charles Johnson's *A General History*, this list, not attributed to any particular pirate, is unique for being so detailed. Johnson, or Mist, found this list in a competitor's newspaper: *The Weekly Packet* of London, 24 Oct 1719. The newspaper clearly identified Edward England as the pirate who took these vessels [one was in error, however – *Eagle* Pink was the capture of Howell Davis]; therefore, it was included in Johnson's chapter on Edward England:

Captain England took a Ship called the *Pearl*, Captain Tyzard Commander, for which he exchanged his own Sloop, fitted her up for the pyratical Account, and new christen'd her, the *Royal James*, with which he took several Ships and Vessels of different Nations at the Azores and Cape de Verd Islands.

In the Spring, 1719, the Rovers returned to Africa, and beginning at the River Gambia, sailed all down the Coast; and between that and Cape Corso, took the following Ships and Vessels.

The *Eagle* Pink, Captain Rickets Commander belonging to Cork, taken the 25th of March, having 6 Guns and 17 Men on Board, seven of which turned Pyrates [actually taken by Howell Davis].

The *Charlotte*, Captain Oldson, of London, taken May the 26th, having 8 Guns and 18 Men on Board, 13 of which turned Pyrates.

The *Sarah*, Captain Hunt, of London, taken the 27th of May, having 4 Guns and 18 Men on Board, 3 of which turned Pyrates.

The *Bentworth*, Captain Gardener, of Bristol, taken the 27th of May, having 12 Guns and 30 Men on Board, 12 of which turned Pyrates.

The *Buck* Sloop, Captain Sylvester, of Gambia, taken the 27th of May, having 2 Guns and 2 Men on Board, and both turned Pyrates.

The *Carteret*, Captain Snow, of London, taken the 28th of May, having 4 Guns and 18 Men on Board, 5 of which turned Pyrates.

The *Mercury*, Captain Maggott, of London, taken the 29th of May, having 4 Guns and 18 Men on Board, 5 of which turned Pyrates.

The *Coward* Galley, Captain Creed, of London, taken the 17th of June, having 2 Guns and 13 Men on Board, 4 of which turned Pyrates.

The *Elizabeth and Katherine*, Captain Bridge of Barbadoes, taken June the 27th, having 6 Guns and 14 Men on Board, 4 of which turned Pyrates.

The *Eagle* Pink being bound to Jamaica, the *Sarah* to Virginia, and the *Buck* to Maryland, they let them go, but the *Charlotte*, the *Bentworth*, the *Carteret*, and the *Coward* Galley, they burnt; and the *Mercury*, and the *Elizabeth and Katherine* were fitted up for Pyrate Ships, the former was new nam'd *Queen Ann's Revenge*, and commanded by one Lane, and the other was call'd the *Flying King*, of which Robert Sample was appointed Captain. These two left England upon the Coast, sail'd to the West-Indies, where they took some Prizes, clean'd, and sail'd to Brasil in November; they took several Portuguese Ships there, and did a great deal of Mischief, but in the height of their Undertakings, a Portuguese Man of War, which was an excellent Sailor, came a very unwelcome Guest to them, and gave them Chace; the *Queen Ann's Revenge* got off, but was lost a little while after upon that Coast; and the *Flying King*, giving herself over for lost, ran ashore: There were then 70 Men on Board, 12 of which were kill'd, and the rest taken Prisoners, of whom the Portuguese hang'd 38, of which 32 were English, three Dutch, two French, and one of their own Nation.

The following is the original from *The Weekly Packet,* 24 Oct 1719:

We have reciev'd the following List of Ships taken by the Pirates this Year, In the River of Gamboa [Gambia], which tho' very particular, we are well assur'd our Readers may depend upon as authentick. The Eagle Pink, Capt. Rickets Commander, belonging to Cork, was taken March the 25th, having 6 Guns and 17 Men on board, seven of which turn'd Pirates The Charlote, Capt. Oldson, of London, was taken May 26th, having 8 Guns and 18 Men, thirteen whereof turn'd Pirates. The Sarah, Captain Hunt, of ditto, was taken May the 27th, having 4 Guns and 18 Men, whereof three turn'd Pirates. The Bentworth, Capt. Garner, of Bristol, taken May the 27th, having12 Guns and 30 Men, 12 whereof turn'd Pirates, The Bank Sloop, Captain Sylvester, of Gamboa, was taken May the 27th, having 2 Guns and 2 Men, who both turn'd Pirates. The Carteret, Capt. Snow of London was taken May the 28th, having 4 Guns and18 Men, vhereof 5 turn'd Pirates. The Coward Galley, Captain Creed, of ditto, Was taken June the 17th, having 2 Guns and 13 Men, whereof 4 turn'd Pirates. The Mercury, Captain Maggot, of ditto, taken May the 29th having 4 Guns and 18 Men, 5 whereof turn'd Pirates. The Elizabeth and Katherine, Captain Bridges, of Barbados, was taken June the 27th, having 6 Guns and14 Men, whereof 4 turn'd Pirates.

The 3 first were sent to Jamaica, Virginia, and Maryland, the two last made Pirates, and the rest burnt. They were taken by the Royal James, Captain Edward England, formerly the Pearl, Captain Tyzard; she now mounts 30 Guns, and 16o Men. The

Mercury is now call'd the Queen Ann's Revenge, and carries 14 Guns, and 30 Men. The Elizabeth and Katherine is nam'd the flying King, has, 8 Guns and 14 Men, Robert Sample Commander.

The following is Johnson's continued history on Edward England, with certain serious mistakes:

England, in going down the Coast, took the *Peterborough* Galley of Bristol, Captain Owen; and the *Victory*, Captain Ridout; the former they detained, but plundered the latter, and let her go. In Cape Corso Road, they saw two Sail at Anchor, but before they could reach them, they slipp'd their Cables and got close under Cape Corso Castle, these were the *Whydah*,[1] Captain Prince, and the *John*, Captain Rider: The Pyrates upon this made a fire Ship of a Vessel they had lately taken, and attempted to burn them, as tho' they had been a common Enemy, which if effected, they could not have been one Farthing the better for it; but the Castle firing warmly upon them, they withdrew, and sail'd down to Whydah Road, where they found another Pyrate, one Captain la Bouche, who getting thither before England arrived, had forestall'd the Market, and greatly disappointed their Brethren.

Captain England, after this Baulk, went into a Harbour, clean'd his own Ship, and fitted up the *Peterborough*, which he call'd the *Victory*; they liv'd there very wantonly for several Weeks, making free with the Negroe Women, and committing such outragious Acts, that they came to an open Rupture with the Natives, several of whom they kill'd, and one of their Towns they set on Fire.

When the Pyrates came out to Sea, they put it to a Vote what Voyage to take, and the Majority carrying it for the East-Indies, they shap'd their Course accordingly, and arrived at Madagascar, the Beginning of the Year 1720. They staid not long there, but after taking in Water and Provisions, sail'd for

---

[1] An error; Wrecked on the coast of Massachusetts 26 Apr 1717.

the Coast of Malabar[2], which is a fine fruitful Country in the East-Indies, in the Empire of the Mogul, but immediately subject to its own Princes: It reaches from the Coast of Canara to Cape Camorin, which is between 7° 30, and 12° North Lattitude, and in about 75° East Longitude, counting from the Meridian of London. The old Natives are Pagans, but there are a great Number of Mahometans inhabiting among them, who are Merchants, and generally rich. On the same Coast, but in a Province to the Northward lies Goa, Surat, Bombay, where the English, Dutch, and Portuguese have Settlements.

---

[2] This narrative skips the taking of *Cassandra* at Johanna or Anjouin, August 1720, by these pirates.

The London Journal, 17 February 1722

Included here because it may include other ships taken off the coast of Africa 1718-1720 by the pirates found in this book. The list was probably composed from Admiralty records and various newspaper articles.

The Names of all the Ships taken by the Pyrates for five Years last Past [1718-1722], with a particular Account of every one that has been destroy'd by them, or otherwise treated in any extraordinary and barbarous manner:

The *Widdah*. The *Kent*. The *George*. The *Dolphin*, destroy'd by the Pyrates. The *Ludlow*. The *Mary*. The *Henry and John*. The *Weymouth*. The *Sea Nymph*. The *Ann Galley*. The *Dover*. The *Berkeley*. The *Tanner Frigate*, this they stript of all her Goods and Ship Materials, as Guns, Anchors, Cables, etc. murthered some of her Men, and set the Ship on Fire, and left her burning. The *Sarah Sloop*. The *Samuel*. The *Buck Sloop*, this was carry'd off by the Pyrates, and burnt on the Coast of Guinea. The *Betsey*. The *Margaret*. The *Emperor*. The *Neptune*. The *Minerva*. The *Bridge Town*. The *Kingston*. The *Eagle*. The *Pearle*. The *Mary*. The *Alexander*. The *London*. The *Crowne*. The *King of Prussia*. The *Protestant*. The *Colston*. The *Society*. A Sloop. Two Sloops. The *Charlotta*. The *John Galley*. The *Victory*, burnt on the Coast of Guinea.[3] The *Petersborough*. The *Temperance*, sunk by the Pyrates on the Coast of Guinea. The *Mercury*. The *Sea Nymph*. The *Essex*. The *Fame*, destroy'd on the Coast of Guinea. The *Indian Queen*. The *Mediterranean*. The *Experiment*, burnt on the Coast of Guinea. The *Comrade*. The *Queen Mary*. The *Mary and Elizabeth*. The *Success*. The *Queen Elizabeth*. The *Prince Eugene*. The *Morrice*, destroy'd by the Pyrates at Guinea. The *Guinea Hen*. The *Tarlton*. The *Princess*. The *Leopard*. The *Dove*, the *Sarah Galley*, both destroy'd on the Coast of Guinea. The *Indian Queen*. The *Mediterranian*. The *Experiment*, burnt on the Coast of Guinea. The *Comrade*. The *Queen Mary*. The *Prince Eugene* [vessel of Ostend]. The *Morrice*, destroy'd by the Pyrates at Guinea. The *Guinea Hen*. The *Tarlton*. The *Princess*. The *Leopard*.

---

[3] Probably *London*, vessel of Capt. William Rideout.

The *Dove*, the *Sarah Galley*, both destroy'd on the Coast of Guinea. The *Royal Hind*. The *Elizabeth and Katherine*. The *Jacon and Jael*. The *Westbury*. The *Onslow*. The *Martha*. The *Robinson*. The *Sarah*, burnt by Pyrates on the Coast of Guinea. The *Sierra Leon*, destroy'd in Sierra Leon River. The *Dragon*, burnt. The *Heroine*. The *Edward and Steed*. The *Society*. The *Margaret*. The *Loyalty*, burnt at Guinea. The *Frederick*. The *Katherine*, sunk at Newfoundland. The *Expectation*, sunk also. The – Capt. Square, sunk also. The – Capt. Russel, his Masts and Rigging cut down and plunder'd. The *Willing Mind*. The *Commerce*, burnt at Newfoundland.

Note: The remainder of the article refers to events following July 1720 and most pertain to Bartholomew Roberts. This excerpt and the next can be found in full at E. T. Fox, *Pirates in Their Own Words*.

The London Journal, 24 February 1722

Excerpts included here because it may reference other ships taken by the pirates found in this book. Most of the references in this article, also found in full at E. T. Fox, *Pirates in Their Own Words,* include Samuel Bellamy, Edward "Blackbeard" Thache, Stede Bonnet, Bartholomew Roberts, Richard Worley, and others.

... *Amity* Sloop, 80 tons, Capt. Tho. Palmer, bound from Dartmouth to Carolina, taken in the Latitude of 32 Deg. 45 Min. and plundered, bu a French Pirate Ship of 30 Guns and 250 Men, one Lebous [Olivier LeVasseur de la Buse], Commander... *Ludlow,* 170 tons, Capt. Arthur Lone, bound from Carolina to London, taken on the Banks of Newfoundland, and plundered. *Glascow,* 140 tons, Capt. DeLapp, bound from Glasgow to Jamaica, taken in the Latitude of Bermudas, plundered and put into Carolina, these three [sic] by a Pirate Ship of 36 Guns and 300 Men, commanded by a Frenchman named Louis Lebore [prob. LeVasseur]... *Mediterranean,* 200 tons, Capt. Arthur Lone, bound from Guinea to Carolina, taken on the Coast of Guinea and carried off. The *Carteret,* Capt. Tho Lynche, bound from Guinea to Carolina, taken on the Coast of Guinea and burnt, these two by three Pirate Ships, one of 20, one of 26, and the other of 30 Guns, all under the Command of one England... *Minerva,* 140 tons, Capt. John Smyter, bound from Madera to Carolina, taken off the Bar of Carolina, and plundered. *Atalantis,* 170 tons, Capt. Rumsey bound from New England to Carolina, take off the Bar of Carolina, and plundered. *Sea-flower,* 80 tons, Capt. Jeremiah Brown, bound from Rhode Island to Carolina, taken off the Bar of Carolina, and carried off, these Three by a Pirate Ship of 30 Guns and 200 Men, commanded by one [William] Moody.

Snelgrave Letter – 30 April 1719

William Snelgrave, "William Snelgrave to Humphrey Morice," 30 Apr 1719, *Humphrey Morice Papers of the Bank of England*.

Hon^d. Sir

On the 4th instant I arrived on this coast to your great loss and my sad mishap, being taken by pirates after this manner, Mr. Jones who had behav'd himself well all ye passage was got in liquor ye day as made ye land, so durst not trust him to carry ye ship in, but haveing an extract of Capt. Gordon's Journall went by that tell twas dark, and anchord of[f] ye Cape 1 1/2 mile from the shore; between 7 & 8 a clock in ye evening ye officer of ye watch told me a boat was very near uss, I went on ye deck haild her, & was answerd they belonged to ye 2 friends Capt. Ellott from Barbados, Mr. Jones said then they are friends, and called for lantherns, I said would trust no boat and orderd all hands to be called, ye words were hardly out of my mouth but there was a volly of small arms fir'd at uss, I commanded ye people to their quarters, but before half of ye men could get in the steridge ye pirates were on ye decks & prevented laying the grateings; I call'd to ye people to go forward with me and sally up through ye forecastle, but ye confusion and noise was so great was not regarded, and they call'd out for quarter upon wch ye pirates ceas'd fireing, haveing shot Hugh Ross in ye side and Capt. Gordon's black in ye arm. The Quarter master of ye pirates came down into ye Steridge, asking were was ye Comdr. told him I was, he asked me what was ye reason I order'd a great gun to be fired at ye boat and ye people to defend ye ship, I replied it was my duty, upon wch he clapt a pistoll to my breast, but putting it one side with my hand it fir'd under my arm, he then beat me with his Cuttlash unmercifully, and order'd me with ye people on deck, as soon as came up, ye boatswain of ye pirates told me they never gave quarter to any Comdr. who offer'd to defend his ship, and strikes at me with his broad sword but God was pleased to cause ye blow to take ye raise on ye quarter deck, otherwise had been cleft down, then they beat me again, but all my people beg'd they would not abuse me, saying they never were with a better Comdr. upon wch they left of[f] and fell to beating them, Mr. Richardson was cut on ye head wth several others that suffer'd. They had turn'd their boat adrift haveing drank damnation to one ye other if they did not take ye ship, so order'd me to send one of my boats with 4 hands to take up theirs but if they did not return declar'd would pistoll me, Mr. Jones offers readily to go & tho' very dark luckily found her, but as he came along side would have had ye people given 3 chears, they had more prudence then to comply for not one would have been left alive if they had done it. By this time ye Pirates ship was come down and fir'd at uss, then they sent me onboard, Mr. Jones going with me, I was treated civil enough, and they told me should have no further hurt to my person, provided ye people gave me a good charcter.

I had not been 1/2 an hour onboard ye pirate, but ye master tells me my chiefe mate had enter'd with them, and advis'd to take ye ship for their own use, saying she sail'd well and was much fitter then their own, this extreamly surpriz'd me, I got an opportunity of cautioning him of his folly, he denied it which ye master overhearing, threatned to cut him down for lying; and further told me, Mr. Jones had desir'd to be seemingly forc'd. The next day Mr. Jones being sober signs their articles, excusing himself to me his circumstances were bad at home, and y^t. he had no love for his wife, upon this thought proper to converse as little wth him as possible. The next day he persuades ye people to enter saying I design'd it my self, so he got 9 to do it. God only knows whether this man had any hopes of meeting with pirates here when he advis'd to touch at this place, for Phas. Christopher one y^t has enter'd & afterwards repented told me wth tears in his eyes, y^t he said to him ye day before came in here he was in hopes to meet with pirates.

The day after I was taken [5th April] they concluded to keep ye ship for their own use, theirs being old, so took up ye deck to make a teer of ports fore and aft, saying they would make me a voyage by bestowing ye cargo on me and would give me of my own all but what they wanted, I represented your goodness to sailors & beged order might be taken to save ye goods which they promis'd; Capt. Glynn was so kind to come onboard when he heard of my misfortune, and there being 3 pirate ships here went and spoke to ye 3 Captains who all promised much more then perform'd; for the Cargo was strangely dissipated, much was thrown overboard besides what they kept for their own use, & a great deale given to ye white people & blacks onshore, The rest through Capt. Glyns assistance with his sloop & a briganteen [Rising Sun?] wch ye pirates had quitted is saved, but most of ye peice goods were wetted by ye malt spirrits and rain, for they open'd the cases throw'd ye goods Loose, & if did not take them so fast as they fancied often threw some overboard.

Have not yet had time or weather to dry & overhaule all ye goods y^t is saved for tis but 3 days past since ye pirates are gone [27th April], and ye white people onshore promise to deliver what they have got + if will allow them salvage, but doubt their being so good as their words.

I have lost most of what I had; what is saved have mention'd at ye foot of this Letter, for my sole comfort in this sad misfortune is, that if I approve myself an honest tho' unfortunate man I shal not loose ye favour of ye best of masters; and ye reason I mention what I sav'd of my own is because cannot now inform what is sav'd of ye cargo, for some of my people has pretended to part of ye goods for salvage & because refus'd their unreasonable request has ass poss'd me as if did design to convert them to my own use, but in a day or two design in ye presence of Capt. Glyn & some others with ye people y^t comes with me to take an inventory of all y^t is saved, and shal then resolve what to do wth y^m for am in a very great streight at present what to resolve on should have come in this ship but ye care of ye goods prevents me, she is to stop at Repungo, so hope shal not be long after her; Capt. Glyn & my selfe with about 12 of my people shal come about days days hence in ye Parnall snow Capt. Morris bound for Bristoll, ye rest has shipt themselves for ye West Indies, except ye Carpenter & Mr. Fox who comes in this w^th.out asking me, ye last haveing taken pett because I reprov'd him for standing still when he saw me working in drying ye goods.

The Pirate as took uss had been here a month, ye others came in 10 days after, have gent down in ye list ye ships taken here by y^m. All ye people with myself were detain'd prisoners tell just before ye Pirates sail'd, haveing us'd those as would not enter with them wth great barbarity; & have given me for them but 1 barrel flower and one of beefe, besides haveing y^m naked, but as I know your goodness allows every thing in reason, so shal endeavor to provide for ye people as comes with me: The Almighty has been graciously pleas'd to support me in this severe tryall, & my hope is in his good time to return to my native country and approve my self to you an honest tho' unfortunate Ser^vt.

Accot. of goods sav'd of my private adventure ..
4 1/2 hhgs french brandy
10 Box Irons
20 peices of course cherryderries
3 peices of buckram

Wm: Snelgrave
River Sierrelion April 30th.
1719

Pirates Names.
Windham Capt. Cocklin. 34 Guns. 90 men. late ye Bird Gally
King James C. Davis - 32 Guns. 130 men.
Duke Ormond. C. Le Booze 22 Guns. 95 men; late Sarah gally

Ships taken by these.
1. Mons. Channel; Society . . London. . . Plunder'd, but little
2. Jno. Bennet .   Robt. & James. Do . . . . Burnt
3. James Chrichton, Nightingall . Bristoll . . . Plunder'd
4. John Thompson _   Jacob & Jaell . London . . Burnt
5. Henry Morris _   Parnall .   Bristoll . . Plunder'd
6. _ _ Ellott . Two Friends. Barbados . Carried wth. ym. for a tender
7. Davd. Chrichton .Queen Elizabeth. London -   Plunderd but little
8. James Nisbett . Edwd. & Steed . Barbados - Plunder'd
9. Jonathn. Lamb[ert]. Sarah Gally. . London . . taken for a privateer
10. Wm. Snelgrave . Bird Gally . . Do. - -   Do.

11. De Vitry . .   Saint Antonio . St. Malloes - Plunder'd & run ashore
12. -- Willson . . Dispatch -   African company.. Plunder'd . .

Snelgrave Letter – 1 August 1719

William Snelgrave, "William Snelgrave to Humphrey Morice," 1 Aug 1719, *Humphrey Morice Papers of the Bank of England.*

Hond. Sir

My last was by the Queen Elizabeth informing of the sad misfortune befallen us in ye river Sieraleon by Pirates: The next day after she sailed Capt. Glynn & my self went amongst ye white people to demand ye goods given them by ye pirates, some where so just I believe as to deliver all they had, but others not only demanded salvage but believe they kept above half what they had recd, tho' I read to them ye act of parliament against piracy: so was obliged to take what they thought fitt to deliver up. As soon as got ye goods all dried Capt. Glynn & I in ye presence of ye people as remain'd with me took an Inventory of all that was saved, consulting what might be best for ye interest and concluded for ye reasons exprest on ye Inventory to ship them home but ye Captain would not take any Holland goods except brass; so was forc'd to leave those behind mention'd in ye paper sign'd by Mr. Robt. Glynn and Capt. Morris knowing there was no other ship: would not carry them under fivety pound which was obliged to comply with: Capt. Glynn propos'd to me to let him have as much goods as amounted to fivety pound sterling prime cost, wch. he would oblige himself to pay for in England or in ye country as you should please to chuse, wch. I complied with and hope you'll please to approve it, for indeed I had all ye assistance from him in his power. The Pirates haveing given me but one barrel of Irish beefe with one of flower, and 14 of ye people designing to go with me, I bought two teirces of Irish beefe of Capt. James Nisbett (several being left onboard him wch. ye pirates did not find out) but he would take no goods, so have presum'd to draw on you for eight pound sterling payable to him, relying on y^r. goodness to pardon it. Wee sailed from Sieraleon ye 14th of May, having had a tedious passage of 11 weeks with many hardships, and arriv'd here yesterday, where had y^r. most generous Letter from Mr. [Lewis] Cassamajor, and humbly beg leave to show my gratitude for so much goodness in saying 'tis unparoled [unparalleled] considering how unfortunate I have been to you, 'tis not in ye least in my power to make any return only still to persevere in ye integrity I owe you and in my prayers to God for ye wellfare, Capt. Glyn was inform'd by ye postmaster an express was going last evening, & had but a minute to write a line wch. I fear was not sence; I mention'd in y^t. by ye Queen Elizabeth 14 people design'd to come with me; there did but 10; two of wch. died in ye passage, and that presume to give ye rest 10 shillings a man to carry them to London, knowing full well nothing pleases you more than acts of humanity; Mr. Casamajor is extream kind to me, but that have no occasion to take any money haveing now Eight pounds of y^{rs}. being part of what sold ye ships boats for at Sieraleon, this morning went to ye Custom house with him, but they would not allow liberty to Send the goods 'tell an order from London, wch. Mr. Casamajor will inform their reasons for: The ship will not be at key [or bay] 'tell monday; and will have ye goods then Examin'd onboard because ye wett they recd at Sieraleon (tho' well dried) may have occasion'd further damage.

The paper inclos'd No. 1 is ye inventory of goods saved wth. Capt. Glyn'[s] opinion about shiping them home.

No. 2 is accot. of Goods wch. Capt. Morris would not take onboard, wth. Mr. Robt Glyns rect. for them; a Copy of ye prizes to sell all & my instructions Left with him.

No. 3 is Capt. Glyns rect. for goods sold him.

No. 4 is acct. of what gave ye white & black people for working.

No. 5 is ye Invoice of goods shipt on ye Parnell Snow, in wch. there is no more goods of Holland then ye bras & Sheets.

No. 6 is accot. of goods recd from ye white people being part of the Inventory, but that leave tell I come to London informing how villanously most of them acted; There is likewise ye bill of ladeing from Capt. Moris. Before came to Seraleon did not deliver ye Cooper his goods because could not well come at y^e

cases, he told ye pirates what quantity he had, & as they pretend one reason for their villanies is to do justice to sailors, they bid him to throw as much as he would into Capt. Glyn's Sloop Chargeing me to let him have them, wch. I did afterwards upon his request as far as ye order, so here is likewise ye Letter to you wth. his rect. on it, and those goods have taken no notice of in ye Inventory.

My hope and comfort is y^t. I shal appear to you to have acted with integrity and to ye best of my power in this unhappy accident, haveing had ye greatest proof of y^t. goodness in not judgeing of things by ye success, I remain with ye deepest sence of gratitude Hond. Sr.

Bristoll August ye 1st 1719   Y^r
                                     Most Obedient Servt.
                                         Wm. Snelgrave

Shal wait y^r. orders when you please to
Send for me to town; wch. if necessary
forthwith, ye 3rd. mate y^t. is with me
can See ye goods Landed.

Snelgrave Deposition – 20 January 1721

HCA 1/54, f. 128

Offm Dni promot ton	The Informon of William
Edwardum Hogbin	Snelgrave of Mile End in
	the County of Middx Mariner

taken before the worshipful Eoton Sayer Dr of Laws
and of the Commissrs of Oyer & Terminer
and Goal Delivery for the Admiralty of
England in the Common Hall of Doctors
Commons London in the presnce of
Brian Rushworth Notry Publ

This Informant saith that on or about the fourth Day of April in the year of our Lord 1719 he the Informant being then Comander of the Bird Gally in the River Ciralone [Sierra Leone] on the Coast of Guinea was taken by a piratical Vessel called the Maroon (whereof one Cocklyn was Comander) And a few Days afterwards one Edward Hogbin (who then lived on Shoar there) came on board the Informants sd Ship & there conversed with the Pirates then on board of her, And after the sd Pirates were all gon out of the sd River, he the Informant understood that the Inhabitants on Shoar had received several parcels of Goods from the said Pirates And thereupon he the Informant went to them & demanded a Sight of the sd. Goods And the sd. Edward Hogbin then produced several peices of Harlem Stripes, Nittacrees, blew Bafts, Cotton Romalls, ffotaes(?), Sleasys & other Goods of the value of fifty pounds or upwards and he the sd. Hogbin then told the Informant & he the Informant believes that the said Goods were taken by the sd. Pirates out of the sd. Bird Gally & given by them to him the said Hogbin, and that he had kept the same for the use of the Owners of the sd. Gally & desired that he might have Salvage, and thereupon he the Informant allowed him a third part thereof for ye Salvage of the same. And beleives that the said Hogbin had more Goods by him which had been taken out of the sd Gally than he had then produced to ye Informant & saith yt ye Lading of ye Gally were ye goods of Humpfrey Morris Esqr.

Wm. Snelgrave

Jurat 20mo. Juny [Jany?] 1721
Coram me

Ex: Sayer presente me

B. Rushworth N. P.

Three Lasinby Narratives – March 1722

"Mr. [Richard] Lasinby's Narrative of the Proceedings of the Pyrates," 19 Mar 1722, IOR L/MAR/B/313A London Journal, ff. 165-171

First Version (taken first on board *London* and read in court 22 March 1722):

I Omitt ye particulars of our Engagement & being taken, because do not doubt but Yr Honrs have had a Satisfactory acct: of that from Capt: Macrae; & likewise in what manner I was taken from him. the first night I came on board. & ye time came for those people to Sleep their was a watch orderd on my Acct: which made some of Y:m so angry as to say, that if they saw me out on ye Deck on any Acct: soever would Knock my brains out which did not a little concern me; Some who were in ye Cabbin bad[e] me be of good Cheere but not to venture on ye: Deck for fear of ye worst, the Chief Surgeon in particular who took care to lat me down on ye Cabbin floor by him, more to prevent my Escape y:n any good nature in the Villain; which found afterwards when rose in ye night by his following me into ye Gallery, and telling me if I offerd att Escapeing they would oblidge Capt: Macrae to find me or else would take all from him again & burn ye Ship [Fancy, given to Macrae by the pirates].

The next morning they got unmoored & hove short for sailing; Capt: Macrae came on board and interceeded much for me but to no Purpose; he left me & soon after they got under sail designing to proceed for India, where they arriv'd some time in Octb: the day before they made ye Land; saw 2 Ships to ye E'ward whom att first sight took to be English, whereupon ye Capt: call'd for me and Threatend to Cutt me in pieces If I did not Immediately tell him the Signalls between us & our

Consorts from England. I made him answer I knew nothing of none, or ever had Occassion to make any

--- 165b

Dureing our Company together; He then Abus'd me; by Calling Scurillous Names, and shook his Broad Sword att me, saying he would Plague me like a Dog as I was & had better tell him; they came up with the Ships soon after, which prov'd to be two Small Moor Ships come from Muscatt with Horses, which they took by fireing a Gun or two, They brought on Board their Cap:ts & Merch:ts, putting y:m to torture to make y:m Confess of their money & riches beleiving they were come from Mocha. They continued all night riffling, & tormenting ye people and the next Morn made ye Land; att the same time a Fleet in Shore Plying to ye No[rth]ward. they Inst:ly held a Councill what to do with the forementioned Ships, some were for sinking y:m Men & horses in them, Others for throwing their Sails overboard, Others again for Cutting away their Masts, & all was they said for fear of being Discover'd on the Coast, after their Debates were over, the[y] brought them to an Anchor in 35 f:m [fathom] water, throw'd all their Sails overboard & Cutt one of ye Ships Masts half thro.

When att an Anchor one of the forementioned fleet bore away to y:m. She made y:m & hoisted English Coulours the Pyrates answering with red. The rest of y:t day they Imploy'd in takeing all their water from y:m & att night they weigh'd with the sea wind & left ye two Moor Ships to Stand to ye Noward after the fleet, which they came up with about 4 the next Morning

---166

Just as they Got under Sail with ye Land Wind Makeing no Stop butt ran thro y:m, fireing their small Arms & Great Guns, on both sides as fast as Could. Load & fire, till day light, y:tt saw their Mistake, haveing all along taken y:m for Angria's fleet, they were in a Great Consternation, not knowing what to do _ whether to run from y:m or pursue, being so much inferior to y:m in Strength, haveing no more y:n 300 men in both Ships, & 40 of y:m Negroes; besides the Victory att yt time had 4 Pomps att work, and must inevitably have perisht some time before, had it not been for ye hand pumps & severall pair of Standards they took out of ye Cassandra; Observing the Indifferency of the Fleet, the[y] took Courage to Chase rather then run, which did; when they sea wind came in, but were to leeward about a Gun shot, Some a head (Especially the great Ships) & some a Stern, which were afraid to tack upon beleiving y:m to be fire Vessels. The Great Ships began to gain on y:m tow:ds sun sett: they Continued ye same Course all night, Do see severall boats pass they had cutt away the next morning were all out of sight, only some few Gallevats & a Small katch to leeward which they bore way after, the ketch perceiving itt embarqt their people on board a Gallevatt, & sate fire to her, they then left of Chace the Gallevats being to nimble for y:m, about an hour after, they see a Gallevat to ye NW which they Chaced & took being come from Gogo, & bound for Callecut, Loaded with Cotton,

---166b

They asked y:m after ye fleet, beleiving were in itt, butt ye Fellows told y:m they had not seen a Ship or boat before y'day since they left Gogo, and Notwithstaning the poor fellows pleadings, they threw all their Cargoe overboard, tormenting y:m by Squeezeing their Joynts in ye vice; to make y:m Confess of the fleet, they kept the boat with y:m all yt night, and part of ye next day, but blowing fresh E:terly they Splitt ye Gallevat sail, so that She could not keep Company with the Ship; They then put the People into their Boat, haveing nothing but a Small Try Sail, no Provisions & about 4 Gallons of Water half Salt, & y:m out of Sight of ye Land, they then resolvd of Cruizeing S:ard, ye next day were between Goa & Carwarr, att noon heard Guns fire att Carwarr, they Instantly Came to an anchor, & att night sent their boat to discover what Ships there was in ye road, who return'd about 2 in the Morning giveing an Acct: of 2 Grabs att an Anchor there, they then weigh'd & ran nearer to they bay and Anchord again att Lay light the Grabs haveing sight of y:m weigh'd & ran out to get under India Diva Castle, which they did with much Difficulty; The Pyrates were so much Displeased att itt, wanting water, that had a Councill whether Should make a Descent yt night & take ye Island, They Could not agree on itt So proceeded to ye So:ward, the next Morning See a Small Ship att an Anchor in Onnore road, which in the evening they took haveing noe one on Board butt a Dutch man & 2 Portuguese

---167

The Capt: & his officers being gone on Shore, the next morning they sent on Shore to acquaint the Capt: that if he wer to Supply y:m with some water & fresh Provisions Should have his Ship again, att night he sent on board his Mate nam'd Frank Harmless with a letter to y:m that if they would deliver the Ship into possession over ye Barr would Supply y:m with what water & provisions they wanted, and not before; they not likeing his Proposals the mate Said he would Carry y:m where Should gett what they wanted, they not willing to trust him being a Stranger, resolv'd of Seeking water att the Lacker Diva Islands, which they put for directly, where they arriv'd in 3 days after the same day of their arrival, they took a Small Manchew with the Govr: of Carwarr's pass on Pod: who Gave y:m an Acct: that there was no anchor ground among ye Islands, they then being near ye Island of Melindra sent their Boat on Shore to see of their was any water, or whether ye Island was Inhabited, they returnd giveing an Acct: of their being good water & abundance of houses but that ye Inhabitants att ye sight of the Ships were fled of in boats to ye Adjacent Islands, only Abundance of Women & Children, which they found a day or two afterwards, hid in ye Bushes; & forct y:m in Barbarous Manner, to their lascivious Inclinations; Destroying their Cocoa trees and every thing they mett wth:, Setting fire to Severall of the Houses, & Churches, Had fresh Gales of wind whils't there which Occassioned their Looseing 3 or 4 Anchors there, the Ground being so

---167b

Rockey, and lastly with a hard Gale of wind were forc't from ye Iland where they left about 70 People black & White & most of their water Casks, In about 10 Days they made Shift to find ye Island again where they fill'd their Water took their people on

Board, Provisions being very Scarce among y:m they now resolv'd of proceeding to Cochin, & see what they Could Get from their good friends the Dutch whom they said, were Confident would not fail of supplying any of their Proffesion.

Three days after they left the Island they arriv'd off from Tellichery where they took a Small Vessel Belonging to Govr: Adams, Jno: Tawke Master, whom they brought on Board very Drunk, He having before heard of my Misfortune enquir'd for me haveing been Acquainted with him in my former Voyage to Bengal in ye Duke of Cambridge; He began presently to tell me yt My Old Capt. Macrae was fitting out after y:m, att which news ye QrMaster told me to prepare for the next Day Swore he would hang me like a Dog as I was, Not Doubting he said but if I was Clear'd from y:m would take ye first Opertunity, to come and fight against y:m as Capt. Macrae had, whom they said, like a Villain as he was they had us'd so civily, in Giveing him a Ship to Carry him from Joanna. And Swore y:n for ye future if in his po?? would Carry the Masters & Officers of all Ships they ever overpower'd, to Plague y:m like Dogs as they were to abuse civily

---168

They thence proceeded to Callecut where they endeavourd to take a Large Moor Ship our of ye Road but were Intercepted by some Guns y:t was Mounted on Shore; I was down below as usual thinking the Story Capt: Tawke told y:m was forgot, but unknown to me ye Capt: & QrMaster were so Malicious to order me to ye Braces on ye Booms in hopes Should there be Shot; When they got Clear of Road they Call'd me up to know ye reason why was not on ye Deck according to their order, I reply'd had no Business there att y:t time entreating to be put on Shore, The Q:Mter Answerd y:t if ever he knew me off ye Deck in time of Action would Shoot me thro ye head, I told him twas better directly to do itt, then keep me in Misery there, att which he beggd the Capt: to Correct me for my Impudence, he being Lame of his hands, according to his Desire he fetch his Cane and began to Labour me unmercifully which some of their people seeing came to hinder him & said he might be asham'd to abuse me in such manner, for nothing saying they would do their endeavour to have me putt on Shore att Cochin with Capt: Tawke.

The next day in their Passage down came up with a Dutch Galliot bound for y:t place with Limestone, they sent their Boat on Board with Capt: Tawke which the forementioned people seeing, came to ye Capt: & told him he might as well y:n let me goe as not and press'd itt very hard, but ye Capt: answer was; that if

---168b

they had a mind to oversett their proceedings by letting a Dog go who had heard their Designs & Resolutions for ye ensueing Year, they might but he would never Consent to itt, Abundance of ye Capts: party also Objected against itt which Occassioned a Strong Debate, & so farr enraged ye Capt: yt he swore if I went he would have a Limb of me first to his Share, he likewise added yt my Going there might be a hindrance of their haveing a Supply from ye Dutch.

Capt: Tawke was sent away in ye Galliot, The next Day they arriv'd off Cochin, where, by a fishing Canoe they sent a Letter on Shore, and in ye Afternoon with ye Sea Breeze ran into ye Road where they Anchor'd, Saluteing ye Fort with 11 Guns each Ship, ye Fort returning their Salute, Gun for Gun, Att night there Came on board a Large boat Laden with fresh Provisions & Liquors, with ye Servt: of an Inhabitant of yt: place Vularly Called Jno: Trumpett, who told y:m they must Immediately Weigh & run farther to ye So:ward where they shou'd have a Supply of all things they wanted, as well Navall Stores as provisions, they had not been long att an Anchor before had severall Canoes on Board with Inhabitans as well White as Black, which never ceased more or less during their stay there; Att nighht Came on board ye foremention'd Jno: Trumpett bringing with him a Large Boat with Arrack

---169

Which they Receiv'd with Abundance of Joy Asking if Could have any More, he Said yt: had Procured all on ye Place for Y:m which was About 90 Legors & 60 Bales of Sugar, which they Should have off before he left y:m, which did in about 3 Days the Boat Going and comeing as fast as Could, The 2nd Day they sent on Shore a fine Table Clock was taken in our Ship a Present to ye Govr: also a Large Gold Watch to his Daughter, who in Return sent y:m 10 Bales of Sugar.

When they had all on Board, Said Mr. Trumpett his Money gave him 3 Cheers & 11 Guns each Ship, throwing handfulls of Ducattoons into his Boat as he put from ye Ship; that night being little Wind they did not Weigh, & Ye Next Morning Jno: Trumpett returnd with More Arrack, & w Large Chests of Piece Goods, & ready Made cloaths, bringing with him ye Fiscall of ye Place, att noon they Saw a Sail to ye So:ward which they Immediately Weigh'd after & Chac'd, butt She haveing so Good an Offing got to ye Noward of y:m and yt night Anchord a Small Dist: from Cochin Fort, which in ye Morning they had Sight of & Gave her Chace She Standing into Cochin Road & They after her, being Assured, by ye Forement: Gentlemen, that they Might take her from under ye Castle; without any Molestation, Begging Withall not to Carry her away, for would Purchase her, & Give as Good a price as any one; The Capt. beg'd y:m to Go into their

---169b

Boats and he Would talk with y:m after he had Taken ye Ship, They Stood in Boldly to Board her, but When were within About a Cables lenght [length] or two of her ye Fort fired 2 Small Guns att y:m The Shott falling Close almost to their Muzles, Att Which they Instantly Bore out of ye Road and Made an Easy Saile to ye So:ward Where att Night Anch[ored] in the Former Berth, att Night A Great boat Was Sent by Jon: Trumpett to Gett y:m Water, and to let y:m Know if they Would Stay there Some few Days Longer there Would be a very Rich Ship Pass by, Commanded by the Generall of Bombay's Brother, That Night they Spent in Getting of Water &

in ye Morning Weigh'd to Continue their Cruize So:ward, haveing Disbursed for Liquors Provisions & Between 6 & 7 Thousand Pounds. After finishing their Affairs With ye Dutch some Were for Proceeding to Madagascar forthwith, Others to Stay & Cruize for a Store Ship for y:m, the latter att Last agreed. on they Ply'd to ye So:ward, Where some time after, they see a Ship in Shore, but She haveing the Wind of Y:m they Could not Gett near her till Ye Sea Wind, Sett in, Which Was very faint, Night Comeing on They Seperated, One Ship to ye Noward & ye Other to ye So:ward, Thinking in Ye Morning to have her Between Y:m Butt Contrary to their Expectation. When day Broke instead of their Chace were very near 5 Sail Who Immediately Made Ye Signall to bear ?? Y:m Which Putt Y:m In Great Confusion, the Consort being then 3 Leagues to ye So:ward

---170

of Y:m, They Immediately Stood to their Consort And Joyn'd him, the Fleet Chaesing y:m being att first very much Dejected beleiveing itt to be the forementioned fleet Commanded by Capt. Macrae, they Made all Saile from y:m Possible & after 3 hours found yt none of Ye fleet Came up wth y:m only one Grab who Came very near half way Between y:m & the Fleet, began to take Courage & Rejoyce; itt Presently After fell Calm & so Continued till Night, When with ye Land Wind they ran directly off Shore and in ye Morning finding ye fleet out of Sight were Extreamly Satisfied not Desireing any of Capt. Macrae's Company, they now thinking themselves out of Danger propos'd to Carowze & keep their Christmass before they Would Stir any farther, which they did in a most riotous Manner, destroying all their fresh Provisions, they had & 2/3ds in Waste I beleive, this Lasted near 3 days, when they then Propos'd to Go to ye Island Mauritius there to repair their Leakey Ship being in a very bad Condition, yt being agreed on, Made ye Best of their way there, In their Passage Expected the Leakey Ship to Sink every day, they were Going severall times to quitt her & I beleive had were itt not for ye Scarcety of Provisions & Water another thing being there a Great Quantity of Arrack, The Allowance among y:m att yt Timewas one Bottle of Water pr man a day and not Above 2 pound of beef & a

Small Quantity of Rice for 10 Men pr day, which had itt not been for ye Arrack & Sugar must ye Greatest part of y:m have Perish'd

---170b

In this Condition they arriv'd att ye Island Mauritius about the Middle of February [1721] where they found very good Refreshment, Refitted & Sheathed their Leakey Ship, & on ye 5th of Aprill they Sail'd in Order for ye Island Mascarine [Boubon or Reunion], where Arriv'd on ye 8th Do in ye Morning, where they found Lying there a large 70 Gun Portugueze, whom they Immediately took With very little Resistance, She haveing Lost all her Masts & Likewise Guns Save 21 In a Storm they had mett with in 13: So Latitude. She had on Board When they Took her the Vice Roy of Goa & Severall Other Gentlemen that were Passengers who came on Board that Morning beleiveing they were English Ships, Haveing an Acct: of Another Ship an Ostender yt Lay to Leeward of ye Island made ye Best of their way to y:m & took her, She was formerly the Greyhound Galley belonging to London.

There happened a Great Caball among ye Pyrates on ye Vice Roys Acct: Some being for Carrying to Mozambique & make him Ransome, Others Saying they did beleive ye Rich Prize had taken Might Partly belong to him & said itt Was better to Take a Small Ransome there then be troubled Wth: him, Which was att Last Agreed on for 2000 Dollars [Piastres]. I then Begg'd to be Sett on Shore which was Granted accordingly was on ye 10th with His Excellence & ye Rest of ye Prisoners. The Govr: of ye Place Interceded as Also ye Vice Roy, very much to leave a Ship to Carry the Prisoners away alledgeing that the Island

---171

Was not in A Condition to Maintain So many People, they with Smooth Promises, said Would Call a Councell About itt to see what Might be Done, butt Contrary to that in the night Sail'd away, Carrying With y:m ye Best of ye Men that they had taken in ye 2 Ships, besides, 200 of Mozambique Negroes in ye Portuguese, Disghning for Madegascar, there to Clean The Cassandra, and from thence to the Red Sea Where if Mett With no Suckcess, Would to their Old friends Att Cochin & Sell their Diamonds they had Taken in The Portuguese Ship (which since as the Vice Roy told me were to the Value of Between three & four Millions of Dollars) & thence to Make ye Best of their Way into the China Seas, beleiving their might be Men of Warr or Other Ships fitted out in Pursuit of y:m.

Dureing my Stay on ye Island there arriv'd in May two Ships from france bound to Madegascar for Slaves & from thence to Misisipy, the beginning of June Arriv'd Another from St. Maloe for China and in her way to Settle the Island Pullecondore, haveing on Board her A Govr: 2 Engineers & about 100 Soldiers and Officers, They made butt very little Stay, when they Sail'd I took Care to write to China to acquaint Your honrs: Ships of What is herein Mentioned.

On ye first of Novbr: Last Arriv'd the Triton French Ship from Mocha last from ye Island Mauritius Where had Stay'd 40 days dureing Which time had taken Possession of ye Said Island; by Erecting a Large

---171b

Cross & leaveing A French flagg flying. The Governour of this Place had Some time before been in Expectation of Ships from france for yt: Purpose, but none Comeing had began to Build a Small Vessel to send up there with People to Settle itt, Much Fearing that the Ostenders would do itt before y:m which he had an Acct: they intended.

Haveing now an Opertunity Embarqu't with ye Vice Roy & Severall Others for France but luckeyly touching att Ye Isle St Hellena mett Capt. [William] Hutchenson, who was so Oblidgeing to take me on Board, being almost Starv'd in ye French Ship.

Richd: Lasinby

read in Court 22nd March

---172

[blank]

Second Version (outline prepared after first version):

"Short Heads of Mr. Lasinby's Narrative," IOR L/MAR/B/313A London Journal, ff. 173-174.

---173

Their Threats to knock my brains out if See me out on Deck, the Surgeon's following me & their offering to burn ye Ship gave to Capt. Macrae if, Attempted Escapeing.

Proceeded Directly from Joanna to ye Mallabar Coast, Barbarity to ye 2 Moor Ships from Muscall Laden with horses, Chaceing a fleet, Takeing a Calevatt threw their Cargoe overboard & tormenting their people, Chaceing 2 Grabs off Carwarr, Takeing a Small Ship att Onnore Carrying her to ye Laker Diva's Broke her up for fire wood Water'd their Ships there & bound to Cochin to their friends ye Dutch who were abused would never fail of Supplying any of their Proffession, in their Way took Capt Tawke who Gave an Acct Capt Macrae's Comeing in pursuit of them, y:n their Threats to hang me, a Small Dutch Vessell Mett ye Day before they arriv'd there, their Sending away Capt: Tawk in her Do Gave the men belonging to ye Vessell Some Scarlett Cloth & Money, ye next Day they arriv'd off Cochin & Sent a letter on Shore, in ye Afternoon Anchord in ye Road & Saluted with 11 Guns each Ship ye Fort return'd ye same, att night ye Boat Came with Provisions & arrack with ye Servant of an Inhabitant of yt Place Vulgarly Call'd Jno: Trumpett, who told y:m to weigh and run farther Down ye Coast in ye Morning Came on Board Jno:

Trumpett with a great boat of Arrack, he Stay'd on board and sent for More, when had all was about 90 Legors & 60 Bales of Sugarr

---173b

I am certain to Jno: Trumpett haveing known him 2 former Voyages the Man he brought with him his 2d: time of Comeing the pyrates told me he Said itt was ye fiscall, the Clock sent on Shore Said to be for ye Governor ye watch said to be for his Daughter, they Rec'd in return for yt: from her 10 bales of Sugarr 2 Boats sent to gett y:m Water, their Chaceing the Ship into ye Road & ye Pyrates told me they did assure y:m might take y:m from under ye Castle without any Molestation, their was on Board all the time they lay there canoes going & comeing all day long with Cloaths & all manner of Necssary's which never ceasd more or less dureing their Stay there, many of ye people yt Came in ye Canoes were Dutch men, att their Departure from Cochin & Trumpett went away they Saluted him with 11 Guns each Ship and throw'd handfulls of Ducatoons in his boat after him, He after yt Informs of a Rich Ship Comeing up ye Coast Commanded by ye Generall of Bombays brother, ____ From thence they went to ye Island Mauritius where Refitted & Sheathd their leaky Ship, from thence to ye Iland Mascarine where they took a Portugueze Ships & an Ostender, forceing most of their men with y:m, when on Shore found here Capt. Conden who Commanded a pyrate And was come he & about 40 of his people in upon ye french Kings act of Grace whereof Remain att present not above 18 on ye Iland some of y:m Marry'd ye Capt: also Rems: there came home Passengers in ye French Ship about The rest being Dead, I enquir'd of y:m whether had any news of more pyrates who told me that when they came from Madegascar knew of no more yn: themselves, they burnt their privateer & Sunk ye Moors prize they had taken in ye Port of St Mary's & left most of the people that Stay'd behind there Sick.

Third Version (official polished version distributed by EIC court and to the Secretary of State and the Dutch VOC):

---175

[Outside page 178:]

"Mr. Lasinbys' Affidt. of his being taken by the Pyrates & of their proceedings

Memd. he Swore to 3 of ye Same Tenour and Sent to ye Secry. of State - one to ye Dutch Company a 3d. for this Company to keep," IOR L/MAR/B/313A London Journal, ff. 175-177b

[text:]

Richard Lasinby of London Mariner maketh oath that he this Deponent was in the Year of Our Lord One Thousand seven hundred and nineteen Entertained Second Mate of the Ship Cassandra Captain James Macrae Commander employ'd in the Service of the United Company of Merchants of England Trading to the East Indies and Bound out on a Voyage to Bombay in the said East Indies That the said Ship Sail'd from England in the Month of March in the later end of that year [years ended in March in the 18th century] and in her Outward bound Voyage Touch'd at the Island Johanna for Water & Refreshments where being Assaulted by a Pyrate Ship call'd the Fancy & afterwards by her Consort pyrate call'd the Victoria, the Cassandra was after a long and brave Defence overpiwer'd and taken on the 7th of August [8th according to Greenwich's log] following many of the People belonging to her being kill'd but those which Surviv'd by Swimming and the help of the Ships Long Boat got ashore at Johanna aforesaid and Fled into the Countrey That after some time the pyrates consented to give Capt. Macrae their Ship Fancy aforesaid to carry him & his Men to Bombay aforesaid being Induc'd thereto (as it was generall reported) by some among them who knew Capt. Maccrae and gave him a good Charcter for his

Kindness to his Men in former Voyages and because she was so much Shatter'd as render'd her unfitt for the pyrates further Service Whereupon the said Captain Maccrae and his Ships Company of which this Deponent was one went on board her but after some time the said pyrates came out and by Violence took away this Deponent & carry'd him on board the Cassandra then their prize as aforesaid Notwithstandg. Capt Maccrae's earnest Entreatys to the contrary _ And this Deponent further saith That he understood by said Pyrates discourse That one Seegar was Commander in Chief of both the aforesaid Ships and was in the Fancy [probably not; Barnes' journal states he commanded *Victory*] during the Fight and one Taylor was Deputed by him to Command the Victoria [Taylor did not command either vessel until after removal of Edward England from *Victory*] _

That to this Deponents best Remembrace the Said Pyrate's Stay'd at Johanna about Six weeks after the Capture of the Cassandra and then both said Ships Sail'd for the Coast of India where arriving in October following they took two Moors Ships Greviously Torturing the people on board to make them discover their Money and Riches and after that seeing some Ships at Sea and wanting to Learn what they were the next day the said Pyrates took a Gallevat bound from Gogo to Callicut with Cotton and Tortured the people on board her by Squeezing their Joynts in a Vice to make them Confess what news they had of said Ships seen the day before as aforesaid _

And this Deponent further saith

---175b

[Note that this "official" version omits the embarrassing battle between the pirates and the first EIC fleet (*London, Defense, Prahm*, etc.) that they encountered immediately after dismissing the Moors ships.]

That the said Two Pyrate Ships Victoria and Cassandra wanting Water did speedily after Proceed to the Laccadiva Islands to supply themselves therewith but being told by the people of a Munchua they had taken there was no Anchor Ground at the Island they then were at they did proceed to the

Island Melindra and there Water Comitting the Vilest Barbaritys to the Women & Children (for the men Spying two Ships coming in had fled to a Neighbouring Island Burning their Houses and Churches and Cutting down their Cocoa nut Trees.

And this Deponent further saith That whilst the pyrates ashore were doing this and getting their Water aboard A hard Gale of Wind forced both Ships from the said Island leaving about Seventy of their people and most of their Water Casks ashore about ten days after they return'd and got their people and Water Cask aboard but provisions being very scarce The Pyrates aboard said two Ships resolv'd to proceed to Cochin being confident as they said from the Accompts given them by some Old Pyrates they had talk'd with That the Dutch at Cochin would not fail to Supply any of their profession Whereupon both said pyrate Ships Set Sail and in three days arriv'd off Tellicherry where they took a small Vessell belonging to Mr. Adams the chief of the English Factory at Callicut and in her one John Tawke her Master whom they brought aboard the Cassandra this Tawkes having known this deponent formerly and hearing he was taken by the pyrates Enquir'd whether he was on board and being told he was the sd. Tawkes being brought to this Deponent and very much disguised by drink said to this Deponent words to the Effect following Your Captain Maccrae is fitting out after the pyrates On this the Quarter Master of the Cassandra in great Rage bid this Deponent prepare for the next day when he should be hang'd like a Villain as he was Exclaiming against capt. Maccrae as an Ungratefull wretch for the kindness they show'd him.

And this Deponent further saith that in two or three days after both said Ships Cassandra and Victoria arriv'd in the Offin off Cochim and sent a Letter on Sh[ore] In the afternoon they run in and anchor'd in Cochin Road Salut'd the Fort each with Eleven Guns The Fort return'd the Salute Gun for Gun The same night there came aboard the Cassandra a large Boat Laden with provisions and Liquors and in her a person who said he was Servant to an Inhabitant of Cochin named John Trumpet This person told the Pyrates that both their Ships must immediately weigh and run further to the Southward where they should have a supply of all things they wanted as well Navall Stores as provisions accordingly both Ships weigh and Anchor about a League further to the Southward.

---176

And this Deponent further saith that soon after their Anchoring severall Canoes from Cocin came on board both the said Ships bringing Divers Sorts of Necessarys as Cloaths Fowles Hogs & Liquors and in the said Canoes were many people both Whites and Blacks The Whites Dutch men the others Natives of the Countrey which as they said (and was Universally believed) were Inhabitants of Cochin That the Evening following the aforesaid John Trumpet came aboard the Cassandra in a large Boat with Arrack which the Pyrates receiv'd with abundance of Joy and desiring to have more the said Trumpet told them he had procur'd for them about ninety Leagers of Arrack and Sixty Bales of Sugar which was all the place could then Spare that they should have it off before he left them and it was brought aboard in about three days the Boat going and coming as fast as it could.

And this Deponent further saith That when he saw the said Trumpet he remember'd him again being acquainted with him at Cochin he this Deponent having been twice there in Ships belonging to the English East India Company which Touch'd at Cochin in their Voyages but he hath been Inform'd his Right name is not Trumpet though he goes by that name at Cochin.

And this Deponent further saith that during the said Two Ships lying at Anchor as aforesaid there was a continued Resort of Boats and Canoes which came to them from Cochin and that in about Two days after the said Ships Coming to an Anchor The said Pyrates sent to Cochin a Fine Table Clock which they got in the Cassandra for a present as they said to the Governour of Cochin and a large Gold Watch to his Daughter and this Deponent saith that he saw Ten Bales of Sugar brought aboard the Cassandra which the pyrates said was return'd to them as a present from the Governours said Daughter.

And this Deponent further saith that when the said pyrates had got the Arrack & others Supplies on board their Ships and had clear'd accounts with the said John Trumpet They gave him three Cheers or Huzzahs each Ship fir'd Eleven Guns and they threw in hadfulls of Duccatoons into his boat as he put from the Ship That night being little Wind the Ships did not weigh.

Whereupon the next Morning said John Trumpet return'd to them with more Arrack and two large Chest of Peice Goods & ready made Cloathes and brought with him a person which the said Trumpet assured them was the Fiscall of Cochin and at noon the same day Spying a Sail to the Southward the pyrates weigh'd and chased her but she having a good Offin got to the Norward of them and anchor'd that night at some distance from

---176b

Cochin Fort The next Morning the pyrates getting sight of her and she of them she weigh'd her anchors and made the best of her way to get under the protection of the said Fort and they Chased her till they saw her Anchor under the Command of Its Guns.

And this Deponent further saith That the said John Trumpet and the other person said to be the Fiscall were on board the Cassandra when she with her Consort first chased said Ship and continued on board till next day and that it was the Generall discourse among the Cassandra's Ships Company that said Two persons had assured their Captain he might take the said Ship from under the Fort without Molestation and at the same time desir'd she might not be carry'd away because they would give as much for her as any others Whereupon the Captain having desir'd the said Two persons to go into their Boat then along the Cassandra's side telling them it was time enough to talk of that matter when she was taken, he caused the Cassandra and Victoria to stand in Boldly into Cochin Road to board said Ship and they were within a Cables length or two of her but then the Fort Fir'd Two of their small Guns at them which this Deponent believes were not done with design to

378   Sailing East

hurt either because he saw the Shot fall short of them however both said Ships thereupon instantly bore out of the Road making an easy Sail to the Southward and Anchor'd at night at Mud Bay a place where the Dutch have a House and their Ships sometimes ly at[.] That Night a great Boat was sent to said pyrates at Mud Bay to get them Water and to acquaint them If they would stay there some few days longer they might expect a very Rich Ship to pass by Commanded by the General of Bombay's Brother whereupon the next morning the pyrates weigh'd and Cruiz'd to the Southward.

And this Deponent further saith that by the best Calculate he could make from the discourses of the pyrates on board the Cassandra of what they paid for the General Ships Stocks of liquors and Necessarys and what particular _____ persons disbursed on their single accounts for their supply aforesaid he believes the whole came to between Six and Seven Thousand Pounds _ Sterling _

And this Deponent further saith That while both said Ships were on their cruize they spy'd a Ship near the shore but she having the Wind of them they could not then get to her and therefore at night they seperated One Ship to the Norward and the other to the Southward thinking in the morning to have her between them but when day broke the Cassandra which stood to the Norward spy'd Five Sail of Ships bearing down towards he[re] which the people apprehending were the Fleet John Tawke

---177

had acquainted them were fitting out against them under Captain Maccrae as aforesaid The Cassandra made from them and joyn'd the Victoria as soon as she could and the said Fleet continuing the Chase, said Two pyrate Ships made the best of their way from them and at last got out of sight.

And this deponent further saith that after severall days of Jollity for getting clear of said Fleet both pyrate Ships proceeded for the Island Mauritius to repair the Victoria which was so Leaky they would have sunk her but that they could not by reason of the weather get out the Water and provisions on board her for there was a scarcity of both among them.

And this deponent further saith That about the middle of Febry following both Ships arriv'd at Mauritius where the Victoria was sheathed and Refitted and both Ships got plenty of Refreshments That on or about the 5th of April following they left that Island and about three days after got to the Island Don Mascarenhas where finding a Large portgeez Ship of Seventy Guns that had Lost her masts in a Storm and all her Guns but Twenty one the said pyrates took her with the Vice Roy of Goa and many other persons of Quality on board soon after hearing an Ostend Ship formerly the Greyhound Galley was to the Leeward of the Island they proceeded & took her.

And this Deponent further saith that on his Earnest Enteaty he at last prevailed on the pyrates to Set him ashore on the said Island of Don Mascarenhas on or about the 10th of the said April and that soon after he heard the French Governour there and also the aforesaid Vice Roy interceed with the Captain Quarter Master and others belonging to the Cassandra then on Shore to Leave either the Portugeez Ship or Greyhound to carry away the people belonging to said two Ships which they had turned a shore alledging as a reason that the Island was not in a Condition to Entertain them they pretended to Consult about it but this Deponent saith that he heard some of the Pyrates say among themselves they would not but would proceed for Madagascar to clean the Cassandra there and from thence to the Red Sea where if they met with no Success they would go to their Old Friends at Cochin and Sell the Dyamonds they had taken in the Portugeez Ship which were reported to be of a very great Value & the said Vice Roy assured this Deponent some time after that they were so this Deponent further saith that the said Two Pyrate Ships did Sail away the following night with their Two prizes and the best of the men then aboard.

And this Deponent further saith that during his stay at the said Island don Mascarenhas he saw & discoursed with Capt. Condon and about forty of his people Who had been a

---177b

Pyrating that they told him they had taken a Rich India Ship which they brought to Madagascar and Sunk her at or near Port St Marys and from thence came to don Mascarenhas on the Encouragement of the French Kings Act of Grace that about 15 of them came from thence taking passgage on a French Ship called the Tryton Bound for Europe on which this Deponent also took passage in November last That Captain Condon and about Eighteen more continued on the Island and the rest were dead That this Deponent understood from the French Directore there that the French East India Companys orders were that if any of the pyrates on the Island dy'd leaving a Wife his Widow shou'd enjoy the Effects belonging to the deceased but if not then such pyrates were not allow'd to give away any of their Effects at their death & this Deponent saw the Directore take into his possession the Effects of Two ____ of said pyrates immediately after notice of their Decease.

And Lastly this Deponent saith That the said Ship Tryton in her homeward bound passage Touching at St Helena found there the Ship Sunderland belonging to the United English Company aforementioned on which this deponent came to England.

Detail of HMS *Phoenix* Log Entries
22 February - 24 April 1718

Date	Bearing & Dist of Known head Lands last seen	Remarkable Observations &c
22 Feb 1717/8	Standing off & on of Harbour Island	Fresh gales and Squally Lay too all night att 6 this morning Saw Harbour Island bearing SSW 3 Leagues stood off & on till noon making of Signalls for a Boat but none appear'd
23 Feb 1717/8	Lying too off Providence Harbour	Moderate and fair bore away for Providence att 10 this morning was off that Harbour; where lay severall Ships & Sloops with Colours of all Nations Flying I then brought too & sent my Lieutenant a Shoar with a Flagg of Truce & his Majesties Royall proclamation of the Act of Grace

24 Feb 1717/8	Att Anchor in Providence Harbour	Ditto Yesterday in the Afternoon my Lieutenant Returned aboard and Informed me that he was receiv'd by a great number of Pyrate with much Civility to whom he read Publick the proclamation and they accepted the same with a great deall of Joy all their Commanders did the like and sent me Information that a Sloop call'd the Lark was att anchor att Bushes Key with a design to goe out upon the Account again where upon I made saill thither I found under Saill with Resolution to push out Between the Shoals but after I had fired severall Shott att her she bore down to me so I sent my Lieutenant on board and took Possession of her she had but 16 Men wch: pretended she for going into the Harbour to Surrender them selves to me and to Accept of his Maj:ties Pardon in the Evening prov'd little wind and Continued all night so that I did not gett into the Harbour till 7 this morning att which time I anchored in 3 fathom & was Saluted by two of the pyrates Ships; Some of thes Commanders and Ringleaders came on board and Informed me that my taking the Sloop had very much alarm all the Pyrates in Generall beleiving that the Men taking [taken] in her would be Executed therefore the Said Commanders Assured me that my Setting att Liberty these Prisoners would be a very great means to induce these People to Surrender and Accept the act of Grace; which I accordingly did and this Confirm'd them all of his Majesties goodness towards them.

25 Feb 1717/8		Squally with rain here we found 5 ships 3 of them from 18: to 36 guns also 9 Sloops which were Traders with these Pyrates but pretended they never did itt till the Act of Grace was Published one of the Dutch man of 36 guns & another of 26: one an English Pink one a Bristoll Gally & the other a French Ship of no Force
26 Feb 1717/8		Squally weather a great many pirates came on board & Surrender'd themselves and accepted his Majesties most Gracious Pardon & took my Certificates for their Protection to carry them to Government
27 Feb 1717/8		Fresh gales Severall Pyrates came on board & Surrenderd themselves
28 Feb 1717/8		Ditto a Sloop came in from Carolina Severall Pirates took Certificates
1 Mar 1717/8		Hard gales and Squally att 10 last night our anchors came home and the Ship Taild a ground att midnight hove off again itt being then high water and the wind abated the Pyrates sett one of the ships on fire this morning hoisted all our Colours & att noon fired 15 guns being his Royall Highness Prince of Wales birth day
2 Mar 1717/8		Moderate gales the Ship grounded att Low water these two Tides past
3 Mar 1717/8		Fresh gales
4 Mar 1717/8		Moderate gales this morning Unmoored and new birth
5 Mar 1717/8		Three Sloops Sailed Severall of the pirates that took Certificates went them Passengers

6 Mar 1717/8		Ditto Last night John Nichols my Gunner Departed this Life
7 Mar 1717/8		Ditto fired 8 guns att the Buriall of my Gunner
8 Mar 1717/8		Fresh gales struck yds & topmast & got them up again
9 Mar 1717/8		Moderate gales and fair weather
10 Mar 1717/8		Ditto
11 Mar 1717/8		Ditto Severall pirates for these ten past took my Certificate
12 Mar 1717/8	In Providence Harbour	Fair weather and moderate gales
13 Mar 1717/8		Ditto
14 Mar 1717/8		Ditto four Sloops sailed: for Carolina, Bermuders Rhode Island and Virginia Severall Pyrates that took Certificates went in them Passengers
15 Mar 1717/8		Moderate and fair
16 Mar 1717/8		Ditto
17 Mar 1717/8		Ditto two Sloop came in from South Carolina
18 Mar 1717/8		Ditto Last night 16 of the pirates went away in a boat to the W:ward with a Design to goe a pirating again
19 Mar 1717/8		Ditto this morning I had Information that 24 of the Pirates went away with a boat from the Shoar in order to joyn those that went the night before
20 Mar 1717/8		Ditto Loosd Foretopsaill for Sailing & made a Signall for all Masters of Merchant men

21 Mar 1717/8		Little wind this day the Pyrates in their boats took a Sloop come from Jamaica coming in to the Eastward
22 Mar 1717/8		Ditto att 1 this morning sent my Pinnace Man'd & Arm'd to Surprize the Pyrates on board the above mentioned Sloop; but they being too Strong she was Oblidged after Exchanging severall small Shott to return'd on board I Summon'd the Inhabitants to Assist me in Surprizing these pirates but by their Actions; they Seem'd more inclinable to Assist y:m [them] then to Reduce them
23 Mar 1717/8		Fair weather and Small gales Last Evening I sailed in Company with 4 Sloops to see them safe off the Coast which was under apprehension of falling in the Pirates hands att 8 AM Spoke with a Sloop from Harbour Island & prevented here from being taken
24 Mar 1717/8	Att Noon Providence Harbour SSW Distance 3 Lgs	Ditto att 9 Last night parted Company with the said Sloops then stood off and on to prevent any Trade from going into Providence which if they had must unavoidably fall into the hands of the Pyrates this morning Saw the Pirates sloop among the Island with a Red Flagg att her Mast Head
25 Mar 1718	Providence SBW [South by West?] 4 Lgs	Small gales and fair weather stood off & on this 24 hours
26 Mar 1718	Booby Rocks SEbE 3 Leagues	Ditto
27 Mar 1718	Providence So: 3: Lgs	Ditto this morning Spoke with a Sloop from Jamaca which now keeps me Company

Date		Position	Log
28 Mar 1718		Att Noon Providence SWBS 5 Leagues	Little wind and fair weather I Yesterday Streched off the Harbour mouth of Providence and made a Signall for a boat, but none came off so I stood off to Sea again with the Said sloop in Company
29 Mar 1718		Att Anchor in Providence Harbour in 3 fathom the Castle SSE Hogg Island yst: [at?] NW	Little wind sometimes Calm this morning bore away for Providence the said sloop in Company att 10 anchored in 3 Fathom in same birth as formerly, Since I went out a Cruizing the Pirates Burnt the biggest of the Dutch Ships and the Bristoll Gally and the other Dutch Ship of 26 guns they sett adrift ashore on Hogg Island where she now has Bilg'd
30 Mar 1718			Ditto this morning Hesl'd ship and Scrub'd her
31 Mar 1718			Ditto This morning the Pirate sloop which is the Jamaca Sloop I formerly mention'd they had taken with their boats anchored to the Eastward of the harbour with a Sloop called the Lark which they had taken 2 days agoe off Harbour Island
1 Apr 1718			Ditto last Evening a boat came from the Pirates with several hands on board her I fired Severall guns with round Shott & patridge att her to Command her a board Notwithstanding which she push'd a Shore

Date	Location	Entry
2 Apr 1718		Fresh gales and fair weather: Yesterday 2 Sloops appear'd coming in to the Eastward, where the Pirates lay att anchor which I expected to be the Sloops from Harbour Island bound on the Racks whereupon I Loos'd my Topgt. sailes and hoisted them with the Sheets flying and fired severall guns as signals to them to attack the Pirates but they proving to be trading sloops and so fell into the hands of the Pirates
3 Apr 1718		Fresh gales and fair weather
4 Apr 1718	In Providence Harbour	Moderate and fair Yesterday the Lark sloop on board of which the Pirates removed themselves weighed and hoisted a Black flagg att her Masthead not Long After they anchor'd of[f] the Point and ridd with the said Flagg flying in the night they put to Sea & was not Seen this morning
5 Apr 1718		Ditto this morning unmoard
6 Apr 1718		Fresh gales Yesterday moar'd This morning 3 Sloops came in from Harbour Island bound on the Racks
7 Apr 1718		Yesterday an accident happen'd by the neglect of the Carpenter and his people, who were healing some pitch in the Fore Castle which boiled over and sett the ship on Fire but was soon extinguished; I Confin'd the Carpenter for beither him self nor any of the Crew attended the pitch when on the Fire neither had any direction from my Self or any of his Superior Officers to make use of any att this timr

Date		Position	Log entry
8 Apr 1718			Moderate & fair att 6 AM made a signall for Masters of Merchant men
9 Apr 1718		Att Noon Providence So: 2 1/2 League	Ditto this morning made a signall for Masters of Merchant Men & to weigh att 10 Sailed but had the Misfortune to run aground coming out of the harbour on the Et:most Bank but in a small time back off again without receiving any Damage that we know off 5 Sloops sailed in Company with us 4 of which parted Company not Long after we came out which was bound on the Racks
10 Apr 1718		Providence Harbour So: 1/2 E 7 Leagues	Ditto Last Evening spoke with a Sloop from Bermudus for providence att 7 AM not being able to weather Abbaco I tackt and stood to ye: S:ward
11 Apr 1718		Att Noon the South most part of Abbaco bore So: 62 Wt: Dist 22 M[iles?]	Ditto Yesterday PM Saw a Saill to the Westward to which I gavew chase att 3 came up with here: she prov'd to be French ship Piratically taken from the French & was now Loaden with hides; which Hornogold had also taken from the Dutch I found in her in Possession of 15 Men; that were all Lately Pirates therefore I Seiz'd her for his Majestie took most of the Men out & Mann'd her out of his Maj:ts ship under my Command and then made Sail having given directions to my Gunner who I put in Commander of her to keep me Company and to Observe my Signalls according to the Instructions I gave him She was called the John & Elizabeth
after 12 Apr 1718			[From here... *Phoenix* sailed north, past Abaco Island to Virginia, and then on to New York]

Letter 139 James Naish on board the House of Austria off of the coast of Dover to the Court reporting that their ship was taken by the pirates after some resistance – 15 June 1720

IOR/E/1/11 ff. 226-227v : 15 Jun 1720

Hon:ble Sr:s   139 (red marker) 226 (circled in pencil)

I cannot doubt the St. Joseph & Brussels Gally arrival Ostend & Therefore conclude You have been advis'd to Expect Several Letters by me, But Tis my Misfortune to Inform Your Hon:rs that they were Seiz'd on by the Officers of the Dragon Pirate, in Expectation of Intelligence other Ships & their Cargoes, Tho it Concerns Me to Assure You they then Knew too well when & where to Cruize for, & fall in with Many; but from a Particular Account of their designs I am to Begg You will at Present Excuse me, & Therefore Please to lett it Suffice That on Feb:ry 9/20, after as Good a Resistance as we were capable of making, we fell into their hands with The Loss of Chief Third mate & Two Seamen, & many others Slightly wounded; She [Dragon] Sails Princely Well, Mounts forty Guns, & Twenty Brass Pieces upon Swiffles on their Gunnil, Two of them also, with one Chorn, in each Top & Small Arms for Twice her Complement, being Three hundred & Twenty Men when I left them on Feb:ry 16/27; they were compleately Stored with Ammunition, & Provision at full Allowance for fiveteen Months. We found them a Generous, tho' Common, Enemy, for Our Loss inconsiderable in the Ships Large & Valuable Cargoe; Our Greatest Suffering was the Necessity he Put us under of Running to Bahia de Todos Santos for a fresh Supply of Provision, In my Passage to That Place I sent my Boat ashoar to your Hon:rs Island St. Hellens & in a Letter to the Governours Council a brief Account Our Misfortune desiring it will Personally give them a More Exact Information of the Pirate's designs, Signals, & Other Circumstances which thought being to:? be foreever ??? ?? to your

Hon:rs Settlement ?? ???? by the Ship That annually Calls at the Island Outward bound; & Very Probably be with them Sooner then the Pirate Which be there Cruizing, but the Gov:r(?) came to understand that my Intelligence was not worth his Notice, That he Exulted at My Misfortune, & That I might be Sure Not to mistake him in his Aboundant Humanity Positively Refus'd to take a Letter. which I sent Purposely With Desire to be forwarded to My Family, that they might not be in Pain, by my being an absent Ship, & this Digressive Observation I Should have Omitted, had he not Justified himself by your Hon:rs Instructions, Which I will Never Believe directed him to Such an illnatur'd Refusal, Because I have had The Honour to Serve under them, & will Still hope to be again Thought Capable, it being my greatest Ambition to Demonstrate that I am

Hon:ble S:rs

Your Most Devoted, Most Obed:t
& Most Humble Serv:t

James Naish

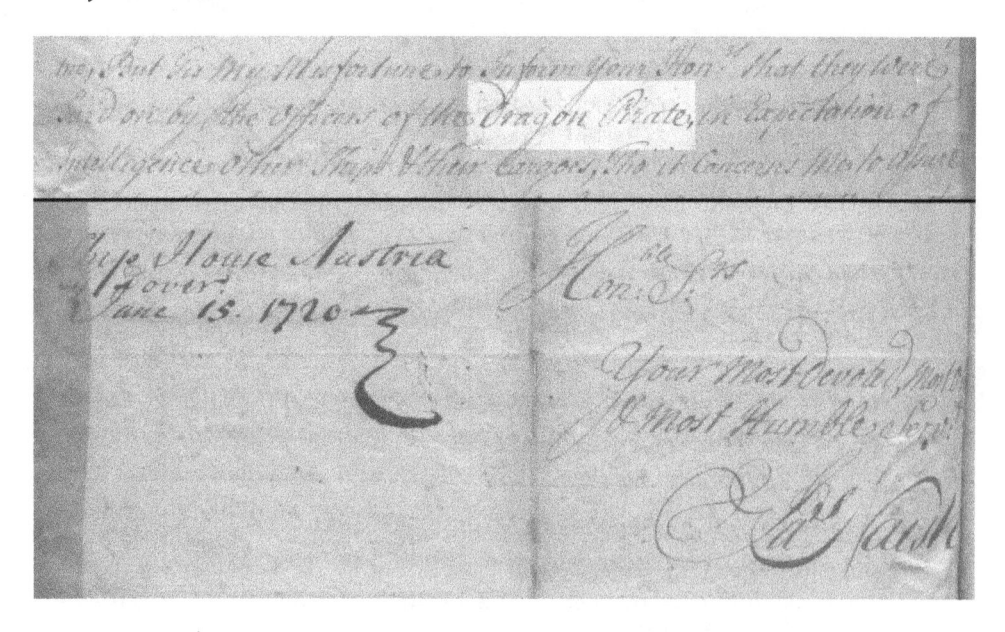

This document clearly shows that the name of the pirate ship that attacked *Prince Eugene* and *House of Austria* near the Cape of Good Hope was named "*Dragon.*" Edward Congdon was the only pirate known to have used this name for his vessel. The document also

gives an excellent first-hand description of *Dragon*. Another detail of note is the use of a double entry dating style. As Catholic Imperial nations of the time were already using a Gregorian Calendar and since James Naish was an Irishman then working for a Catholic nation, he would have been familiar with using two different dates, 11 days difference, representing the Julian dates (still in use by 18th-century Britain) and the Gregorian style utilized by France, Spain, Belgians, Ostenders, etc. Naish understood that officials from both Britain and Ostend might read his letter and he indicated both dating styles, as shown in the photo from page 1 of the document:

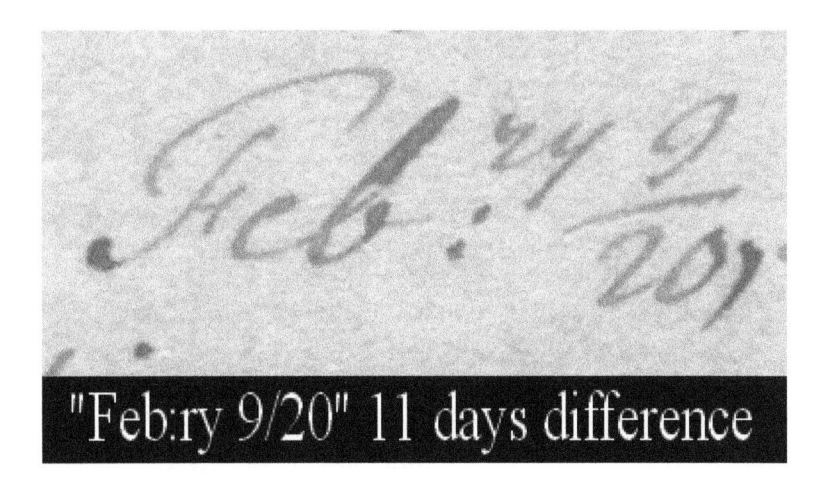

"Feb:ry 9/20" 11 days difference

Southampton Archives (UK), SC9/4/81, Examination of Richard Vavastour, 25 Jul 1719

Vavastour was a crewman of John Thompson's on Jacob & Jaell, who was held for "six weeks," meaning that pirates had been at Sierra Leone since about 15 March. He took passage on a French ship to the island of Guernsey, then to Southampton, arriving 24 Jul 1719.

Southampton Archives (SC9/4/81):

Vill & Cond Southton ss The Exaiacon [Examination] of Richd. Vavastour
    taken on oath the twenty-fifth day of
    July Anno Dom. 1719

This epaiant [deponent] saith that on the twelfth day of March last past he this epaiant [deponent] being on board a Ship called the Jacob & Jaell John Thompson Master was taken by pyrates in Shilone [Sierra Leone] on the Coast of Guinea and by them kept a prisoner for the space of six weeks and by a ffrench Ship arrived at Guernsey from whence he arrived at this port of Southton the day before the date hereof [24 July 1719].

Jurat did y anno saprad,
Coram Md   Charles Smith Mayor

Observations On Board the Lyon at Charnocke Point On the Island of Madagascar. Being the place where the Pyrates are said to Rendevous --- HCA 1/54, ff. 138-139

April 27: 1722 This day Commerd: Mathews sent a Shore to the Beach Several Dozen Bottles of Liquor. ----------

Do: 28 This day wee had word brought off from Charnock Point that 2 white Men were on Shore there. One Nam'd as was said Jemmy Deering. the Other Jns. Plantine which were reported to have formerly belong'd to the Pyrates, and left behind at this place w:th their Riches they Had plunder'd. I observ'd from On Board a Body of black men [note: "black men" here not capitalized like "white Men"] Arm'd came down On the Beach opposite to the Shipp. W:th a St. Georges fflag flying before E'm amongst whom was said to be the twp white Men abovemention'd Jemmy Deering & Jno: Plantin[.] Upon the arrival of these Men the Commodore went soon after a Shore to them, (On the Beach), & immediately afterwards sent off an Order to Me to Spare him 2 Puncheons of the Kings Arrack. Which I Comply'd w:th And the Said Arrack was then Sent On Shore to the Commad:r w:th a Pipe of Madera wine which was Said to be Dispos'd off On Shore to this aforem'd Jemmy Deering & Jno. Plantin at a very great Price. I observ'd the St. Georges fflag was kept flying on the Beach the whole Day. ---

29 - This day the two white Men aforenam'd were Said to be gone into the Country, upon Intelligence as was reported that the Town where they dwelt was going to be Attack'd, they went away w:th So much Precipitancy that they left behing them the two Puncheons of Arrack And the Pipe of wine Sent On Shore yesterday. This Evening finding the Said Liquor was Deserted, the Commadore Order'd the Longboat On Shoar to fetch it off, which was accordingly Comply'd w:th and the Aforesd. 2

Puncheons of Arrack and Pipe of Madera wine was rec:d On Board again

April 30 - This Morning at 8 We Sail's and Stood to the No:W:d Carrying away w:th Us the 2 aforesd. Puncheons of Arrack and pipe of Madera wine. ---

Excerpts from H. C. V. Leibbrandt, *Precis of the archives of the Cape of Good Hope*, Vol. 1
(Cape Town, W. A. Richards, 1896) that may pertain to pirates Taylor, LeVasseur, England, Congdon, and the Royal Navy fleet sent after them as they passed the Cape of Good Hope to enter the East Indies.

These records come from the Dutch administration at Cape Town, South Africa.

1720

[Date of Edward Congdon's capture of *House of Austria* and *Prince Eugene* at the cape was Febuary 9th [J: Feb 20] 1720]

February 22 - Arrival of the "Assenburgh" from Amsterdam. Reports that on the 13th, and 60 miles from the coast, it had been attacked by a pirate about 104-6 feet long, carrying about 26 guns and 230 men. A large portion of the latter were black. It had twice been beaten off, but had followed the "Assenburgh" until within sight of the Cape. Most of the damage was suffered in the masts and rigging. The pirate had striven to make the "Assenburgh" helpless by shooting away its masts. Only five men were slightly wounded. News at once sent to the "Amazone" in Saldanha Bay to be on its guard, and prepared for battle should the pirate visit that bay to repair damages.

February 24. - The "Postlooper" sent out to cruise and warn the rest of the return ships to be prepared for battle, and to remain together.

March 5. - Arrival of the return ship "Hopvogel," which some days ago had met with two pirates which had captured an English vessel within sight of the "Hopvogel."

1721

April 5. – Arrival of two English vessels, the "Mary" and "Cardonna," which reported that in May last [1720] the English outward bound ships "Cassandra" and "Greenwich," when at one of the Mayotte islands named Anjouan (or Johanna), had been attacked by a heavily-armed pirate. The first was captured, but the other escaped. The pirate was afterwards reinforced by two others, and then the trio decided to cruise for some time off Ceylon, in order to capture the Surat, Bengal and Moorish ships. The Governor of Bombay had sent out some armed vessels against them. Another pirate had also taken a Moorish (Indian) ship, and found in it 13 lac rupees in cash. These pirates, he said, had 14 first-class vessels at sea, the smallest carrying 30 guns, to attack any ship of whatever country it might be. It was further stated that they intended to settle at Mauritius.

June 6. – [G: 27 May] Arrival of the English King's ships "Lion and "Shoreham" from Portsmouth to Bombay. They would not salute the Castle according to the usual custom.

June 7. – One of the officers landing to-day asked for refreshments for the ships. They were granted; but the Governor to see beforehand the ship's papers, in order to convince himself that they were really men-of-war; and also that they should salute the flag of their High Mightinesses. The officer replied that they really were King's ships, and therefore not obliged to salute or to show their papers, but if the Castle wished to welcome them with a salute, they would reply to the same with the same number of guns. The Council hereupon met and decided as per resolution.

June 22. – [G: 11 Jun] Arrival of the English ship "Exchester" [*Exeter*], which saluted the Castle with 13 cannons, and was thanked with 11; but as it was also a King's ship, it is to be presumed that the salute was intended for its consorts lying here.

June 24. – [G: 13 Jun] The three English war ships leave. The "Exchester" [*Exeter*] only salutes, and receives a reply from the Castle.

July 3. – Return of the "Zeelandia" from De la Goa, which it had left on the 7th June. The three hookers had arrived there on the 9th March, and the commander had taken possession in the name of the Company. We were, however, sorry to hear that the Commander Willem van Taak and 15 others – officers and men-had died there in a short time, and when the vessel left many others were mortally sick. All further particulars are to be found in the letter from that place.

July 4. – The first sworn clerk sent round to the members of Council with the following communication: - That as a large number of the men had died at De la Goa, and a large number was lying ill, whilst the servants there gave good hopes for the place if they were only provided with what they required, so that in course of time the Company would ly benefited, the small vessel "D'Uno," now ready to leave, should be detained, in order, after a reperusal of the papers, to be despatched to De la Goa with the necessary men and requirements. This proposal was unanimously adopted. See Resolution of 5th July.

July 8. – [G: 27 Jun] Arrival of the English war ship "Salisbury," without saluting the Castle.

July 19. – [G: 8 Jul] The English ships "Hartford," "Grantham" [50 miles behind *Salisbury*; they met the next day at sea] and "Salisbury" leave. Only the "Hartford" salutes.

August 12. – The "Uno" and "Zeelandia" leave for De la Goa with the resolution of the Council, that in the place of the deceased W. van Taak, the Secunde there, Casparus Swertner, had been appointed commander, and Fred. Christian Lappenbergh as his "Secunde."

December 7. – The "Zeelandia" also arrives from De la Goa, but brings no particular news. Things were as bad there as when the two other hookers left.

December 28. – The "Caap" [*Comptoir Hollande*] leaves for De la Goa.

1722

April 10. – Departure of the return ships – 17 in all. The "Gouda" arrives from De la Goa, bringing fortunately no dead, but unfortunately bad news from that station. Sickness was very bad there. Amongst others the Commander Swertner and the Secretary Fred. Christ. Lappenbergh had died. Trade weak.

Hardly any food for the garrison, and nothing to buy from the natives. Affairs there in a deplorable state.

1723

July 12. – The "Schoteroog" arrives from Rio de la Goa, which it had left on the 23rd June. Only one sick on board. Reports that the Residency there had last year [22 Apr] been attacked by two strong pirates and a brigantine, one with 64 and the other with 36 guns; with 900 men in all, white and black. They had sacked the station, taken what they liked, and destroyed almost what remained. They had also taken with them the hooker "de Caap" [*Comptoir Hollande*], with all the men on board, so that affairs there are pretty considerably in a confused state. The contrary would have been desirable.

1724

June 20. – Arrival of the "Jacoba" in good condition. Had only been slightly damaged in masts and rigging during its encounter with the pirates. She carried 250 men.

N.B. – The Journal of 11th June states that the officers of the "Wickenburg" [Ostender who sailed with *Prince Eugene* in 1719?] which had just arrived, had reported that the "Jacoba" had in latitude ___ and longitude ___ been attacked by two powerful pirates, one under the English flag, and well manned and armed (on the 6th April). After a fight of seven glasses, the pirates were beaten off and sailed away. The "Jacoba" had a few killed, and seven slightly wounded.

1725

August 28. – As the "Zeepost" might fall in with the pirate, her departure for Rio de la Goa os postponed, the office there requiring no immediate assistance. [Paranoia?]

Information of Clement Downing late a Midshipman on board of his Majesty's Ship Salisbury - 16 Oct 1724

HCA 1/55, ff. 79-80

Offin Dni promot con
Thomam Matthews - [part of the investigation of Thomas Mathews for his Courts-Martial in 1724]

The Information of Clement Downing late a Midshipman on board of his Majesty's Ship Salisbury now living at the house of Mr. Woodall in Bell Savage Yard London aged 28 years taken before the worshipfull John Andrew Dr. of Laws one of the Commiss:rs of Oyer & Terminer & Gaol Delivery for the Adm.y of England at his Chambers in Drs Comons London on the 16th Day of October 1724 in the presence of Brian Rushworth Not.y Publick

This Informt. saith that in the Month of April in the year of our Lord 1722 his majestys Ships the Lyon[,] Exeter[,] & Salisbury were at Charnock Point at the Island of Madagascar, and he the Informt. with the Boats Crew & some of the Officers of the Salisbury went on Shoar to water the Ship but before they went on Shoar (to wit) the next Morning after the Arrival of the Ships at the sd Point, Mr. Crawford one of the Leiftenants, with one of the Midship Men of the Lyon (whereof Captain Thomas Matthews the Comodore of ye sd. Ships was Comandr) brought Orders on board the Salisbury from the sd Comodore that she the Salisbury should sail directly for St. Marys which is about[?] some few Leagues ---- from the sd Point & which she accordingly did, & they there found great Quantitys of Goods which were much damaged (to wit) Pepper[,] Ginger, & broaken China which lay in large heaps upon the Shore & some very good Forax [Borax?*] and Gym Libanum [Gum Olibanum**] all which Goods (as the Informt. believes) had been left there by the Pirates And when the Salisbury had been at Anchor there for a short time, the sd Leiftenant returned on board the Lyon in order (as he declared) to inform the sd Comodore of the sd Goods & soon afterwards a Signal was made on board, the sd Comodore for the Salisbury to weigh Anchor & return to the Point which she accordingly did & imediately afterwards the sd Comodore on board the Lyon in company with the Exeter sailed for St. Marys & the Salisbury lay at Charnock Point to refit the head of her foremast, and when he the Informt. with the Boats Crew & Officers were on Shoar to water the Ship as beforementioned they saw a white Man coming down towards the Shoar with about 20 or 30 black Men armed with fire arms & when they were come down the sd white Men asked what the said Ship were & from whence her came & Mr. Davis the mate of the Salisbury telling him that they were merchants Ships & that they lay there for water & Provisions he replied in these or the like words (No No I know better. You are the Squadron of Men of War that are come to look for us (meaning as the Informt. apprehended & believes) himself & other Pirates And then ye sd Mr. Davis asked him what his name was, And he then declared that his Name was William Plantin that he was born at Chocolat Hole at Jamaica & that he had belonged to a Pirate Ship called the Dragon & that he had got great Wealth by taking a Ship that came from Judah off of the Streights of Babliamendum [Straits of Bab-el-Mandeb], & another Ship with the portuguese Vice Roy on board out of Don Maskareen Road [La Réunion] bound for Europe & that he lived with his family upon an Island which he had fortified & given the name of Ranter Bay & that the Natives inhabiting the sd Island sung Songs in praise of Plantin the king of Ranter Bay or to that effect[.] And also saith that the Exeters boat with one Mr. ffrost a Midhsip Man & also a Carpenter of the Exeter being on Shoar to cut a flying Jibb Boom they went off in order to give Information] on to the Squadron concerning the sd Plantin. And the said Plantin also declared that the Pirates had fitted out the Cassandra to carry 40 Guns (meaning as the Informt. apprehended & believes) a Ship called the Cassandra belonging to the East India Company and which was reported to have been taken by the Pirates) & that they had also fitted ye sd. portuguese Ship to carry 70 Guns & that they were gon out with ye sd. Ships & then asked where ye Informt.s Captain & Leiftenant were[.] And farther saith that there were afterwards carryed on Shoar from ye Lyon in the Salisbury's long Boat several Baskets or hampers of glass Bottles & some small Casks of Arrack & the Comodore & Captain Cockburn Comander of the Salisbury went on Shoar in the Salisbury's Barge & they then went with the Informt. & others of the Boats Crew up into the Countrey to meet some Oxen which the Comodore had bought for fresh Provisions & when they had got about a Mile & half they met Charles Collins one of the boats Crew of the Salisbury coming down who told them that Mr. Davis (the mate) & Mr. Bassett a Midshipman of the Salisbury) were coming down with the Oxen[.] And then the Comodore asked them when ye white Men would come down & the sd Mr. Davis told him that they would come in a Day or two[.] And then the sd. Comodore & Captain Cockburn & the rest of the Men returned on board & ye sd. Casks[,] Baskets[,] or hampers with a pit silver Mug[,] a Silvers knives & fforks a ffirken of Butter a parcel of Sugar[,] Candy[,] & other Goods were kept in the Boat all Night & the next Day the sd. Comodore[,] Capt. Cockburn[,] the Informant & others went on Shoar again & then ye aforesaid Goods were delivered out of the Boat on Shoar[.] And he the Informt. saw the same delivered to the Servants or Afents of the aforesd. Plantin by the sd. Mr Davis & Mr. Bassett & he the Informt. heard ye Comodore order ye sd Mr. Bassett to go to ye sd Plantins house & to see ye sd. Goods safely delivered & to be very carefull in his Accounts & the next Day about four in the afternoon the sd Mr. Bassett came down again & he the Informt. then being with ye Salisburys Barge on board the Lyon was ordered by ye Comodore & Captain Cockburn to fetch the sd. Mr. Bassett on board the Lyon which ye Informt. accordingly did[.] And he the sd Mr Bassett afterwards (to wit) on ye same Day told the Informt that he had paid the said Comodore the Money for the aforesd Goods & that he had rec'ed of the sd Plantin and delivered to ye sd Comodore five Barrs or Wedges of Gold & several Diamonds & then showed the Informt a Diamond about the bigness of a large Pea which (As he told the Informt,) he ye sd Mr Bassett had for himself[.] and farther saith that at another time there were carryed on Shoar from the Lyon several large Puncheons of Arrack & a Butt of Madera Wine, & he the Informt. & the rest of the Company on board the Salisbury saw a St. Georges fflag coming down towards ye Shoar & the Comodore then imediately went on Shoar & he the Informt. & others on board the Salisbury were informed by the Boats Crew that ye Comodore feasted with the sd Plantin & 2 other white Men (to wit) James Deering[,] a scotch Man & the other a Dane the greatest part of the Day & that ye sd white Men had rec'ed Advice that Ranter Bay was attackt by the Natives & that thereupon they were gon away in a hurry & had left their Liquor in the Woods[.] And saith that ye Salisburys Boats went on Shoar to assist in ye bringing off the sd Liquors & the sd Mr. Bassett (who went on Shoar with the sd Boats) told ye Informt. that the sd Liquor was carryed on board the Lyon[.] And farther saith that when they were at Sea ye sd Mr Bassett showed the Informt. ye Money which (as he declared) he had reced of the said Plantin for the last parcel of Goods before mentioned & told the Informt. that he was going on board the Lyon by the Order of the sd Captain Cockburn to pay ye same to ye Comodore & saith that ye sd Money was all Gold (to wit) Cuppers & Cherquins [may refer to Dutch coins] & the Informt. verily believes that the Bagg wherein the sd Gold then was did by the Bulk of it) containe between 4 & 5 hundred pounds Sterling[.] And the sd Mr Bassett did then carry the same on board the Lyon.

Clement Downing

16th. Oct 1724. Jurat corum me   J. Andrew Sent to me B: Rushworth N:P:

----

*Borax is a salt formed by the combination of boracic acid with the marine alkali or soda. It is brought from the East Indies, where it is said to be found at the bottom or on the margin of certain lakes, particularly in Thibet. It is said to be artificially prepared in Persia, like niter. It comes in three states. 1. Crude borax tinkal, or chrysocolla, from Persia, in greenish masses of a greasy feel, or in opake crystals. 2. borax of China, somewhat purer, in small plates or masses, irregularly crystallized, and of a dirty white. 3. Dutch or purified borax in portions of transparent crystals, which is the kind generally used. It is an excellent flux in docimastic operations, a styptic in medicine, and useful in soldering metals.

**Frankincense (also known as gum olibanum), is an aromatic resin used in incense and perfumes, obtained from trees of the genus Boswellia in the family Burseraceae, particularly Boswellia sacra (prob. B. thurifera, Indian frankincense).

The farther Inform[ati]on of the before named Clement Dow[n]ing – 28 Oct 1724

HCA 1/55, f. 93

Offm DNI con Pratum
Capneum Mathews [part of the investigation of Thomas Mathews for his Courts-Martial in 1724]

The farther Inform.on of the before named Clement Dow[n]ing taken before the worshipfull John Andrew Dr of Laws one of the Commiss.rs of Oyer & Terminer and Gaol Delivery for the Admiralty of England at his Chambers in Doctors Commons London the 28th Day of October 1724 in the presence of Brian Rushworth No.ry Publick.

This Informt. saith that on the 26th. instant one Richard Moor living (as he declared) at the house of one Rose at the kings head in Wapping owned & confessed to ye Informt. at the house of one Stoney ate the white hart in Wapping that he the R Moor & one Gyles Neal & John Thurston had been forced into the Service of the Pirates & that he [they] had been in their Service in the East Indies between 3 & 4 Years, And that he well knew a Pirate Ship called ye Dragon that had cruised there & that he well knew one Plantin a Creolian & one Deer[,] a reputed Scotch Man[,] & another who (as the sd Moor declared) was a reputed Dane & that the said Plaintin & Deer & the sd Dane had belonged to the sd Ship the Dragon & that she had taken a Ship with a Portuguese Vice Roy on board of her[,] for which he the sd Moor belonged/had been at Madagascar & that they had there found some Letters which Comodore Mathews had left there with the Natives for Captain Cockburn the Comander of the Salisbury & that they had thereby discovered the Names[,] force[,] & Station of the Squadron of English Men of War that were sent out to seek for the Pirates & that upon the reading of the sd. Letters one Taylor (who was the Quarter Master of the sd pirate Ship) uttered these or the like Words (Damn my Blood God forgive me for swearing heres a Squadron of Men of War sent to look after us but they dont much care for the seeing of us[;] they are more upon the trading account[,] but however lets stand one by another and take Care of ourselves.)

Clem.t Downing

Jurat 28.vo Oct 1724
coram me
J Andrew

present me B: Rushworth N: P:

Information of Gyles Neal living at the house of Wm Brown a Butcher in Market Lane in St. James Market – 28 Oct 1724

HCA 1/55, ff. 93-94

Offm Dni con Pratum
Capneum Mathews [part of the investigation of Thomas Mathews for his Courts-Martial in 1724]

The Inform.on of Gyles Neal living at the house of Wm Brown a Butcher in Market Lane in St. James Market taken as before

This Informt. saith that on the 26th instant one Richard Moor at a publick house at the Sign of the white hart in Wapping owned & confessed in prsence of the Informt. & his fellow Witnesses Clement Downing & John Thurston that he was on board one of ye Pirates Ships whence the Squadron of english Men of War went to look for them in the East Indies & that there were four of the sd. pirate Ships & that he the said Moor belonged to the same Ship which Quartermaster Taylor belonged to & that the sd. Pirates were then refitting a great Ship which they had taken from the portuguese Vice Roy & that the sd Pirates hearing that the sd. Squadron of english Men of War were in Persuit of them they had made all the Dispatch they possibly could to fit her & get her away, from St. Marys Island about 3 or 4 Leagues from Charnock Point at the Island of Madagascar & that from St. Marys they went to Port Dolphin [Dauphin] upon ye sd Island of Madagascar & from thence to St. Augustines upon ye same Island &

that they there found amongst the Natives a Letter which had been left with them by Comodore Matthews for Capt Cockburn ye Comander of the Salisbury & that the sd Letter was publickly read by the sd. Quarterma[ste]r Taylor before all the Company of the sd. pirate Ship & that he ye sd Taylor then declared before all the sd Ships Company that he knew what Strength the sd Men of War were of & that he knew that they did not come there to seek for the Pirates but to force a Trade[.] And he ye sd. Richard Moor then also declared that he knew one Jemmy Deer & one Plantin & that they had been Pirates on board the Dragon, & that the sd Ship the Dragon had taken a rich Ship from Judah [Jeddah?] or to that effect.

     Giles Neale

Jurat 28.vo Oct 1724
coram me
J Andrew

    Pr[e]sente me
    B: Rushworth No.rio Pub.co

Many more primary sources can be found in the "Pirate Library" on my website at http://baylusbrooks.com

Index

A General History, i, 26, 28, 31, 32, 87, 88, 89, 95, 96, 101, 102, 116, 119, 126, 131, 135, 144, 162, 190, 192, 214, 343
Aberdeen Creek. See Pirate's Bay
Act of 1696, 4
Act of Grace, 9, 194, 376
Act of Union (1707), 7
Adams, Robert, 178
Addison, Secretary Joseph, 42
Adventure Galley, 16, 214
Africa, 5, ii, 9, 11, 13, 17, 21, 22, 25, 36, 37, 38, 40, 44, 45, 51, 64, 70, 73, 74, 75, 80, 93, 95, 99, 100, 103, 107, 108, 118, 128, 129, 136, 140, 142, 155, 156, 189, 198, 202, 203, 274, 277, 297, 300, 313, 319, 329, 330, 343, 348
Aguevisse, J., 211
Albany, 196
Alexander, 195
Alimah III, 155
Allen, Sir John, 212
Álvarez, José Manuel Serrano, 297, 298
Ambodifotatra Bay, 144, 266
American Rebellion of 1715-1718, 9
American Revolution, 8
American Weekly Mercury, 196
Amsterdam, Holland, 134, 276, 277
Anabon Island, 5, 81, 85, 86, 116, 125, 128
Ancestry.com, i, 39, 40, 99, 131, 135, 192

Anchuthengu. See Anjengo
Ancré, Marie-Catherine, 210, 211, 213
Andrew, John, 290
Andrik, Erderik, 230
Anglican Church Records, 124
Angrey, Konhoji, 168, 169, 170, 249, 258
Angrian, of Konhoji Angrey, 168, 169, 170, 171, 172
Anjadip Island (Southern Goa, India), 175
Anjango, India, 171
Anjediva. See Anjadip Island
Anjengo Fort & Town (India), 179, 184
Anjou, Île d', see Île Marotte
Anjouan. See Johanna, See Johanna
Anne, 40, 114
Annobon, Island of, 40
Anomabo (Africa), 18
Anstis, Thomas, 297, 300
Antankarana (people), 287, 336
Antigua, 40, 54, 64, 103, 106
Antongil Bay, 268, 269, 270, 325, 335, 336
Arabia, 155, 160, 239
Arabian Sea (N. Indian Ocean), 5, 140, 165, 217
Armstrong, Sir Thomas, 245
Arnaudov, Plamen Ivanov, 6
Arnett, Thomas, 299
Arrack (drink), 181, 261, 271, 272, 363, 364, 365, 368, 372, 373
Ashworth, Leigh, 51, 64, 188

Assumption, port of (Madagascar), 203
Atlantic Ocean, 3, 13, 300
Aurengzeb, King, 5
Aux Cailles, Île. See Île aux Forbans
Avery, Henry. See Henry Every
Ayrshire, Scotland, 145, 164
Badillo, J. Gerónimo, 298, 301, 302, 304, 305, 307, 308, 310, 316, 317, 318
Baguet, Jeltin, 133
Bahama Islands, 10
Bahamas, 6, 7, 9, 18, 22, 26, 36, 50, 51, 52, 64, 84, 102, 187, 188, 189, 190, 194
Bahía Escocesa. See Scot's Bay
Baía da Lagoa. See Delagoa Bay
Baldridge, Adam, 5, 11, 12, 13, 19, 260, 335
Bane, Thomas, 320
Bank, 111
Bank of England, i, 40, 42, 66, 349, 353
Barbados, Island of, 31, 36, 46, 49, 70, 95, 99, 100, 101, 103, 104, 106, 112, 114, 296, 300, 313, 345, 349, 352
Barnes, John, 143, 144, 148, 149, 150, 151, 152, 153, 154, 155, 159, 160, 161, 258, 370, 1
Barrow, Thomas, 8, 9, 10, 18
Batchelor's Delight, 19
Battle of Cape Passaro (1718), 297
Bay of Campeche, 318
Bay of Honduras, 318
Baye de Tombeau. See Carpenter's Bay
Beker, Henry, 204, 205
Bellamy, Samuel, ii, 25, 26, 27, 33, 42, 64, 65

Bellomont, Lord, 16
Bengal, India, 178, 362
Benito, Don, 92, 319, 320
Benjamin, 11, 26, 187, 188
Bennet, John, 54, 55, 65, 352
Bentinck, Henry. See Duke of Portland
Bentinck, Lady Elizabeth Noel, 296
Bentworth, 111
Berkeley galley, 98, 99
Bermuda, 9, 38, 64, 187, 188
Betsimisaraka, 340
Betsimisaraka (people of East Madagascar), 205, 269, 270, 271, 336
Bialuschewski, Arne, 38, 100
Biddulph, John, 19, 20, 203
Bight of Benin, 40
Bijepur, Odisha, India, 168
Bird galley, 34, 38, 40, 52, 313
Blackbeard, aka Edward Thache, 8, 27, 28, 33, 69, 96, 102, 103, 106, 124, 157, 189, 190, 246, 297, 314
Blackston, Thomas, 113
Blanckley, Thomas Riley, 39
Blanco, Isla Morro, 30, 31
Blincko, Richard, 42, 43, 44, 66, 72, 73, 78, 79, 80, 81, 93
Board of Trade, 4, 5, 6, 8, 11, 14, 19, 45, 55, 128, 294
Bois, John, 106
Bombay, 5, 23, 131, 135, 144, 145, 147, 150, 153, 156, 158, 160, 162, 163, 165, 168, 170, 171, 172, 173, 183, 202, 238, 244, 249, 255, 256, 258, 260, 261, 274, 321, 347, 364, 370, 374
Bombay, India, 161
Bombetoke Bay, 234
Bombétoke Bay (W. Madagascar), 255, 282

Bonket, Phillipus, 109
Bonnet, Stede, 33, 64, 89, 91
Boone, Charles, 162, 163, 164, 170, 173, 184, 185, 239, 260, 321
Bordeaux, France, 213
Boston News-Letter, 8, 27, 28, 55, 65, 97, 98, 103, 127, 190, 195, 296, 318, 319, 320
Boston, Massachusetts, 8, 27, 28, 55, 65, 97, 98, 103, 104, 127, 190, 195, 296, 297, 318, 319, 320
Bouche, la. See Olivier LeVasseur
Boucher des Forges, Antoine, 213
Bourbon, Île de, 5, 6, 120, 139, 143, 159, 164, 197, 202, 203, 204, 205, 206, 207, 208, 209, 210, 213, 215, 217, 218, 219, 220, 221, 222, 223, 225, 226, 229, 231, 232, 233, 234, 235, 236, 237, 245, 249, 259, 261, 262, 268, 269, 279, 290, 300, 323, 324, 325, 326, 327, 328, 329, 330, 331, 332, 333, 335, 336, 338, 339
Bourbonnais (people), 331
Bouse, la. See Olivier LeVasseur
Bowen, Capt., 87
Bradford, Alexander, 128, 129
Braithwaite, Samuel, 260
Braund, William, 291
Brazil (South America), 36, 82, 106, 142, 189, 195, 196
Brehoit, John, 22
Brice Galley, 146
Brice, Randal, 146
Bridges, Thomas, 114

Britannia, 172
British Library, i, 22, 80, 133, 145, 146, 148, 151, 159, 165, 202, 239, 247, 258, 290, 291, 313, 314
Brittany (France), 74, 209, 210, 212, 214
Brown, Ignatious, 195
Brown, John, 26
Brown's Garden, 148
Browne, William, 146
Buck, 36, 42, 60, 62, 96, 111, 113, 114, 344, 348
Buck, le, 86
Bucquoy, Jacob de, 5, 19, 241, 257, 269, 275, 277, 278, 279, 280, 281, 282, 283, 284, 285, 286, 287, 288, 289, 327
Buffet, Henri, 197, 207, 210, 211, 212, 213, 214, 215
Bull, Jonathan, 103
Burchett, Josiah, 247, 251, 252, 253, 290
Burgen, Hans, 271, 272
Burgess, Douglas R. Jr., 4, 259
Burgess, Josiah, 187
Burin, François de Ricquebourg, 210
Buse, la. See Olivier LeVasseur
Bushell, Nathaniel, 99
Butler, James, 67, 68, 70
Butler, Thomas, 68
Butscher, Capt., 195
Buzzard. See Olivier LeVasseur
Byng, Sir George, 245, 246
Cadogan snow, 95, 96, 97, 100
Calabar (African port), 39, 40, 41, 93, 101, 130, 236
Calais, France, 25, 67, 80, 83, 338, 339

Calicut, 13, 160, 163, 174, 178, 179, 180
Callabar Merchant, 93, 116, 126, 128, 129, 130, 131, 134
Camocke, George, 245, 246
Candler, Bartholomew, 297, 300, 310
Cap d'Amber (N. pt. Madagascar), 274, 286
Cap de Monte, Liberia 79
Cap de Palmes, Liberia 79
Cap de Trois Pointes, 64, 80, 93, 115, 116, 125
Cap Saint-Marie (S. point of Madagascar), 252, 274, 286
Cape Coast Castle, 18, 33, 40, 60, 142
Cape Comorin, SE India, 13, 160
Cape Lopez, 40, 83, 85, 86, 89, 93, 128
Cape of Good Hope, 5, 71, 123, 127, 130, 249
Cape Tiberon (West. Hispaniola or Haiti), 105
Cape Town, South Africa, 116, 130, 134, 248, 289, 329
Cape Verde Islands, 34, 36, 54, 96, 189, 256
Capetown, 249, 252
capitalism, 7, 17, 23, 221
Caribbean, 8, 19, 67, 70, 95, 109, 118, 235, 300, 318
Carlisle, 22
Carnegie, James, 12, 40, 64, 101, 129, 142, 189, 330
Carpenter (Skinner), Mary, 99
Carpenter, Capt., 261
Carpenter's Bay (NW Mauritius), 261
Carré, Jacques, 79
Carteret snow, 114

Carteret, John Lord, 111, 114, 124, 128, 293, 306, 309, 312, 344, 345
Carwar. See Karwar
Cassandra, 5, 42, 62, 90, 93, 95, 109, 117, 120, 124, 126, 131, 132, 135, 140, 141, 142, 143, 144, 145, 146, 149, 150, 152, 153, 154, 155, 158, 159, 160, 161, 162, 164, 166, 167, 170, 171, 172, 173, 174, 175, 176, 177, 178, 180, 181, 182, 184, 185, 190, 215, 217, 223, 225, 226, 228, 229, 230, 231, 234, 238, 239, 241, 245, 247, 249, 256, 259, 260, 264, 269, 274, 275, 279, 284, 285, 292, 299, 300, 301, 302, 303, 304, 305, 306, 307, 308, 309, 310, 311, 313, 314, 315, 316, 317, 318, 319, 320, 346, 359, 366, 370, 371, 372, 373, 374, 375
Cassle, Capt., 189
Catholic, 3, 20, 210
Cayenne (Guyana), 93
Ceylon, Island Nation of, 185
Chandos, 146, 160, 170
Charles II, 5
Charles VI Galley, See Prince Eugene (Ostend)
Charlotte, 111, 113, 115, 343, 344, 345
Charnock Point, 121, 264
Charnock's Point, 268
Chavonnes, Maurits Pasques de, 251
Christiana, 103
Christopher, Thomas, 49
Church of Our Lady of the Assumption, Lorient, France, 210
City of Ostend, 230, 231, 234, 235, 236, 275

Clayton (Cleyton), John, 323, 328
Coast of the Cafres. See Mozambique
Cochin, India, 5, 160, 161, 163, 165, 176, 178, 179, 180, 181, 182, 183, 184, 217, 218, 247, 361, 362, 363, 364, 366, 368, 371, 372, 373, 374, 376
Cockburn, John, 243, 247, 248, 255, 257, 270, 271, 273
Cocklyn, Jeremiah, 9, 31, 34, 35, 36, 37, 38, 39, 41, 48, 49, 50, 51, 54, 55, 57, 58, 60, 62, 63, 64, 65, 66, 67, 70, 71, 72, 73, 78, 79, 81, 82, 83, 84, 85, 86, 89, 90, 93, 107, 110, 112, 116, 119, 120, 124, 125, 127, 135, 139, 142
Code Noir or "Black Code", 221
Comorros Islands, 255, 274
Collin, Jean, 62, 107
Compagnie des Indes Orientales (CDI), 139, 205, 210, 236, 325, 326, 328, 329, 330, 331, 338
Comptoir Hollande, 275, 277, 283
Comrade, 70, 71, 72, 73, 78, 79, 81, 83, 86, 89, 90, 119, 125, 348
Concordia, 146
Condent. See Edward Congdon
Condent, Christopher. See Edward Congdon
Condent, Jerry, 192
Confederate States of America, 69

Congdon, Edward, 5, 24, 72, 87, 88, 96, 97, 99, 120, 121, 131, 132, 134, 158, 187, 189, 190, 191, 193, 194, 195, 196, 197, 198, 200, 201, 202, 203, 204, 205, 206, 207, 208, 210, 211, 212, 213, 214, 215, 217, 218, 221, 231, 232, 268, 269, 290, 328
Cooke's Bay (SW Île Saint-Marie), 266, 268
Cooker, 204, 205
Corisco Island, 73, 81, 125, 128
Cornelissen, Jan, 109, 122n41
Coulston, 96, 97, 98, 99, 100, 101, 189, 195
Courchant, Joseph de Beauvoilier de, 204, 205, 207, 208, 211, 213, 227, 228, 231, 327, 328
Craggs, James, 128
Creed, Thomas, 111, 113, 114, 115, 121, 272, 344, 345
Creichton, David, 61
Creichton, James, 49
Crumpe, Isaac, 99
Curaçoa, 11
Cygnet, 19
Da Gama, Vasco, 275
Dahomè, 40
Daily Courant, 133, 194, 236
Daily Post, 102, 108, 109, 113, 114, 149, 195, 299, 300
Darien, Scots settlement of, 301
Dauphin, 189
Davids, Jean, *See* Howell Davis
Davies, Henry, 268
Davis, Howell, 31, 32, 34, 35, 36, 42, 50, 54, 63, 64, 67, 86,

95, 96, 97, 98, 100, 101, 107, 109, 110, 112, 113, 119, 123, 124, 343
De Bry, John, 133, 193, 194, 214
De Campo, António, 275
De La Bourdonnais, Mahé, 220
De Menezes, Comte d'Ericeira ,Luís Carlos Inácio Xavier, 223-225, 397
De Nyon (engineer), 222
Dearlove, Peter, 22, 23
Deer, James "Jimmy", 271
Defense, 278, 285, 286, 299, 300, 324, *See Nossa Senhora do Cabo, See Nossa Senhora do Cabo*
Defiance, 84, 119
DeFoe, Daniel, 19, 28
Delagoa Bay, 276, 277
Delagoa Bay (S. Mozambique), 244, 257, 274, 275, 278, 289
Dent, Digby, 297, 309
Deoghur, 170
Deventer, Marinus Lodewijk, 276, 277
d'Hermitte, Hyacinthe, 324, 325, 326, 328, 329, 331, 332, 336, 337, 338
Diggs, Cole, 201
Dina Morgabin. See Île de Bourbon
Doale, William, 198
Domascaicus. See Île de Bourbon
Don Mascarin Island. See Ile de Bourbon
Donnan, Elizabeth, 12, 17, 40, 50, 56, 60, 65, 101, 112, 123, 129, 130, 142, 189, 319, 330
Douarin, le, J., 211
Downing, Clement, 117, 118, 119, 120, 121, 122, 123, 136, 137, 140, 141, 142, 144, 156, 157, 158, 159, 161, 162, 163, 164, 167, 170, 171, 172, 173, 174, 217, 222, 223, 239, 245, 250, 256, 257, 258, 260, 261, 265, 266, 268, 269, 270, 271, 272, 273, 274, 290, 291, 303
Dragon, 87, 96, 97, 120, 121, 133, 189, 190, 193, 194, 195, 196, 198, 200, 205, 214, 268, 269, 271
Dreijer, Gijs, 132
Duckin(g)field, John, 99, 127, 202
Duke of Cambridge, 178, 362
Duke of Ormond, 38, 54, 55, 56, 62, 65, 66, 67, 70, 71, 72, 73, 79, 112
Dumas, Pierre Benoît, 326, 327, 328, 332, 333, 336, 337, 338, 339, 340
Dunwich, Robert, 198, 200, 201
Dutch Cape Colony, 251, 275
E. T. Fox, ii, 33, 36, 38, 63, 66, 69, 72, 73, 87, 103, 113, 147, 162, 165, 167, 168, 190, 202
Eagle, 35, 38, 39, 106, 109, 111, 343, 344, 345, 348
East India Company (EIC), 5, 2, 5, 6, 7, 12, 16, 20, 23, 42, 43, 66, 79, 95, 121, 130, 131, 133, 134, 135, 138, 140, 142, 145, 146, 147, 149, 151, 153, 155, 156, 157, 159, 160, 162, 163, 164, 165, 167, 168, 169, 170, 171, 172, 173, 176, 184, 197, 198, 202, 232, 237, 238, 239, 246, 247, 250, 260, 275, 277, 290, 291, 292, 300, 305, 310, 313, 314, 316, 318, 320, 321, 325, 329, 369, 371, 373
East Indies, 5, 9, 12, 14, 16, 18, 20, 23, 25, 28, 71, 72, 83, 93, 109, 117, 126, 127, 131, 137, 138, 139, 140, 142, 144, 147, 178, 196, 204, 219, 224, 235,

247, 268, 281, 300, 319, 340, 370
Edward Low, 27, 102, 300
Elizabeth (aka Queen Elizabeth), 12, 17, 40, 42, 49, 61, 65, 66, 101, 112, 113, 114, 129, 137, 142, 146, 189, 296, 330, 344, 345, 348, 352, 353, 354
Elk, Capt., 284
Elliot, William, 46, 49, 54, 58
Elton, Abraham Jr., 146
England, Edward, 7, 9, 33, 61, 93, 95, 96, 97, 98, 100, 101, 102, 103, 104, 106, 107, 108, 109, 110, 112, 113, 115, 116, 117, 121, 122, 124, 125, 126, 127, 128, 130, 131, 132, 134, 135, 136, 139, 140, 143, 144, 147, 150, 152, 157, 158, 161, 162, 166, 167, 178, 190, 194, 195, 215, 217, 265, 268, 279, 320, 324, 343, 345, 370
English Mediterranean Fleet, 291
Ericeira, Count of. See De Menezes
Ethiopia, 140, 274
Ethiopian Ocean. See Indian Ocean
Evans, Benjamin, 320
Evening Post, 132, 191, 317
Evening Star, 192
Every, Henry, 5, 6, 7, 10, 14, 80, 123, 139, 140, 141, 143, 217, 259
Exeter, 254
Expedition, 141
Fame, 87
FamilySearch.org, i, 39

Fancy, 5, 6, 7, 109, 116, 117, 122, 123, 124, 125, 127, 131, 135, 136, 140, 142, 143, 144, 149, 150, 151, 152, 153, 154, 158, 159, 160, 162, 163, 166, 170, 269, 358, 370
Fantasy. See *Cassandra*
Fauré, Michael, 341
Fazakerly, William, 170
Fellows, John, 42, 360
Fenn, John, 297, 300
Feuquieres, Marquis de Pas, 92
Field, Timothy, 247
Fielding, John, 314
Fiery Dragon. See *Dragon*
Fiscal (admiralty officer), 183
Flanderin, André, 230
Flemish (of Flanders), 132, 134, 193, 204
Fletcher, Benjamin, 11, 12, 131, 135
Florida, 3, i, 64, 68, 69, 133, 187, 194, 294, 320
Flying Dragon. See *Dragon*
Flying Gang (Bahamas), 9, 26, 64
Flying King, 109, 114, 344
Forbans, Île aux, 243, 244, 245, 264, 266, 269, 274
Forbin, Piérre, 213
Foreward galley, 113
Fort Anjediva (India), 175
Fort Cochin, 183
Fort Dauphin. See Port Dauphin
Fort James, 35, 50, 65, 109
Fort Lijdzaamheid, 253, 274, 275, 277, 280
Fort St. David, 163

416 Sailing East

Fort St. George (Sumatra), 145, 160, 163, 170, 180, 185
Fougeray-Garnier, de, 236
Foulpointe, Madagascar, 335
Foynard, Jean, 213
France, i, 3, 21, 25, 32, 61, 67, 68, 69, 70, 71, 73, 74, 88, 92, 139, 158, 190, 203, 204, 205, 207, 209, 210, 211, 215, 218, 220, 221, 222, 223, 236, 238, 267, 324, 325, 329, 330, 331, 332, 336, 339, 341, 367
François-Louis, 212
frangourin (drink), 208
Freeman, John, 234
Freetown, Sierra Leone, 45, 55
French Windward Islands, 92
French, Anthony, 195
Frenchman's Bay. See Pirate's Bay
Frost, John, 27, 28
Frost, Midshipman, 268
Gabon (Africa), 81, 86, 89
Gambia River, 31, 34, 35, 36, 38, 50, 65, 108, 113, 118, 120, 127
Gargan, Richard, 146, 149, 151, 160
Garner, Capt., 111
Gascoigne, 202
Gasser, Dr. Jacques, 62
Gee, Michael, 118, 121
Gence, César, 212
George I of Hanover, 9, 67, 69, 279
Gerrebrants, Matheus, 63
ghurabs (frigates), 169
Gilbert, Thomas, 146, 163
Glorious Revolution (1688), 15, 16, 67
Glover, Robert, 12
Glynn, Henry, 50, 51, 52, 53, 54, 58, 60, 64, 65, 351, 353
Godolphin, 320

Gogo (town in India), 174, 360, 371
Gold Coast (Africa), 71, 72, 74, 120, 127, 137
Golden Age of American Greed, 8
Golden Age of Piracy, 7, 74, 192
Golding, Mathew, 34
Goletérie, Joncheé de la, 210
Good Fortune, 300
Gordon, John, 45, 349
Gouzronc, Renée le, 213
Grabs. See Ghurabs
Graham, Mungo, 109
Graham, Richard, 109
Grand Caymans, 297
Grand Port (SE Mauritius), 220
Grand Sestre (Grand Cess), 76
Grantham, 247, 249, 258
Grave, Sieur, 232
Greenhill, David, 313
Greenwich, 143, 144, 146, 147, 148, 149, 150, 151, 152, 153, 154, 159, 160, 161, 162, 164, 171, 232, 258, 370
Grenadines, 30
Grey, Charles, 88, 130, 131, 134, 135, 142, 143, 144, 163, 165, 239
Greyhound. See Comptoir
Holland, See City of Ostend
Griffin, James, 48, 61
Grout (SW of Portobello, Panama), 298, 301, 303, 305, 309, 311
guarda-costa, 318, 319
Guelderland. See Nossa Senhora do Cabo
Guernsey, Island of, 211
Guët, M. I., 208, 209, 234, 323, 324, 325, 326, 327, 338
Guinea (Africa), 5, 12, 18, 35, 39, 40, 42, 45, 50, 51, 53, 54,

64, 67, 70, 72, 73, 80, 83, 86,
92, 103, 104, 106, 117, 118,
121, 123, 124, 127, 128, 137,
147, 189, 195, 196, 197, 272,
320, 329, 348
Guinea Hen, 36
Gulph of Persia, 14
Gunsway, aka *Gang-i-Sawai*, 5
Hague, The, 251
Hais, Edouard, 77, 78, 81, 90
Hais, Guillaume, 73, 74, 76, 78,
79, 81, 82, 84, 85, 87, 88, 89,
90, 91, 124, 142
Halsey, John, 132
Hamilton, George, 294
Hamilton, Lord Archibald, 293
Hamilton, William, 103
Hancock, John, 15
Harper, Robert, 99
Harris, Barrow, 297, 301, 309,
318
Harris, Joseph, 39
Harvey, Capt., 162
Haskett, Elias, 22, 23
Havana, 7
Hego, Jacques, 124
Hellevoetsluis, 43
Henrietta, 200, 202
Henry, 40, 55, 81, 103, 128, 140,
313, 348
Henry and Temperance, 52
Herbert, Richard, 200, 202
Heroine, 42, 43, 44, 66, 72, 73,
78, 79, 80, 83, 86
Heywood, Peter, 293
Higginson, Richard, 163
Hill, Thomas, 74, 86, 88
Hispaniola, 26, 104, 105, 106,
109
Hitchins, John, 99
HMS *Albemarle*, 245

HMS *Assistance*, 297
HMS *Boyne*, 245
HMS *Bredah*, 297
HMS *Deale Castle*, 245
HMS *Enterprize*, 319
HMS *Exeter*, 247, 248, 260, 264,
265, 266, 268, 274, 291
HMS *Falkland*, 297, 300, 309,
316
HMS *Kent*, 245
HMS *Kingston*, 296
HMS *Launceston*, 297, 300, 309,
310
HMS *Lion*, 247, 248, 249, 254,
255, 256, 261, 264, 265, 266,
268, 271, 272, 273, 274, 291
HMS *Lyme*, 113
HMS *Mary*, 69
HMS *Mermaid*, 297, 301, 303,
307, 308, 311, 313
HMS *Namur*, 291
HMS *Phoenix*, 9, 36, 187, 194
HMS *Portland*, 245
HMS *Rye*, 198
HMS *Salisbury*, 117, 121, 136,
243, 247, 248, 256, 262, 264,
265, 268, 269, 272, 273, 274,
291
HMS *Sandwich*, 290, 291
HMS *Scarborough*, 30, 113
HMS *Shoreham*, 247, 248
HMS *Swallow*, 118, 296
HMS *Windsor*, 297
HMS *Yarmouth*, 245
Hogbin, Edward, 52, 53
Holland, Rich, 320
Hollat, Joseph, 198
Holmes, James, 274, 290, 291
Honfleur, France, 213
Hooke, Abraham, 202

Hornigold, Benjamin, 26, 27, 187
Horsburgh, James, 177
House of Austria, 133, 134, 197
Hume, Francis, 31
Hunt, Henry, 110, 112, 113, 126, 128
Hurricane of 1715, 8, 64
Hutchinson, William, 238, 367
Ianantsony. See San Augustin Bay
Île de France. See Mauritius
Île St. Laurent. See Madagascar
Indian Ocean, 5, 1, 3, 25, 136, 139, 155, 156, 170, 203, 209, 249, 255, 291, 300, 328, 340
Indian Queen, 74, 86, 87, 88, 90, 131, 139, 144, 146, 147, 148, 149, 348
Ireland, 6, 44, 68, 143, 198, 211, 294
Island of the Pirates. See Île aux Forbans
Isle of Pines (New Caledonia, Panama), 301, 303
Jacob and Jaell, 42
Jacoba Galeij, 109, 116, 122n41, 126, 131
Jacobite, 7, 32, 68, 70, 245, 278, 279, 294
Jacobite Rebellion of 1715, 7, 68
Jacobitism, 66, 69, 70, 293
Jacquin, 40
Jamaica, 8, 40, 42, 50, 51, 64, 66, 86, 95, 99, 103, 109, 111, 112, 114, 123, 128, 135, 198, 268, 292, 293, 294, 296, 297, 300, 303, 305, 307, 308, 311, 312, 313, 344, 345
James I, 138
James III. See Pretender
James, Edward, 64

Jennings, Henry, 51, 64, 187, 188
Joeans, Thomas, 211
Johanna, 146
Johanna Bay, 93
Johanna, Island of, 5, 7, 62, 90, 124, 126, 132, 140, 144, 145, 146, 147, 148, 151, 155, 159, 160, 161, 166, 171, 255, 274, 320, 346, 370
John, 66, 313
John and Mary, 319, 320
John and Rebecca, 13, 14
John Gally, 135, 139, 140, 142
John III (Portuguese), 275
Johnson, Adam, 328
Johnson, Charles, 190, See Nathaniel Mist, See Nathaniel Mist
Johnson, Isaac, 196
Johnson, Lawrence, 19
Johnson, Sir Robert, 188, 189, 247, 248, 256, 260
Jones, Cadwallader, 6
Jones, John, 319
Jones, Simon, 45
Jouane, Pierre, 104, 105, 106
Judith, 42
Kaapkolonie. See Dutch Cape Colony
Karwar, Karnataka, India, 175, 176
Katherine, 40, 112, 114, 344, 345
Kelly, J., 211
Kennedy, Thomas, 128, 129, 133
Kennedy, Walter, 63
Kidd, William, 12, 14, 15, 16, 20, 23, 132, 140, 214, 335
King George II, 293
King James, 34, 36, 37, 58, 63, 66, 67, 68, 86, 138, 352

King of Ranter's Bay, 269, See Plantain, John, James, or William
King v. Joseph Stratton, 198
King, Stephen, 125
King's Head, 291, 303
King's Town. See Mustamudu
Kingston, Jamaica, 309
Kirby, Richard, 146, 147, 148, 149, 150, 151, 152, 153, 154, 159, 160, 161, 162, 164, 171, 232
Kozhikode. See Calicut
Kru Bay. See Pirate's Bay
l'Akion, 331
L'Bouse. See Olivier LeVasseur
l'Heureaux Avanteuries, 115, 124
L'Orient. See Lorient
l'Union de Nantes, 84
La Concorde, aka *Queen Anne's Revenge*, 103
La Coruna, Spain, 5
La Duchesse de Noailles, 232, 234, 326, 339
La Gazette de Paris, 235, 236, 237
La Méduse, 324, 325, 328, 329, 332, 338
La Rochelle, France, 76, 78, 212, 328
Lambert, Jonathan, 38, 55, 56, 65, 73, 109, 112
Lards, François de, 212
Lasinby, Richard, 151, 153, 158, 159, 160, 161, 162, 164, 165, 166, 167, 168, 171, 172, 173, 174, 175, 176, 177, 178, 179, 180, 181, 182, 183, 184, 185, 217, 223, 227, 232, 234, 235, 237, 238, 358, 367, 369
Lawes, Nicholas, 293, 300
Laws, Joseph, 290, 297, 301, 303, 304, 305, 306, 307, 308, 309, 310, 311, 312, 314, 315, 317, 318
Le Bon Secour, 62, 107
Le Croisic, Brittany, France, 211, 213
Le Lesabes de Nantes, 63, 79, 80
Le Mercure, 104, 190, 191, 203, 204, 205, 206, 207, 214, 224
Le Preni de Nantes, 79, 87, 88, 91
Le Solide, 82, 83, 84, 89, 120, 142
Le Victorieux, 73, 74, 75, 76, 77, 78, 79, 81, 82, 83, 84, 85, 86, 90, 124, 127, 142, 243, See Victory
Le Victorieux, crew of, 91
Lebous. See Olivier LeVasseur
Lenox, 251
Leslie, Francis, 187
Leslie, William, 103
Lestock, Richard, 246, 291
LeVae, Adolphe, 63, 134
LeVasseur, Olivier de la Buse, 5, ii, 9, 19, 24, 25, 26, 27, 28, 30, 31, 32, 33, 34, 35, 36, 37, 38, 39, 50, 51, 53, 54, 55, 57, 58, 62, 63, 64, 65, 66, 67, 70, 71, 72, 73, 74, 78, 79, 80, 81, 82, 83, 84, 85, 86, 87, 88, 89, 90, 93, 107, 110, 112, 116, 119, 120, 124, 127, 131, 132, 135, 139, 142, 144, 145, 146, 147, 149, 157, 164, 166, 176, 178, 180, 181, 215, 217, 223, 226, 229, 230, 231, 232, 233, 234, 235, 238, 243, 244, 245,

249, 269, 270, 274, 275, 278, 279, 280, 281, 284, 285, 287, 289, 290, 300, 323, 324, 325, 326, 327, 328, 329, 332, 333, 335, 336, 337, 338, 340, 341
Liberia, 75
Libertalia (website), 327
Library of Congress, 10, 192
Lind, André, 211
Lisbon, 22, 195, 196, 234, 236, 237, 248, 256
Livingston, Robert, 16
Llandaff Court, Cardiff, Wales, 245
London, 146, 160, 165, 166, 168, 170, 172, 176, 178, 181, 182, 183, 238
London Journal, 113, 114, 123, 151, 159, 164, 165, 195, 303, 317, 348, 358, 367, 369
Lord Fairfax, 22
Lords of Trade, 3
Lorient, Brittany, France, 158, 210, 211, 329
Lougher, Walter & Richard, 86
Lowrie, John Cameron, 177
Lowther, George, 300
Lowther, Robert, 31
Loyal Merchant, 34
Loyalty, 114
Luanda Bay, Angola, 87, 88
Lucy, Philippe, 211
Luengo Bay. See Luanda Bay
Lunsford, Virginia, 139
Luntly, Richard, 36, 38, 62, 63
Lynch, Thomas, 114, 124
Lyon, Mr. (of London), 173
Mackett, Henry, 114
Mackett, William, 163
Macrae, James, 5, 62, 95, 116, 122, 127, 144, 145, 146, 147, 149, 150, 151, 152, 153, 154, 155, 156, 157, 158, 159, 160, 161, 162, 163, 164, 166, 170,

172, 178, 179, 180, 184, 185, 238, 279, 320, 321, 358, 362, 365, 368, 370
Madagascar, 1, 3, 4, 5, 6, 7, 8, 9, 10, 11, 12, 15, 16, 18, 19, 20, 21, 22, 23, 24, 71, 74, 79, 80, 85, 88, 93, 114, 116, 117, 118, 119, 120, 123, 125, 126, 127, 129, 132, 135, 136, 139, 141, 142, 143, 146, 156, 160, 161, 162, 164, 167, 176, 184, 189, 195, 197, 198,199, 200, 201, 202, 203, 204, 205, 206, 207, 208, 209, 212, 218, 220, 221, 231, 234, 235, 239, 241, 245, 254, 255, 257, 258, 259, 260, 261, 264, 267, 269, 270, 271, 272, 274, 277, 282, 283, 286, 289, 290, 291, 299, 301, 320, 323, 324, 325, 326, 327, 328, 329, 330, 331, 332, 337, 341, 346, 364, 375, 376
Madame, Îlot. See Île aux Forbans
Madeira, Island of, 30, 104, 195, 196, 248
Madras, India, 138, 145, 160, 163, 170, 179, 180, 185, 249
Maelcamp, Jacques & Charles, 132-133
Maggot. See Henry Mackett
Maguire, Hugh, 146
Mahajamba Bay. See Bombétoke Bay
Maharashtra. See Maratha
Mahebourg (Mauritius). See Warwick Bay
Malabar Coast (India), 19, 20, 126, 142, 145, 160, 175, 179, 218, 247, 260, 269, 346
Malacca, 13
Malagasy (people), 19, 23, 80, 136, 254, 269, 331, 336
Malindi, 155

Mann, Horace, 247
Maputo, Mozambique, 275, 281
Maratha (people), 168
Marennes, Charente-Maritime (SW France), 213
Margaret, 189
Margibi, 75
Marie, 105, 211
Marquaisac, de, 330
Marques, Lourenço, 275
Marquis de Prié, 63, 134
Marquis del Campo, 63,
Marshalsea, 22, 115
Marosy Island, see Marotte, l'Îsle
Marotte, l'Îsle (in Antongil Bay), 287, 330, 331, 338
Marquaisac, de, 328
Marques, Lourenço, 273
Marshalsea, 22, 114
Martinique, 82, 83, 91, 92, 104, 120
Mary Anne, 26
Maryland, 56, 65, 81, 112, 195, 344, 345
Masaliet River, 282
Mascaragne. See Île de Bourbon
Mascarenes, 71, 139, 219, 220, 221, 222
Mascarenhas, Dom Pedro, 219
Massachusetts, 8, 16, 25, 296, 297, 346
Massailly (people), 206, 282, 283
Massaly, Madagascar, 335
Mathelage Bay, See Bombétoke Bay
Mathews, Thomas, 5, 117, 140, 239, 241, 243, 244, 245, 246, 247, 248, 249, 254, 255, 256, 257, 258, 260, 261, 264, 265, 268, 270, 271, 273, 274, 275, 282, 290, 291, 292, 299
Matthews, John, 72, 78, 86, 87, 88, 89, 103, 135, 142, 144, 147
Matthews, Thomas, 249
Mauritius (Indian Ocean), 13, 79, 80, 93, 139, 161, 162, 164, 184, 208, 214, 215, 218, 219, 220, 221, 222, 223, 225, 226, 227, 228, 245, 260, 261, 262, 269, 328, 329, 330, 331, 335, 336, 365, 367, 369, 375
Mayne, Covill, 247
Mayotte, Island of, 144, 146, 147, 149, 255
McDonald, Kevin P., 18, 19
Mecca, 5, 13
Melindra (Kavaratti?), 176, 361, 371
de Menezes, Luís Carlos Inácio Xavier 222, 226, 227, 228, 229, 230, 233, 234
Merchant, 86
Mercury, 104, 105, 106, 111, 112, 114, 196, 197, 296, 344, 345, 348
Merina Kingdom, 200
Meunier, Pierre, 76
Michel, Jean, 91, 275, 329
Middlesex, England, 66, 113, 114
Miles, Morgan, 198, 201
Mist, Nathaniel, i, 28, 31, 32, 33, 35, 88, 89, 101, 102, 131, 134, 190, 193, 194, 196, 343
Mocha, Yemen, 13, 14, 155, 168, 236, 238, 272, 359, 367
Mogadishu, 155
Moghul Indian Empire, 168

Moheli Sultanate, 155
Molewater, Bastiean, 44
Mollo, Pièrre, 211
Mombasa, 155
Monkey Key. See Grout
Monrovia, 75
Montadouin, René de, 92
Moody, William, 31, 37, 38, 55, 62, 64
Moor, Richard, 12, 63, 71, 72, 73, 74, 85, 86, 89, 90, 103, 119, 120, 125, 126, 135, 140, 141, 142, 144, 145, 161, 167, 168, 180, 190, 202, 215, 217, 227, 243, 244, 249, 258, 259, 260, 264, 269, 271, 290, 291, 299, 301, 302, 303, 313, 359, 362, 368
Moore, John, 319
Morel, Nicholas, 82
Morgan, Evan, 202
Morice, Humphrey, i, 35, 37, 40, 42, 43, 44, 45, 48, 61, 66, 72, 78, 127, 313, 314, 319, 321, 349, 353
Morning Star, 192, 300
Morris, John, 65, 351, 352, 353, 354
Mousell, Thomas, 320
Moville Trader, 96, 189
Mozambique, 132, 140, 231, 235, 236, 264, 274, 275, 278, 281, 288, 289, 329, 330, 331, 366
Mughal, 5, 6, 12, 140, 184, 217
Mumvil Trader. See Moville Trader
Murrane, 32, 35, 37, 38, 53, 54, 55
Murud-Janjira, 168
Muscat, Oman, 12, 168
Mustamudu, Anjouan, 155
Mystic Seaport Museum, 193
Nadreau, Jacques, 84

Naish, James, 88, 133, 134
Nantes, France, 73, 74, 75, 90, 92, 103, 211, 213, 243
Narcissism (Trump-era), 281
Nassau Town, New Providence Island, Bahamas, 187
National Archives (London), i, 31, 35, 40, 65, 66, 87, 100, 114, 121, 129, 131, 134, 135, 189, 190, 195, 198, 200, 201, 241, 249, 261, 262, 263, 265, 272, 303, 316
Neal, Gyles, 234, 241, 243, 244, 258, 271, 274, 290, 291
Negré, François, 63, 79, 80
Negus, Jonathan, 39, 40
Netherlands, 43, 277
Nevis, Island of (Windwards), 31
New Caledonia (Panama), 301, 303
New England, i, 9, 12, 112, 119, 214, 235, 320
New Granada (1717 - modern Colombia, Ecuador, Panama, and Venezuela), 297
New Jersey, 27
New Providence Island, 6, 8, 9, 10, 11, 35, 36, 50, 51, 83, 84, 88, 96, 113, 187, 189, 194, 195, 247
New York, 5, 11, 12, 13, 14, 15, 16, 18, 19, 106, 138, 163, 187, 192, 196, 203, 246, 259, 297, 335
New-England Courant, 296
Nichols, Thomas, 187
Nightengale, 49
Nossa Senhora do Cabo, 5, 132, 217, 218, 223, 224, 225, 226, 227, 229, 230, 231, 235, 237, 241, 244, 249, 279, 299, 326

Nosy Boraha, see Île Saint-Marie
Nosy Hibrahim, see Île Saint-Marie
Nosy Mangabe, see Île Marotte
Notre-Dame de l'Assomption, Lorient, France, 213
Nova Scotia, 27
Ogle, Chaloner, 296, 319
Ogot, Bethwell A., 155
Old Bailey, 16
Onslow, 117, 118, 121, 122
Opperhoofd, 275, 277
Orangefield, Ayeshire, Scotland, 164
Ostend (Belgium), 87, 109, 131, 132, 133, 134, 146, 149, 150, 151, 193, 194, 204, 230, 231, 234, 235, 237, 326, 339, 375
Ostend East-Indies Company (GIC), 132
Othniel Davis, 189
Oulson, Branson, 111, 115
Owen, Henry, 52
Oyer and Terminer (court), 290
Paesie, Rudolf, 122
Paimboeuf, France, 75
Panama, 297, 298, 299, 300, 302, 310, 311, 318
Parmentier, Jan, 133, 146
Parnall snow, 65, 66, 351, 352
Pascal, Joseph, 85, 328
Patterson, Alexander, 82, 83, 84, 119
Pearce, James, 313
Pearce, Jeremiah, 42, 43, 50, 65, 66, 313, 314
Pearl, 109, 111, 112, 343, 345

Pearse, Vincent, 9, 36, 50, 51, 187, 194, 195
Pendergrass, Mrs., 69
Penguin Island group (W. South Africa) (W, 248
Perkins, Samuel, 12, 14
Pernambuco, 40
Perry, Micajah, 42
Persia, 155, 161
Peterborough, 85, 99, 103, 126, 127, 346
Petite Sestre (Sobo?), 75, 76
Philadelphia, 14, 123, 178, 196, 197
Philipse, Frederick, 5, 11, 12, 19
Phipps, Col., 60, 142, 189, 201
Piat, Denis, 213, 214, 326, 330
Pirate Island, Île Saint-Marie. See Île aux Forbans
Pirate Wars, 4, 6, 7, 9, 10
Pirate's Bay (Africa), 45, 46, 61, 62, 63, 109, 135
Pitt, George, 144
Pitts, John, 258
Pius, Antoninus, 144
Plantain, John, James, or William, 117, 118, 119, 120, 121, 122, 123, 124, 125, 136, 141, 142, 144, 161, 167, 215, 245, 260, 268, 269, 270, 271, 272, 291, 336
Planter, Guillame, 328
Plattel, Capt., 232
Plowman, Daniel, 315
Plumb, Abraham, 42, 63, 64
Plummer, Capt., 125
Plymouth, England, 189, 190, 210, 212, 235, 247
Popple, William, 128

Port Dauphin (Madagascar), 139, 200, 201, 220, 243, 261, 262, 264, 274
Port Louis (NW Mauritius), 220
Port Louis, Lorient, France, 210, 211, 212
Port Mariel, Cuba, 26
Port Royal, Jamaica, 69, 268, 294, 297
Portland of London, 297
Portland, duke of, 293, 294, 295, 296, 297, 303, 304, 305, 306, 307, 308, 309, 310, 311, 312, 314, 315, 316, 317, 318
Porto Bello, 7, 303, 305, 317
Portobello (Panama), 5, 40, 135, 292, 293, 297, 298, 301, 303, 304, 306, 308, 309, 313
Portsmouth, England, 145, 172, 297
Portugal, 64, 196, 197, 224, 225, 235, 236, 248, 316, 339
Portuguese, 23, 53, 55, 64, 73, 78, 81, 82, 83, 84, 85, 123, 132, 139, 140, 155, 157, 164, 168, 175, 176, 195, 196, 203, 219, 224, 225, 226, 229, 230, 231, 235, 236, 237, 241, 249, 269, 271, 275, 280, 281, 286, 287, 289, 299, 344, 347, 360, 366
Post Boy, 103, 147, 153, 156, 158, 160
Post Man Historical Account, 97, 98
Postilion, 26
Poulain, Constance (lady of Montgogue), 210
Poulier brothers, 189
Prahm, 170, 172, 174, 371
Prescott, William, 150
Pretender, or James III, 49, 67, 68, 69, 70, 294

Prince, 40, 45, 99, 134, 193, 194, 198, 202, 293, 329, 346, 348
Prince Eugene (Bristol), 193, 194, 197, 198, 200, 201, 202
Prince Eugene (Ostend), 99n6, 132-134, 193, 194, 197, 204, 348
Prince, Lawrence, 42, 65
Princess, 42, 63, 64, 80, 348
Principe Island, 5, 64, 80, 81, 82, 84, 123, 124
Pringle, Patrick, 121, 163, 192
Pronis, Jacques, 220
Prosperous, 117, 118
Prudent Hannah, 320
Pullecondore, Island of, 238
Quarry, Robert, 14
Queen Anne, 7
Queen Anne's Revenge, 68, 103
Queen Anne's War, 7, 20, 297
Queen Ann's Revenge (not Thache's), 112
Rade des Tortues, 220
Rajapore, 12
Randolph, Edmund, 11
Ranter's Bay. See Antongil Bay
Rappahannock River, Virginia, 128
Ratocaffe, King, 206, 282, 283
Rawley, James A., 42, 43
Rebecca, 200, 202
Red Sea, 12, 13, 17, 19, 140, 142, 167, 366, 375
Reddish, Edward, 247, 248
Redwood Island (SW Île Saint-Marie), 266
Resolution, 12
Réunion, Île de. See Île de Bourbon, See Île de Bourbon
Revenge, 172
Rhode Island, 117, 300
Ricketts, William, 111

Rideout, William, 103, 104, 106, 124, 127, 348
Riebeeck, Jan van, 251
Rio de Junco, 75
Rising Sun, 36, 37, 38, 48, 50, 58, 351
River Medway, 290
Robert, Lt. L., 233
Robert, Sieur, 330
Roberts, Bartholomew, 33, 42, 55, 63, 103, 119, 123, 124, 297, 300, 319
Roberts, Thomas. See Bartholomew Roberts
Rogers, Woodes, 9, 24, 36, 42, 84, 96, 189, 190
Rose, Mr., 291
Ross, Hugh, 47, 349
Rotherhithe, England, 133
Rotterdam, 43, 44
Rouen, France, 213
Rover, 189, 195
Royal African Company (RAC), 17, 18, 50, 52, 55, 56, 65, 108, 123, 330, 331
Royal Fortune, 119
Royal James, 63, 68, 108, 109, 111, 112, 113, 116, 343, 345
Royal Navy, 24, 69, 121, 123, 164, 193, 239, 243, 244, 257, 270, 274, 278, 279, 290, 292, 298, 306, 312, 313, 314, 315, 317, 319
Royal Ranger, 83, 86
Royal Rover, 63
Ruby snow, 313
Rye House Plot, 245
Saint Domingue (Haiti), 26, 83, 92, 104, 105, 106

Saint-Denis, Bourbon, 197, 204, 206, 207, 218, 228, 230, 233, 234, 327, 328
Sainte-Catherine, 211
Saint-Marie, Île, 5, 18, 23, 24, 117, 120, 121, 135, 139, 141, 143, 144, 164, 193, 197, 198, 200, 201, 204, 205, 214, 233, 241, 243, 244, 249, 259, 260, 264, 265, 266, 269, 270, 274, 282, 325, 335, 336
Saint-Maries, Île, 265
Saint-Omer, 210
Saint-René, 214
Salamanga (king, generic), 283
Salim, Sultan, 155
Samana Bay, Hispaniola, 104, 297
Sample, Robert, 114
Samson, Thomas, 70, 119
San Augustin (SW Madagascar), 13, 136, 199, 231, 234, 235, 241, 243, 244, 249, 254, 255, 256
São Tomé, Island of, 82, 126, 131
Sarah, 38, 55, 56, 65, 73, 109, 110, 111, 112, 113, 114, 115, 126, 343, 344, 345, 348, 352
Saturday Evening Post, 35, 86, 318
Saunders, Edward, 99, 100
Scot's Bay, Hispaniola, 104
Scotland, 7, 15, 109, 145, 163
Seager, Jasper, 10, 93, 131, 141, 143, 144, 149, 152, 157, 162, 166, 171, 181, 190, 215, 217, 226, 231, 243, 269, 279, 320
Seager, Thomas, 143
Segnor Joseph, 38
Senegal, 330

Seudre, la (river in France), 213
Shoreham, 254
Siddy, 168
Sierra Leone (Africa), 18, 31, 34, 35, 36, 37, 38, 41, 43, 44, 45, 50, 52, 54, 55, 57, 61, 62, 65, 70, 72, 75, 95, 101, 109, 110, 111, 112, 119, 136
Siger, Capt.. See Jasper Seager
Skinner, Peter, 51, 95, 96, 97, 98, 99, 100, 101, 189, 195
Slade, William, 36
slavery, 17, 68, 221, 222, 324, 329
Smith, James, 99
Smith, John, 319
Smith's Tribe, Bermuda, 188
Snear, Mr., 299
Snelgrave, William, 31, 34, 35, 36, 37, 38, 39, 40, 41, 42, 43, 44, 45, 46, 47, 48, 49, 50, 51, 52, 53, 54, 55, 56, 57, 58, 60, 61, 62, 63, 64, 65, 66, 67, 72, 108, 110, 112, 313, 349, 352, 353, 355, 356
Society, 189
South Carolina, 55, 69, 188, 189, 191, 192, 300
South Sea Company, 40, 42, 109, 121, 135, 313, 314
Spanish Empire, 3
Spanish Town, Jamaica, 124
Speedwell, 71, 72, 73, 78, 79, 81, 83, 84, 85, 119, 125, 126
Spencer, Thomas, 195
Spotswood, Alexander, 128, 129, 198
Sri Lanka. See Ceylon
St Joseph, 133
St. Albans, 251
St. Catherine's Anglican Church, St. Jago de la Vega, Jamaica, 314

St. Christophers (Windwards), 26
St. George's Bay. See Pirate's Bay
St. Helena, 13, 83, 109, 376
St. James Market, London, 291
St. Lawrence, Île of. See Madagascar
St. Mary. See Ile Saint-Marie
St. Mary's. See Ile Saint-Marie
St. Paul, port of (Madagascar), 203
St. Paul's, Bourbon, 215, 230, 262
Stanhope, 238
Stanhope, Lord Charles, 68, 69, 128, 239
Stadt Oostende, See City of Ostend
Stevenson, John, 142
Stoney, Mr., 290
Stratton, Joseph, 99, 193, 198, 199, 200, 201, 202, 204
Stahremberg, 146, 149, 150, 153, 160
Stuart, 6, 15, 16, 66, 67, 68, 69, 138
Sunderland, 238
Surat, India, 5, 138, 155, 160, 168, 202, 236, 346
Surinam, 103
Susanna Galley, 198
Swallowfield, 145
Swansea, Glamorgan, 198
Sylvester, Capt., 111, 113, 114, 344, 345
Syrène, 332
Tamana, *see* Deoghur
Tankarana Region (N. Madagascar), 287
Tate, James, 150
Tawke, John, 178, 180, 362, 363, 368, 371, 374

Taylor, Richard, 5, 9, 31, 36, 42, 60, 62, 66, 71, 72, 73, 79, 80, 81, 86, 112, 119, 120, 139, 142, 145, 158, 161, 166, 171, 176, 180, 188, 215, 217, 230, 244, 246, 258, 269, 270, 271, 274, 275, 278, 284, 285, 292, 293, 299, 300, 301, 304, 305, 306, 307, 317, 319, 320, 327
Tellicherry, India, 160, 178, 179, 371
Temple Hall, Jamaica, 294
Tenerife, Island of, 189
Terrible, 117
Tew, Thomas, 5, 140
Thames River (England), 88, 291
The Successful Pyrate, 7, 10
Thomas Freke & Co., 198
Thompson, John, 42, 54, 352
Timerly River (W. Madagascar), 255, 282
Tizard, Edward, 109
Toaka (drink), 283
Tolinaro, *see* Fort Dauphin
Tookerman, Richard, 69, 70
Tortuga, 26, 27
Travers, Tim, 168
Trevor, Tudor, 297
Triangular Trade, 4
Triton, 236, 238, 367
Trois Amis, 211
Trott, Nicholas, 6
Trumpett, Jonathan, 181, 182, 183, 363, 364, 368
Tsaratanana Mountains, 287
Tunbridge, Robert, 51, 98, 99, 100
Turnberry Castle, 145
Two Friends, 46, 49, 54, 58, 352
Tyzack. See Tizard

Tyzack, Timothy, 202
Tyzard. See Tizard
Upton, William, 146, 170, 171, 172, 173, 238
Van Nassau, Maurice, 220
Van Warwyck, Wybrand, 220
Vane, Charles, 9, 70, 188, 246
Vaughan, Hugh, 80, 99, 100, 101, 220, 221, 222
Vaughan, Megan, 220, 335, 336
Venezuela, 30
Verenigde Oostindische Compagnie (VOC), or Oude Westindische Compagnie (WIC), 43, 138, 251, 275, 276, 277, 369
Vergne, de la, Simon de Villeneuve, 210
Verguin, J., 329, 330, 331, 332, 335
Vernet, Du, 204
Vernon, Edward, 69
Viceroy of Goa, 5, 159, 164, 217, 219, 224, 227, 232, 235, 236, 299, 300, 305
Victory, 73, 74, 75, 85, 90, 103, 106, 124, 126, 127, 139, 142, 144, 150, 152, 153, 154, 158, 160, 162, 164, 165, 166, 170, 171, 172, 173, 174, 175, 176, 177, 178, 180, 181, 182, 184, 185, 215, 218, 220, 223, 225, 226, 228, 229, 230, 234, 241, 247, 249, 256, 257, 260, 261, 269, 300, 346, 348, 359, 370
Vierge de Cap. See *Nossa Senhora do Cabo*
Vierges de Grâce, 210
Ville d'Ostend, La, See *City of Ostend*

Virginia, 39, 40, 69, 101, 112, 128, 129, 193, 198, 199, 201, 202, 221, 300, 319, 320, 344, 345
Voisy, William, 198, 200, 201
Vos, Joannes de, 133
Voyages (database), i, 39, 40, 41, 49, 60, 80, 81, 97, 100, 101, 103, 108, 109, 111, 119, 122, 123, 127, 130, 135, 190, 319, 320, 368, 370, 373
Wackee, Isaac, 106
Wade frigate, 106
Walker, John, 202
Walpole, Horace, 247
Wapping, London, 88, 290, 291, 303
Warwyck Bay (Mauritius), 220
Washington, DC, 192
Webley, Capt., 189
Webley, John, 99
Weekly Journal, 35, 86, 134, 196, 236, 318
Weekly Journal and British Gazette, 236
Weekly Journal and Saturday Evening's Post, 134
Weekly Packet, 33, 34, 35, 36, 54, 55, 65, 66, 96, 97, 98, 100, 102, 108, 109, 112, 113, 114, 190, 343, 345
West Indies, 1, 2, 3, 9, 10, 11, 14, 15, 18, 20, 21, 22, 23, 25, 26, 35, 38, 63, 69, 74, 82, 103, 104, 106, 107, 113, 127, 140, 143, 189, 194, 278, 284, 285, 292, 293, 296, 298, 299, 300, 306, 313, 315, 318, 321, 340, 351
Whidaw. See Whydah
White Hart Tavern, 290
White, John L., 192
Whorwood, Thomas, 198
Whydah, 214
Whydah (Africa). See Quidah & Judah
Whydah, Africa, 329
Widdaw. See Whydah
William & James, 300
William III, 15, 16, 68, 143, 294
William of Orange. See William III
Williams, Chalonce, 202
Williams, John, 117
Williams, Palsgrave, 35, 36, 64, 65, 188
Williams, Palsgraves, 26
Windham. See Bird
Windham, William, 67, 68
Winter, Christopher or Robert, 95
Wirtemburg, 133
Woodard, Colin, 70, 88, 95, 246
Wooddrop, William, 31
Wooley, Thomas, 290
Woolley, Thomas, 134, 247, 248, 290
Wyat, Samuel, 99
Yeo, John, 319
York River (Virginia), 101, 128, 201, 202, 319, 320
York Town, Virginia, 198
Zeeland (W Netherlands), 122

Keep that looking glass out!

Quest for Blackbeard
The True Story of Edward Thache and His World

Available at Lulu.com, Amazon, Barnes & Noble, Alibris, and other fine online retailers!

baylusbrooks.com

CPSIA information can be obtained
at www.ICGtesting.com
Printed in the USA
BVHW030225181021
619184BV00007B/70

9 780359 047925